YOUR
MEDICAL RIGHTS

YOUR
MEDICAL RIGHTS

HOW TO BECOME AN EMPOWERED CONSUMER

Charles B. Inlander

and

Eugene I. Pavalon

LITTLE, BROWN AND COMPANY
BOSTON　　　TORONTO　　　LONDON

First Edition

NOTE: For reasons of privacy, many names
in this book have been changed.

Library of Congress Cataloging-in-Publication Data
Inlander, Charles B.
    Your medical rights: how to become an empowered consumer / by
Charles B. Inlander and Eugene I. Pavalon.
        p.   cm.
    ISBN 0-316-41885-4 — ISBN 0-316-69546-7 (pbk.)
    1. Patients — Legal status, laws, etc. — United States — Popular
works.   2. Consumer protection — Law and legislation — United States.
I. Pavalon, Eugene I.   II. Title.
KF3823.Z9155   1990
344.73′041 — dc20
[347.30441]   90-32148
                                                                          CIP

HC 10 9 8 7 6 5 4 3 2

PB 10 9 8 7 6 5 4 3 2

MV PA

Published simultaneously in Canada
by Little, Brown & Company (Canada) Limited
Printed in the United States of America

Contents

Preface

TRUST ME, I'm a doctor." Maybe you have seen small campaign-style pins proclaiming that message. A friend gave me a button with the "TRUST ME . . ." on it. She had picked it up at a medical convention.

While the pin may be intended as a joke, the deeper implication is not funny. In fact, my sense of humor about things medical is waning at a rapid pace.

One of the reasons for my descent into medical despondency is the fact that many doctors lie. And, frankly, when I or anyone else confronts them with their lies, they lie again.

Let me give you an example: we are in the midst of a cesarean section crisis. More than 25 percent of all children born in the United States are the products of cesarean births. In Canada the figure is nearly 20 percent and in England, where cesarean sections recently reached 11.3 percent, doctors themselves expressed concern.

Every woman I know who has had a cesarean section has told me the reason the doctor gave for doing it was that either she or the baby was in distress. A C-section was absolutely necessary, the doctor said, in order to survive a crisis.

In a recent article on "needless births by cesarean" in the London newspaper *The Sunday Times,* Dr. Colin Francome, a senior sociology lecturer, pointed out an important dichotomy concerning the C-section issue:

"If you ask doctors why the cesarean rate is up they say it is because we are scared of being sued, or because of time pressures or staff shortages. But when you ask women, they are never told this. They say it is because the baby had problems or because they needed it. It is obvious they are not being told the truth."

On several occasions when I have been at meetings where doctors were railing about being sued, I have asked the outraged speaker if he had told the patient that the reason a particular procedure was done was because of fear of litigation. "Of course not!" they bellow.

Then they go on to tell another lie about how they themselves have never performed an unnecessary anything.

Doctors want it both ways. They want to be able to tell their customers one thing and the newspaper something else. They want to perform unnecessary tests, which they tell their patients are critical, then run off to medical meetings and complain about "having" to perform unnecessary tests to protect themselves.

Doctors want us to trust them, but they give us little basis for doing so. Why should I trust a doctor who lies to me?

If my auto mechanic tells me my engine is shot and I need a new one, and later, after I replace it, I find that the real problem was my transmission, you can rest assured I will never trust or use that mechanic again. In fact, I might very well sue him for fraud.

Should doctors have the same standards applied to them? There is no question — they should.

Obviously, not all doctors are bad people. But most lie. And the reason they do so is to protect themselves, not their customers. Organized medical groups, such as the American Medical Association, have created a "we" (the doctors) versus "them" (the consumers) mentality about American medicine. They complain that consumers are too litigious. They blame malpractice suits on greedy lawyers. They point fingers at patients for not following their advice. They conduct massive public relations campaigns to try to gloss over their shortcomings. Too often they try to divert our attention from the real issues confronting consumers with campaigns to ban boxing or convert the equivalent of a hospital candy-striper into a primary-care nurse.

Then they want us to love them . . . to trust them. However, by tacitly approving of such specious conduct, organized medical groups have set their members up for a major consumer revolt.

Americans cannot tolerate being lied to for very long. We have forced a president of the United States to resign from office for lying. We have shipped business executives to jail for it. Why do doctors think we will allow them to operate under a double standard very much longer?

"TRUST ME, I'M A DOCTOR" is a message American medicine has wanted us to accept for more than 100 years. Most Americans have done just that, and many have suffered because they did not question or get up and leave when they should have.

But today that message is an example of a profession in trouble. It represents all that is wrong with the most important service any person uses.

Let's start making a button of our own — one that we wear each time we visit a doctor or hospital. On it would be the first words that every doctor states when he recites the Hippocratic Oath: "FIRST DO NO HARM."

Charles B. Inlander
President
People's Medical Society

Eugene I. Pavalon, Esq.

Acknowledgments

AUTHORS do not produce books alone. Many hands and minds participate in the creation. In this case, special recognition is due to several individuals without whom this project would not have progressed beyond the idea stage.

Bruce Wexler deserves the lion's share of credit for his skill, craftsmanship, and abilities. Without his talents, so much of *Your Medical Rights* would not have been written.

Special thanks to our editor, Jennifer Josephy. Her enthusiasm, commitment, and guidance made our work all that much easier. Heartfelt thanks as well to Jennifer's assistant, Alice Ma, and to our copyeditor at Little, Brown, Elizabeth D. Power. These behind-the-scenes people make manuscripts into books.

The staff of the People's Medical Society once again put their typical efforts beyond the call of duty into this project. Thanks to Mike Rooney for assembling Appendix A; Bill Bauman for coordinating the phoning and fact checking; Linda Swank, Gayle Ebert, and Miriam Flexer for making the verification calls; and Karla Morales and Paula Brisco for assistance throughout.

Once again, sincere thanks to our literary agent, Gail Ross. Her dedication to, and love of, the People's Medical Society is the reason *Your Medical Rights* is the latest in what is becoming a long line of books to help medical consumers produced from the People's Medical Society. She is one of a kind.

And, finally, we wish to dedicate this book to the men and women who take an active part in consumer organizations and coalitions throughout this country and who have thereby created a better environment for all.

YOUR
MEDICAL RIGHTS

Introduction

THIS is a true story. In Palm Beach County, Florida, a woman entered the hospital for some tests that resulted in a minor procedure being performed. She remained in the hospital a few days, and when it came time for her to be discharged, the hospital accounting office demanded payment for the services not covered by her insurance company. The amount owed for these noncovered services was quite small, for items like television and phone calls. The patient asked that the hospital bill her and said she would gladly send a check. That was not possible, replied the clerk; the hospital policy was pay when you left or you could not be discharged.

The woman's husband stood by listening in disbelief to the clerk. Calmly, he walked over to the pay phone and called the county sheriff. He told the sheriff that his wife was being held for ransom, which is illegal in Florida (as it is in every state). A few minutes later, a sheriff's deputy arrived at the hospital with handcuffs. He told the hospital administrator to either release the woman or face arrest. She was released.

Medical consumers — all of us — are constantly intimidated by doctors, hospitals, insurers, and just about everyone else in the health professions. The intimidation paralyzes us to such a degree that we either forget or are afraid to exercise our rights. Mistreatment and disrespect we would not tolerate from any other service provider are too often the rule.

Sadly, medicine has remained America's last bastion of non-consumerism in an era when lawmakers have raced to pass laws that protect consumers from bad products and shoddy service.

When one compares medical and health services to any other service industry from the standpoints of disclosure, accountability, and consumer respect, one finds a report card with many failing grades.

For example, banks issuing mortgages must inform the customer, in writing, of the interest rates, the payment amounts, and all fees associated with the mortgage, as well as other complicated information.

This is called disclosure. It is the heart of consumerism. It is the basis by which individuals know their rights. And the laws have been written, over the past 20 years, to put the onus of disclosure responsibility onto the provider of service.

But not so with medicine. While doctors are required to tell you side effects of medications, the cost of their own services, and even the likelihood that a procedure will be successful, there are no laws that will ensure that they do so without your asking.

That is what makes your medical rights different from other consumer rights. Simply put, the onus falls more on the consumer than on the provider. Unless you know your medical rights, there is a good chance they will be violated.

This book is designed to make you a more informed and knowledgeable consumer. We have written it to guide you through your rights and the concepts you need to understand to exercise them. We are convinced that people who know their rights, understand how the system works, and utilize that knowledge get better medical care than those who do not.

The old expression "There ought to be a law" is an interesting one when applied to health care. Most people think that there are no laws to protect them. They think whatever the doctor does, whatever the hospital clerk says, or whatever the insurance company claims department ordains is the law. Medical consumers travel through the maze of services confused and therefore vulnerable.

What this book does is to show you that there is a law. In fact, there are many laws that protect medical consumers from being victims of intimidation and outright bullying. Often these laws are not specifically written to protect your medical rights, but they apply. For example, the incident described at the beginning of this introduction is a perfect example of that fact. Being held for ransom is being held for ransom, be it by political terrorists or medical terrorists.

As consumers we have been led to believe we are mentally incapable of understanding medicine or our rights. We are treated as medical idiots by those who provide the services. In almost every encounter with the medical system, we are placed in a position of weakness, rather than strength. Think about it.

Most doctors call their patients by their first names, while the patient is expected to call the practitioner "doctor." Hospital admissions clerks make consumers think that the release they sign upon entering is a blanket approval to do whatever the facility wants. It is not.

Everything the medical professions do is tinged with intimidation, intentionally or unintentionally. As a result, what we have come to accept as normal consumerism has been nonexistent in medicine.

But as medical consumers, we are also the victims of the powerful medical lobbying and trade organizations. Groups like the American Medical Association and American Hospital Association have developed a power base in this country unequaled by any other sector. In fact, they have even gone beyond the realm of trade association and presented themselves as quasi-scientific groups.

By publishing journals, supporting scientific studies, and developing massive public relations mechanisms, they have created a mystique about health and medicine. This mystique implies that those who practice or provide medical care are somehow anointed with superior intelligence. Of course, then, those of us who receive care are mere mortals with lesser abilities.

Through this process, they have been able to train their members most effectively to develop techniques and tactics that essentially place the provider of care into a position of parent, while putting us, the users of their services, into a childlike state.

As a result, American health care users have become docile and dependent on the provider not only to give care but to serve as their advocate. Even medical schools teach their students that they are a patient's best advocate, ignoring the built-in conflict of interest any care giver has in this relationship.

Another reason we consumers are intimidated is the sheer size of the health care system. Any individual is easily put off by an industry that is so dominant. How does one question a hospital? "How could my doctor be wrong? Doesn't America have the best health care system in the world?"

But most of us are intimidated by the system because of the lack of information made available to us. Most people passively accept what happens to them in medical matters because they are unaware of routes of recourse. People get unnecessary hospital chest X rays on admission because they *think* it is the law, not some profit-driven hospital "policy." Hospitalized consumers accept a doctor's explanation that an infection in a surgical wound is a "common complication," when the facts are clear that most are caused by unsterile equipment or negligent operating room procedures.

Intimidation works only when the party being intimidated is uninformed. Armed with information and knowledge, one cannot be intimidated. In fact, well-informed consumers are fairly intimidating creatures themselves.

Medical care should be a partnership. We go to practitioners for help. They have a certain body of knowledge that we seek to benefit from. But we have knowledge as well. Not only do we know a great deal about medicine (remember that 85 percent of all medicine delivered in this country is self-care), we also know that practitioners who bully and attempt to intimidate are often those who provide the poorest care.

Your Medical Rights is designed to make your encounter with the medical world a safe and satisfactory one. We have designed and written this book so that it is a tool, an instrument for you to use to ensure the highest-quality outcome.

While the book describes many cases of people whose rights were violated, whose lives were lost, or who were injured, its purpose is to help you avoid being one of those victims.

Your Medical Rights is also meant to demonstrate that you can win. Whoever said "You can't fight city hall" was wrong. You can fight back and you can win. No medical consumer need be a victim. No medical consumer need be shoved around or ignored. Not a single patient should be treated as though the medical system is doing you a favor by treating you.

Medical care is America's largest business. It consumes 12 percent of the gross national product. That is double the amount spent on defending the United States each year. It is now America's largest employer in most urban areas. Almost all of us see a doctor once a year on the average. Thirty-five million people are operated on yearly. Thirty-two million people are Medicare beneficiaries. Hundreds of millions of prescriptions are filled annually. And yet, most Americans have little knowledge of their rights.

But that is now changing. Americans are demanding to know more. They are standing up to the medical world and saying in loud and clear words that the time has come for change.

Your Medical Rights is a part of that change. The day of the uninformed medical consumer is over. This book is meant to help you become a leader in that change.

AUTHORS' NOTE: For the sake of convenience, the male pronoun has been used throughout to refer to patients, physicians, and others.

What You Don't Know
Does Hurt You

IN THIS COUNTRY, certain groups should never take their rights for granted.

Women, senior citizens, gays, and blacks — groups that are traditionally discriminated against — should know and exercise their rights.

Health care consumers fall into this category. If that surprises you, think about the last time you were in a hospital and felt as though you were in a prison. Or about the arrogant, condescending attitude of some doctors you know. Or about the way a nursing home treats its residents. Or about the story in the paper detailing the gross misconduct of a doctor being sued for malpractice.

When you enter the health care system, you enter a world over which you have little or no control, in which you meekly follow orders.

At best, it's a humiliating experience. At worst, it's a life-threatening one. Your only defense is your rights as a consumer. If you don't exercise those rights, bad things can happen. Here are four examples. The names have been changed, to protect not the guilty doctors but their innocent victims.

THE CASE OF THE CLOSEMOUTHED DOCTOR

Betty Wilson went into the hospital for surgery on her obstructed bowel. A few days later, Betty met with Dr. Ivan Denby, her surgeon. Dr. Denby explained that he had removed a tumor along with part of her lower intestine; she could go home soon and no further therapy was needed.

So Betty went home, assuming that the problem was solved. Shortly thereafter, Betty began experiencing pain and other bowel-related difficulties. This time, she went to another doctor at a different hospital who examined her and told her she had cancer.

Betty was shocked. It was the first time a doctor had used that word to describe her condition. Even her new doctor was startled that her former doctor had failed to inform her about what was wrong. After the operation, even a green medical student would have spotted the cancer. Dr. Denby was a surgeon with years of experience. He had to have known about the cancer, yet he hadn't said a word about it to Betty.

Subsequently, Dr. Denby explained that he had consulted a hospital oncologist after Betty's surgery and that the oncologist had told him that "given the nature of the tumor, no further therapy was indicated." Dr. Denby said he decided not to worry the woman by telling her about the cancer "and let nature take its course."

It took its course and Betty died. If she had begun chemotherapy immediately after the operation, her life might have been prolonged.

In this instance, Betty's rights were violated. She had the right to know everything about her condition. The doctor failed to disclose that information to Betty. It's possible if she had known about her rights, she might still be alive.

THE CASE OF THE SAFE-SEX DOCTOR

Sandra McCoy was a young black unwed mother of five. She went into the hospital to have a cyst removed from her ovary. After the operation, her surgeon, Dr. William Whitney (who was white), told her that he had not only removed the cyst but had cut her tubes. "We removed the cyst and its benign," he said. "You know, you've had enough children out of wedlock. I fixed it so you can have all the fun you want with your little playbox, and you don't have to worry about getting pregnant." He then patted her on the head.

Sandra had the right to know what her doctor was going to do before he did it. Even more important, Dr. Whitney had absolutely no right to cut her tubes without suggesting the procedure beforehand and obtaining Sandra's consent. Dr. Whitney did not have the right to play God.

THE CASE OF THE CURE
WORSE THAN THE DISEASE

Dan Tilden consulted Dr. Steve Conroy, a board-certified dermatologist, about psoriasis. It was a painful condition, and Dan wasn't satisfied with another dermatologist's treatment.

Dr. Conroy gave him methotrexate. Methotrexate's primary use is in cancer patients undergoing chemotherapy. But the *Physician's Desk Reference (PDR)*, a listing of all drugs and their effects, also recommends it for treatment of disabling psoriasis. The *PDR,* however, specifies that the drug can harm the liver and kidneys, and doctors prescribing it should monitor liver function regularly.

Dan took the drug for five years, and Dr. Conroy never once ordered a liver function test. After five years, Dan began losing weight; he felt lethargic and his skin was turning yellow. Dan went into the hospital where his illness was diagnosed as jaundice. Before long his liver failed and he died.

Dan had the right to competent medical care. By failing to monitor Dan's liver, Dr. Conroy proved himself incompetent.

THE CASE OF THE WRONG DIAGNOSIS

Donna Willis's 3-year-old child, Sally, had had a fever and respiratory problems for 10 days. Suddenly, her temperature shot up to 105 degrees and Sally became listless and unresponsive. Donna was alarmed and rushed her daughter to the emergency room of the local hospital.

When they arrived, a nurse recorded the medical history, including the fact that Sally had been taking penicillin. After a 45-minute wait, an emergency room physician, Dr. Ahmed Ali, saw the child.

But he didn't examine her. He merely looked at what the

nurse had written on the emergency room record and added, "Pharyngitis [inflammation of the throat], continue penicillin-type medication." He then sent Donna and Sally home.

Sally's condition worsened. Donna took her to a pediatrician, who delayed making a treatment recommendation for 2 days. Finally, he recommended a spinal tap.

The spinal tap revealed that Sally had spinal meningitis. Treatment had been delayed too long. Sally was brain-damaged and had to be placed in an institution.

If the spinal tap had been done when Sally went to the emergency room, she quite likely would have been cured; her type of spinal meningitis was caused by hemophilic bacteria (a result of influenza) and is treatable with erythromycin. Sally's symptoms clearly suggested spinal meningitis was a possibility, and because Dr. Ali failed to recognize that possibility, he was negligent. He should have examined her and recognized that a spinal tap was called for.

Sally had the right to competent medical care. Dr. Ali was both incompetent and negligent.

In the Dark

As you read about these cases, you probably thought: this can't happen to me; the odds are against it; the individuals were victims of bad luck and circumstance.

We'd like you to consider another explanation: that these cases are just the tip of the iceberg; that they represent problems that are commonplace; that variations of these cases are played out in every medical setting in every part of the country every day.

Why? Well, the answer is complicated, but let's approach it from a few different perspectives.

First, most people aren't aware of their medical rights. And what you don't know can hurt you. As a medical consumer, you make certain assumptions when you enter a doctor's office or a hospital — assumptions that are often incorrect.

For instance, you assume that a doctor can withhold information from you, either because you wouldn't understand it or because it would make you worry. In almost all cases, however, doctors must provide you with complete information about your condition, including diagnosis and prognosis. If the doctor fails to do so — and especially if that failure results in additional medical, financial, or personal problems — you have the right to sue him for malpractice.

Many people assume that once they are hospitalized, they can only leave the hospital when given permission to do so. Though that might be the impression hospital administrators would like to foster, it's false. The hospital isn't a prison and the doctor isn't your jailer. In fact, if they try to keep you there against your will, you have the right to sue them for false imprisonment. If a hospital administrator tells you that you can't leave until you've paid your bill, don't believe him. You can leave any time you want.

Here's another assumption related to hospitals: you have to submit to examination by all medical personnel — interns, residents, medical students — who come into your room. Absolutely not. You can refuse to be a training device for future doctors. In fact, you can say no to any order, whether you're in the hospital or in the doctor's office. Remember, it's your body; you haven't donated it to science. Unless you give your permission, no one can do anything to you.

As medical consumers, we make hundreds of incorrect assumptions like these. The common thread of the assumptions is that health care practitioners can do what they like, when they like, how they like. But we are protected if we know what our rights are.

Records

Doctors and hospitals keep written records about your condition and treatment under lock and key. If you ask for those records, they'll often react like CIA agents asked to turn over top-secret documents.

It's far easier for other parties to get those records than it is for you. Insurance companies, employers, law enforcement agencies, and state officials can obtain them with relative ease. These groups often have little need to know all they are given. But the laws ironically favor the providers rather than the recipients of medical care, turning your records into an open book for those who care to read them.

Why is it so difficult for you? First, if mistakes in treatment have been made, doctors and hospitals don't want a documented record of those mistakes in victims' hands. Second, they want to maintain control; doctors don't want you looking at your records and questioning what everything means. Health care professionals have an obsessive need to maintain the upper hand in dealings with consumers. Knowledge is power, and they don't want you to have either.

Only 13 states have laws mandating patient access to all records (doctor, hospital, and mental health). Even in those states, the health care establishment is often resistant. If you have ever been in a hospital, think about asking the nurse who took your temperature what it was. Odds are, she replied, "Oh, I can't tell you that until the doctor comes back." Given how difficult it is to obtain that simple bit of information, imagine the reaction when you ask for your records.

Those records are vitally important to you. They give you the information necessary to talk to your doctor on common ground; they're your ammunition if a mistake is made. Without those records, it's difficult for you to question or challenge physicians. As you will see later in the book, there are ways to secure your records, even when statutes do not specifically authorize you to do so.

Intimidation

Doctors intimidate. Hospital rules and regulations confound and confuse. Physicians' arrogance contributes to your feelings of helplessness.

Here's a typical situation. You go to the doctor's office and are forced to sit in the waiting room for a half hour; then you're escorted into an examining room, where you wait another 30 minutes, unclothed and extremely vulnerable, on a cold metal table. When the doctor finally arrives, he asks what your problem is, quickly examines you, utters a few oohs and ahs, and perhaps writes a prescription in illegible penmanship on a scrap of paper. He calls you by your first name, while you are expected to call him doctor. If you ask a question, he might give you a curt, technical answer that you don't really understand. He's always in a hurry; his impatience suggests that your problems aren't worth his time.

The whole process is intimidating. You're literally stripped of your defenses, of your dignity. You're made to feel like a helpless child rather than an intelligent adult. It's an environment that encourages subservience.

There's ample evidence suggesting that doctors view patients as children — as docile, uninformed, and helpless. Medical ethicist Sissela Bok studied physicians trained at or affiliated with the Harvard Medical School and concluded that they talk about lying to their patients "in a cavalier, often condescending way. . . ." Thomas Preston, M.D., in his 1981 book *The Clay Pedestal,* writes that a doctor "assumes that his superior knowledge and experience enable him to judge what the patient needs. Since the patient is presumed to be unable to make an informed decision and likely to choose wrongly even if fully informed, it is standard practice for physicians to manipulate information in order to persuade patients to accept recommendations. . . ."

By and large, physicians are terrible communicators. The illegible handwriting on their prescriptions is a symbol of their inability to articulate their thoughts and feelings. According to a September 23, 1985, article in *Medical World News,* a study at UCLA's Cancer Rehabilitation Project found that "9 in 10 physicians had never received any formal training in how to disclose a cancer diagnosis" to the afflicted patient.

That inability to communicate is a contributing factor to patient intimidation. People naturally fear the unknown or the incomprehensible.

The problem is a lack of consumerism. Years ago, if you took your car in for a tune-up, returned four hours later, and were handed a bill for both a tune-up and a brake job, you had little recourse. Now, all states require auto service departments to provide written estimates, to have repairs preapproved by customers, and to return replaced used parts to verify the work.

Doctors don't provide estimates. They often fail to disclose the full nature of treatment, and they don't feel obligated to receive fully informed permission before treatment. And they never return your parts.

Though doctors might not be as physically intimidating as the aforementioned auto mechanic, their attitudes achieve the same effect.

Accountability

There are doctors out there with scores of malpractice suits filed against them; who are addicted to alcohol or drugs; who have overcharged patients or Medicare to the tune of millions of dollars; who call themselves specialists yet have no special training. Your physician may fall into any of those categories. If so, it's unlikely that you'll know about it or that he's being punished for his mistakes.

You have the right to honest, competent medical care. Unfortunately, the health care profession rarely safeguards that right. Let's look at some of the ways they fail to do so.

Licensing

Once a physician obtains his medical license, he usually keeps it for life. There's no guarantee that the doctor who obtained his license when he was 25 is still competent at 50. Not a single state requires a physician to take an examination after passing his first one. A driver with three drunk-driving convictions is far more likely to have his license revoked than a doctor with three malpractice suits against him. It also might surprise you to learn that state licensing boards are often unaware of doctors who are found guilty of, or plead guilty to, medical malpractice; most states don't require courts to report these verdicts to boards.

In most states, doctors aren't required to take continuing education classes to retain their licenses; only 20 states have that requirement. Equally disturbing, many continuing education programs are nothing more than a few lectures aboard a luxurious cruise ship. Given the rapid evolution of medical knowledge, comprehensive continuing education programs seem essential. A physician can be woefully behind the times — unaware of effective new treatments or old treatments now considered dangerous — without fear of disciplinary actions.

It's true that a significant number of doctors are board-certified specialists. Of the twenty-three boards recognized by the American Board of Medical Specialists, recertification procedures are mandatory for some, but others are voluntary. Anesthesiologists and colorectal surgeons, for instance, have no recertification requirements.

About 163,000 of this country's 500,000 physicians aren't certified as specialists. Yet these uncertified doctors are free to practice in any area of specialized medicine — from brain surgery to heart surgery — with impunity. A doctor can say he's a cardiologist, talk, act, and charge his patients like a cardiologist, but he may well not be trained as a cardiologist.

This approach to licensing fosters a dangerous illusion on the part of consumers. You naturally assume that a licensed physician is a competent one. You see his framed certificate on the wall and automatically accept it as a sign of competence. In many cases, it's nothing of the kind. Most people who are harmed or have had their rights violated by physicians are the victims of licensed practitioners.

Let's Be Careful Out There

There's a need to hold our health care system accountable, as the following attests:

• A Harvard University study of 500 doctors and 504 medical students revealed that 59 percent of the doctors and 78 percent of the students had used psychoactive drugs at some time in their lives and that during the year completed before the study, 25 percent of the doctors had treated themselves with these drugs; 10 percent had used drugs for recreational purposes (*New England Journal of Medicine,* September 1986).

• 98.1 percent of hospital bills of $10,000 or more contain errors, 73 percent in the hospital's favor, according to a study by the Equifax Corporation in 1984.

• A nationwide, 32-hospital study compared 1800 clinical diagnoses made on living patients to anatomical diagnoses made at autopsy. They found the error rate was nearly 20 percent. About half of those mistakes probably led to death. (Washington University in St. Louis *Feature Service,* September 1985)

• The number of foreign-trained doctors practicing in the U.S. is growing rapidly — doctors whose training is often inferior to that received in this country.

• Statistics indicate that the number of incompetent and dangerous physicians is between 5 and 15 percent of those practicing.

• The average hospital makes up to 60 medication errors an

hour; errors include giving patients the wrong medicine, the wrong dosage, or the right medicine at the wrong time.

If these facts aren't sufficiently alarming, consider the October 1987 "Report and Recommendations of the State of New Jersey Commission of Investigation on Impaired and Incompetent Physicians." Here are just two examples cited in the report.

• . . . the office assistant of an allegedly senile specialist in internal medicine . . . became concerned about her liability for the physician's treatment of patients. . . . "Main concern was absence of sterile technique and reuse of needles on more than one patient without sterilization."

• . . . the hospital's chief surgeon had appeared on occasion with alcohol on his breath and had "the shakes" . . . had appeared drunk during crisis admission situation and was "rarely in the emergency room without alcohol on the breath."

Though these examples are from just one state, they're indicative of problems throughout the country.

Discipline

A number of different bodies exist with the power to discipline physicians: state medical boards, hospital boards, various professional societies. Yet rarely do they do anything more than slap a few wrists.

Sidney M. Wolfe, M.D., of the Public Citizens Health Research Group, reported that in 1983 between 136,000 and 310,000 people were injured or killed because of medical mistakes. In that same year, only 563 doctors were put on probation or had their licenses revoked.

Obviously, something's wrong.

What's wrong is that the system is rigged like an old-time political election. The boards that are empowered to discipline doctors are composed of doctors. It's naturally very difficult for a board member to revoke a colleague's license. It's not unlikely for the board member to know or have worked with the offending physician; the board member would have trouble passing a "death sentence" on a fellow physician, in any case, because doctors are part of a brotherhood that eschews back-stabbing.

The American Medical Association strongly advocates "peer

review": physicians monitoring, warning, and punishing misdeeds of fellow physicians. The concept is much like putting the fox in charge of the chicken coop.

Time and again, we see doctors getting away with assault, battery, and worse. An orthopedic surgeon in Washington (state) twice operated on the wrong limbs of two different individuals and was sued each time. After the out-of-court settlements, the physician had to agree to a $50,000 deductible on his insurance policy to cover future suits. Though that might force him to purchase a less expensive Mercedes, it's certainly a far cry from eye-for-an-eye justice.

Or there's the Chicago plastic surgeon who had 18 malpractice suits filed against her before an Illinois disciplinary board took any action. Though they finally revoked her license, they held out the possibility that she could get it back if she kicked her drug habit.

It's not unusual to find physicians with numerous malpractice guilty verdicts on their records being allowed to practice. Sometimes, the problem is administrative: it takes months or years for overworked, understaffed licensing boards to reach a decision. Other times, doctors are merely placed under "supervision" — watched but not disciplined. Still other times, court actions aren't even reported to licensing boards.

In many instances, board investigations of doctors are kept secret. In 1985, the *New York Times* reported that two-thirds of 30 state medical boards studied failed to disclose disciplinary proceedings against doctors until they were completed.

The problem, of course, is that these doctors continue to treat people who are unaware that their doctors may well be negligent.

What it comes down to is this: most incompetent physicians will either escape punishment or receive minor penalties. They'll continue to practice. Even if a surgeon has botched scores of operations, it's entirely possible that he'll be free to wield his scalpel, leaving a never ending trail of unsuspecting victims.

Have You Been Wronged?

It's not always easy to know whether you've been wronged. Think about your medical experiences. Was there a time when a doctor prescribed a drug that had serious side effects — side effects he didn't tell you about?

Or maybe you went to one doctor who recommended surgery. You had the procedure done, and months or even years later, a second doctor told you the operation was unnecessary. Was the first doctor at fault?

Think about a bill you received from the hospital. Did it seem as though there were charges for services you never received?

Were you forced to undergo a series of X rays that, in hindsight, proved unnecessary? That may have done more harm than good?

The possibilities are endless. The problem is especially acute for persons who, for one reason or another, have trouble exercising their rights — children, senior citizens, and the mentally ill. Unless they have a strong advocate — an aggressive friend or family member — their rights are often ignored and abused.

Consider the plight of those residing in nursing homes. Under federal regulations, nursing homes must have written policies governing patients' rights. Yet many don't. Even those that have them often abuse them.

For instance, nursing home residents have the right to be fully informed of their medical conditions, to help develop their treatment plans, and to refuse to participate in experimental research. These rights, however, are often ignored. Some nursing home physicians view residents as guinea pigs, unprotesting candidates for the latest experimental drug.

It is not unusual for nursing home administrators to take advantage of residents, especially financially. Though residents should be given a regular accounting of financial transactions made on their behalf, it's easy for administrators to ignore this requirement.

Whether a senior citizen or a strapping youth, you should never assume that your rights will be respected. To paraphrase Murphy's Law: if a right can be abused, it will be abused.

What can you do? Let's take a look at the four cases discussed earlier in this chapter and the actions the victims might have taken.

WHAT BETTY SHOULD HAVE ASKED

If Betty had only known about her rights, she could have taken a number of steps to protect herself from Dr. Denby's incompetence.

First, she had the right to full disclosure about her condition. One question anyone having surgery should ask is: "What are you looking for?" Or: "What are the possibilities?"

The answers to those questions would have told Betty that cancer was a possibility.

After the surgery, the logical question would have been: "Is the tumor cancerous?" Or: "Is it life-threatening?"

In addition, Betty had the right to ask for a second opinion before surgery. She also had the right to see her medical records.

If Betty's rights had been respected, she would have learned that she had cancer. Upon discovering that fact, Betty probably wouldn't have passively accepted Dr. Denby's recommendation that no further treatment was necessary. She would have been justifiably worried and acted upon that worry, insisting on seeing another doctor, who, if he was competent, would have begun treatment immediately.

What happened to Dr. Denby? He's still practicing, despite losing a medical malpractice suit.

HOW SANDRA MIGHT HAVE AVOIDED UNNECESSARY SURGERY

As a black woman, Sandra was victimized not only by Dr. Whitney's medical arrogance but also by his social attitudes.

If Sandra had known about her right to be fully informed about treatment, she could have insisted on knowing exactly what Dr. Whitney was going to do before he operated. Though she had no way of knowing that Dr. Whitney was going to cut her tubes, it's quite possible that this irresponsible doctor might have suggested the possibility if questioned. At that point, she could either have found another doctor or insisted that he do no such thing.

Sandra also didn't realize that she could have responded to Dr. Whitney's disrespectful attitude and his performance of unauthorized surgery by filing a grievance with the state medical licensing board. A competent board would have ruled he had no right practicing medicine.

As of this writing, however, Dr. Whitney continues to practice.

HOW DAN COULD HAVE SAVED HIS OWN LIFE

When Dr. Conroy prescribed methotrexate, Dan had the right to know everything about the drug: what it was primarily used for, its side effects, its advantages and disadvantages compared to other drugs.

In addition, when Dan purchased the drug at a pharmacy, he should have asked the pharmacist for the package insert that comes with every shipment of drugs. The insert would have alerted Dan to methotrexate's dangers and the need for regular liver function monitoring.

Dan, like Sandra and Betty, simply assumed that he was in the hands of a competent physician. If he were aware of his rights, he wouldn't have made that assumption and would be alive today.

Given Dr. Conroy's gross incompetence and a successful malpractice suit against him, it's amazing that he is still practicing.

HOW DONNA MIGHT HAVE HELPED HER DAUGHTER

When Dr. Ali saw Sally in the emergency room and did nothing more than tell her mother to continue the medication she was on, Donna should have recognized that the doctor was negligent.

She had every right to expect an examination. When Dr. Ali refrained from performing one, Donna should have protested immediately. She should have voiced her displeasure not only at the lack of an examination, but at the doctor's insistence on maintaining the same medication when it was obviously doing no good.

Donna should also have contacted her pediatrician the moment she left the emergency room and asked him to examine Sally. Even if Dr. Ali was incompetent and failed to test for spinal meningitis, her pediatrician, with his superior knowledge of children's diseases, probably would have recommended a spinal tap.

Unfortunately, it's unreasonable to expect that Donna

would do the things recommended here. Like other health care consumers, Donna had never been taught to ask the critical questions she should have asked.

Dr. Ali, like the other doctors involved in these cases, is still practicing medicine.

Knowledge Is Power

Think about the four cases described. Consider the false assumptions people make about their rights and the health care system.

Contemplate how difficult it is to get your medical records, the intimidation practiced by hospitals and other health care providers, the lack of physician accountability.

Remember how difficult it is to know if you've been wronged; how you sometimes are unaware that your rights as a patient have been violated.

Having done all that, how do you feel? Outraged? Helpless?

Then it's time to do something. It's simply a matter of knowing your rights and fighting for them.

After all, you can be a victor as easily as a victim. How?

• If you have a general understanding of what you can and cannot do — and what health care practitioners can and cannot do

• If you learn the strategies and tactics to use in specific situations, ensuring that your rights will be honored: before surgery, when you're in the hospital, when a doctor seems unresponsive to your needs, and so on

• If you understand what your alternatives are when you've been wronged — from filing complaints with hospitals to seeking legal action

In the following chapters, we'll help you understand your rights and provide you with tools to enforce them. At this point, we hope we've given you enough information so that you realize both problems and solutions exist.

Look at it this way. At some point, you or a member of your family is going to be sucked into the health care system. You can be either a passive observer or an active participant.

Given the dangers of being a helpless patient, we don't think you'll take what happens lying down.

CHAPTER TWO

Be Prepared

A HOSPITAL ADMINISTRATOR asks you to sign a form that gives surgeons carte blanche to remove any organ or limb from your body.

You're looking for a new personal physician, and you're trying to find someone who will treat you with care and competence rather than as a contributor to his bottom line.

Your doctor suggests you enter a hospital for treatment, but you're reluctant to go to the recommended hospital; the local newspaper just ran a story about the unusually high number of medical malpractice suits against that hospital's surgeons.

These situations aren't uncommon. It's likely that you or a family member will face them. You can go into them blind, crossing your fingers and hoping luck is on your side — or you can be prepared. As you have seen in the previous chapter, health care consumers can protect themselves by asking questions in advance of treatment, anticipating potential problems, and speaking up for themselves.

If you're an active participant in the health care process, you're less likely to be a passive victim. Remember, numerous studies published in such prestigious publications as the *New England Journal of Medicine* show that the more assertive you are, the better health care you receive. And it makes no difference if you are rich or poor.

How do you start? Well, the first and best place involves choosing a doctor who is competent and who respects your rights.

Looking for Dr. Right

Many people have been led to believe that choosing a doctor is a game of chance — you roll the dice and hope for the best. They've been convinced by the medical profession that because they lack medical knowledge, they aren't capable of discerning a doctor's skills.

Though it's true that you can't listen to a doctor talk about his skill in heart surgery and determine whether he's a butcher or a virtuoso with the scalpel, you can learn a great deal about his abilities through a number of techniques. And you need to use every device available to you to ensure competence, because as we've stated previously, not a single doctor in any state is required to take a competency exam after receiving a license.

Let's say you're looking for a primary-care doctor to be your personal physician. The first step is to compile a list of potential candidates. You can do that in a number of ways:

1. Ask friends for recommendations. If they have doctors they trust — and those doctors are accepting new patients — put them on your list.

2. Consult doctor-referral services operated by medical societies and hospitals. Doctors listed are members of the society or are affiliated with the hospital. Remember that simply being listed is no guarantee of quality.

3. Check newspaper ads. One caveat: doctors who advertise might have a reason for doing so; they may be young and just starting a practice or simply be so bad that they're desperately in need of "customers." Furthermore, in most major cities there is a surplus of doctors. As a result, many physicians have begun advertising certain services, such as lens implantation. But just because a doctor advertises doesn't mean he is good — it only means he can afford to place an ad.

4. Call your medical insurance company. Although they are not a usual source, some do give recommendations.

5. Try your company personnel office. Ask the personnel director for the names of doctors other employees like *and* dislike.

6. Look up listings in the telephone directory. Use these cautiously. One study of yellow-pages listings of doctors found that many of them did not have certification in specialties they had advertised. Two doctors listed weren't even licensed to practice medicine in the state.

7. Seek referrals from doctors you know socially. But remember that being a friend of a doctor does not ensure competence or good recommendations.

8. Ask a nurse. If you know a nurse, ask about doctors to see or to avoid. Nurses know more about good and bad doctors than any other health professionals.

It's important to remember that getting the name of a really good doctor is only a very early step. Now the real work begins.

Conducting Interviews

Once you've compiled a list, it's time to arrange interviews. That's right, an interview. Look at the process as if you were interviewing candidates for a job — for a very special job with an enormous amount of responsibility.

Call the doctors and set up "get-acquainted" visits. If a doctor refuses to accommodate your request for a visit, cross him off your list. Such a refusal is a good indication of the doctor's attitude toward the people he treats.

The Doctor Information Worksheet (pages 28–29) is an excellent tool for obtaining information and comparing the responses of different doctors.

Let's examine the most important question on the worksheet. First, is the doctor board-certified? Though board certification doesn't guarantee competence, it does guarantee that the doctor has passed a rigorous test in his discipline. While that alone doesn't demonstrate competence, it does show that the doctor took the time not only to study further but to be tested. This is especially important if you're looking for a specialist. As we pointed out in the previous chapter, doctors are allowed to practice any specialty without board certification.

Second, is the doctor a sole practitioner or is he part of a group practice? There aren't many sole practitioners left. Most have formed groups, and it's wise to know the make-up of the group.

Some are multispecialty groups, while others focus on a general area such as family medicine. If the doctor is part of a multi-specialty group, be aware that if he has to refer you to a specialist, it's likely to be someone in his group. That specialist might not be the best doctor for your needs, but he'll probably be recommended simply because he's part of the group. During the interview, ask your doctor what his group's referral policy is.

Third, fees and payment schedules vary. Don't be embarrassed to ask questions about costs and billing procedures. It's your pocketbook that's at stake. It's also your right to get truthful and accurate information. Asking these questions could save you a great deal of money or make it easier for you to pay your doctor's bills.

Fourth, will he allow you access to your medical records? In 26 states, this is your right. In others, you must negotiate. The previous chapter demonstrates why this is important. If the doctor has a policy against access, he probably isn't the one for you.

Fifth, where does the doctor have admitting privileges? Again, you have the right to know. If it's at a hospital with a bad reputation — or not one you would choose to go to — you will have to weigh his qualifications against the hospital's drawbacks.

Besides the questions listed on the sheet, judge the doctor by his credentials. Did he go to a medical school you've heard of? How many years has he been practicing? Is he on the faculty of a major medical school?

That last question is important. Appointment to the faculty of a major medical school is a good indication that a doctor has distinguished himself in his field. On the other hand, don't be overly impressed if a doctor tells you he's an instructor in clinical medicine or a lecturer or adjunct professor. Many doctors volunteer to work with residents and interns, and this is no sign that they've achieved anything significant.

Ask the doctor if he has ever been sued for malpractice and lost or settled. He is obligated to answer honestly. What should you do if you learn that a prospective doctor has a number of medical malpractice suits filed against him? Certainly you should be wary, but it's not necessarily a sign that the doctor is incompetent. We know of a neurosurgeon at a leading Chicago hospital who's been sued a dozen times. The problem is that he's in a

THE DOCTOR INFORMATION WORKSHEET

NAME OF DOCTOR	Doctor 1	Doctor 2	Doctor 3	Doctor 4
Is this doctor accepting new patients?				
If "no" when will he/she accept new patients?				
Is this doctor an M.D. or Doctor of Osteopathy?				
Is this doctor board certified in his/her specialty?				
Is this doctor an alternative doctor?				
Does this doctor provide get-acquainted visits?				
How much time will I be given on this visit?				
How much will it cost?				
Does this doctor publish a list of his/her fees?				
What is the cost of a regular office visit?				
What is the charge when the doctor makes a hospital visit?				
Is payment demanded at the time of service?				
Does this doctor permit a flexible payment schedule?				
Is this doctor's location convenient to where I live?				
Is public transportation to the doctor's office available?				

Is there adequate parking at the doctor's office?					
Is this doctor in a solo or group practice?					
If group, are doctors same specialty?					
If group, are doctors different specialties?					
Do patients have direct telephone access to the doctor?					
Are there specific call-in times? When?					
Does this doctor make house calls?					
What is the cost of a house call?					
Does this doctor offer lab work and other services in the office?					
What is the cost of these services?					
Does this doctor have convenient office hours?					
Does this doctor have office hours on weekends?					
Will my medical insurance coverage be accepted?					
Will the doctor file all insurance claims?					
Does this doctor accept Medicare Assignment?					
Do I have access to my medical records?					
Do I have access to a summary of my medical records?					
Will I receive copies of all lab tests ordered by the doctor?					
Where does the doctor have hospital privileges?					
Is this hospital my first choice?					

high-risk field, and he's frequently called in as a consultant on cases. When lawsuits are filed against other doctors in these cases, his name is added to those of the defendants because he was one of a number of doctors involved. This neurosurgeon is highly skilled, yet you'd be misled if you judged him only by the number of suits filed against him. That doesn't mean other high-risk specialists aren't incompetent. It behooves you to have the doctor explain the circumstances of a lawsuit he may have been involved in; then decide for yourself.

If a doctor doesn't practice in a high-risk area and he has a number of suits filed against him, he may well be incompetent. You have to judge those suits individually, determining such things as whether the doctor was the primary-care physician, the grounds for the suit, and so on.

One last point: asking all these questions of a doctor may ultimately affect his attitude toward you. It doesn't necessarily mean you'll receive better or worse treatment. But the doctor will view you differently; he'll remember that you're the one with all the questions. It might make him a little more reluctant to dismiss you with a curt word; he'll realize that you are not a passive patient and won't tolerate a cavalier or unresponsive physician. On the other hand, he may announce that he doesn't want you as a patient. If that's the case, leave with a smile, because you have just significantly reduced your chances of becoming a victim.

Before You Let Him Do Anything . . .

At some point in your relationship with a doctor, he's going to recommend a specific action. It might involve giving you drugs, ordering tests, surgery, hospitalization, or a host of other possibilities. Before you let him have his way, ask questions. Don't meekly nod your head and accept his recommendation.

Treat your doctor's statements as if he were a politician and you were a journalist. Ask who, what, where, when, how, and, especially, why. Those questions might make him uncomfortable. But unlike a politician, your doctor doesn't have the luxury of saying, "No comment." In fact, the law says he must answer all your questions honestly.

When your doctor makes a recommendation for treatment, here are some of the questions that you might ask:

1. What's the purpose of the treatment? What do you hope to accomplish by it?

2. Is the procedure painful or dangerous? Is the pain or danger worth the benefits that will result from the procedure?

3. Are there alternatives to the procedure? What are they, and what are their advantages/disadvantages compared to the one recommended?

4. How much will it cost?

5. What will happen if I don't have the procedure done?

6. Who will be responsible for my treatment? What are their credentials? Where will it be done, and is that a good place for it?

Why are these questions so important? Because even the best doctors are human and make mistakes. And the worst ones are inhuman and have little regard for what's best for you. Remember, your doctor must answer your questions and cannot do anything until you give him permission based on information he has given you.

Here are two examples of the advantages of asking questions.

A newspaper reporter's mother had a lump in her breast. Her doctor said a biopsy had to be done, and he asked her to sign a form giving him permission to do a mastectomy if a malignancy was found.

Fortunately, the reporter had a healthy skepticism about form-signing. She called other medical experts, who all said the same thing: "Don't let your mother sign the form!" They told the reporter that after a biopsy, a number of questions had to be asked and answered: What is the "stage" of the cancer? What is the prognosis if a lumpectomy is done? Would radiation therapy be a better alternative given the mother's age and health? In the end, the reporter's mother exercised her rights and did not sign the form. Instead, she gave her permission only for a biopsy to be performed.

It turned out that a mastectomy wasn't necessary. Though there's no way of knowing if the doctor would have performed a mastectomy had the patient signed the form, it is quite possible the doctor would have yielded to temptation. Never give a doctor carte blanche when carte blanche isn't necessary.

Here's an even more telling example. James Blackstone, a leading midwestern lawyer, had an accoustic neuroma, a benign tumor of the hearing nerve. The problem was that the tumor was growing and, if left untreated, his doctor said, would put pressure on the brain stem and paralyze Blackstone's breathing. So he had an operation to remove the tumor. The operation, however, left Blackstone deaf in one ear and paralyzed half his face.

For 15 years after the operation, no other problem occurred. Then, when the lawyer was 53, a small, new benign tumor was discovered in the same place. His doctor insisted on surgery to remove all the tumor, even though it could result in a total hearing loss and complete facial paralysis.

Blackstone started asking some questions. He used the same logic that he would apply to a tricky point of law. He began with the supposition that it would take another 15 years for the tumor to grow to the point where something had to be done. Because the tumor was benign, he didn't have to worry about it spreading beyond its site behind the ear. He also assumed that in 15 years there would be surgical advances; that new laser treatments would be better refined, allowing doctors to operate with less risk of paralysis or hearing loss.

He presented his argument to a well-known neurosurgeon in Boston, requesting that he remove only as much of the tumor as would avoid further paralysis and impairment of hearing in his undamaged ear, something his local doctor refused to do. The doctor, after considering the suggestion, looked at him and said, "You know, that's a great idea. I'll do the surgery as you request, and in 15 years surgical techniques may be so advanced that any needed surgery at that time could probably be performed without risk to you." The surgery was performed without damage.

Like James Blackstone, use your common sense when contemplating a medical decision.

The Hospital

Hospitals are not all the same. They differ in terms of policies and practices, types of personnel, and fees. They're like hotels: some are grand institutions with superior service, and others are flophouses.

Preparing for the hospital experience means more than packing toothbrushes and pajamas. It's important that you exercise your right to information before you agree to be admitted to a hospital. Here are some basic questions to ask before and during your hospital stay that will help protect your medical rights and your health. They might even save your life.

Why does the doctor recommend that you go to this particular hospital?

It's not necessarily because it's the best hospital for you. It may be that it's the hospital where most of your doctor's hospitalized patients are; it's the most convenient one for him. Or it might be that he has a quota relationship with the hospital: he delivers a certain number of patients in exchange for a hospital-supplied office.

You want a hospital that is skilled in the treatment you're being hospitalized for. If you're going in for heart surgery, ask him about the hospital's cardiac unit. Your doctor might have admitting privileges at a number of area hospitals, so there could be a choice to be made. If he doesn't have privileges at a hospital you want to go to, find another doctor who does. Your doctor must answer your questions truthfully and with direct information. A statement such as, "It's the best," is an opinion and not fact. Press your doctor for facts and statistics.

What type of hospital is it?

Many different types of hospitals exist. Each type has advantages and disadvantages, and you should choose the one that makes sense for you.

There are specialty hospitals and general hospitals, teaching hospitals and nonteaching hospitals, community hospitals and medical centers. There are also osteopathic hospitals and outpatient surgery centers.

Specialty hospitals, as the name implies, specialize in one or several types of treatment: cardiac surgery, for instance, or cancer treatments. If you need a specific type of treatment, a specialty hospital might be appropriate. On the other hand, specialty hospitals are limited by their specialties. They're often unable to handle medical problems outside of their area of specialization. If, for instance, you go into an orthopedic hospital for surgery and you experience cardiac arrest during the operation, they might not have the expertise to treat that condition. Therefore, it's a good idea to ask about a hospital's backup services. You should also inquire about the mortality rate (deaths that have occurred) at the hospital among people who have had the same procedure that you are considering and compare it to other hospitals in your region and against national averages.

If your doctor informs you that he'd like to put you in a teaching hospital, that might sound attractive. After all, these hospitals often have the most sophisticated technology and the most prestigious doctors. The downside is that you may not be seen by a prestigious doctor, and the high-tech equipment might be irrelevant to your treatment.

At a teaching hospital, be prepared to be exhibit number one. Interns will constantly be at your bedside, poking and prodding. Sure, you'll receive a lot of attention. But it may well be unwanted attention. A University of Chicago study revealed that patients at teaching hospitals were less satisfied with the quality of care than those at nonteaching hospitals. Remember, though, you have the right to refuse to allow a student, intern, resident, or anyone, for that matter, to touch you or treat you. Teaching hospitals may be learning centers for students or new doctors, but you have the right to refuse to be one of their subjects.

The only way to determine which hospital will meet your needs best is to ask your doctor questions about the hospital. Ask him about the hospital's reputation, about its strengths and weaknesses, about its costs. Some people are better-off at small community hospitals, where treatment is more personalized. Others might require a new state-of-the-art machine available only at a major medical center. Whatever your needs are, you have the right to choose your hospital.

Do I have to sign these forms?

Yes, but you can do so under protest and with reservations. You can also make modifications. When you're in the hospital, you will undergo a number of specific procedures. You should be given a consent form for each procedure. However, most of the time, you will not. Instead, you will be asked to sign the blanket release you were handed when you were admitted. Do so, but demand a consent form for each procedure proposed. A consent form should say what the hospital intends to do, what is involved, what the risks are, and what, if any, are the alternatives.

When you get the form, read it and, if necessary, revise it. Pay special attention to who the form specifies will do the procedure. You have the right to insist that you will not agree to the procedure unless Dr. X performs it; that intern Y can't do it, etc.

Make sure that the procedure described in the form is the same one that your doctor described to you. If it seems that the form grants permission for other procedures that you weren't aware of, don't sign the form until that point is clarified.

Remember, these forms aren't set in stone. In fact the form is provided by the hospital. It is not the law. It should lay out the information you need to make a decision. If the information appears wrong or unclear, don't consent. The form is a contract that's subject to revision, and you have the right to revise it. And you also have the right to say no to anything proposed.

What does the hospital do to prevent infections?

Not enough. Nosocomial (hospital-acquired) infections are the result of microorganisms that are common in hospitals. They can make you sick or kill you. Some estimates of infection-related deaths are as high as 100,000 annually. Almost 10 percent of patients entering a hospital will get such an infection. Fifty percent of these infections are preventable.

That's why you should ask a simple question: what's the hospital's rate of nosocomial infections? Is it above average? If the answer is yes, you should choose another hospital.

Even if the answer is below average, you should take certain steps to reduce the odds of infection. They include:

1. Demanding that hospital personnel wash their hands before they touch you. It's the easiest way of decreasing the odds of infection, and you have every right to make this request.

2. If your hospital roommate has an infection — or you're worried that he or she has something you might catch — ask the doctor about the risk. If there is a risk, request a transfer to another room.

3. If parts of your body will be shaved prior to surgery, don't let this happen the night before surgery. Nosocomial infection rates are significantly higher for those who are shaved the night before surgery.

4. Ask the nurses to check drainage of urinary catheters and maintain the cleanliness of the hospital room. Be alert to infections. Many patients who have acquired nosocomial infections have been bluffed into thinking it's a normal complication. It's not. It can be costly — and even deadly.

Is this operation necessary? Are there possible side effects to this drug? Are you sure your diagnosis is correct?

It might be difficult for you to ask these questions. After all, you're questioning your doctor's competence.

On the other hand, you have valid reasons for doing so. Consider:

• *The New England Journal of Medicine* reported a Harvard hospital study showing that 10 percent of all patients who had died might have lived if they had received the correct diagnosis. In some categories of disease, the misdiagnosis numbers were as high as 24 percent.

• *RN* magazine conducted a poll of more than 12,000 nurses; 46 percent thought 30 percent of surgery was unnecessary. Heart specialist and author Robert G. Schneider, M.D., suggests that between three million and six million unnecessary surgeries are performed annually.

• *Postgraduate Medicine* (January 1980) estimates adverse drug reactions in hospitalized patients at 18 percent or higher. Kenneth Barker, a pharmacist at Auburn University, estimates that an average 200-bed hospital makes 60 to 90 drug errors each day.

The three questions listed at the beginning of this section should be followed up with other, more detailed, questions. For instance:

• Is there another drug you might give me that has less harmful side effects?

• This isn't the same color as the pill I've been taking for the last week. Was my medication changed? Why? Was a mistake made?

• Are there nonsurgical alternatives to the operation you propose? What are they and what are their success rates? What is the success rate for the surgery you're suggesting?

• What is the basis for your diagnosis? Explain to me how the tests you had taken confirm that diagnosis. Is there a possibility that the tests aren't 100 percent accurate, and that other tests should be conducted before you make a diagnosis?

Specialists

The treatment you receive for a specific condition is often a result of a specialist's bias. Because specialties often overlap — you can see either a neurosurgeon or an orthopedist for a back condition, for instance — you may well be choosing your treatment by choosing your specialist.

A closed-circuit seminar at the Mayo Clinic focused on ulcerative colitis. The panel was divided into two groups of specialists: gastroenterological surgeons and internists. All the surgeons believed operations — permanent colostomies — were necessary. The internists disagreed; they believed the surgical risks were significant and careful monitoring of the condition was a better option.

Whom should you believe? Good question. But that's exactly why you need to ask questions.

Here's another example. A man went into a hospital with a serious circulation problem in his finger. A hand surgeon was to amputate the finger. The night before the operation, the man had second thoughts about the amputation and simply walked out. The next day, he consulted a vascular surgeon, who told him that the finger could be saved by transplanting one of the man's arteries into it. Both were viable options. Only by questioning and exercising your rights can you assure yourself of the best outcomes.

How do you prepare for the biases of specialists? When specialties overlap, consult both types of specialists. Hear their treatment recommendations and the reasons behind their recommendations. Compare the alternatives. You might even want to call in your personal physician to help you analyze each specialist's position. Don't forget second, or even third, opinions. Even in the same specialties, doctors disagree. That's because medicine is far more art than science. Some doctors don't keep up with new developments in their fields. Some are incompetent. They can be blamed afterward for bad results or mistakes, but the fact remains that you will still be injured. By pursuing your rights, you can improve your odds of a satisfactory outcome.

Children's Rights

As difficult as it is for adults to prepare themselves to deal with the health care system, problems multiply when children are involved.

The problems begin when doctors are forced to address two consumers: the child and his parents. Two sets of rights are involved, because what the doctor feels is best for the child might not coincide with the parents' feelings, and conflicts arise.

For instance: a critically ill newborn will survive only if extraordinary measures are taken, measures that will leave the child severely handicapped. The doctor believes the treatment is appropriate. The parents believe the baby should be allowed to die rather than live a miserable, pain-filled life.

Contrary to what you might think, doctors don't have the final authority in these decisions. As a parent, you have the right to act as your child's advocate. In most instances, the courts have supported the rights of parents over the recommendations of doctors. Though there are exceptions, especially in life-threatening situations, parents can and should participate in the treatment of their child.

But how much authority do you have? Consider the following frequently asked questions:

What should I do when the doctor insists that I wait outside while he examines my child?

Refuse. You have every right to be with your child during examinations and treatments. Other than an emergency, or if you have an older child receiving highly personal medical care, a doctor can't separate you from your child.

What should I do when the doctor dictates a course of treatment for my child?

Bringing a sick child to the doctor is often an emotional situation. You're concerned and upset, and your tendency is to look to the doctor as a savior. You desperately want to believe in his healing powers.

But every doctor is fallible, and you know things he doesn't. You have the right to informed consent before the doctor does anything to your child. In other words, he has to explain to you why the treatment is necessary, what it involves, what its consequences are, and treatment alternatives. If the doctor informs you that a significant minority of children experience severe allergic reactions to the drug he's recommending, you might want to consider alternative treatments or talk to another doctor.

My child is in the hospital, and the doctor says I can't stay with her. What can I do?

You can refuse to sign the consent form. Though the hospital can refuse to treat your child unless you sign, they might then be guilty of abandonment if they've already admitted the child or if it is an emergency. Usually, if a parent insists on remaining with a child throughout the hospital stay, they'll agree, albeit reluctantly.

I've heard certain vaccinations are dangerous to my child's health. Do I have the right to refuse vaccinations?

Yes. First talk to a physician about the risks versus the benefits of a specific vaccine. If the risks outweigh the benefits — even in the case of required immunizations for school-age children — you can obtain a medical exemption for your child in the form of a written statement from your doctor. You also might reside in one of 22 states that allow exemptions based on a parent's "philosophical objections." (See Appendix A.)

SPECIAL CONSIDERATIONS FOR CHILDREN

As we point out elsewhere in this chapter, protecting the medical rights of a child is sometimes different from protecting your own. The main difference is that the child cannot represent himself in as informed a way as an adult. In addition, most children have no legal standing.

But ultimately their rights are the same as yours. The key is to make sure that from a rights standpoint, the child's rights are protected with the same zeal as an adult's.

While most medical people tend to pamper and cuddle kids, they are often not concerned with their rights. In fact, some get downright ornery when a parent raises questions or issues that imply the practitioner may be doing harm to the little child.

Often, a well-meaning doctor or nurse may try to coerce a child into accepting a treatment without first consulting a parent. Even if the procedure is as minor as taking a blood sample, this should never be tolerated.

So here are some tips to keep in mind when it is your child who is being treated at the doctor's office or the hospital. Don't hesitate to use them. Don't be shy. Your child cannot speak for himself and is relying on you for protection.

• Always go into the examining room with your child. Ask the questions you would ask for yourself. The only time a doctor can legally deny a parent access to the examining room is if he suspects child abuse. Even in such cases, a witness other than an employee of the doctor should be present with a child.

• Never let the doctor do something to your child, at the office or in the hospital, without first getting your permission to do it. Children have the same rights to informed consent as adults; however, for a minor the parent or guardian is the only one authorized to give permission. Informed consent for a minor is really consent by an authorized adult.

• If your child is hospitalized, have someone present 24 hours a day. This is difficult, and may be resisted by the hospital personnel, but it is very important. Most children are incapable of asking the right questions when a nurse or doctor comes in to do something. Sometimes this occurs at night or at odd hours. Try to have someone present at all times who will stick up for the child's rights. You have the right to be with your child 24 hours a day, as long as you are not hindering the treatment of your child or others.

• If you are unable to have someone be with the child at all hours, and your child is capable of using the telephone, tell him to call you when someone wants to do something that you have not told him would happen. Let the hospital personnel know you want them to call you before any changes or alterations to the procedures are made.

• Inform the hospital personnel in friendly, but firm, words that you expect to be a part of your child's care. Emphasize that you are holding them responsible for the child and that anything less than full responsiveness is intolerable.

• If you feel your hospitalized child is not receiving the care or treatment required, in a timely and humane fashion, go see the hospital administrator immediately. You have every right to lodge a complaint and should do so if you have a legitimate concern. Don't worry if you are labeled a troublemaker, because troublemakers tend to get better care.

• Keep a record of all interactions and events. Keep track of who treats your child, what they do, and when. You may be surprised to find out that your records are better than theirs. The idea here is not to have a record so that you can sue them later, but rather to ensure that there is consistency in the treatment your child receives.

• Do not assume a special "children's hospital" is any less dangerous than a general hospital. While special children's hospitals may concentrate on children and their conditions, their potential for violating your child's rights are as great as any other hospital's. In fact, they might be even greater, because many people assume that children get better treatment than adults. The point is simple: the only advocate whose sole interest is your child is you.

Having a sick, injured, or medically needy child is a scary and traumatic experience. All we want is for the child to get the best care and get better. We must put our trust into

doctors and hospitals. But we must make sure they earn
that trust. We have to monitor their actions to safeguard
our children's medical rights.

Senior Citizens

Health care professionals often treat senior citizens much as
they treat children: as passive creatures who lack the ability to
participate in their own treatment.

Preparing for doctors and others who adopt this patronizing
attitude is essential. Your own attitude should be, in the words
of poet Dylan Thomas, to refuse to "go gentle into that good
night." In other words, don't let them push you around.

That means asking the same questions we've discussed earlier:
questions about treatment, reasons for treatment, side effects,
and so on. If you don't feel you'll be able to ask those questions,
designate someone as your advocate — a friend or family member.

There are a number of specific issues of concern to senior citizens. Let's look at some of the most important ones.

*My doctor has recommended a procedure, and I wonder if it's
worth doing. Maybe if I were 55, but I'm 78. Isn't age a factor in
treatment?*

In many situations, age *is* a determining factor for treatment. There are doctors who prey on the elderly, who know
Medicare will pay them for a given operation or procedure.
Yet the treatment often has more risks than rewards. For instance, removal of cancerous tissue is often unnecessary. Because cancers grow far more slowly in the elderly than in younger
people, it often makes sense to avoid operations and treat the
cancer with nonsurgical procedures. Yet doctors are quick to
recommend the scalpel, either because they're inexperienced in
dealing with elderly patients or because it's an easy way to make
a fast buck.

Therefore, get second, and even third, opinions before you
consent to major medical procedures.

Do all doctors have to accept Medicare?

No. Before a doctor begins treatment, ask him if he accepts
Medicare. Your local Social Security Administration office or

the Area Agency on Aging will help you locate a doctor who does.

Along the same lines, you should know that Medicare is not a financial long-term solution. It won't pay for an extended stay at a nursing home. It will, however, cover most short-term health care costs.

My doctor recommends that I move into a nursing home. It's true that I can't get around the way I used to, but aren't there other options?

There are and you should explore them. One possibility is in-home care, which might involve an ambulatory service such as dialysis. Another possibility is home-sharing — living cooperatively with other senior citizens in a house where a resident/manager makes sure everything runs smoothly. You can also contract for outside services that meet a specific need: Meals on Wheels programs, adult day-care centers, homemaker services, and telephone reassurance programs.

If these options prove unworkable and you decide to enter a nursing home, shop around. The quality of care and financial arrangements vary considerably. One home, for instance, might have excellent physical therapy resources — resources you need. Another might be staffed with registered nurses skilled in long-term care, as opposed to a home that has relatively few skilled personnel.

Remember: don't enter a home simply because your doctor tells you he can get you in. You wouldn't buy a house sight unseen, and neither should you make an investment in a nursing home without checking out the facilities and the costs.

SPECIAL CONSIDERATIONS FOR SENIORS

Senior citizens use the health care system more than any other group. More tests and procedures, operations and treatments, drugs and medical equipment are doled out to Americans 65 and older each year, and the numbers are only getting bigger.

Senior citizens are also more vulnerable to having their medical rights violated than any other group. Children, at least, most often have a parent or guardian who can help to protect them. That is not always the case with older medical consumers.

There are many important considerations senior citizens should take into account when dealing with the medical system. Here are some tips they and their families and friends should use to protect their rights.

• Always take someone with you into the examining room at the doctor's office. Many elderly people are at a disadvantage at the doctor's office, because they can be hard of hearing, nervous out of fear, or just not fully aware of what is going on. Having someone along ensures that questions are asked and answers are heard.

• If you have no one to take along with you to the doctor's office, take a small tape recorder with you. Tell the doctor you want to record the examination or session so that you can remember what he said or advised. The doctor may balk at this out of fear that you might be setting him up for a lawsuit. But explain that he keeps a record, and so do you.

• Say no to anything you do not understand. In the hospital, seniors are often cajoled into having something done to them by staff or physicians who treat a senior citizen like a child. Don't let this happen. If you do not understand what they are proposing, say no to it, and tell them to explain in a way you fully understand. This is your right, and they have no business trying to bypass it.

• Use every means you have available to exercise your rights. For example, if you feel that the hospital or doctor has overcharged Medicare for services rendered (or not rendered) to you, call the Department of Health and Human Services, Office of the Inspector General's Medicare Fraud Hotline (for phone number see Appendix A).

• Ask for it in writing. Hospital and medical personnel often explain things quickly, often too fast for an older person to comprehend. Later, after damage has been done, the medical people say they advised you of your rights. Even though you did not understand what they told you, they may have the law on their side. So tell them to put what they are proposing in writing, and take the time to review it (bring in someone to help if necessary) before you make a decision.

• Don't be afraid to call in others. Many senior citizens become stubborn about acknowledging their shortcomings. While this is certainly understandable, the problem this attitude may create in medical matters is that you get second-rate care. Get friends and relatives involved in your care. They will protect your interests better than you may your own in some instances.

• Don't be afraid of offending a doctor. Many senior citizens feel that doctors and hospitals are doing them a favor by treating them. As a result, they often do not seek second opinions, are afraid to question their doctor, and sometimes are reluctant to leave a doctor they know is not competent. Don't worry about offending the doctor. It is your health that is at stake. It is your right to get second or third opinions, ask questions, and change doctors.

It is a sad commentary on the medical establishment that older Americans are so vulnerable to abuse and rights violations by a profession and industry that are designed to serve and to do so with compassion. But the fact is that many senior citizens are sitting ducks for such abuse. And once again, we must be on guard to protect our own and our loved ones' rights.

Be Your Own Advocate

Asking questions and speaking up for your rights is a logical response to the health care system.

You wouldn't jump out of a plane without a parachute.

You wouldn't enter a foreign country without first finding out whether the political conditions were on an even keel.

You wouldn't cross a busy street without looking both ways.

You wouldn't buy a car without shopping around.

When you enter a potentially dangerous situation, it's sensible and appropriate to take precautions. Yet for many years, Americans have jumped into the health care system without first testing the waters; without surveying its surface and depths for problems; without looking for sharks. In other words, Americans have been naive, poorly prepared health care consumers.

No more. Americans are starting to realize that up and down the line, our health care system has faults. Mistakes are routinely made. Incompetence is a danger, and few effective safeguards exist to discipline or monitor the actions of incompetent physicians. Hospitals, nursing homes, and other health care settings frequently treat patients as second-class citizens, ignoring and abusing their rights.

Prepare for the worst and you're likely to avoid it. Question everyone from physicians to nurses to administrators. Be on the lookout for the doctor who might be making a critical mistake in your treatment. Be skeptical of the nurse who is about to draw your blood for the fourth time that day. Make sure there's a reason for what she's doing and that you're not simply feeding the vampires in the laboratory.

Learn to use your greatest consumer gift — your mouth. Ask questions. Say no to things you do not understand. Be assertive when you can, and when you can't, bring someone with you who can stand up for you.

Prepare for a health care system that turns many bright, idealistic medical students into money-hungry, insensitive physicians. Your doctor has been through a gauntlet of sleepless nights, low pay, and crushing work loads. From medical school to internship to residency, he's been through the equivalent of boot camp — boot camp that's lasted 10 years or more. By the time he gets out, he's likely to be cynical and in debt. He's in his early 30s and ready to get his slice of the pie. The system hasn't encouraged him to develop ethical standards or compassion for his patients. Instead, it's made him bitter and arrogant.

Not all doctors fit this profile. But enough of them do so that you should be prepared for the sizable percentage who are like this. You have a right to be treated like a human being, not like a piece of meat.

You are the only person available at all times to protect your rights. Being your own health advocate is the best way to do that. Advocacy means many things: it means speaking out for yourself and others; it means learning the way the system works and taking actions so that it works for you; it means asking questions and demanding answers; and it means being prepared for situations that can cause you or loved ones harm.

Remember, in health and medical care, harm that has been done is often irreversible. You may win some money; you may get revenge; you may even stop the practitioner from practicing. But you may never be whole again. Don't be afraid to be an advocate for yourself.

CHAPTER THREE

Disclosure

How MUCH are you entitled to know? When you go to your doctor and he recommends a medication, how much does he have to tell you about that drug's efficacy and its side effects? How much should you know about the surgeon whom you're referred to and who may operate on you; how many times has he done the operation, and what is his success rate?

From a strictly legal standpoint, the health care profession isn't obligated to tell you much. There are no state or federal laws that mandate disclosure of all the information you really should have. Most of the information you get is usually the result of your prodding or questioning.

On the other hand, pressure from consumers and organizations like the People's Medical Society is being brought to bear on health care practitioners to disclose that information. For instance, medical malpractice suits are making doctors think twice about holding back facts about treatment. Malpractice insurance underwriters say that doctors' failure to explain potential risks and outcomes of treatment is a common cause of suits. Some states have passed laws that require doctors to explain the risks of certain procedures.

Still, doctors and other health care practitioners are miserly when it comes to dispensing information. Some of them just don't want to be bothered; others claim they're too busy. There are physicians who assume that their patients won't understand what they're telling them, so what's the point? Still others believe that a little information is a dangerous thing — consumers will worry themselves to death. And remarkably, some doctors don't even know the risks associated with procedures they perform, medications they dispense, or treatments they prescribe. Since most people don't ask, why bother to keep current?

Don't accept these attitudes. You have every right to this information. You need to make informed decisions about your care. Without it, you're in the dark; you have no control. With it, you can make educated decisions about what's best for you.

Disclosure is more than your doctor's telling you that you need an operation, that you'll be in the hospital for a week, and chances for a full recovery are 95 percent. Disclosure means knowing the relevant facts, statistics, and evidence that support a doctor's recommendation to do or not to do something. If, for instance, the mortality rate for the operation is 20 percent, he should tell you that. He should explain typical postoperative symptoms. He should clearly communicate what will occur during the operation: the steps in the procedure, how long it will take, who will be operating, the surgeon's qualifications for performing the operation, and so on. In fact, not only should this be provided — it should be in writing. This is the consent form we said you should demand whenever a major or questionable procedure, treatment, or medication is recommended.

You have a right to all the facts. Without them, you might end up like the following victims of the health care system.

THE POSTOPERATIVE SCARS

Marilyn was a thirty-five-year-old woman who wanted to have breast implants to enlarge her bust. She visited a cosmetic surgeon who explained the relatively simple procedure, clearly communicating how the procedure would improve her appearance.

Marilyn was excited and gave her consent for the operation, agreeing to pay the substantial fee the cosmetic surgeon requested.

The operation went smoothly, and Marilyn came through it well, with the fuller breasts she desired.

There was only one problem: highly visible, raised whitish scars where the surgeon had cut, called keloids. This type of scar is permanent.

Marilyn was, naturally, quite upset. Given that the purpose of the operation was to improve her appearance, she had every right to be angry. If she had known that her larger breasts would be accompanied by scars, she wouldn't have agreed to the operation.

Marilyn's surgeon failed to inform her that a significant minority of the population "throw keloids." True, the majority don't. But Marilyn wasn't informed of this risk and therefore wasn't able to factor it into her decision.

RADIATION OVERDOSE

In 1970, Lucy had cervical cancer. Doctors operated and removed the cancerous tissue. They also followed up with radiation treatments; Lucy received ten treatments of 2500 rads each.

Ten years later, there was a recurrence of the cervical cancer. Lucy had a complete hysterectomy. Afterward, her doctor mapped out a program of radiation therapy. After the radiation treatments, Lucy became seriously ill, but not from the cancer. Instead, her intestines were slowly deteriorating to the point where she now needs constant blood transfusions and is fed intravenously.

Lucy was suffering from radiation enteritis, the result of excessive radiation.

What didn't Lucy's doctor disclose? The fact that radiation has a cumulative effect. At some point, he should have said to Lucy, "There's a risk with radiation; too much of it can result in a radiation overdose. It builds up in your body over time." He should have asked Lucy whether she had had radiation therapy earlier.

If he had told her that and asked her about previous treatment, Lucy surely would have reminded him that she had radiation treatments 10 years ago and the course of her treatment could have been altered to avoid the terrible consequences of the enteritis.

THE FOOTBALL INJURY

Steve was a standout high-school football player, over six feet tall and able to bench-press 400 pounds. He was a top college prospect until he made a head-on tackle of a bruising fullback.

The bolt on the side of his helmet was loose and, in the collision, dug into the side of his face. After the game ended, Steve went to the hospital, complaining of dizziness and double vision.

It seemed as though he was okay, though he had a concussion. The opthalmologist said he also had a blow-out fracture of the orbit of one eye, but as long as the ocular nerve wasn't trapped, he'd be fine.

Still, the double vision didn't go away. Steve's parents took him to a leading plastic surgeon, who didn't seem overly concerned about the double vision. He did, however, say that he recommended reconstructive surgery for the damaged orbit, explaining that without such surgery, Steve would have a scar. He added that during surgery they could check out the eye, but that Steve shouldn't worry because the ocular nerve wasn't trapped. Steve decided he didn't care if he had a scar and declined the surgery.

Yet the double vision persisted. Two weeks later, Steve's parents took him to another well-known surgeon. The surgeon took one look at Steve and said, "You need surgery immediately. Any fool can see the optic nerve is trapped. If you wait, the optic nerve will atrophy and you'll have permanent double vision."

Though this is a case of misdiagnosis, there is also an important disclosure issue involved. Neither the opthalmologist nor the plastic surgeon disclosed the dangers of a trapped optic nerve; neither of them mentioned the possibility of permanent double vision. If they had, Steve and his parents would have been justifiably alarmed; they certainly wouldn't have waited two weeks before visiting another surgeon.

Forms of Disclosure

Anyone who has ever left the doctor's office with more questions than answers knows the importance of disclosure. You've visited your physician, and he's prescribed a drug; or he's told you, "We're going to have to watch that condition carefully"; or he's said that your symptoms indicate that you might have a certain disease. This kind of talk can mean several things.

For example, he may not be willing to commit himself to a specific diagnosis. This is common. But just as likely, it may mean he has no idea of what is wrong and is afraid to acknowledge his ignorance with an honest, "I don't know what's wrong."

Invariably, as you're driving home, scores of questions occur to you. It's as if your doctor has opened a Pandora's box of worrisome thoughts by his ambiguous, unclear statements. Even if you had the doctor's undivided attention for hours, you wouldn't know where to begin.

But here's a start. Most encounters with health care practitioners are divided into certain categories. You should be sure to request and receive from the practitioner information in each of them.

Questions About the Hospital Recommended or Used

• In the past year, how many times has the hospital performed the procedure recommended for you, and what have been the outcome statistics (success, failure, complications, etc.)? Studies show the more a procedure is done at a hospital, the better the outcomes tend to be.

• What is the hospital's nosocomial (hospital-caused) infection rate? The procedure may be fine and done with skill, but the national average for infections acquired in hospitals is growing to the point where some studies indicate almost 1 in 10 consumers gets a nosocomial infection. Other studies note up to 80 percent are avoidable, unnecessary infections.

• What are the number and types of accidents in the hospital? This is important. Many people are injured in hospitals as a result of slippery floors, improperly fitted railings on beds, etc. Ask how many workers' compensation claims have been filed during the previous year. If workers are getting hurt, imagine what could happen to you!

• What are the number and types of malpractice claims against a hospital, including specific hospital personnel involved in the suits? What were the outcomes of the suits? Hospitals are reluctant to provide this information; insist on having it.

• What sort of experimental treatments (related to your specific area of concern) were done during the past year? Has the Institutional Review Board commented on any of those experiments? What were their comments? Don't be a guinea pig for your doctor's medical education. Make sure you are fully informed if any aspect of your care, all of it or part of it, is experimental.

• What are the hospital's morbidity (nonfatal complications) and mortality statistics for your procedure? While this does not tell you everything, it gives you a measure for comparison of one hospital with another.

Questions About Treatments and Procedures

• What is the treatment? Exactly what does it involve? Make sure you're told in detail and that the information is given in writing and without prejudice (i.e., there are no threats not to treat you if you do not go along with the recommended procedures). Remember, the law says this information must be disclosed. There are absolutely no exceptions other than life-threatening emergencies.

• What are the risks and benefits, as well as the success rate? If there is going to be only a 20 percent chance of full recovery, would you still risk the procedure? In addition, make sure you are told what could happen to you if you elect not to have the procedure and on what basis that determination is made.

• What is the cost of the treatment? This is important. Medical care providers tend not to disclose full costs. Demand that this be done in writing and in full. Indicate to the doctor that you are holding him to that figure. Also, indicate that any proposed changes must be discussed and approved by you.

• After the procedure is done, what's next? Are there follow-up tests and other monitoring procedures? Most procedures, particularly invasive ones, require a significant amount of after-procedures and after-care. You have the right to know the specifics before you consent to the treatment.

• What literature exists about the procedure, both favoring it and against it? Where can that literature be obtained? You have the right to see or be referred to the evidence that supports the doctor's claim. Don't be shy or put off by this. Remember, you usually read a large amount of literature about an automobile before you buy it. Do the same about the procedures being proposed.

Questions About Your Practitioner

• What are the doctor's credentials: education, experience, qualifications, board certification, institutional and professional affiliations, publications, license information, and states where he is licensed? Don't be misled by titles or names a doctor bestows on his practice, such as "holistic" or "the women's center." These are self-applied "advertising" gimmicks and not valid indications of competence.

• Has the doctor been involved in any disciplinary actions, including malpractice suits? What was the outcome of these actions? Check with the state medical licensing board for actions against the practitioner. Ask the practitioner if he has ever been sued and what the outcomes were.

• What does the doctor charge for "typical" procedures? Ask the doctor for a fee schedule. Ask if he accepts Medicare assignment. If the doctor will not put his fees in writing, confirm what he told you in writing after you are given a price.

• Does the doctor have any financial interest in a health care or other, related, facility? Doctors often own all or part of the service organization they refer you to. Ask if your doctor has an ownership stake. If so, there may be a conflict of interest. The doctor is obligated to tell you if you ask. In Pennsylvania, such information must be disclosed up front.

Records

When it comes to health care records, think of yourself as someone who keeps two sets of books: one will be provided by various health care practitioners and facilities; the other will be your own.

Both are important. The more information you have about your medical history, the better you'll be able to safeguard your medical future.

You should routinely request records from doctors, hospitals, and laboratories. If you don't request those records, odds are that you won't receive them. Request them verbally at first. If that doesn't work, put your request in writing.

Be insistent. Health care practitioners don't like to part with what they feel are their records. But they're about you, not them. You have a right to obtain copies of your hospital medical charts, lab tests, diagnostic tests, annual check-up results, and so on. If your doctor is reluctant to part with those records, you might decide to be reluctant about paying his bills. After all, documentation of what has been done to you is part of the service you've contracted for.

Not all states have laws that assure you of getting your records. So negotiate this point with your doctor. Tell him that as a condition of your being his patient, you want copies of your records upon request.

Don't wait to obtain those records. They have a habit of getting lost after a period of time. Hospitals' records can be especially problematical. After a number of years, old records are often thrown away. Another problem is that hospitals close, and records disappear after closings.

Records can disclose information to you that might not otherwise be forthcoming. Consider all written information from health care practitioners a record, even bills. For instance, a woman went into a hospital for a biopsy, and the doctor told her the results were negative. She was relieved until the bill arrived. Besides the various charges for the biopsy, the bill stated that tissue from the biopsy was found to be malignant. Luckily, the woman read her bill carefully. She contacted her doctor and he checked the results; indeed, the bill was right and he was wrong. Keep copies of all your medical records as long as you can.

Don't depend only on "outside" records. Keep your own medical diary. During or after a visit with a doctor, write down what he said. Note whatever tests or procedures are done, and the results. Keep a running list of medications — what they are, when you first began taking them, side effects.

It is equally important to jot down what your doctor tells you. In some instances, what he says and what he does can be two different things entirely.

A man visited his doctor, complaining of stomach problems.

The doctor assured him nothing was wrong and didn't recommend any tests or treatment. Later, the man learned he had gastric cancer. He sued the doctor for malpractice. Though the doctor claimed he had recommended a gastroscopy (examination of the interior of the stomach), there was nothing in the records to confirm that. In addition, the man's notes from his meeting with the doctor contained no mention of a gastroscopy.

Here's another reason to write your own medical history: medical records sometimes are incomplete or altered. It's not unusual to find a record of a doctor's visit with a patient to contain only the following: "Saw patient today, examined him." It's also relatively easy for a doctor or nurse to add a few words to the medical record after the fact, reshaping the truth to their advantage.

Finally, maintaining your own records gives you a better understanding of the medical facts. For most people, medical jargon is confusing; it's easy to misinterpret or misunderstand what a physician tells you, especially if that physician isn't a good communicator. If you have trouble remembering or understanding what the doctor tells you, then disclosure won't do much good. (See Your Medical Record, Appendix C.)

Medical Products

What do you really know about the medical products you purchase — such things as pacemakers, birth control devices, vitamins, self-test kits? In most cases, not enough. From a legal perspective, you have a right to know more than you do, especially if there are potentially harmful side effects or if there is some defect in the product.

Take, for example, home test equipment designed to determine if there's occult blood in your feces or for pregnancy or for blood pressure measurement. What harm can these tests cause? A lot, if people misuse them because of poor or misleading label instructions or because certain information was omitted.

Let's say you're worried because you've had intestinal pain, loose, irregular bowel movements, and other symptoms that make you suspect you have a problem. You purchase a self-test kit and are relieved to find that you test negative; no occult blood. You figure you don't have a serious problem, such as cancer, and ignore your symptoms. But the symptoms persist.

Months later, you go to your doctor; he administers more sophisticated tests and finds that you have a malignant tumor in your small intestine, a tumor that, if it were treated earlier, might have increased your chances for survival.

If the warning label on the test didn't clearly indicate that it wasn't 100 percent accurate — that x percent of the time users get a false positive or negative — then it's quite possible you have grounds for a lawsuit.

Other tests pose other problems. One might have poorly written instructions that cause you to misread the results. Another might be highly inaccurate, resulting in a false positive that could cause you a great deal of worry and expense — you go to your doctor and insist he perform a series of expensive tests because of the false positive.

Another area of concern is defective medical devices or products. As soon as a company learns its product is defective, they must immediately inform you of that fact. If they don't do it quickly enough — or even worse, if they attempt to suppress or minimize the problem — then you have the right to take legal action if you've suffered as a result.

Here's an example. A company that manufactures pacemakers learned that a batch of pacemakers had defective cases, allowing bodily fluids to enter the pacemaker and cause malfunctions. The company immediately issued a recall on all the pacemakers, sending letters to a list of doctors informing them of the recall. The doctors, in turn, notified their patients.

One elderly woman, upon receiving a note from her doctor about her defective pacemaker, became quite upset. In fact, she was so upset that she had to be rushed to the hospital. Because of her hospital stay and the operation to remove and replace her pacemaker, she incurred thousands of dollars in hospital bills.

The manufacturer refused to reimburse her for those bills. They claimed that though her pacemaker was indeed one of the batch thought to be defective, they had examined the device and found it to be in working order.

She filed a lawsuit, which the company's attorney was, naturally, eager to settle. The woman had every right to be reimbursed for a problem caused by the manufacturer. Here are some of the most frequently asked questions (and answers) about disclosure requirements:

Do I have the right to my medical record?

It depends on the state in which you reside. (See Appendix A for your state agencies.) If there is a statute that grants you access to your medical records, and your doctor refuses to give them up, then contact the appropriate governmental agency — usually the state's attorney or attorney general's office. They'll contact your doctor and enforce compliance with the statute.

Without a statute, the law is fuzzy. Technically, a doctor doesn't have to give his records to you. That's because, unlike an X ray or test you paid for, they're his personal records, not yours. On the other hand, the state may well consider the matter a public policy issue. Because his medical record affects you so personally, it might be determined that your right to that record supersedes other considerations.

Is my doctor required to tell me if he has been sued or has judgements against him for malpractice?

No. But if you ask him that question and he refuses to answer, then you should immediately be suspicious.

Do I have the right to have copies of my test results?

Yes, but remember they're copies, not necessarily originals. You may have to pay for the copying expenses, which can be considerable when records are several hundred pages long. You might want to request copies only of specific, relevant sections of the results, thereby cutting down on your costs.

Is my doctor required to tell me if he owns, fully or partially, the laboratory or any other service to which he sends me or my specimens?

It depends on the state. In Pennsylvania, for example, the doctor is required to disclose such information. That's not true in many other states. Federal legislation is pending that would require such disclosure. Contact your state attorney general's office for your state's requirements.

Can I find out if a doctor who moved into my state has had disciplinary actions against him in other states?

Yes, if you know the state where he formerly practiced. Contact the medical licensing board in that state. (See Appendix A for addresses and phone numbers.) A federal law that went into effect in 1989 requires a national data bank of such information, but Congress prohibited public access to that data bank.

Can my doctor lie to me?

In certain cases. If, for instance, he can demonstrate that he lied because the truth would have been medically detrimental, then courts have allowed the practitioner to lie.

However, if you agree with your doctor that he will tell you the truth — no matter what it is — he has an obligation and you have a right to the unadulterated facts.

This can be a problematical area, especially when doctors, out of a sense of compassion, can't bring themselves to tell a patient that there's no hope, that his condition is terminal. In most cases, however, compassion is no substitute for the truth. The majority of people don't want to be deceived about their conditions.

At the other extreme, doctors lie to protect themselves. For instance, a physician ignored a man's complaints that the cast on his broken leg was too tight. Subsequently, the doctor learned that the bones were misaligned, but he told the man, "This is a typical problem. Nothing could have been done about it earlier." As a result of his mistake, the doctor was forced to operate and insert a plate, and infection (osteomyelytis) resulted.

From a legal standpoint, a doctor's lie creates the basis for a legal action for fraud, and fraud extends the statute of limitations for legal action. Therefore, if you discover years later that your doctor lied, you still have time to file a lawsuit. In addition, the lie can be a basis for punitive damages against the physician.

Is the standard release form I am forced to sign when I enter the hospital binding?

It depends on what the release form says. If it's a release against negligence on the hospital's part, it doesn't really matter if you sign it. It's unenforceable. Generally, such forms have been held to be against public policy.

Some hospitals have created another type of release form, one in which you waive your right to file a lawsuit in common court and agree to arbitration as a resolution for malpractice. Again, these releases have been held to be unenforceable because they're considered "contracts of adhesion" — the hospital has such a tremendous bargaining advantage that you're placed in an unequal position.

The hospital might also ask you to sign a consent form for a specific procedure. Don't sign a blanket consent, allowing them to do anything they feel is necessary. Consent only to the procedure that you've been informed about and agree is necessary.

If you refuse to sign a blanket consent form, the surgeon may refuse to operate. He has that option in some instances. He doesn't have that option, however, if any delay in the operation might result in negative consequences — if you have a ruptured appendix, for example.

When children are involved, it is important to be aware of considerations that are particularly relevant to their care.

Can my child have an abortion without my consent?

Yes, if she is of legal adult age, as determined by state law.

Can our family doctor withhold information about my child's condition?

Yes, if your child is of legal adult age, he or she can instruct the doctor to keep certain things confidential.

Can my 15-year-old son or daughter enroll in a drug treatment program without my permission?

Yes, if 15 is adult legal age in your state.

I don't want my child to have certain inoculations. But the school says I can't enroll him unless he receives them. Can they do that?

Maybe. The law requires inoculations in most states, but many states also have medical, religious, and other exemptions. (See Appendix A for more information.)

Can a doctor keep me out of the examining room while he examines my child?

Under only two circumstances. First, if he suspects child abuse by either parent or guardian, he may keep you out while he questions or examines the child. Second, if you are hindering or getting in the way of proper medical care, he may ask you to leave. Otherwise, you have the right to be there.

Senior citizens should be aware of disclosure requirements in several areas, such as the following:

Is the doctor required to take Medicare assignment?

No. And unless you ask if he takes Medicare, he also doesn't have to disclose this fact prior to treatment.

Can I negotiate fees with my doctor?

Absolutely. Just because you're elderly and your insurance or Medicare will pay for part or even all of the treatment, don't let your doctor dictate fees. Negotiate. Since fees are made up by doctors there is room to discount. Those who negotiate usually win.

My spouse is hard of hearing and not always aware of what is going on. Can I be present at all examinations?

Yes. You may also ask questions, seek more information, and assist your spouse in whatever way is necessary to make more informed medical decisions.

My husband told the doctor not to tell me if he finds I have cancer. Can he do that?

Yes, but the doctor can't withhold such information unless he has sound reason to believe that telling you would make your condition worse. If you're worried about this possibility, tell your doctor you want to know the results, regardless of what your spouse tells him.

Do I have the right to stop heroic measures from being taken to prolong my life?

Sometimes. Only 39 states have living will laws that allow you to set the terms of your own death relative to heroic measures. Generally, if you are of sound mind, you can insist that all treatments be stopped, and the courts (if it comes to that) will back you up. The problem arises when you're not of sound mind — if you're in a coma, for instance. In those instances, hospitals will feel obligated to do everything possible to keep you alive, despite the wishes of family members.

The prescribing and dispensing of medications is a topic of great importance to the empowered consumer.

Is there a law that requires I be given the package inserts that explain the side effects of medications prescribed for me?

There almost was. In 1980, Congress passed a law that would have required that the ten most prescribed medications include such inserts with each filling. However, President Reagan made this law his first veto.

Is my doctor required to tell me the side effects of medication he prescribes for me?

He should, but usually won't unless you ask. Make sure you demand detailed information about side effects.

Can my pharmacist prescribe medication?

Only in Florida.

Must my physician inform me if there is a generic drug available in lieu of the brand name he prescribed?

In most states, only if you ask. You can also ask the pharmacist for a generic equivalent.

May I bring prescription medication from foreign countries into this country if it's not approved in the U.S.?

Not legally.

Certain disclosure issues pertain only to women. The following questions are ones women are most likely to ask, and the answers provide information that will make you a more empowered consumer.

Do I have the right to an abortion?

Yes. The only question is who pays for it. Federal monies can't fund it, and some states prohibit their monies from being used for this purpose.

Can a doctor do a cesarean section without my permission?

Only in emergencies. Still, they're done far too often. Doctors make a great deal of money from C-sections, and they're more convenient for the doctor (they can schedule them as they do any operation, rather than running to the hospital in the middle of the night).

Doctors should perform C-sections only when a normal delivery presents increased risk to mother or child. If a doctor insists on doing a C-section, he should clearly explain what the risk of normal birth is, such as the possibility of a mother's venereal disease being passed on to the child, or the child's position in the womb hindering the delivery.

If you suspect that the doctor performed a C-section for some other reason, you may have grounds for a malpractice suit. If specific damages result from the C-section — such as weakening of muscles from the incision, or scar tissue — you might want to consult a lawyer.

Can a doctor do a hysterectomy without my approval?

No.

May I request that another woman be present during a gynecological exam?

Yes, and you can choose that woman. You may also request that your spouse be there.

I think I once had a Dalkon Shield IUD inserted. Now I read that I have the right to collect damages from the manufacturer. Can my doctor deny me the information I need to determine if I did have a Dalkon Shield IUD?

No, but many women are being denied that information. Some doctors are not aware that they're not liable for prescribing the Dalkon Shield. The federal court case that set up the damage fund specifically prohibited such action. Still, doctors' ignorance of this prohibition has caused some of them to assume that they could be sued. Set your doctor straight and demand the information.

I am about to remarry. Can my future husband obtain a copy of my medical record from my doctor without my knowledge?

No. Even when you're married, he can't obtain it without your written permission.

CHAPTER FOUR

Prisoner or Patient?

IF YOU'VE EVER BEEN HOSPITALIZED, the odds are you have a horror story to tell. It might not be anything catastrophic — the food made you sick, a bullying nurse refused to answer your questions, you were charged for services that weren't rendered. Or it might have been more serious. You were given the wrong medication, a major surgical error was made, you acquired a staph infection.

Everything that's wrong with health care tends to become worse in a hospital setting. Hospitals, because of their size, structure, and policies, systematically encourage a denial of their customers' rights. The horror stories are partially a result of that denial. Robbed of your ability to exercise your common sense — to speak out and question a particular treatment or policy — you are particularly vulnerable to the system's abuses.

Despite appearances, the hospital is not a prison. From the moment you check in to the time you check out, you're entitled to question, criticize, refuse, leave, consult, and consider alternatives. In this chapter, we'll show you how to do so.

Let's begin with a few hospital stories.

THE DELAY

Mark Copely visited his doctor, complaining about stomach pain. The doctor told him not to worry about it, but if it persisted, to come back and they'd run some tests. The pain not only persisted, it intensified. Mark was rushed to the hospital emergency room when he began vomiting blood.

X rays were taken and Mark was kept in the hospital for four days. During that time, he was in agonizing pain. Yet no one was sure what was wrong. His symptoms didn't quite fit the pattern for any particular condition. Mark instinctively recognized that something was terribly wrong, but when he spoke to the doctors who examined him, they spoke of "waiting and seeing what develops." Mark accepted their advice; he felt he had little choice in the matter.

After four days, one of the doctors noticed that Mark's white blood cell count was high. It wasn't quite clear why no one had noticed it before. But the high count immediately suggested the obvious: Mark had a burst appendix that had led to peritonitis. His life was hanging in the balance, and an emergency seven-hour operation was performed.

Luckily, Mark pulled through. His recovery was going along smoothly; then he received a $25,000 bill from the hospital, most of it for the emergency surgery.

Mark was justifiably outraged. Not only had the hospital's inaction almost cost him his life, but they were trying to make a profit out of their negligence.

Mark consulted a lawyer, who, in turn, contacted the treating doctors, requesting Mark's records as well as their explanations of what had happened. Amazingly, none of the doctors admitted making a mistake. As one of them put it, "It was just one of those things. We had to explore all the possibilities."

More likely, they failed to explore and act upon the most likely possibility. They failed to listen to Mark, who was certain something was seriously wrong. They failed to watch his white blood cell count and match it up with his symptoms. Perhaps Mark's doctors were overworked and weren't able to give Mark's case the attention it deserved. Perhaps the doctors were relatively inexperienced and didn't have the knowledge to read the obvious signs. Perhaps they were simply incompetent.

Whatever the reason, Mark had a right to obtain prompt medical treatment. Even the meanest criminal has the right to a speedy trial. If Mark had known he had the same right to a speedy diagnosis, he — or a friend or relative — could have demanded that something be done about his condition. If the doctors hadn't waited four days, Mark would have had a simple appendectomy. The hospital not only put Mark's life in jeopardy, they charged him far more than they should have. Mark successfully maintained an action for malpractice against the treating doctor and hospital.

THE HEALTHY KIDNEY

Margie Klopek complained to her doctor about urinary pain. The doctor immediately suspected a problem, since Margie had one diseased, marginally functional kidney. A test was done, and it indicated there was indeed something wrong with her healthy kidney.

The doctor put Margie in the local hospital. Exploratory surgery was scheduled, before which the doctor had her sign a general consent form.

During the exploratory surgery, the doctor removed Margie's "good" kidney. Afterward, the doctor explained that he had identified a malignant tumor and thought it best to remove the kidney immediately.

Margie was aghast. The doctor hadn't even mentioned the possibility of removing her kidney before the surgery, though the general consent form did contain a clause allowing him to "perform whatever additional surgery is deemed necessary."

Margie contacted a lawyer, who eventually brought a successful malpractice suit against the doctor and the hospital. The basis of the suit was that the doctor should never have abridged Margie's rights by removing the kidney without her express permission. By doing so, he was dooming her to a life dependent on a dialysis machine. Furthermore, the suit alleged, the doctor should first have done a frozen section of the suspected tumor to confirm the malignancy. If it was malignant, then he still should not have removed the entire kidney; proper procedure would have called for removing only the malignancy and monitoring the kidney to see if a malignancy reappeared.

But the doctor's negligence didn't end there. The pathologist's report stated that there was no tumor and the kidney was healthy.

The doctor responded that he knew it was malignant because he "eyeballed the tumor, and I should know it was malignant because I've seen so many of them." When asked why there was no evidence of a tumor, the doctor responded, "Well, I guess when they were carrying the kidney from the operating room the tumor fell off the tray."

Again, this is a clear and common rights violation. If Margie had known that the hospital's general consent form was giving the surgeon carte blanche to remove her only kidney, she would never have signed. Or at the very least, she would have amended the form's language, allowing him to do only a frozen section.

EARLY DISCHARGE

Harry Peters was in the hospital, recovering from major abdominal surgery — the resection of an intestine. The typical recovery period for the operation was seven days, but Harry still felt weak and dizzy on the eighth day.

The hospital wanted to discharge Harry, but he didn't feel it was safe for him to leave; Harry was an elderly man who lived alone, and he'd be going home to an empty apartment with no one to take care of him. The hospital knew this, but they persisted, trying to persuade Harry to leave. They sought a second opinion, and the consulted doctor concurred that Harry should be discharged.

At this point, Harry had no choice but to leave; he would have to pay for the room if he stayed. After the second opinion was communicated to Harry's insurance company, the company had refused to pay for even one more additional day in the hospital.

Harry went home. That night, Harry fainted, fractured his hip, and was readmitted to the hospital.

Subsequently, he filed a successful lawsuit against the hospital. The hospital had no right to put Harry at risk by sending him home prematurely. In effect, they used the insurance company's refusal of payment to blackmail Harry into leaving.

Check It Out Before You Check In

Mark, Margie, and Harry realized too late that their rights were being violated. The damage was already done. With hindsight, each one of them would tell you that the best time to understand and exercise your rights is the moment you learn that you're going to be hospitalized.

It's unlikely that an emergency will prompt your hospitalization — only about 5 percent of people who are hospitalized come via the emergency-room route. You'll probably have sufficient time to check out a hospital before you check in.

Begin by visiting a facility you and your doctor have agreed upon. You're not presumptuous to ask for a tour. It's a logical request that is well within your rights. If you keep your eyes and ears open, you'll probably be able to determine whether the hospital is the type of place you want to stay.

Typically, the hospital will assign you a nonmedical guide — probably someone from the public relations department. He or she will take you on a prearranged trip through the hospital, designed to impress you with all its bells and whistles: high-tech equipment, state-of-the-art operating rooms, and so on. Look beyond the hype. Here are some specific things to watch for and inquire about:

• Is the place clean? Do the hallways smell unpleasant? Are people jammed into waiting rooms while they attempt to deal with an unresponsive bureaucracy? What's your gut response to the hospital's environment?

• Are the rooms sufficiently large, or did you mistakenly think a room was a closet? Are the bathroom facilities equipped with grab bars on the toilet and bathtub?

• Where's the call button in relationship to the bed? How much effort will you have to make to reach it? Watch and see how long it takes for a nurse to respond when a patient presses the button.

If possible, talk to the patients. Ask them for their impressions. Do they have specific complaints about nurses, doctors, food, noise, beds? Don't let your guide screen you from these people. You're not visiting a foreign country where the host has the power to keep you away from "undesirables."

During your orientation tour, request that you be allowed to talk to hospital staff. Find out about hospital facts and policies like visiting hours, nurse-patient ratios, special programs, such as a patient representative (ombudsman), or support groups and so on. The more you learn, the better equipped you'll be to take advantage of the hospital's facilities once you're there.

Planning Your Arrival

Just because the doctor says you should check in on Thursday doesn't mean you have to. Because of sky-high hospital costs, you might want to take care of some business prior to your arrival. Call the admitting office, make an appointment, and talk to them about the following:

• Insurance coverage. Find out how much of your treatment will be covered. What papers do you need to bring along? How will you be billed, and what forms of payment are acceptable? Should you call your insurance company before being hospitalized to check on coverage of specific treatments you anticipate?

• The billing procedure. What's the payment schedule? What's the difference in room rates (private versus semiprivate)? What time of day does billing begin and end?

• Complaint procedures. If you're dissatisfied with something during your hospital stay, whom do you complain to? Does the hospital have a patients' rights advocate? If there's a problem with a nurse as opposed to a doctor, whom should you talk to about it?

It's possible that you can chop a day or two off your time in the hospital simply by taking certain tests on an outpatient basis before you're admitted. You can also fill out a number of forms before that first day in the hospital.

A final suggestion: avoid entering the hospital on Friday afternoon or evening. Most lab facilities are closed on weekends, and it's likely you'll languish in your costly hospital bed until Monday without anything being accomplished. Also, July is a bad month to be hospitalized. At this time, interns descend, ready to "doctor" for the first time.

Solving Anticipated Problems

If, in this preadmission process, you find things that you don't like, you have two options. First, you can negotiate changes. If, for instance, you hear from other patients that the nurse assigned to your room is a fire-breathing martinet, you can try to negotiate being assigned another nurse or a room in a different nurse's section. You'll be surprised to learn how many issues are negotiable.

Second, if problems seem insurmountable — during your tour, you found the hospital to be unacceptable — then tell your doctor you want to go to another hospital. You are not obligated to stay in the hospital that your doctor recommended. If your doctor does not have privileges at another facility, maybe you should seek another physician. Doctors are as much a reflection of the hospitals that keep them as hospitals are a reflection of the doctors they keep.

Be Careful What You Sign

When you arrive at the hospital, be prepared for consent forms. You'll find yourself confronted with a general consent form as well as one for specific procedures.

Read them carefully. If you don't sign them, it's likely that either you'll be refused admittance or that a procedure won't be performed. On the other hand, you have every right to amend those forms to your liking. You can also write on the form what phrases you object to and that you're signing doesn't mean you agree to those odious phrases.

The procedure consent form is between you and your doctor. Be on the lookout for anything in the form that gives your doctor permission to do anything beyond what you've been told he'll do. If there's a discretionary power clause — something to the effect that the doctor can take any additional measures he deems necessary — strike it. Remember, always put your initials next to the changes you make on the forms. If you're confused by the language of the form, get your doctor to translate it into understandable layman's terms before you sign it. More than one person has learned upon reading the forms that his treatment involves more than he'd previously been told. Ask your doctor to clarify any confusion and justify additional procedures.

You might also want to insist that the form include your denial of permission for anyone beyond your treating doctor or surgeon to operate on you. In other words, he can't bring in an intern or resident to do the work, even if he's in the operating room.

How will hospital administrators and doctors react to these changes? It will vary, and some might try to convince you that you should sign the form as originally written. Most, however, will bow to your wishes. They realize that standard consent forms frequently deny patients their rights and, fearful of lawsuits or other complaints, will grudgingly allow you to make certain changes.

Tests

Sometimes a hospital resembles a prison. Other times, it seems like a school, given the number of tests its "pupils" are subjected to. Though some of those tests are certainly necessary, you shouldn't feel obligated to take every pop quiz that is sprung on you.

Hospitals order too many tests: blood tests, X rays, scans of various body parts, urine tests, cell analyses. Why? Partly because tests are profitable; sometimes because of fear that they'll lack the necessary documentation if a malpractice suit is filed; sometimes because the younger medical staff (interns and residents) are overly concerned about covering all the bases; and sometimes because the tests have become part of the routine.

None of those reasons is valid. You have every right to protest and refuse redundant or irrelevant tests. Not only are they a drain on your pocketbook, but they can be harmful to your health.

Chest X rays, for instance, have long been a routine test for anyone entering a hospital. But they rarely benefit the patient, and they are costly. Even more serious, they expose you to harmful radiation. The American College of Radiology has taken the position that routine hospital admission chest X rays be eliminated unless a very specific need has been cited.

If your hospital insists you have a chest X ray — and if they can't provide you with a reasonable explanation of why you should have one — refuse the test.

How do you know if a test is necessary? A little common sense combined with a few questions of your doctor should tell you.

Let's say you had a lower-gastrointestinal (GI) X ray prior to entering the hospital. Once you're there, they tell you that you're going to have another one. Ask your doctor why, reminding him of the previous test. One study demonstrated that, of nearly 250 patients who had tests performed before entering the hospital, 71 percent of the tests were repeated, and in 14 percent of those patients the tests were unnecessary.

What if you have a test done in the hospital and, a few days later, they want to do the same test again? Ask why. It might be that the technician messed up the test. At the very least, you shouldn't be charged for his mistake. And if it's a test that exposes you to radiation, you should tell your doctor you're worried about the additional dose of radioactivity and question whether the benefits from the second test outweigh the danger of another radioactive dose.

What if the nurses keep coming in to draw your blood? Too often, a battery of tests is ordered, and each test requires some blood for analysis. Because the tests are run by different people in the lab, they don't consolidate your blood sample. Each expects to have his own tube of fresh blood. You might want to suggest that the lab draw from the same tube of blood for all your tests. Again, do not be afraid to speak up.

Intensive Care

If you or a family member has ever been inside an intensive care unit (ICU), you know they offer around-the-clock monitoring of patients and the latest technology to do so. ICUs can, and do, save lives.

They also cost an arm and a leg.

The more technology and time expended, the higher the expense. And it's an expense that's not always justified.

A George Washington University study concluded that as many as 25 percent of ICU patients shouldn't be there, because they were either too healthy or too sick to reap the advantages of the ICU. Those who are too healthy can often benefit more from close monitoring in a private room or the use of one piece of equipment found in the ICU. Those who are too sick are in the ICU simply to postpone the inevitable — the moral implications of such a postponement are the focal point of much debate.

In addition, the ICU can have a harmful effect on some people. The very intensity of the environment — you're the constantly observed organism on a microscope slide — can be disconcerting. Psychologically, it can make you feel more dependent and ill than you really are.

If you're placed in an ICU, you're probably in no position to protest — odds are you've just had a heart attack. If, however, a family member is sent to an ICU, ask your doctor why the ICU was chosen as opposed to other alternatives. According to Robert Wilson, M.D., "the ideal ICU patient appears to be one who needs very sophisticated monitoring and intensive care for a short period of time and has a good chance of survival and subsequent enjoyment of life for at least several years." If your family member doesn't fit that description, start asking questions.

Common Concerns

During your hospital stay, you're going to be confronted by a bewildering series of events, decisions, and problems. Some will be relatively minor. Others will be crucial, affecting your treatment, recovery, and bill. The following will identify those areas and give you some tips on how to assert your rights:

You believe your doctor or nurse is rude, uninterested, or just plain incompetent.

There's no worse feeling. You're lying in your hospital bed and the nurse is treating you like an incompetent infant. Or your doctor is talking to you about your treatment and mistakenly referring to tests you're sure he never performed.

What can you do?

If it's a matter of inattention or rudeness, talk to the offending party and express your feelings. Sometimes, hospital personnel are overworked and don't realize how they're behaving. A few pointed words might do the trick. If it doesn't, complain to the hospital administrator or the patients' rights representative (if there is one).

If the situation is more serious, make some noise. Tell the hospital administrator that you're contemplating legal action if a doctor strikes you as obviously incompetent. That threat should get them to assign you another doctor, as well as alert them to a problem they should monitor.

According to statistics, one of every ten doctors is either incompetent or mentally or physically impaired (drug and alcohol addiction among physicians is a serious problem). No one should tolerate a doctor with alcohol on his breath or a mind that can't remember simple medical facts. If that is the case, protest long and loudly until something is done.

You are worried about a hospital roommate who has an infectious disease or about an unsanitary bathroom.

Despite appearances, a hospital isn't the perfectly sterile place it's supposed to be. Nosocomial infections — those acquired in the hospital — are common. Five to 10 percent of hospital patients (about 2 million people) acquire them annually, and it's estimated that they result in at least 100,000 deaths each year.

Though you can't protect yourself against all causes of these infections, you can reduce your risk. For instance, if you're worried about catching what your roommate has, ask your doctor or nurse about the risk. If there is a risk, insist upon a transfer to another room.

If hospital personnel fail to wash their hands before they touch you, tell them to keep their hands off until they wash.

If you're going to undergo surgery, don't let them shave you until the morning before the surgery. According to a number of studies, shaving the day before increases your risk of infection.

The medication you're receiving makes you feel terrible.

Drugs are dangerous. Even when administered by trained personnel, they can cause acute, unanticipated reactions.

If you become violently ill shortly after you are given a drug, tell someone. There are usually a number of alternative drugs you can take, and you should be informed of what they are.

It's also possible that your doctor or nurse has given you the wrong dosage or even the wrong medication. According to Kenneth Barker, a pharmacist at Auburn University, hospitals with the best drug-problem records make mistakes 2 to 3 percent of the time.

One way to protect yourself from errors is to learn the dosages, colors, and sizes of your medications. When you're given a pill, if it doesn't conform to what you expect, don't take it until your doctor or nurse double-checks that it is what has been prescribed.

Your doctor is avoiding you.

Don't take it lying down. If he's not stopping in once every other day (once every day is preferable), then confront him. Tell your physician you're upset and that you will not pay for services that haven't been rendered.

Doctors fail to visit their hospitalized patients regularly for a number of reasons. It's possible that a string of emergencies has prevented your doctor from finding the time. Or it might be that he's not particularly concerned about your condition and he's been out playing golf. Or it could be that he's incompetent.

It's perfectly reasonable for you to know the reason for your doctor's absence. If he's not concerned about your condition, for instance, it may be that you should no longer be hospitalized. Your doctor is accountable to you, and it's up to you to make him accountable.

Your surgery has been postponed and you don't know why.

Most people, upon hearing that their surgery has been postponed, react by imagining all sorts of horrific scenarios. "They've decided my condition is inoperable," or, "I've developed a more serious problem they don't know how to deal with."

More than likely, it's none of those things. A scheduling mistake, a surgeon who's become sick, or some other minor snafu has caused the postponement.

But you should immediately ask your surgeon about the reasons for the postponement. For one thing, postponements can be expensive. If you have to hang around the hospital for an extra few days, you could be accumulating additional thousands of dollars in bills. You might want to go home and wait out the postponement rather than stay in the hospital. Also, if the postponement is the fault of the hospital, talk to the billing department to be sure they adjust their billing accordingly.

Everyone keeps looking at your chart but you. You want to know what it says.

Contrary to what you might have been led to believe, your chart is not for the doctor's eyes only. It's your chart, not his, and you should be allowed to examine it.

Try asking your nurse first. She'll probably be more receptive to your request than the doctor. Ask her to interpret the jargon you don't understand. If there's something on the chart that confuses you and the nurse can't explain it, ask your doctor to tell you what his comment implies.

If both the nurse and doctor refuse to let you see your chart, complain to the hospital administrator. If that doesn't work, call your lawyer and see if he can apply some pressure.

Taking Your Leave

When and how you leave the hospital brings up a number of rights issues. It's not always a simple matter of packing your pajamas and strolling out the door. Unfortunately, many people aren't aware of the problems that can occur, and that's when your rights are most likely to be violated.

Let's take an extreme situation. You're in the hospital and you decide you want out. Perhaps you've consulted with another doctor, not affiliated with the hospital, who's told you your operation is unnecessary. Or maybe you've concluded that the hospital is a hell hole and an extended stay is likely to worsen your condition rather than better it.

Despite the protests of doctors and administrators, you demand to be released. In hospital nomenclature, this is called a discharge against medical advice (AMA).

The hospital will ask you to sign an AMA release form, which essentially states that you give up your rights to file a lawsuit. Don't sign it. If the hospital tries to prevent you from leaving, call your lawyer. If your lawyer advises you to sign it, do so, but write on the form that you're signing under duress and why you're leaving.

A more common leave-taking issue involves bills. The hospital will try to get you to pay your bill upon discharge, saying something like, "See the cashier before you leave." They may imply — or even insist — that you can't leave until you pay your bill.

They're wrong. One reason they'd prefer you pay immediately is that they don't want to give you the time to examine the bill carefully for errors. That's exactly the reason you should take the bill home and go over it item by item. If there's something you don't understand or that you suspect is a mistake, call the hospital billing department and ask for clarification.

You can also reduce the amount of the bill by taking a few simple steps upon departure:

• As soon as you are told by your doctor that you can leave, arrange for the earliest possible departure. If you leave after noon, rather than before noon, you might be charged for an additional day.

• Don't accept any medications unless you have been assured that you won't be charged for them. Your neighborhood pharmacy will charge you less than the hospital.

• Don't pay a doctor's discharge fee if he's not there personally to discharge you.

Finally, don't leave the hospital without talking to your doctor about posthospital care, diet, exercise, and so on. Ask him what signs you should look for that might indicate problems associated with your condition. Does he feel you need some type of after-care and, if so, what type? Are there follow-up treatments, and when and where will they be performed?

Don't leave the hospital without answers to those questions. They're critical bits of information that will have an impact on your physical and emotional health.

Malpractice

The three examples with which we began this chapter all re-sulted in successful malpractice suits. All were results of mistakes made in the hospital.

Yet how do you know if you have been a victim of malprac-tice? And if you suspect you are a victim, what should you do?

Let's take a typical scenario. You went into the hospital for an operation on your back; the operation was designed to elim-inate excruciating pain in your lower back. After the operation, your entire right arm was numb. Despite the surgeon's reassur-ances that the numbness will go away when you're recovering at home, it doesn't. Though your back is fine, you've lost the use of your right arm. Because you work at a job that can't be done without both arms, you can't return to work.

You consult a personal-injury lawyer, who agrees to take the case. The lawyer requests and receives all your medical records from the hospital, talks to the medical personnel involved in your case, and turns everything over to a reviewing medical specialist who determines whether the hospital personnel complied with minimum accepted standards. If they did, you don't have a case. If they didn't, and the lawyer is convinced you have a meritorious case with the potential for recovery of damages you suffered, he'll file a suit.

Depending on the jurisdiction in which the case is filed, it might take years before the suit is resolved through litigation. Or there might be an earlier out-of-court settlement.

That's the basic scenario. Now let's examine some of the questions this scenario raises:

How do you know if you have a viable malpractice suit?

First and foremost, you need definable damages of consequence. In other words, if the operation had left you with only a partially numb finger of one hand, it's unlikely that would meet the criteria (unless you happened to be a concert pianist). Death, the loss of a limb or organ, intense and documented pain, are examples of damages of consequence. Other damages might be economic, such as loss of income, medical costs you might not have otherwise incurred, costs for custodial care. Disability and disfigurement are also damages of consequence. Psychological damages — such as traumatic neurosis, or the loss of a spouse — might also be recoverable in a suit, though, because these damages are hard to document, they aren't as likely to provide a basis for proceeding with a case.

I've heard that people win malpractice suits based on pain and suffering. What's the rationale behind those awards?

There's been a great deal of criticism leveled at the pain and suffering concept, mostly from physicians. But their criticism is uninformed; they don't understand how our legal system works.

Our system is designed to "make whole" victims of negligence. When a person suffers a significant injury or disability, he can never be fully compensated. Something's been taken from his life that no amount of money can restore. If we confined awards to economic damages, we would not be considering all the factors necessary to make a person whole. So we include subjective damages, like pain and suffering, the nature and extent of the injury, and resulting disability. The money someone receives is designed to make up partially for the quality of life that was taken from that person. He's no longer the whole person he would have been if it were not for a health care professional's negligence.

If I have an operation and the results don't meet my expectations or are not what my doctor told me they would be, do I have grounds for a suit?

Not necessarily. The Standard of Practice doctrine states that you are entitled to receive a minimal acceptable level of care. If, for instance, an operation has only a 50 percent success rate, it will be difficult to prove that malpractice occurred if the operation failed (unless, of course, an egregious, provable mistake was made by the surgeon). In the eyes of the law, a doctor does not have to perform at the highest level possible.

Consider that approximately one-third of all appendectomies are unnecessary. Yet they're done because the symptoms of appendicitis — pain and vomiting — often cause doctors to misdiagnose and operate immediately, especially if a relatively young person comes into the hospital with those symptoms. A top-flight doctor wouldn't misdiagnose the case symptoms — he'd have some additional tests made to determine whether the problem truly was appendicitis. But that's a higher level of performance than the standard level of care calls for.

Similarly, it's rare to win a malpractice case based on a hospital-acquired staph infection, which is considered an acceptable consequence of surgery.

The Standard of Practice doctrine can become highly problematical. Let's say you're diagnosed as having lung cancer, and a hospital tells you there's nothing they can do for you. Another hospital, however, has developed a state-of-the-art treatment program that's helping a significant percentage of lung-cancer patients successfully battle the disease. Is the first hospital guilty of negligence because they turned you away? No. But should they have at least informed you that the other hospital was getting terrific results and referred you there? Of course. Still, you can't sue them for what they failed to do.

My eighty-nine-year-old grandmother, who had Alzheimer's disease, went in for routine surgery on her leg, but the anesthesiologist made a mistake and she died. Is this a winnable malpractice suit?

Probably not in terms of meaningful recovery. The problem is with the damages. The grandmother was a financial burden to the family when she was alive — her death eliminates the nursing home costs. Because of her age and condition, it would be enormously difficult to recover damages for her family despite the obvious mistake during surgery.

What if a doctor fails to diagnose my condition or makes a misdiagnosis?

That can be grounds for a malpractice suit if the best-chance doctrine applies. If a reviewing doctor testifies that a person lost his best chance (to save his life, limb, organ, etc.) because of a failure to diagnose or a misdiagnosis, then there might be a case.

Failure to diagnose cancer frequently brings this doctrine into play. With cancer, the rule is: the earlier the detection, the more favorable the outcome.

The hitch here is that some cancers are highly virulent and that even if they had been diagnosed earlier, the patient wouldn't have been much better off.

Some juries will rule against the plaintiff if a testifying doctor says that there is only the possibility that an earlier diagnosis would have benefited the patient. They require probability before they'll employ the best-chance doctrine.

If I can document a mistake that was made and damages that I suffered, will a lawyer automatically accept my case?

No. Medical malpractice cases are enormously expensive. Not only do they require a great deal of time, but there are numerous other expenses involved in gathering evidence and paying experts to testify. For those reasons, medical malpractice lawyers want to be reasonably sure that they have not only a viable case but one where a significant amount of damages can be collected.

The lawyers aren't as selfish as they might seem. Medical malpractice cases take a toll on plaintiffs. Not only do they require a lot of time, but they are also emotionally taxing. To put someone through that process without the possibility of a substantial award is unethical.

What are my alternatives besides a malpractice suit?

It depends on what your objectives are.

Let's say you want to be financially compensated for what happened to you in the hospital, but either you don't want to go through legal proceedings or you don't have a case that will stand up in a court of law.

Some states allow arbitration as a dispute-resolution forum. Most often, a neutral panel hears the case and renders a decision that might involve financial compensation. The verdict usually can't be appealed.

When you agree to arbitration, you are asked to waive your right to a trial in a court of law. Be aware, however, that you cannot be coerced into signing an arbitration agreement. Don't let anyone force you either to sign such an agreement or to forego medical care. It's illegal.

Another option is to write the hospital administrator and inform him that you are going to consult your lawyer unless the hospital compensates you for problems that occurred during your stay. If the administrator is sensible and agrees there was a problem, he might be willing to reduce your bill because of it (or because he fears legal action).

What if I don't care about financial compensation — if all I want to do is stop a negligent doctor from harming anyone else?

There are a few different routes open to you.

As strange as it seems, you might want to complain to your treating doctor if he wasn't the cause of the problem. If another doctor at the hospital was negligent, or if it was a nurse or technician, he might be willing to respond to your complaint. Your doctor might be in the best position to alert the hospital administration of the ticking time bomb on the premises and cause them to get rid of it.

You can also contact your state's medical licensing board or the attorney general's office. In the past, complaints to these bodies haven't produced much action. In Illinois, for instance, only six doctors lost their licenses in 1987, and the reasons were drug abuse or other criminal conduct. (In fact, one doctor jailed for drug abuse was found still to have his license!) But this tolerant attitude is beginning to change, partly because of public outcry against doctors who are allowed to practice despite records of repeated negligence.

Can medical malpractice suits result in some form of punishment for the offending doctor beyond financial damages?

They should, but too frequently they don't. A surprisingly large number of plaintiffs file suits and tell judge, jury, and lawyer that they don't want any money; they just want to make sure that the guilty physician is no longer allowed to practice.

Judges will respond to these people by sending trial transcripts to state departments of education and registration.

Unfortunately, neither the state agencies nor the hospitals readily revoke licenses or privileges.

Admittedly, hospitals are in a difficult situation. When they revoke a physician's privileges, that physician often turns around and sues the hospital, claiming he's been denied due process and that his privileges should be reinstated. From a legal standpoint, the physician may be right; hospitals often fail to conform to due process standards. As a result, hospitals are wary of revoking a doctor's privileges.

WOMEN AND HOSPITALS

It is an unfortunate fact that, in our society, many women are conditioned to believe that their bodies are medical disasters waiting to happen. (Male) doctors often foster this belief, looking upon women as even more helpless and servile (if that's possible) than their male patients. It's not unusual for a physician to prescribe sedatives or psychotropic drugs in response to women's "silly" complaints, assuming the problem is "all in her head."

The problems this attitude leads to are exacerbated in the hospital. This is especially true regarding surgical procedures. Since six out of every ten operations are performed on women, you should be aware of the four areas where most abuses occur and what you can do to prevent those abuses.

Hysterectomies

Hysterectomy is one of the most frequently performed "unnecessary" operations: more than 600 women die annually from complications following hysterectomies or from preexisting conditions worsened by the operation. In addition, hysterectomies can result in serious hormonal and sexual complications and dysfunctions.

There's no medical reason that justifies removing a healthy uterus. Don't let a doctor convince you that it should be removed because it's prolapsed (sagging), because a cancer might develop there (though it hasn't yet), or as a foolproof method of contraception.

Hysterectomies are profitable, and avaricious physicians view these operations as easy ways to make a buck.

Cesarean Sections

We talked about this abused operation earlier (page 6). Don't undergo it if natural childbirth is a viable option. Remember, too, if you had a C-section in the past, you don't necessarily have to have one in the future. Vaginal deliveries are often possible even though your last child was delivered via C-section.

Childbirth

Home births, birthing centers, the use of midwives, and other alternative approaches to childbirth are frowned upon by many physicians. While they may claim safety concerns are their reasons for opposition, studies indicate that such delivery options are as safe or safer than traditional hospital deliveries. They may really dislike these alternatives because they take control of the birth out of their hands and money out of their pockets.

If your doctor opposes the alternative delivery you've chosen, find out why. If he tells you it's a matter of safety, ask him for specific facts documenting why and how it's unsafe. You might remind him that Holland, where one-third of all births take place at home, has the lowest infant mortality rate in all of Europe.

Breast Cancer

In cases where the cancer is localized (about 60 percent of all cases), lumpectomies are just as effective as mastectomies. Lumpectomies are also quicker, cheaper, and less dangerous.

Beware of the slash-happy surgeon! He's the one who, following a biopsy that reveals a malignancy, immediately performs a mastectomy. The anesthetized patient isn't given a chance to get a second opinion or explore alternative treatments such as radiation therapy. Before the biopsy, make sure your surgeon understands and agrees that nothing beyond the biopsy will be done until he discusses the results of the biopsy with you. Negotiate, ask questions, and have a family member or friend available who can express your concerns and represent your interests if you are unable to be an effective advocate for yourself.

MEDICARE PATIENTS

If you are a Medicare patient, you cannot be discharged because your "DRGs" (see page 137) or Medicare payments have been used up. The hospital must issue you a form when you are admitted verifying this federal law. If they don't, be sure to ask for it.

If you have doubts about whether you are really ready to be discharged, you have the right to have your case reviewed by a PRO (Peer Review Organization), which will determine whether a further stay can be covered by Medicare. PROs are groups of doctors appointed by the government to monitor the hospital care of Medicare patients. For more information, see chapter nine.

EMERGENCY ROOM

The most nerve-racking visit to the hospital is made when you have no time to plan, no time to investigate facilities ahead of time — in short, when you have an emergency on your hands.

Emergency-room visits are dangerous not only to your health but also to your rights. Despite the training of emergency-room personnel for crisis situations, the sheer speed

and frantic pace of those rooms often produce rights abuses.
Here are some things you should watch out for:

• If your child has swallowed poison, if your spouse is
having a heart attack, or some other life-threatening emergency is taking place, you have the right to immediate medical treatment. You are not subject to "restaurant" rules —
being seated in order of arrival. A true emergency
supersedes everything else, and you should demand speedy
service.

You also have the right to information. Don't let the
treating physician cop out with "It's too early to know anything yet." Find out what he suspects is wrong, even if he's
not sure. At the very least, a little information might ease
some of your worries.

• If it's a real emergency, you should give the doctor as
much information as you can about the problem. Obviously,
that's not always possible, especially if you're unconscious
or in agonizing pain. But if you brought someone in and
have observed the symptoms, make sure you tell the doctor
what you've seen. Don't let him brush you aside. Though
it's true that you shouldn't be in the treatment area in most
instances (unless the patient is your child), you have every
right to convey what you know about the sick person's condition to the doctor.

• You can't be turned away from the emergency room if
you are critically ill or if you don't have health insurance.
In a number of states, hospitals that turn people away can
be criminally liable. The same is true if they hold you in a
waiting area, saying that they're going to transfer you to
another hospital (usually the city's public hospital). A delay
in treatment can have an adverse effect on your condition,
and you shouldn't tolerate a delay. If necessary, threaten to
call an attorney if they insist on transferring you before
treatment.

• Don't go to the emergency room unless it's absolutely
necessary. Treatment there will cost you twice as much as
it normally would at a physician's office, and you're doing a
disservice to those who are truly in need of emergency care.

• Try calling your own physician or his answering service before you leave for the emergency room. Often, your doctor will meet you there, thus expediting the "triage" process that goes on. Also, your doctor may call the hospital to alert the emergency room about your arrival.

CHILDREN

As frightening and uncomfortable as hospitalization can be for adults, it's even worse for children. As a parent, you can do a number of things to reduce your child's fear and, more important, ensure that his rights are safeguarded.

Here are some steps you can take:

• If your child wants to stay with you (or you want to be with your child), don't let a heartless nurse, physician, or administrator separate you unless there is a justifiable medical reason. Simply because visiting hours are over isn't a good enough reason. Despite a nurse's protests, you can stay in the room overnight if you feel it is necessary, and some hospitals will even bring a cot into the room for you to sleep on. The only caveat is that you cannot interfere with normal treatment.

• If your child is hospitalized for a long time, make sure he's not isolated from friends or siblings. Ignore rules about hospital visits from underage children. Those visits are critical for a hospitalized child's psychological well-being. Negotiate this with your physician, who can help if hospital personnel are reluctant to cooperate.

• Pay attention to what your child says, how he reacts to medication and treatment, and his general mood during the hospital stay. You know your child far better than the nurses and doctors. The hospital personnel can easily misinterpret or misunderstand what a child tells them. Because many children can't speak up for themselves, you have to speak up for them. Do not be shy. As a parent, you are your child's legal surrogate, and you have every right to ask questions, grant or deny permissions, and lodge complaints.

CHAPTER FIVE

None of Your Business

How MUCH PRIVACY are you entitled to in health care situations? That's a difficult and controversial question, the focus of increasing debate in medical and legal circles.

If you have a sexually transmitted disease, do you have the right to refuse to name the names of your sexual partners?

If your daughter asks her doctor for a birth control device, do you have the right to be informed about it?

If you have been hospitalized for psychiatric reasons, do you have the right to prevent your employer or insurance company from learning about it?

These are all cutting-edge privacy issues. They are all subject to a great deal of confusion — on the part of both consumers and health care practitioners. Because of that confusion, it's important to know what you can do to safeguard your right to privacy.

Rules and Rights

Your right to privacy in a health care setting is guaranteed by a number of formal and informal rules. There are the doctor-patient confidentiality, the informed-consent doctrine, the first amendment, and a potpourri of state laws.

Unfortunately, just because these doctrines and laws exist doesn't mean they're enforced. In some cases, there are conflicts. For instance, all the controversy swirling around the abortion issue and AIDS is a result of the conflict between the first and fourteenth amendments — your right to privacy versus the government's right to do things that benefit the common good.

In other circumstances, privacy requirements are ignored or abused by health care practitioners: A hospital may give an insurance company more information about your medical history than they're entitled to know; or a doctor may tell your spouse about your condition with the hope that the spouse will persuade you to consent to a certain type of treatment.

Under any circumstances, invasions of privacy can be embarrassing and distressing. Because of the intensely personal nature of medical treatment, however, privacy violations can be even more harmful.

Later in this chapter, we'll talk about what you can do to enforce your privacy rights. First, we'd like to share with you an extraordinary illustration of what happens when an individual's privacy rights are abused. It's a story that not only spotlights a growing area of abuse but also conveys the medical establishment's attitude toward the privacy issue.

THE BILLION-DOLLAR MAN

In 1976, John Moore first met Dr. David Golde of the UCLA Medical Center. Moore was suffering from a rare blood disorder known as hairy cell leukemia. Dr. Golde recommended that Moore have his spleen removed.

The following account of the John Moore case comes from court filings and an amicus curiae brief filed by the People's Medical Society in the Supreme Court of California.

Before performing the surgery, Dr. Golde instructed a team of UCLA researchers to take a piece of Moore's removed spleen and some of his blood cells for use in Dr. Golde's research — research that was unrelated to Moore's treatment.

The operation was successful, and Moore returned to his Washington (state) home, making periodic visits to UCLA over the next seven years because of Dr. Golde's recommendation of additional treatments.

The treatments, however, were designed to help Dr. Golde and a colleague develop a cell line, a new generation of cells, from Moore's tissues.

In 1979, Dr. Golde applied for a patent on Moore's cells,

and in 1981, he received it, listing himself and his colleague as "inventors" of the line. As inventors, they were entitled to share in royalties and profits produced by the line. Working with a company called Genetics Institute and a pharmaceutical company named Sandoz, Golde and his colleague reaped hundreds of thousands of dollars. It was estimated that the products resulting from the cell line would be a $3 billion business by 1990.

Moore claims that no one told him about any of this. In fact, according to Moore, Dr. Golde insisted that his blood cells had no financial value.

In 1983, Dr. Golde gave Moore a consent form — which Moore signed — that would allow them to do research using his tissue. Later that year, Dr. Golde asked Moore to turn over all rights and products attached to his cell line, as well as the rights of his offspring. Moore refused.

Eventually, Moore learned of Dr. Golde's actions and filed a suit, which the Supreme Court of California is now hearing (as of this writing).

A Growing Problem

What happened to John Moore isn't unusual. As gene-splicing and other biotechnological sciences advance, such experiences are becoming increasingly common. According to the *Wall Street Journal* (January 29, 1986), there was a 300 percent increase in patents with origins in patients' tissues from 1975–1979 to 1980–1984.

On the most basic level, there is something morally wrong about doctors removing a part of your body and using it for their own financial gain — especially when they keep you in the dark about what they are doing. Some doctors would argue that once something leaves your body, it's no longer yours. The purpose of this chapter isn't to get into a semantic argument, so we won't debate the issue.

What are the consequences if a doctor takes something from you and uses it for personal gain without your permission?

Obviously, there's the loss of significant profits — profits that you're entitled to, since without you, those profits wouldn't be possible.

But there are far more serious consequences. First, there's the relationship between profit and treatment. This is a clear conflict-of-interest situation, and it can threaten your health: what's best for the doctor might not be best for the patient. The procedures that yield optimal research results might not conform to the best treatment. It's possible that research-biased treatment could be harmful to the patient's condition.

Equally disturbing is the psychological impact on the patient. John Moore, for instance, claims that he suffered significant emotional distress, assuming that Dr. Golde's insistence that he return to UCLA for periodic treatments meant that his condition wasn't improving; that it might be growing worse. Moore claims that because Dr. Golde never told him the real reason for his continuing treatments, he naturally assumed there was a problem.

There is nothing more frightening than a series of unexplained medical procedures. In a way, they're a form of psychological battery, committed by a physician who has no compunction about hurting a patient's mind.

Finally, Moore bore the financial burden of numerous trips between Washington and California, as well as medical bills. It is the ultimate insult for a doctor to inflict a financial burden on a patient when the primary purpose of his prescribed regimen is personal financial gain.

If You Think You're a Research Victim

The first thing you can do is insist that your doctor tell you if he decides to initiate any new treatments or procedures. Also demand to know the reasons for the treatment changes. What you are doing is serving fair warning that you won't tolerate any unexplained deviations from what you expect to happen. It will make him think twice about using you to further his research.

Second, carefully read over hospital consent forms, noting if there's a reference to "experiments with tissues." If there is, ask your doctor if your tissue will be used for experimental purposes. If he says it might, ask him if your tissue has any commercial value. If he says yes, and you don't mind its being used, try to strike a financial agreement regarding profits from his research. If he refuses to cut you in on the profits, or you don't want your tissue to be used in research, strike the relevant language on the consent form, and write your reasons for crossing it out in the margin.

If your tissue is used without your informed consent, you, like John Moore, may have grounds for a lawsuit. If so, contact a lawyer.

The Larger Issue

The Moore case illustrates many doctors' attitudes toward their patients' right of privacy. A significant percentage of physicians operate on the principle that what's yours is theirs. It's as if once you enter the hospital or their office, you lose your proprietary rights to your body.

If you're a victim of this attitude, don't remain silent. Though it might not be life-threatening, it can cost you money, time, or even your job. Let's look at some common problems and what you can do about them:

I was in the hospital and my doctor told me that I had to make a decision about an operation. I wanted to talk about it with my wife in private, but the doctor remained in the room while we were discussing it; he even interrupted me a few times. Did I have the right to ask him to leave while I discussed the operation with my wife?

Yes. You could have insisted that he, as well as any other hospital personnel, leave the room while you made your decision.

I've noticed that a number of people stop by the nurse's station and look at the charts — including my medical chart. Should it be on view for everyone?

No. Insist that your medical record be seen only by those people involved in your treatment. After you're discharged, insist on the same confidentiality. Give the hospital a list of people — your doctor, surgeon, nurse — whom you'll allow to see your chart.

When I entered the hospital, they gave me a form to fill out that asked lots of personal questions. Did I have to answer all of them?

No. If a question doesn't seem related to your treatment — and no one can explain to you why it's relevant — refuse to answer it.

I recently underwent an operation under local anesthetic. I noticed about 10 people in the observation room, and it made me nervous and embarrassed. Should those people have been there?

No. It's not uncommon for students, visiting medical dignitaries, and others to be invited to view operations. If such a practice makes you uncomfortable, tell your doctor. Operations are intensely personal experiences, and you have the right to keep them private affairs.

My father, who is 80 years old and in a nursing home, has been in increasingly poor health the last few months. I've tried to get him to tell me what's wrong, but he refuses. I asked his doctor to tell me, but he also refuses. Since I'm paying my father's medical bills, don't I have a right to know?

No. Just because you're paying the bills doesn't mean confidentiality can be breached. Your father and his doctor have every right to exclude you.

There's a hospital in town that I refuse to go to; I've been there twice, and both times I had bad experiences. What happens if there's an emergency and they take me there for treatment? Can I tell them to keep their hands off and take me to another hospital?

Probably not. If it's a real emergency, the hospital has an obligation to treat you. If they don't and you suffer damages as a result of a delay, they can be sued for abandonment. On the other hand, if it's not an emergency, then you have every right to insist on another hospital.

Sex-Related Issues

With all the controversy and confusion surrounding AIDS, numerous privacy issues have arisen in recent years. One of the most important involves whether an AIDS patient has an obligation to name sexual partners.

The law isn't clear on this issue, and different states have adopted different policies. There is a conflict between the first and fourteenth amendments: does the public's right to know supersede an individual's right to privacy? It's an enormously difficult problem with no clear-cut answers.

Right now, it's advisable to act on the assumption that you

can't be forced to name names; that's true not only for AIDS but for any sexually transmitted disease. If your doctor is insistent, you might want to consult an attorney before supplying those names, ensuring that your doctor adheres to a confidentiality agreement.

In Illinois, a number of laws have been proposed or passed revolving around this issue. For instance, a bill was recently passed making it a crime to have sex without telling the other person you have a sexually transmitted disease. Another bill is pending that would make AIDS testing mandatory before a couple could get married.

Increasingly, the courts and the federal government are throwing these issues back to the states, allowing each state to construct its own policies. It would be wise for you to learn what your state's laws are before you consent to reveal any information you deem private.

Teenagers

Most teenager-privacy conflicts revolve around sex: birth control and abortions.

Can your 16-year-old daughter have an abortion without your consent? Can her doctor give her birth control pills or devices without your knowledge? Can she be treated for a sexually transmitted disease without her doctor informing you? Can the school force her to take sex education classes?

Again, these are loaded questions, and each state tends to dictate different answers.

As a general rule, teenagers have the same right to patient-physician confidentiality as adults. If two teenagers are married, that right is absolute, regardless of whether they have reached the age of majority.

At the same time, some states have attempted to pass laws stating that a teenager can't have an abortion without parental consent. In other states, parents have successfully prevented schools from dispensing information about birth control.

Insurance

Don't assume that insurance companies are entitled to complete access to your records. It's what many insurance companies assume, but they're wrong. Their access is limited.

Under certain conditions, they are allowed to view your medical records. If, for instance, you submit a bill for them to pay, they are allowed to view your record to confirm that you needed and received treatment.

But what stops the insurance company from looking at more than one part of your record? Let's say you are in an automobile accident and you go to the hospital for surgery on two broken legs. While you are in the hospital, you become severely depressed and ask to see a psychiatrist.

Your insurance doesn't cover psychiatric care and you are not asking the insurance company to pay for it. Still, it's part of your medical record, and it's likely the insurance company will learn about it.

They shouldn't. To prevent them from doing so, instruct the hospital to provide the insurance company with the records of Doctor A, who treated you for your broken leg, but not Doctor B, who treated you for your depression. If the hospital asks you to sign an authorization for your records on the bill from Doctor B, don't do it. It's none of the insurance company's business.

An insurance company shouldn't know more than it needs to for a number of reasons. First, they might see something on the patient's record that could influence future payments. Let's say they discover the policy holder received treatments for headaches a few years ago. When the headaches recur and the doctor has to remove a tumor, the insurance company refuses to pay, claiming it was a preexisting condition.

Second, if the insurance company is privy to information, it's possible that an employer will also get wind of it. Suppose the employee once had a drug problem. If his employer learns about it, it may well influence their attitude toward him; it might even lead to his dismissal.

Another problem might be requests from another party's insurance company for medical records. For example, a patient was hit by a car, and the driver's insurance company tries to find out about the accident victim's condition from the hospital. Until recently, insurance companies blatantly disregarded statutes that forbade hospitals from releasing such information without the patient's consent. Though this practice isn't as common today as it once was, it still takes place. Therefore, insist to any hospital you are in that they are not to release any information about your condition to "outsiders" without your knowledge and permission.

Finally, beware of insurance companies' "dirty tricks." In an effort to obtain information a hospital refuses to provide, some companies have been known to ask a friendly doctor to write to a patient's doctor with a request for information. Doctors trade information about patients the way kids trade baseball cards; there doesn't have to be any written authorization. Unfortunately, the doctor passes his knowledge on to the insurance company, and you're not sure how it got there.

The only recourse you have is to insist to your doctor that he not reveal anything about your condition to a fellow physician unless that physician is involved in your treatment.

Lawsuits

What happens to doctor-patient confidentiality when you file a lawsuit?

Though it's true you waive some of your privileges to that confidential relationship, you don't waive all of them. Opposing attorneys can subpoena your medical records and question your doctor. But their access is limited to only those things that relate to your claim for damages. If they try to go beyond that limitation, your attorney should immediately object.

Don't worry that if you file a lawsuit, your entire medical history will be open for examination in court. You still retain significant rights to confidentiality.

If your right to privacy is violated in a health care setting, is it grounds for a lawsuit?

Here are a few things to consider if you're trying to determine if you have grounds for a suit. First, was something done to you without your consent and did you suffer damages as a result? For instance, you asked that only your doctor examine you, but a steady stream of interns and residents poked and prodded you, resulting in your developing a nervous condition. Second, was another party's conduct irresponsible — an insurance company obtained authorization for your medical records without your consent, the information was conveyed to your employer, and you were fired as a result (they learned that you were epileptic).

If you answered yes to one or both of those questions, you should consult an attorney.

CHAPTER SIX

Guinea Pig

GIVEN THE PROLIFERATION of new and experimental technologies, surgeries, and drugs, it is likely that you will come in contact with one of them during the course of medical treatment. The question is, will you be their victim or beneficiary?

It depends on a number of factors, all of which relate to your rights as a health care consumer.

Before we discuss those factors, let's define the difference between new and experimental. As the name implies, experimental means that something is fresh off the drawing board (or straight from the laboratory) and has little history of practical use. An experimental drug, for instance, might be approved by the FDA for use by a handful of doctors at a few selected hospitals. Experiments are risky; in many cases, not only is the treatment's efficacy unknown but so, too, are the short-term and long-term side effects.

A new treatment, on the other hand, is one step beyond experimental. It has received approval from one regulatory body or another. Doctors have more knowledge about the effects of new treatments than of experimental ones. When bypass operations were first performed, they were considered a new procedure. The same was true of hip replacements.

Now that we've differentiated between experimental and new, let's examine some problems that occur with both types of treatments.

Experiments without Consent

Doctors frequently have a vested interest in using an experimental piece of technology or giving you an experimental drug. As you'll recall from the previous chapter, in which we discussed the doctor who stood to make millions of dollars from a patient's cell line, experiments can be lucrative for those who conduct them. Not only is there money to be made, but there is prestige to be gained from experiments that work.

You have the absolute right to know in advance if you are participating in an experiment. Even more so than in "normal" treatment situations, physicians are obligated to inform you in advance and describe the nature of the experimental procedure.

That doesn't mean they always do. Sometimes, they refrain from doing so because they're worried that a patient might refuse to participate, that, for example, he'll balk when informed that one of the wonder drug's side effects is blindness. Other times, doctors determine that the illness is terminal and there is no choice; an experimental drug is the last, best hope.

If you are the uninformed victim of an experiment — and damages result because of it — you have the right to file a medical malpractice suit against the doctor.

The key thing to remember in these situations is to ask if something is experimental, even if the doctor doesn't tell you it is. Look for red flags like a change in medication — the doctor gives you a green pill instead of the blue one you've always taken — or he says something ambiguous like, "I'd like to change your medication; there's a new drug that might be more effective."

Experimentation with Consent

Some physicians might say to you, "We're going to use an experimental procedure, since the traditional ones haven't worked." They are fulfilling their obligation to tell you that the procedure is experimental, but they don't give you any information beyond that; they also make it seem as though you don't have a choice in the matter.

You do have a choice. To make it, you should question your physician about the procedure. For instance, let's say your doctor tells you he wants you to undergo a new cancer treatment. You should ask him exactly what that treatment involves; how long it will take; what the possible side effects are; what has been learned about the treatment from others who have been guinea pigs; what your alternatives are if you refuse the treatment; why the treatment hasn't been approved; and why the doctor thinks the treatment will be effective for your condition.

This way, your doctor will have to say more than that the drug is, for example, a new cancer treatment. He'll say something like, "The treatment involves a regimen of cisplatinum and methotrexate. The dosages are high and they're interspersed with radiation given at intervals of one week each with a rest period of three days between intervals. After a month, we'll probably increase the dosages if it's not as effective as we hoped. The possible side effects are nausea and increased likelihood of pneumonia and a number of other infectious diseases."

Types of Experiments and New Treatments

Contrary to what many people believe, new and experimental treatments extend beyond drugs. Surgical procedures, for instance, are constantly evolving and are often new or experimental.

Just as there's more than one way to skin a cat, there are frequently many ways to perform an operation. Cervical laminectomies (spinal neck operations) generally involve surgeons entering from the back of the neck. However, a few doctors prefer the anterior route. Though the results have been good with this new operating logistic, there's also a greater potential for complications, since the surgeon has to cut through more dangerous territory (he comes closer to more vital organs).

Hip replacements, which we mentioned earlier, also can be done in different ways. There's the choice between the cemented or cementless hip replacement, for instance. The same choices apply to certain types of heart surgery: a bypass versus the newer angioplasty. In some instances, the alternative to traditional surgery might be a new or experimental nonsurgical technique: instead of a gall bladder operation, you can opt for a technique that dissolves gallstones via sonic waves.

New technologies form another category. Because of the great cost that goes into research for these technologies, there's significant pressure on doctors and hospitals to use them. They have made the investment and they want it to pay off. Artificial hearts are one well-publicized manifestation of new technology. Also well-publicized is the physical and psychological trauma suffered by the few who have allowed artificial hearts to be implanted.

Sometimes, seemingly harmless new technologies result in unanticipated problems. Nuclear magnetic resolution imaging (NMRI) is a noninvasive procedure that calls for the patient to be enclosed in a pitch-black tube for about 15 minutes or longer. During that time, there's a tremendous amount of noise. Some people have found the experience uncomfortably claustrophobic and have ended up refusing to complete the test.

Treatments in all three categories — drugs, surgery, and technology — can result in unanticipated problems. That's why what is known should be shared with patients. It's the only way they can make informed decisions about whether they want to participate in new or experimental procedures.

Examples of Abuses

Abuses of new and experimental techniques come in many forms.

At Chicago's Cook County Hospital, pregnant women were given large doses of tranquilizing drugs without their knowledge. A few doctors on the medical staff did so for a research project; the doctors who initiated the experiments were either suspended or fired.

Cataract lens implants also are subject to abuse by profit-hungry ophthalmologists. Though not an experimental procedure, it is relatively new, and there have been well-documented problems with implants. The most serious problem is rejection by the body, which can lead to blindness in the implanted eye.

One doctor, a man who specializes in lens implants, did a bilateral implant — implanting lenses in both eyes — via successive procedures in a relatively short amount of time without waiting to see if there would be a rejection problem. There was, and the patient lost all vision. The doctor had not informed his patient that this was a possibility. Even worse, he did not take the precaution of doing only one implant and waiting to see if the patient's body would reject it, thereby safeguarding her against the possibility of total blindness.

Abuses involving experimental drugs are widespread. They often occur when new drugs are tested, with initially positive results. Doctors rush to use them without sufficient knowledge of their potential drawbacks.

For instance, there's an antidepressant drug called Prozac that has had wonderful results for people who are suffering from depression. A doctor, aware of the drug's growing reputation, prescribed it for a patient along with other drugs. Because he didn't monitor her reaction to the drug carefully — and he didn't know what warning signs to be aware of — the woman slipped into a coma. Though she recovered, she still sustained memory loss and sizable hospital bills.

Many drugs are used for more than one condition. Researchers learn a drug that is commonly used for heart patients is also effective when given to arthritis sufferers. Though the drug is FDA approved and has been subject to extensive use and testing, suddenly it's a new drug. Unfortunately, it's not categorized as such, and that results in problems.

You might recall our discussion of methotrexate from an earlier chapter. A cancer-fighting drug, it's also been found to be effective in treating serious cases of psoriasis. While an oncologist is generally familiar with the drug, a dermatologist might not be. In the case we cited, a dermatologist prescribed methotrexate to a psoriasis patient and failed to monitor his liver condition. Long-term use of methotrexate destroyed the liver, and the patient died.

Therefore, beware of old drugs used for new purposes. In a novice's hands, they can be as dangerous as any purely experimental drug.

Where and When You're Most Vulnerable

Experimental treatment abuses are most likely to occur in nursing homes, county hospitals that serve the poor, state institutions for treatment of the mentally ill, and prisons. These places contain people who are often disadvantaged, docile, and without resources.

If you or a loved one is in one of these facilities, you should be acutely aware that health care rights might be violated because of new or experimental procedures.

People are extremely vulnerable to these abuses if they are desperate. Patients who have terminal conditions or whose suffering has not been relieved by traditional treatment are most likely to become subjects of experiments. Doctors perceive them to be likely guinea pigs because of their condition, but so do they. When a doctor mentions a new, controversial, untested treatment, hopes soar. People are more willing to take a chance — to refrain from asking the questions they normally would ask — because of their situation.

Your Best Defense Is a Good Offense

Because people who are victims of experiments are sometimes in desperate straits, they are more willing to grasp at straws, with no questions asked. As we've stressed throughout this book, that's the worst possible thing to do.

This is especially true when a new or experimental procedure is involved. Experimental procedures are risky; they may result in devastating side effects; the "cure" might be worse than the disease.

Of all the questions to ask prior to treatment, perhaps the most important is: what are my alternatives? This is a critical question to ask when you are faced with a new or experimental treatment. It may well be that you have a choice between two experimental procedures; or between a new and an experimental one; or between a new and a traditional approach.

Find out everything you can about each alternative. Insist that your doctor inform you about the length of each treatment, the side effects, and what has happened to other patients who have experienced the treatment.

If problems result because of experiments or new procedures, you have legal remedies. The most flagrant violation of your rights is experimental treatment that is performed without informing you of the treatment's experimental nature. If you suffer significant damages, you have cause for a medical malpractice suit.

A trickier situation arises when a doctor tells you the treatment is experimental (or new) but fails to provide you with sufficient information. He doesn't inform you about the horrible side effects or neglects to mention that the success rate is only 1 percent.

The likelihood of a successful suit frequently depends on your condition. It's difficult to present a strong case if the illness is terminal, the legal logic being that there really wasn't any other alternative. Even in these instances, however, it might be wise to consult a lawyer. Even if the condition is incurable, that's no justification for cruel and unusual punishment — the too-frequent result of unwise experiments.

Insurance

Look at the language in your insurance policy and you'll probably find an exclusion: the policy doesn't cover "experimental" treatments.

However, what's experimental and what's not can be subject to debate. If you decide to proceed with experimental therapy, contact your insurance company in advance to determine whether they'll pay.

Sympathetic doctors can be of assistance. Many times, their description of treatments will increase or decrease your chances of being reimbursed by insurance.

In addition, the line between new, experimental, and traditional procedures blurs easily. What is viewed as experimental in 1989 might be classified as traditional in 1990. You have only to look at infertility procedures (such as laparoscopic surgery for endometriosis) to see evidence of changing distinctions. Once considered purely experimental surgery, it is now covered by a growing number of insurance companies (in response, in part, to consumer demands).

A Philosophical Issue

Experimental and new approaches have value. Even the most skeptical will admit that they have resulted in significant medical advances. No one should automatically assume that just because a treatment is termed experimental, it's worthless.

At the same time, however, you might not want to be a guinea pig and subject yourself to the inevitable trial and error of new treatments.

Our point is that you have a choice, and you should make it fully informed.

CHAPTER SEVEN

Please Pay the Cashier

HOSPITALS AND PHYSICIANS foster the illusion that they aren't businesses, that they're somehow above the fray, operating on a purer, loftier plane. When you receive a bill from them, it's not like the bill you receive from a department store; it's more like a bill you receive from the IRS for back taxes. Payment isn't to be questioned.

But hospitals and doctors are in business to make money like everyone else. They are subject to the same requirements and consumer protection acts as shoe stores, credit card companies, and limousine services.

Hospitals and doctors have no special privileges. You should scrutinize their bills as carefully and skeptically as you would any other.

Perhaps you should exercise even more skepticism than you normally would. A 1984 study by the Equifax Corporation reviewed hospital bills of $10,000 or more as mentioned previously. They found that 98.1% of those bills had errors. Over 70 percent of those errors were in the hospital's favor, and the average error per bill was $1300.

Are hospitals and physicians engaged in a plot to defraud customers? No. The problem is that hospitals are very much like hotels. Only they are hotels with far more complex problems and services, and they are susceptible to all the administrative mistakes that come with the territory.

You can protect yourself from their blunders, but only if you treat the hospital like the business that it is. They are going to make computer errors. They are going to charge you for services that weren't performed. They are going to dispute bills with third-party payers. They are going to act outraged and threatening if you dare to question a bill.

Don't let a hospital administrator or a physician's collection service bully you. Stand up to them and demand an accounting. If you do, the chances are you'll save yourself more than a few pennies. In some instances, we're talking about thousands of dollars.

Where do you begin? The logical place is the insurance policy tucked away in some dusty drawer. If it's the right type of policy, its pages contain significant protections for consumers.

Insurance

Two people can go into the hospital for the same treatment and come out with totally different bills. One might owe nothing, while the other owes thousands of dollars. The difference is related to a number of factors, including insurance coverage, the hospital and doctor chosen, the laboratories the doctor or hospital uses, discussions with the doctor and hospital prior to treatment.

Let's look at insurance first.

Like many people, you might not have a choice of insurance companies and policies; the choice is mandated by your employer. Still, many organizations are moving toward cafeteria plans (also known as flexible benefits) in which employees do have some significant choices to make in terms of deductibles and coverage areas. If you don't have coverage through your employer, you face a bewildering array of options — there seems to be a new insurance company calling you on the phone or sending you mail every week.

Whatever your situation, it's critical that you be aware of exactly what your coverage entails. With that knowledge, you'll be in a far better position to choose physicians, hospitals, and treatments that make sense economically as well as medically.

Here are some key questions:

• Does the policy pay indemnity benefits or service benefits? Service benefits are generally better, since they pay the hospital or doctor directly for services. Indemnity benefits provide you with a specific amount for each day of hospitalization, and that amount might be less than what the hospital charges.

• How many days of hospitalization does the policy cover? If it's less than thirty days, it's not a particularly good policy.

• Does the policy cover preexisting conditions?

• Does the policy pay for medicines and other services such as X rays, laboratory treatments, etc.?

• Does the policy cover specialty care such as intensive care, coronary care, etc.? If it doesn't pay at least some of the cost for specialty care, you should avoid that policy.

• Does the policy cover outpatient services?

• Does the policy require you to pay a deductible or make co-payments toward expenses?

• How much does the policy pay toward doctor visits when you're in the hospital, and how many visits does it cover?

• Does the policy cover laboratory and diagnostic tests, both in the hospital, and in your doctor's office?

• Does the policy pay a lump sum for surgery, or does it pay the "usual, customary, and reasonable" fee? The latter is preferable.

• What is the maximum dollar amount of coverage provided by the policy you are considering?

• Does the deductible apply to a benefit period or does it apply to each time you file a claim? It's much better if the policy has a yearly deductible.

• Are the co-insurance/co-payment provisions of the policy at least 80–20? (That is, the insurer pays 80 percent and you pay 20 percent of the bill.)

• What is the stop-loss amount at which you stop paying anything toward your medical expenses?

• What services are excluded from coverage?

Shopping Around

Remember our opening to the chapter: hospitals and doctors' practices are business entities. Like any business, they are in competition with each other, and their pricing structures reflect that competition. Hospital room costs, for instance, can vary dramatically, even if they're in the same city. The same is true for fees charged by physicians, tests, and other procedures.

Don't be shy about asking beforehand what something costs. Feeling awkward asking your doctor what he charges is preferable to sticker shock. Far better to ask in advance than discover you could have saved $100 by receiving a check-up from another physician.

When you're shopping around, don't equate price with quality. Just because one hospital charges more than another doesn't mean they provide better-quality services. In fact, it might be just the opposite.

If a doctor has a fashionable address, you may well be charged at a higher rate to support his sky-high rent. Similarly, if a hospital does extensive advertising, part of that advertising cost might be passed along to you.

In many instances, some of the best physicians charge relatively low fees. They're often associated with universities or research foundations and are supported by those groups. Consequently, they have significantly lower overhead and are able to keep their fees down.

You should also compare various hospital fees. Specifically, find out the charges for rooms (private and semiprivate), the treatments your doctor recommends, and lab work. The laboratory facilities a hospital or physician uses can have significant bearing on your total bill. The hospital with an in-house facility might be able to charge far less than one that contracts with an outside lab.

Avoid Duplication

Certain tests are done as a matter of routine. Whether you're going in for your annual check-up or you're in the hospital for a specific procedure, you'll be subject to a series of standard procedures — blood tests, X rays, etc.

Ask your physician the purpose of each and every test he proposes. It might be that some of the procedures can be eliminated, if they're irrelevant to the purpose of your visit.

It's also possible that you've had some of the tests done recently, and they don't need to be repeated. For instance, you might have had blood and urinalysis tests done as a requirement for a new insurance policy. Or you might have had an X ray taken a year earlier. Ask your doctor if he can use the results from those earlier tests and eliminate new ones.

Avoiding Mistakes

As we pointed out at the beginning of the chapter, hospitals frequently make billing errors. Here are some things you can do to prevent them.

First, monitor each bill you receive, especially if you've been in the hospital for an extended period of time. Generally, you won't receive one lump-sum bill. Instead, you'll receive invoices twice a month. Examine the bill carefully. It should break down the amount charged for every service; if it doesn't, demand that the hospital do so.

Pay special attention to the description of each treatment. If you don't understand the description, you're entitled to a translation into plain English. This translation is important so you understand not only what was done but what might not have been done. It's not unusual for people to be billed for procedures that were never conducted. All it takes is for a harried nurse, physician, or administrator to check the wrong item on a piece of paper or for the wrong billing amount to be punched onto the computer's keyboard.

The bill will also contain a column that says "patient amount due." You'll be able to determine what you owe versus what your insurance has paid. If you suspect a discrepancy — the insurance company isn't paying for as much of your treatment as you expected — ask for an explanation immediately.

Another problem can result if the insurance company reverses its decision about your bill. Let's say you receive six bills from the hospital over a three-month period. Each one is for approximately $4000. But you don't worry about the amount because each bill clearly states that you owe only the deductible: $250. A month after the last bill arrives, you receive a bill from the hospital saying you owe $24,000.

After you get up off the floor, you ask the hospital representative to repeat his explanation of why you owe that huge sum.
Apparently, the insurance company has denied coverage.

Do you actually have to pay the money? No! Your argument
is that the length of your hospital stay was dictated in part by
your assumption that your stay was covered — an assumption
confirmed by the statements you received from the hospital. If
you had been informed earlier that your hospitalization wasn't
covered, you would have had the option of leaving earlier or
finding alternative, less-expensive treatment.

Because of the Byzantine coverages offered by many insurance
companies and their slow-moving review committees, this situation isn't unusual. If it happens to you, don't be cowed by the
hospital's insistence on payment. The dispute is really between
the hospital and the insurance company, and it shouldn't involve
any monetary loss on your part.

Other Coverage Problems

What happens when an insurance company gives you and the
hospital fair warning that it won't pay for treatment? Or when it
decides to pay for only a portion of your costs?

Here's a typical situation. You enter a hospital for a major
operation. The operation is successful, but the recovery period
takes longer than expected; perhaps some minor complications
arise. You're still bedridden and not feeling well when the insurance company decides that, as of Monday, they will no longer
pay for your hospitalization. The insurance company's quality-
review committee has monitored your condition and concluded
your hospitalization is no longer necessary. Your doctor believes
you should be hospitalized, but he says there's nothing he can
do.

There is something *you* can do. You have the right to contest
the insurance company's denial of coverage. Talk to your doctor
and other treating physicians about why they believe it's necessary that you remain in the hospital and the potential for your
condition to worsen should you leave. Get them to put it in
writing, and send the information to your insurance company. If
your evidence is sufficiently compelling, it's possible that they'll
reverse their decision.

Another, related, problem involves insurance companies cutting their payment amounts. Many of the larger insurance companies have language in their policies which states that they'll pay for "standard and reasonable care." When they receive your charges from the hospital or doctor, they can decide that care was "unreasonable." Perhaps they state that a specific procedure was unnecessary, a fee was too high, or your hospital stay was too long.

If the hospital asks you to make up the difference, refuse to do so. Your argument is that you were depending on your physician and the hospital to determine what was reasonable. You should not be held accountable for the actions of others.

Excessive Charges

At some point, you have probably received a bill from a doctor or health care facility that you deemed excessive. You were charged $300 for a routine check-up, or a blood analysis laboratory fee was $500. Perhaps you expected outpatient surgery to cost $2000 and instead the bill was $5000.

In all of these cases, the charges seem exorbitant. What can you do?

The first thing is to write a letter to the offending party stating that you are withholding payment until you get an explanation for the charges. That will get their attention, and it's your right to withhold payment.

Next, if the explanation is unsatisfactory — they claim that's what they always charge, it's the standard fee, etc. — attempt to document the reason why you believe the charge to be exorbitant.

If you were given a verbal or written estimate of a lower charge prior to treatment, that might do the trick. It's possible that you can accumulate a list of comparable charges for the same services from other health care providers. If those charges are substantially lower than yours, it might help you.

Remember, though, that free market principles apply. Hospitals and doctors can charge whatever they want. Caveat emptor. Still, if a charge is demonstrably excessive, the health care provider might be willing to reduce your bill.

Hospitals, for instance, might be reluctant to file suit against you to collect a bill if they don't have a strong case. It's not that they're worried about losing the one case; they're concerned that if the suit goes against them, they might not be able to collect outstanding bills from other people who have had the same treatment as you.

Hostage Situations

Don't let a doctor, nurse, or hospital bureaucrat tell you any differently: you have an absolute right to be discharged at any time, even if you haven't paid one penny of your bill. If they try to hold you against your will, they're guilty of unlawful imprisonment. If they forcibly try to restrain you from leaving, they're also guilty of battery.

Despite the law, many hospitals try to bully or bluff patients into believing they can't leave until they pay. When you enter the hospital, the first thing they ask you is the name of your insurance company. During your stay, they try to confirm coverage. Many times, however, they can't confirm coverage by the time you're ready to leave.

This makes the hospital bureaucrats extraordinarily nervous. They might try to do one of two things. First, they might ask you to stop by the cashier on your way out, implying that the cashier holds the key to unlock the prison. Second, they might ask you to sign a note declaring that you are responsible not only for charges to date but for future, undetermined charges.

This last scenario is most likely to occur if you leave the hospital prematurely. Since they haven't completed their record keeping, they haven't tallied up all the charges and are understandably worried about a disputed bill.

You don't have to sign their note. They lack the power to insist you sign a note promising payment on unknown, untotaled charges; it's like asking you to sign a blank check.

Despite what some health care administrators might have you believe, you're free to leave the hospital without passing the cashier. If administrators take a contrary position, they could be the ones who go directly to jail.

CHAPTER EIGHT

Till Death Do Us Part

SINCE THE KAREN ANN QUINLAN CASE, national attention has been focused on such issues as "quality of life" and "the right to die," and on ethical questions about prolonging life in hopelessly ill people. Stories abound of people in comas with incurable diseases who are being kept alive "thanks" to the so-called marvels of modern technology. As Thomas and Celia Scully say in their book *Playing God,* "For the first time in history, physicians have the ability, know-how and sophisticated technology to sustain the physical life of patients beyond any reasonable quality of life they may want to endure."

Traditionally, the physician has been solely responsible for deciding when life is to be allowed to end and when further effort is to be expended to keep the person alive — an awesome power that has too often resulted in the overtreatment of the dying. But in recent years, such medical practices have flown in the face of the burgeoning consumer movement and its attendant emphasis on patients' rights and patient autonomy. The consequence? Change is in the wind and, in many cases, state laws have been influenced.

The right-to-die movement, a movement away from impersonal technology to personal choices, is under way. If it is important to you to die with dignity and to maintain autonomy over future legal and medical decisions made on your behalf, then you need to do some advance planning now. And that is what this chapter is all about.

We will attempt to help you with this planning by explaining how you can use living wills and durable powers of attorney for health care to maintain your autonomy. There's also a section detailing the "latest" definitions of death, from the perspective of both the legal and medical worlds.

Our goal is to put the authority and autonomy in decisions about your health care in your hands and to keep death a personal matter.

Redefining Death

Death used to be simple. If you stopped breathing, your heart stopped, and your pupils dilated, you were dead. Not so today. No longer is the traditional heart-and-lungs concept of death applicable in every case. Therefore, if you are concerned about dying with dignity, it is important for you to understand how the medical and legal world are redefining what once was the most certain thing in life — death.

The changes in the definition of death have come about, according to the *Medico-Legal Journal*, thanks to what has been called the "revolution in intensive-care technology, which now enables artificial ventilation and circulation, feeding by the intravenous route, and the elimination of waste products of metabolism by dialysis machines to be resorted to on bodies whose brains have been irreversibly destroyed." Organ transplantation also changed the accepted definition of death, because for an organ to be of the utmost benefit to the recipient, it must be removed at the earliest possible moment after circulation stops.

As a result, the definition of death has been broadened to include the irreversible loss of all brain function — brain death. In a landmark report in 1968, the Ad Hoc Committee of the Harvard Medical School to examine the Definition of Brain Death laid down four characteristics of a permanently nonfunctioning brain:

1. Unreceptivity and unresponsivity — total unawareness of externally applied stimuli.

2. No movement or breathing — one hour's observation of spontaneous muscular movements, breathing, or response to stimuli. (If the person is on a respirator, absence of breathing must be established by three minutes off the machine.)

3. No reflexes present — fixed and dilated pupils, no eye movement or blinking, no contraction of muscles due to stimulation.

4. Flat electroencephalogram (EEG) — after 10 minutes of recording.

These tests, the report said, are to be done twice, 24 hours apart.

Either through laws or court decisions, most states recognize the concept of brain death but have left the final determination to the doctor. The wording of most of the statutes conforms to what is called the Uniform Determination of Death Act (proposed by the President's Commission for the Study of Ethical Problems in Medicine and Biomedical and Behavioral Research in 1980): *"An individual who has sustained either (1) irreversible cessation of circulatory and respiratory functions, or (2) irreversible cessation of all functions of the entire brain, including the brain stem, is dead. A determination must be made in accordance with accepted medical standards."*

What about the states where there is no legislation? In their 1986 book *The Right to Die: Understanding Euthanasia,* Derek Humphry and Ann Wickett say that decisions about what constitutes death in those states are left up to physicians' own definitions. Your state Bar Association can tell you what applies where you reside.

Unfortunately, even a legal definition of brain death does not completely eliminate the uncertainty surrounding this issue. According to a 1985 report in *Washington Post Health,* the newspaper's weekly supplement, the criteria for determining brain death vary slightly from hospital to hospital. So you may want to call your community hospitals — first try the office of the chief of the medical staff, then go to the hospital administrator, if need be — to find out what "standards" they use to determine brain death. (The criteria should always include total lack of movement, inability to breathe without a respirator, total unresponsiveness to stimuli, and total absence of reflexes.)

But even with recognized and legislated definitions of brain death, and established criteria for determining it, there is uncertainty among some physicians; they question whether it means death of the entire brain, including the brain stem, or just cerebral death, which is partial death of the brain. A September 1987 article in the magazine *Omni* referred to a growing movement to modify the concept of brain death to include people in what is called a persistent vegetative state (PVS), a number estimated to be around 10,000 in this country.

In PVS, only part of the brain is destroyed; the main stem is intact, so the person is capable of reflex functions, such as breathing and sleeping, but incapable of thought or even awareness of the environment. PVS, often called cognitive death, can last for years, with absolutely no hope for improvement.

But the cognitive death idea has many opponents, in both the medical and the lay worlds. There are those who ask, "Where will it all end — in experiments on these people?" Others simply believe the long-term unconscious may someday "wake up." So the debate is liable to go on for years, or even decades, to come.

These are all matters you may want to discuss with your physician, and perhaps with a lawyer knowledgeable in right-to-die issues, so that any advance directives you write encompass all the points about which you believe strongly. Any of the organizations concerned with death (which are listed elsewhere in this chapter) should be able to help you, as well.

Making Your Wishes Known

No one likes to plan his own death in advance, but in today's "what is death" environment, planning may be a necessity.

Basically, there are two legal routes available to help ensure that your passing occurs on your terms: living wills and durable power of attorney.

Living Wills

A living will is a written statement that you do not want life-prolonging medical procedures if your condition is hopeless and there is no chance of regaining a meaningful life. Living wills have been around since 1976, when California was the first state to pass what is called the Natural Death Act. Although called "wills," they have nothing to do with property, but rather with oneself, and are intended to take effect when you are alive. An outgrowth of concern over the loss of ability to direct medical care at the end of your life, a living will is an advance directive, and is operative only if you are terminally ill and unconscious or otherwise incompetent to discuss and decide with your physician what treatment you wish.

Not only a tool to control the extent and type of medical care you receive at the end of your life, a living will can also help reduce the emotional stresses and strains felt by both your family and your doctor, in the event that they must make decisions whether to withhold, withdraw, or continue medical treatment that cannot cure or reverse a terminal condition.

By 1989, 38 states and the District of Columbia had passed some form of law authorizing an individual to make personal decisions about dying. These living will laws go by various names: "natural death acts," "death with dignity acts," "medical treatment decision acts," "right-to-die acts," etc. The laws vary in detail from state to state, so be sure to find out the limitations in yours, including:

• Whether more than the standard two witnesses are required and if notarization is mandatory

• If applicable to you, whether implementation of the living will is prohibited if you are pregnant

• Whether the withdrawal of life-sustaining treatment may include artificial feeding and hydration. (This is one of the most controversial issues of the right-to-die movement. Many states' living will laws specifically prohibit the withdrawal of food and water; others allow it, and some sidestep the issue entirely.)

• Whether you must follow a particular form or are permitted to add personalized instructions

• Whether your state's living will is valid in another state

If you reside in a state without a living will statute, what can you do? Realize first and foremost, as Society for the Right to Die director Alice Mehling says, "Even without a living will law, everyone has the common-law right to refuse treatment." Her recommendation is to execute a general living will form (available from her organization and others) as clear and convincing evidence of what you want.

Must your hospital or doctor accept your advance directive? In their book *The Right to Die: Understanding Euthanasia,* Humphry and Wickett say that some resist obeying living wills, a refusal that in many cases has led to litigation. In point of fact, Mehling tells us, the "growing body of legal opinion is that [failure to comply with a valid living will] is grounds for battery action."

For more information on the role of advance directives in the right-to-die issue; to obtain the appropriate living will document to comply with your state's legislation or the form you should use if your state lacks living will legislation; or to get answers to individual questions concerning living will enforcement and many other issues, contact Concern for Dying or the Society for the Right to Die. (For addresses see pages 131–132.)

---

*Sample**

"LIVING WILL" DECLARATION

Declaration made this ___ day of _____, 19___
I,_____, being of sound mind, willfully and voluntarily make known my desire that my dying shall not be artificially prolonged under the circumstances set forth below, and do declare:

If at any time I should have an incurable injury, disease or illness certified to be a terminal condition by two physicians who have personally examined me, one of whom shall be my attending physician, and the physicians have determined that my death will occur whether or not life-sustaining procedures are utilized and where the application of life-sustaining procedures would serve only to artificially prolong the dying process, I direct that such procedures be withheld or withdrawn, and that I be permitted to die naturally with only the administration of medication or the performance of any medical procedure deemed necessary to provide me with comfort care.

In the absence of my ability to give directions regarding the use of such life-sustaining procedures, it is my intention that this declaration shall be honored by my family and physician(s) as the final expression of my legal right to refuse medical or surgical treatment and accept the consequences from such refusal.

I understand the full import of this declaration and I am

emotionally and mentally competent to make this declaration.

Signed ——————————————————————————

Address ——————————————————————————

The declarant has been personally known to me and I believe him/her to be of sound mind.

Witness ——————————————————————————

Witness ——————————————————————————

Source: President's Commission for the Study of Ethical Problems in Medicine and Biomedical and Behavioral Research, "Deciding to Forego Life-Sustaining Treatment," U.S. Government Printing Office, pp. 314–315.

*NOTE: This is just a sample and not to be taken as necessarily the correct or legally binding form for your needs. Be sure to check the requirements of the statute in your state.

DOES YOUR STATE HAVE A LIVING WILL LAW?

These are the 39 jurisdictions with living will laws:

Alabama	Illinois	North Carolina
Alaska	Indiana	Oklahoma
Arizona	Iowa	Oregon
Arkansas	Kansas	South Carolina
California	Louisiana	Tennessee
Colorado	Maine	Texas
Connecticut	Maryland	Utah
Delaware	Mississippi	Vermont
District of Columbia	Missouri	Virginia
Florida	Montana	Washington
Georgia	Nevada	West Virginia
Hawaii	New Hampshire	Wisconsin
Idaho	New Mexico	Wyoming

Durable Power of Attorney for Health Care

The durable power of attorney for health care is an alternative form of advance directive, a written document that allows you to name someone as agent (also called proxy or attorney-in-fact) with authority to make medical decisions for you (according to

your previously expressed wishes) in the event you become incompetent and are unable to make those decisions for yourself.

You may already know about durable power of attorney in its
standard sense, which is a way of authorizing another person to
make decisions or take actions on your behalf in financial or
property transactions. Indeed, *all 50 states plus the District of
Columbia have durable power of attorney laws,* and these laws
have been used as the basis for health care directives.

Despite that, however, some states have passed legislation creating a durable power of attorney specifically for health care decisions. This is to ensure that health issues are kept separate from
other legal issues, such as matters dealing with your money. But
even in states without a statute concerning a specific durable
power of attorney for health, the courts have generally recognized such documents, according to Concern for Dying. (Check
with your state Bar Association for details on the law.)

The most critical issue is deciding who is the appropriate decision maker, and Ami S. Jaeger, J.D., of the American Bar
Foundation, recommends that you consider these factors:
"Whom would you trust with life-and-death decisions? Who
knows you best — your attitudes and values? Who would respect
your wishes?" Jaeger says most people appoint spouses or close
family members — good choices because they know you well —
but warns that if they are beneficiaries of your estate, there could
be a conflict of interest.

The best strategy is to have both a living will and a durable
power of attorney. A living will is only about the final moments
of life. Considered more flexible than a living will, a durable
power of attorney can be drafted to include the authority to
make decisions about several areas of medical treatment, not just
the termination of life support — on behalf of people not capable of making their own decisions, such as after a serious accident, a permanent loss of consciousness, or an incapacitating
illness.

"For example," Jaeger says, "if [an incompetent] person is
severely diabetic, and the doctor recommends he undergo an
amputation, the living will would not cover the situation, but a
durable power of attorney would."

Concern for Dying and the Society for the Right to Die both
have legal departments that can give you further information on

this topic. The Hemlock Society also distributes copies of the durable power of attorney for health care.

The "Debbie" Case

Euthanasia is the topic of a prominent medical ethics debate in a time when many people are questioning the process of dying in hospitals, expressing profound fears about becoming dependent, and agonizing over whether doctors will provide adequate relief of pain and suffering. The essay "It's Over, Debbie," which appeared in the January 8, 1988, *Journal of the American Medical Association,* and the ensuing brouhaha, illustrate the enormous uncertainty and conflicts of opinion attending the issue of "mercy killing" (or active euthanasia, the more objective term). Clearly, the furor over the story of Debbie's death is not over.

"It's Over, Debbie" is a first-person, unsigned essay that describes how a tired resident physician at an unidentified hospital injected a fatal dose of morphine into a terminally ill, 20-year-old patient with ovarian cancer. The doctor was not her attending physician — indeed, he had never seen her before — but was called to her bedside because she had not slept in two days, was struggling to breathe, and was vomiting unrelentingly. The doctor writes, "Her only words to me were, 'Let's get this over with,' " which he took as a plea to die. Within minutes of the morphine injection, the woman was dead.

By publishing the account, anonymously and without accompanying editorial comment, *Journal* editor George D. Lundberg, M.D., intended to stir up a national debate on the issue of "mercy killing," which he certainly did — and more. "It's Over, Debbie" prompted a Cook County (Illinois) grand jury probe and a subpoena of the *Journal's* records in an attempt by prosecutors to learn the author's identity. In April 1988, citing the failure of the prosecution to prove a crime had been committed, a judge dismissed the subpoena.

What About Your Doctor?

A peripheral controversy emerged as to whether the events actually took place — quite a few doctors and ethicists expressed doubt, although equal numbers acknowledged the story's verisimilitude. The first such "confession" ever to appear in an American medical journal, "It's Over, Debbie" spotlights a nagging question many of us have: *Does this practice occur in hospitals more often than we realize and more often than most doctors are willing to admit?*

Much of the initial outcry came from many physicians who believed that "It's Over, Debbie" would replace the image of the caring physician with that of the killing physician. In a rush to correct the appearance that the American Medical Association supports or is neutral about euthanasia, the AMA reiterated its long-standing dictum against direct medical killing. The AMA position, in short, is that physicians may withhold life-sustaining treatment under certain circumstances but should never intentionally cause death. However, the "line" is often hard to draw.

That's the official word from organized medicine, but what is really going on? Truly, it's hard to tell. Manhattan internist Eric Cassell says, "No one talks about that kind of stuff." Quentin Young, M.D., former medical director of Chicago's Cook County Hospital, says that by its very clandestine nature, active euthanasia is "more prevalent than we have knowledge of. It's a private transaction, although there have been public reports of nurses and others undertaking such actions."

Details of exact numbers, or even estimates, remain sketchy, but some recent polls do seem to substantiate the reports that doctors are performing "mercy killings," or active euthanasia.

• More than 35 percent of Colorado physicians, according to a 1988 survey reported in *American Medical News* (July 1, 1988), said they would have given a lethal drug to terminally ill patients they have treated, if such an action had been legal. And nearly 37 percent said they have knowingly given pain medication that would hasten a person's death.

• In a 1988 poll of physicians by the San Francisco Medical Society, 70 percent said that terminally ill patients should be allowed to choose active euthanasia, and more than half (54 percent) said that doctors should carry out the patients' wishes (*Medical Economics,* June 20, 1988).

• A 1987 survey of California physicians conducted by the Hemlock Society found that nearly 23 percent of them had taken steps to bring about the death of a patient requesting such action. Of the 79 who said they had, 15 had done it once; 35 had taken such steps two or three times, and 29 had done so more than three times. When asked if it is sometimes right for a doctor to take active steps to bring about the death of a patient who has requested such action, 62.5 percent of the doctors agreed that it is.

Around the time of the "Debbie" issue, three separate indictments against doctors for performing euthanasia wound up in court. And in an April 21, 1988, *Medical Tribune* article, Hemlock Society director Derek Humphry said his impression was "that, more and more, doctors are getting into trouble." Nonetheless, no doctor as yet is in jail as a result of mercy killing.

Right and Wrong, Intentional and Incidental Euthanasia — Walking the Fine Line

According to attorneys interviewed for the *Medical Tribune* report, there is a "right way and a wrong way." For example, withholding artificial feeding from a permanently unconscious patient can be legal and ethical, but injecting morphine to get the same result is criminal.

The courts also distinguish between intentional and incidental results. According to the same article, "It is legal to give a patient morphine with the intention of relieving pain, and the incidental effect of hastening death, but it is criminal to give the same patient the same dose of morphine with the primary intent of hastening death." The former distinction has come to be referred to as accidental or "double-effect" euthanasia, a concept that has been around for a few years. Along with many textbooks on cancer care, the 1983 President's Commission report "Decisions to Forego Life-Sustaining Treatment" stated that it is permissible to use morphine for end-stage cancer pain and respiratory distress even if it hastens death.

Another important legal and ethical issue here is the matter of consent. Much of the outcry condemning the "Debbie" case came as a result of the so-called unilateral way in which the resident made his decision. Humphry says it "[demonstrated] in at least one instance how poorly hospitals handle such requests for euthanasia." The consensus among active euthanasia advocates is that it is not a decision to be made by a medical resident in the middle of the night.

Various surveys have found that the majority of Americans favor active voluntary euthanasia for the terminally ill. So there may be more than a little truth in Lundberg's statement that the public is more willing and ready than the medical profession to get physician aid-in-dying. Unfortunately, where this issue is concerned, we are in the midst of uncertainty as well as confusion.

Resuscitation: Your Choice

In hospitals and nursing homes across the country, "DNR" stands for the order Do Not Resuscitate. It means that, should respiration or heartbeat fail, cardiopulmonary resuscitative measures (CPR) will not be started. A DNR order means that the patient will not be given brief emergency CPR, nor will the patient be placed on long-term mechanical life support equipment. Knowing about DNR orders — when, how, and by whom they are issued, and how they work — is an important step in gaining more control over the circumstances of your or your loved one's death.

Historically, in the absence of laws and guidelines, decisions such as when to turn to technology and when to let nature take over have been left to the medical team. For years, only medical and nursing personnel knew whether a person was designated DNR, because doctors believed that it was "inappropriate" to discuss the matter with the patient. An outcome of this secrecy was that there was tacit agreement among the hospital staff to engage in "slow codes" (have the resuscitation team purposely move slowly) or "show codes" (have the team feign a resuscitation effort, for the family's sake). However the DNR status was indicated — by a purple dot on the patient's chart, as one New York hospital did, or by any other esoteric symbol — doctors, nurses, technicians, and all the other members of the health care team knew what to do and not do.

An important nationwide survey of DNR orders in intensive care units (*Journal of the American Medical Association,* January 17, 1986) found that 75 percent of the time, the ICU or attending physicians initiated the DNR orders, and only 8 percent of the time did the family do so. In this 13-hospital study of more than

7,000 admissions, only one patient gave the word, and only one patient had a living will that stipulated no resuscitation.

For the most part, this scenario is changing, and for a variety of reasons, not the least of which is the movement toward greater patient autonomy — and doctors' fear of lawsuits by patients or their families. As of January 1, 1988, all hospitals seeking accreditation by the Joint Commission on Accreditation of Health Care Organizations had to have a policy in place concerning the withholding of resuscitation services to patients. *So it is important that you find out what your hospital's specific DNR policy is.*

A few questions then arise:

Should you routinely, upon admission to the hospital, discuss your wishes for resuscitation? At what point in the course of your illness/hospitalization can the decision about resuscitation best be made? What can you do if your decision about resuscitation changes over time? Clearly, timing is essential. According to a study reported in the July 11, 1986, *Journal of the American Medical Association*, DNR orders are written at a time when most patients are not capable of participating in the decision, although the majority of the people in the survey were considered competent when they were admitted. On the other hand, if a person is critically ill when admitted to the hospital, there is not always enough time to discuss resuscitation.

What should you do to avoid such a devil-and-the-deep-blue-sea predicament?

• Talk to your physician about the appropriateness of a Do Not Resuscitate order — before it is needed, and even before admission to the hospital, if possible. Ask specifically about your illness and the probable consequences of refusing resuscitation. Force the issue, if you must, to ensure that your physician knows what aggressive and expensive medical care would be undesirable to you.

• Discuss the matter with your family so that they will know your wishes and be able to act confidently in your behalf if necessary.

• Document your wishes concerning emergency resuscitation, and have your physician make this a part of your record. According to the Society for the Right to Die, "Most of the 39 jurisdictions with 'living will' laws have for some time allowed people to reject [emergency resuscitation], just as they can reject any other life-sustaining treatment."

• And remember, a DNR order is not an irrevocable decision. If the outcome of another day in the hospital or another hospital stay causes you to have second thoughts, just speak up — and document your decision, of course. Any major improvement in your condition would also nullify the DNR order.

The important thing is to avoid the potential complications that can arise — conflicts between family members, conflicts between your family and the hospital and doctors, and the need for determination by outside parties such as the hospital ethics committee or legal counsel.

We echo the finding of the President's Commission for the Study of Ethical Problems in Medicine and Biomedical and Behavioral Research: "Decision-making about life-sustaining care is rarely improved by resort to courts."

MODEL DNR ORDERS

In 1983, the President's Commission for the Study of Ethical Problems in Medicine and Biomedical and Behavioral Research developed these guidelines related to Do Not Resuscitate orders. Use these recommendations to determine how your hospital's policy stacks up:

• "A competent and informed patient or an incompetent patient's surrogate is entitled to decide with the attending physician that an order against resuscitation should be written in the chart. When cardiac arrest is likely, a patient (or a surrogate) should usually be informed and offered the chance specifically to decide for or against resuscitation."

• "Physicians have a duty to assess for each hospitalized patient whether resuscitation is likely, on balance, to benefit the patient, to fail to benefit, or to have uncertain effect."

• "When a physician's assessment conflicts with a competent patient's decision, further discussion and consultation are appropriate; ultimately, the physician must follow

the patient's decision or transfer responsibility for that patient to another physician."

• "When a physician's assessment conflicts with that of an
incompetent patient's surrogate, further discussion, consultation, review by an institutional committee and, if necessary, judicial review should be sought."

• "[DNR policies] should require that orders not to resuscitate be in written form and . . . delineate who has the
authority both to write such orders and to stop a resuscitation effort in progress."

Undertreatment of Pain — What Can You Do?

Relief of pain and suffering should be the fundamental goal of
every physician, yet new research indicates that physicians
chronically underprescribe medications, thereby causing patients
needless suffering. According to a survey undertaken at Rush-
Presbyterian–St. Luke's Medical Center in Chicago and published in the journal *Pain,* 65 percent of hospitalized patients
reported experiencing unbearable pain at some point.

Why are doctors reluctant to give adequate doses of painkilling
drugs? After all, isn't the ancient medical dictum, "To cure
sometimes, to comfort always"? Doctors underprescribe largely
because they fear that heavy doses of drugs will create addicts.
They hold back even when their patients have only weeks or
months to live. Dr. Russell Portnoy, director of analgesic studies
at Sloan-Kettering Memorial Hospital, calls this a practice based
on "a medical myth." Unfortunately, this misconception persists
despite an important study published almost a decade ago in the
New England Journal of Medicine. Out of 11,882 hospital patients treated with painkilling drugs, only four were found to
have become addicted.

Still, the myth thrives, and not only among prescribing
physicians but among caregiving nurses as well. The Rush-
Presbyterian–St. Luke's survey found that, on the average,
nurses gave patients only one fourth of the doses of painkillers
allowed by the physicians. From this and other studies, it is clear
that misinformation — concerning effective doses, duration of
effects, and dangers of addiction — is rampant and, according to

Portnoy, persists in part because of gaps in medical education. Currently, the typical four-year medical curriculum devotes four hours or less to pain, and most experts agree that is not enough.

This appalling state of affairs is echoed in a 1987 report by the Hastings Center, an eminent think tank specializing in medical ethics. "Guidelines on the Termination of Life-Sustaining Treatment and Care of the Dying" concluded that "many health care professionals have inadequate knowledge about the pharmacology of pain relief and the appropriate use of narcotics and similar agents for dying patients."

So much for the problem. Now, what can you do? If you find yourself in such a situation, realize that you (or your surrogate) must play a major role.

• Specify in your living will that you wish medication to keep you as pain-free as possible.

• Discuss with your doctor your fear of or concern about pain and your desire for adequate medication for control of pain. Pain is a complex symptom, and not all of it is physical in origin; much derives from anxiety, a sense of hopelessness, family stress, fear, spiritual concerns, and more — and all can lower your threshold for pain, thereby creating the perception of more and more pain. Together, discover the cause of your pain.

• But also ask what the adverse side effects of the painkilling drugs are. An article in *Postgraduate Medicine* (June 1988) points out that pain control measures often fail because the patient could not anticipate the adverse side effects.

• Communicate as honestly as you can the extent of your pain. Some experts recommend that doctors ask two key questions: "*Does the medicine ever take the pain away completely? Does the pain return before it is time for the next dose of medicine?*" According to Robert G. Twycross and Sylvia A. Lack, in *Symptom Control in Far Advanced Cancer: Pain Relief* (1987), if no is the first answer, then the dose should be increased. If the second answer is yes, then the dose should also be increased. But don't wait for your doctor to ask the questions. Give him the answers right away.

• Discuss with your physician the alternative therapies for pain relief — for example, biofeedback, hypnosis, relaxation techniques, and acupuncture. While they may not work in every case, they have helped many.

In medical matters, pain and dignity are closely related. This is especially so in the terminally ill patient. It is an inhumane medical system that sits back and allows a person to die in pain when there are means available to control it.

For more information on the treatment of pain, contact: International Pain Foundation, 909 N.E. 43rd St., Suite 306, Seattle, WA 98105-6020. To obtain a list of accredited pain treatment centers, write: The Commission on Accreditation of Rehabilitation Facilities, 2500 Pantzano Road, Tucson, AZ 85715.

Physician Aid-in-Dying

As we have pointed out earlier in this chapter, the physician's role in assisting death is mired in controversy. As national attention to the right-to-die issue turns to the question of active euthanasia, one organization's work stands out. Unlike other right-to-die groups that support only passive euthanasia, the National Hemlock Society also supports the concept of active voluntary euthanasia for the terminally ill, and takes the stance that terminally ill people have the right to end their own lives in a planned manner. In the parlance of the organization, such a suicide goes by a number of names, including "rational suicide," "self-deliverance for the dying," and "autoeuthanasia."

Hemlock's most controversial and, at the same time, best-selling, book on the subject is *Let Me Die Before I Wake*. It is a do-it-yourself suicide manual for the terminally ill, and Executive Director Derek Humphry says that Hemlock "is alone in the world [in putting] out on the free trade and library market [such] a guide." Humphry is quick to point out, however, that the group's view of suicide for emotional and mental reasons is as conventional as anyone else's — to prevent it where you can.

The way Humphry and the Hemlock Society see it — once active euthanasia is legalized (now it is not), people won't need such a book because they will end their lives through their doctors. Now, he says, people cannot do that, "so they take the law into their own hands. It's a very secret crime, and it goes on a great deal without being detected."

But the Hemlock Society is not irresponsible in its view of legalized physician aid-in-dying. In a letter to the editor of the *Journal of the American Medical Association,* a representative of the organization from Illinois states, "The Hemlock Society firmly believes in legalized physician aid-in-dying only when it conforms to the following requirements:

1. There must be adequate legal documentation that the euthanasia was requested by the patient well in advance of its occurring.

2. The physician who aids the patient in dying must have known the patient and must have been fully aware of his/her medical history and desire for aid-in-dying in the event of terminal illness.

3. The physician must have a second opinion from another qualified physician that affirms that the patient's condition is indeed terminal.

4. The rights of physicians who cannot in good conscience perform aid-in-dying are to be fully respected, providing they in no way obstruct the practice of physicians who in good conscience give such aid."

Euthanasia is not legal. But clearly the efforts of the Hemlock Society are making policymakers think long and hard about fulfilling people's wishes at the end of life.

The Biggest Controversy of Them All

More than any other life-sustaining question, the subject of withholding or withdrawing artificial feeding have moved into the forefront of right-to-die issues. Perhaps because of the symbolic significance of nourishment in the minds of many people, sustenance (food and water) appears to be more difficult to discontinue than any other treatment — whether in a person who is expected to die in a relatively short time, or a comatose person whose death may not occur for months or years.

However, amidst all the controversy surrounding the issue, many authorities see an emerging legal trend. Courts in at least 15 states have ruled that patients have the same right to refuse feeding tubes as to refuse other medical treatment — a growing consensus that counts among its supporters the American Medical Association. In 1986, the AMA's Council on Ethical and Judicial Affairs issued a major opinion stating that it is ethically permissible for doctors to withhold all life-prolonging treatment, including artificial nutrition and hydration, from permanently unconscious or dying patients. And in a precedent-setting ruling in 1987, the New Jersey Supreme Court affirmed a lower-court decision (the Jobes case) that had been the first ruling to support removal of life-extending artificial feeding and hydration from a patient not diagnosed as terminally ill.

Generally, competent patients have the right to refuse this treatment and the right is not limited to comatose or terminally ill patients. For incompetent patients, artificial feeding, as with other treatments, can be stopped in accordance with the patient's previously expressed wishes.

In examining your options regarding this emotionally charged issue and your right to refuse treatments, here are some pointers:

• Document your wishes about artificial feeding (as well as other life-sustaining treatments), and be as specific as you can. Our best advice is also that of Alice Mehling, executive director of the Society for the Right to Die: "If you have feelings regarding artificial feeding in your particular case, then write them down. Most assuredly spell them out." Bear in mind, however, that although a written directive is the clearest evidence of an incompetent person's wishes, courts have honored a person's wishes verbally communicated even when they were not in writing. But why take the risk?

• Know your state's living will law (if it has one) — in this case, what it says and does not say about artificial feeding. Even in states with such laws on the books, not every one specifically mentions artificial feeding, and the language in some of the laws actually restricts artificial feeding. Connecticut, Georgia, Missouri, and Wisconsin specifically state that artificial feeding is not a procedure a person can reject under the statute.

• Know the common feeding and hydration treatments available should you not be able to eat in the usual way, and discuss these with your physician. What are the goals of these feedings — to prolong life, deliver calories, or provide comfort? The difficulty comes in determining whether the burdens of feeding are worth the benefits — especially since these treatments are invasive, can be painful, and sometimes are harmful both to unconscious and conscious patients.

The Society for the Right to Die details the following potential complications and side effects of the common feeding and hydration treatments. While these complications do not necessarily occur in a majority of the cases, you need to know them so that your discussions with your doctor can be productive.

1. *Nasogastric tube:* This intervention causes discomfort for the average person, who also runs the risk of food aspiration, pneumonia, vomiting, injuries to tissue, and bleeding into the stomach. (Others have documented additional risk of sinus and lung infections.)

2. *Intravenous feeding:* The risks include phlebitis, hematoma, infection, blood clots, and embolism.

3. *Gastrostomy tube:* The risks are those usually associated with the use of anesthesia, as well as infection and peritonitis.

4. *Parenteral hyperalimentation:* The risks include perforation of the lung, causing collapse, blood poisoning, and massive bleeding.

• Be certain that you know your physician's feeling on withholding/withdrawing artificial feeding. You may even want to familiarize yourself with area hospitals' and nursing homes' policies. According to a report in the journal *Medical Staff Counselor* (Summer 1988), no matter how unfounded the fears may be, some health care providers are still worried about the legal liability for honoring patient preferences — even when these preferences are completely documented in the medical record. Furthermore, there is always the chance that your doctor will prove unwilling, for reasons of conscience, to participate in the rejection of artificial feeding. It is far better to know these things in advance rather than haggle over the issue from a hospital bed or subject your family to the conflicts that may arise.

As a special article in the February 4, 1988, *New England Journal of Medicine* pointed out: "Allowing patients or their surrogates time to choose another physician or facility that will honor their decisions is far preferable to waiting until the patient's condition deteriorates before attempting a transfer."

The Hospice

Hospices were developed to assist dying patients — typically cancer patients who have exhausted the various forms of curative treatment — and to help them live their remaining weeks or months as free of symptoms and as much in control as possible. Deliberately created as alternatives to traditional long-term institutions, hospices provide palliative (or comfort) care to patients and their families, and also provide bereavement counseling for the families following the patient's death.

For people who do not wish to receive further aggressive treatment for a terminal illness, or for whom only palliative care can be provided, a hospice offers an opportunity for the patient and family to help each other during the dying process in a supportive atmosphere.

FURTHER SOURCES OF INFORMATION ON DEATH AND DYING

The following organizations provide information and materials on death and dying. In addition, your state bar association (see Appendix A) can assist in matters relating to living wills and durable power of attorney for health care.

CONCERN FOR DYING
250 West 57th St.
New York, New York 10107
(212) 246-6962

NATIONAL HEMLOCK SOCIETY
P.O. Box 11830
Eugene, Oregon 97440
(503) 342-5748

SOCIETY FOR THE RIGHT TO DIE
250 West 57th St.
New York, New York 10107
(212) 246-6973

ELISABETH KUBLER-ROSS CENTER
South Route 616
Head Waters, VA 24442
(703) 396-3441

NATIONAL HOSPICE ORGANIZATION
1901 N. Fort Meyer Dr.
Suite 307
Arlington, VA 22209
(703) 243-5900

CHAPTER NINE

Years Bring Fears

Y EARS BRING MANY FEARS to people. And a common fear we acquire as we get older is the fear of illness. For the senior citizen, illness may signal diminishing abilities or require major alterations in lifestyle, neither particularly desirable situations.

Another fear that is growing among the senior population, is that of being helpless when having to deal with the medical care system.

While it might be argued that your medical rights are your medical rights regardless of age, senior citizens face special medical and legal circumstances that complicate matters.

First, people 65 years and older use the health care system more than any other group; thus they are exposed to more chances of rights abuse. Second, federal and state entitlement programs, such as Medicare, are not easy to understand or to use to maximum effect. Third, an additional tier of medical services, such as nursing homes and Medicare-approved HMOs available, complicates the picture.

In this chapter, we will look at specific areas where senior citizens often experience difficulty. We will examine your rights concerning Medicare, nursing homes and Medicare, supplemental health insurance (often called "Medigap" because it supplements your Medicare coverage), HMOs established exclusively for Medicare-eligible persons, and some other medical rights issues of particular importance to seniors.

Medicare

Medicare is the largest entitlement program in the world. Over 32 million Americans are Medicare-eligible, and most are beneficiaries. The Medicare program is federally mandated and administered by the Health Care Financing Administration, which is part of the United States Department of Health and Human Services.

Medicare is also one of the most complicated programs ever created. Those under age 65, or otherwise ineligible for the program, believe Medicare is relatively simple. Little do they know. Their misconception of the program runs something like this: when you turn 65 or are disabled, you go to your local Social Security office and register, and the rest is medical nirvana. Nothing could be further from the truth (as any senior citizen will attest).

Because of the complicated nature of the Medicare program, many senior citizens do not get the maximum benefits they are entitled to receive. Sometimes this occurs because the individual does not realize a particular service or treatment is covered. Other times doctors or hospital personnel misinform the beneficiaries of their benefits — not with intent (remember, Medicare is often as much of a maze to them as to you). And still others find the process so complex or difficult to figure out that they do not bother to file claims, dispute decisions, or appeal denials.

While we certainly cannot cover all of Medicare in one section of one chapter (see the People's Medical Society book by Charles B. Inlander and Charles K. MacKay, *Medicare Made Easy* (1989), to learn how to get the maximum benefits from Medicare), we can cover some of the more important questions related to rights that often arise.

I've applied for Medicare and have been told that I'm ineligible. What should I do?

Find out exactly why you are ineligible. (If you filed an application, you should have received a letter telling you the reason.) If you do not meet one of the categorical requirements for the program — for example, you are not yet 65, or are under 65 and not disabled, or are not a U.S. citizen, or are an alien admitted for permanent residence — you should try to alter your status.

There's no way to be 65 faster, but you can consult a lawyer who specializes in disability cases, apply for citizenship or alien resident status, or — if you were found ineligible because you have not worked enough — check your earnings record.

If you believe that a clear error has been made and that it is not being corrected, you can appeal the finding of ineligibility.

You should also check to see if you are entitled on the basis of someone else's earnings. You may be eligible as the wife, widow, divorced wife, husband, widower, divorced husband, child, or parent of someone else.

I applied on the basis of disability, and have been turned down. I want to appeal. What can I do?

Realistically, you have to hire a lawyer. Disability law is complicated, is affected variously by different precedents in different judicial districts, and changes constantly because of court decisions. Beware of lawyers who promise to get you disability benefits. No one can promise that; the outcome depends on the facts of your case. Also, be aware that the federal regulations governing disability limit the fees an attorney may charge you for representation before the Social Security Administration. (The Social Security Administration makes the determination.) The fee is limited to the smallest of the following:

- 25 percent of past-due benefits

- The fee you and the attorney agreed on

- The fee set by the Social Security Administration

If the case goes to federal court, the court may award a fee higher than any of the above, but the amount the Social Security Administration will pay out of past-due benefits awarded is limited to the smallest of the three amounts. You are responsible for any fees above that amount that are awarded by the court. The Social Security Administration does not pay any fees if you lose, because in that case there are no past-due benefits to pay from. In other words, you always have to pay the attorney, but the fee is paid from past-due benefits if you win.

Before paying for an attorney, contact senior citizens' centers, area agencies on aging, and welfare rights projects that are listed in the phone book. No-cost or reduced-cost legal services may be available from them.

I now know that I am definitely not eligible for Medicare. What can I do?

Persons who are age 65 and do not otherwise qualify for Medicare can purchase Medicare coverage just as they would private insurance. This is expensive, running $189.90 per month for combined hospital (Part A) and doctors' bills (Part B) in 1989. (Check with your local Social Security office for the current rate.) If you purchase Medicare, you will still have to purchase supplemental insurance to have a package that really protects you against the financial effects of illness. You may find that it is cheaper to purchase individual coverage from a health maintenance organization (HMO) that offers very comprehensive benefits for one, fixed price, if an HMO is available where you live.

You are permitted to purchase Part B of Medicare (insurance for doctors' bills) if you are a resident of the United States, are 65 or over, and are either a citizen or an alien lawfully admitted for permanent residence who has resided in the United States for the last five years. (It is under this rule that everyone enrolls in Part B.) If you are not eligible for Part A of Medicare, enrolling for Part B entitles you to purchase it. So you have to buy Part B to get Part A.

I want to visit my sister in Canada this summer and have some surgery done while we are together so she can take care of me. Will Medicare pay for a hospital stay outside the United States?

No. People think that Medicare pays for care anywhere in the world. It doesn't. Only care in hospitals in the fifty states and the District of Columbia, Puerto Rico, and the last two U.S. territories, Guam and the Virgin Islands, is paid for. The only exceptions are situations in which you are close to the Mexican or Canadian borders and need emergency care, and the nearest hospital is a Mexican or Canadian one, or if the Mexican or Canadian hospital is much closer to your home than any American hospital and is accredited by the Joint Commission on Accreditation of Health Care Organizations or a comparable body in the foreign country. In these situations, Medicare will pay for services in a Mexican or Canadian hospital.

Please note that doctors' services outside the United States are covered only if they are given during an inpatient hospitalization that is paid for under the circumstances described above.

I am worried that I will have to leave the hospital when my Diagnosis Related Group (DRG) days run out, even if I'm not well.

Don't be. It is illegal for the hospital even to suggest it. During the early days of the DRG system (the system that determines the amount of money Medicare will pay a hospital for the services provided you), there were a number of instances of abuse. Patients were told that they had to leave the hospital "because your DRG has run out" or something similar. Discharging any patient who still needs hospital care because of financial considerations is a total violation of the hospital's contract with Medicare. The hospital has agreed to provide services to you as long as they are medically necessary.

Because of abuses observed, the People's Medical Society (PMS) and the American Association of Retired Persons (AARP) joined forces to ask Medicare to require hospitals to "Mirandize" Medicare patients: just as persons being arrested are told of their constitutional rights, Medicare now requires all hospitals to provide Medicare beneficiaries with an Important Message from Medicare form upon admission for any patient care:

AN IMPORTANT MESSAGE FROM MEDICARE

Your Rights While You Are a Medicare Hospital Patient

- You have the right to receive all the hospital care that is necessary for the proper diagnosis and treatment of your illness or injury. According to Federal law, your discharge date must be determined solely by your medical needs, not by "DRGs" or Medicare payments.

- You have the right to be fully informed about decisions affecting your Medicare coverage and payment for your hospital stay and for any post-hospital services.

• You have the right to request a review by a Peer Review Organization of any written Notice of Noncoverage that you receive from the hospital stating that Medicare will no longer pay for your hospital care. Peer Review Organizations (PROs) are groups of doctors who are paid by the Federal Government to review medical necessity, appropriateness and quality of hospital treatment furnished to Medicare patients.

Talk to Your Doctor about Your Stay in the Hospital

You and your doctor know more about your condition and your health needs than anyone else. Decisions about your medical treatment should be made between and your doctor. If you have any questions about your medical treatment, your need for continued hospital care, your discharge, or your need for possible post-hospital care, don't hesitate to ask your doctor. The hospital's patient representative or social worker will also help you with your questions and concerns about hospital services.

If You Think You Are Being Asked to Leave the Hospital Too Soon

• Ask a hospital representative for a written note of explanation immediately, if you have not already received one. This notice is called a "Notice of Noncoverage." You must have this Notice of Noncoverage if you wish to exercise your right to request a review by the PRO.

• The Notice of Noncoverage will state either that your doctor or the PRO agrees with the hospital's decision that Medicare will no longer pay for your hospital care.

  † If the hospital and your doctor agree, the PRO does not review your case before a Notice of Noncoverage is issued. But the PRO will respond to your request for a review of your Notice of Noncoverage and seek your opinion. You cannot be made to pay for your hospital care until the PRO makes its decision, if you request the review by noon of the first work day after you receive the Notice of Noncoverage.

† If the hospital and your doctor disagree, the hospital may request the PRO to review your case. If it does make such a request, the hospital is required to send you a notice to that effect. In this situation the PRO must agree with the hospital or the hospital cannot issue a Notice of Noncoverage. You may request that the PRO reconsider your case after you receive a Notice of Noncoverage but since the PRO has already reviewed your case once, you may have to pay for at least one day of hospital care before the PRO completes this reconsideration.

IF YOU DO NOT REQUEST A REVIEW, THE HOSPITAL MAY BILL YOU FOR ALL THE COSTS OF YOUR STAY BEGINNING WITH THE THIRD DAY AFTER YOU RECEIVE THE NOTICE OF NONCOVERAGE. THE HOSPITAL, HOWEVER, CANNOT CHARGE YOU FOR CARE UNLESS IT PROVIDES YOU WITH A NOTICE OF NONCOVERAGE.

How to Request a Review of the Notice of Noncoverage

• If the Notice of Noncoverage states that your physician agrees with the hospital's decision:
  † You must make your request for review to the PRO by noon of the first work day after you receive the Notice of Noncoverage by contacting the PRO by phone or in writing.
  † The PRO must ask for your views about your case before making its decision. The PRO will inform you by phone and in writing of its decision on the review.
  † If the PRO agrees with the Notice of Noncoverage, you may be billed for all costs of your stay beginning at noon of the day after you receive the PRO's decision.
  † Thus, you will not be responsible for the cost of hospital care before you receive the PRO's decision.

• If the Notice of Noncoverage states that the PRO agrees with the hospital's decision:

† You should make your request for reconsideration to the PRO immediately upon receipt of the Notice of Noncoverage by contacting the PRO by phone or in writing.
† The PRO can take up to three working days from receipt of your request to complete the review. The PRO will inform you in writing of its decision on the review.
† Since the PRO has already reviewed your case once, prior to the issuance of the Notice of Noncoverage, the hospital is permitted to begin billing you for the cost of your stay beginning with the third calendar day after you receive your Notice of Noncoverage even if the PRO has not completed its review.
† Thus, if the PRO continues to agree with the Notice of Noncoverage, you may have to pay for at least one day of hospital care.

NOTE: The process described above is called "immediate review." If you miss the deadline for this immediate review while you are in the hospital, you may still request a review of Medicare's decision to no longer pay for your care at any point during your hospital stay or after you have left the hospital. The Notice of Noncoverage will tell you how to request this review.

Posthospital Care

When your doctor determines that you no longer need all the specialized services provided in a hospital, but you still require medical care, he or she may discharge you to a skilled nursing facility or home care. The discharge planner at the hospital will help arrange for the services you may need after your discharge. Medicare and supplemental insurance policies have limited coverage for skilled nursing facility care and home health care. Therefore, you should find out which services will or will not be covered and how payment will be made. Consult with your doctor, hospital discharge planner, patient representative and your family in making preparations for care after you leave the hospital. Don't hesitate to ask questions.

Acknowledgement of Receipt — My signature only acknowledges my receipt of this Message from (name of hospital) on (date) and does not waive any of my rights to request a review or make me liable for any payment.

_____

Signature of beneficiary or
person acting on behalf of beneficiary.

The hospital tells me that I have to leave because "my DRG has run out."

Telling you this is (a) untrue, and (b) a violation of the hospital's contract with Medicare. You are entitled to hospital services as long as they are medically necessary. The hospital can always apply for additional payment.

We suggest that you, or someone helping you, first write down the name and presumptive title of anyone who told you this. Then call the administrator's office. State that you are aware that the hospital will be paid the full DRG for your admission and that they can apply for outlier payments. (These are payments from Medicare that reflect a mitigating circumstance or complication that may increase the cost over and above a normal DRG rate.) Ask if this has been done. Then state that the only reason that you can be discharged is that you no longer need hospital care and that hospitals don't discharge people, doctors do. Ask which doctor made the determination that you no longer needed hospital care. Write down all the answers you get from every person you talk to. Then call the Office of the Inspector General at the Department of Health and Human Services (1-800-368-5779). Say that you want to report a case of abuse of the Medicare program. They will take it from there.

I want to have an operation in the hospital, and Medicare has denied me, saying that I have to have it done in an outpatient facility. What can I do?

You can appeal, even though there is generally no problem with outpatient surgery and you may be at less risk than you would be in the hospital. Your proposed admission was turned down because the organization designated by the federal government to review such matters, the peer review organization (PRO), did not find it medically necessary. You can request a reconsideration of this decision, just as you can any other PRO decision. There are specific procedures you must follow when you request a reconsideration or appeal a decision. You can get that information from the PRO listed on the denial decision, any Social Security office, or a Railroad Retirement Board office if you are a railroad retirement beneficiary.

Nursing Homes and Medicare

While nursing homes are not exclusively for senior citizens, the vast majority of their residents are over age 65. In fact, it is estimated that one out of four persons 65 or over will spend at least some time in a nursing home.

Evaluating, selecting, and living in a nursing home are not easy. One of the most heart-wrenching moments in a family's existence is making a decision about placing a loved one in a long-term-care facility.

While this chapter is not designed to give you a comprehensive view of nursing homes and what you need to do to ensure a high-quality placement for yourself or a loved one (see the People's Medical Society book by R. Barker Bausell, Michael Rooney, and Charles B. Inlander, *How to Evaluate and Select a Nursing Home,* 1988, for such a review), it is important that you understand your rights in such facilities as they relate to Medicare.

Let's begin by giving the bad news. Medicare does not cover what people usually think of as "nursing home care." There are three levels of nursing home care:

• *Skilled nursing facilities (SNFs)* offer care delivered by registered and licensed practical nurses on the orders of an attending physician. They offer services such as oxygen therapy, intravenous and tube feedings, care of catheters and wound drains, and physical, occupational, and speech therapy.

• *Intermediate care facilities (ICFs)* provide less-intensive care than do SNFs. Patients are generally more mobile, and rehabilitation therapies are stressed.

• *Sheltered, or custodial, care* is nonmedical. Residents do not require constant attention from nurses and aides but need assistance with one or more daily activities or no longer want to be bothered with keeping up a house. The social needs of residents are met in a safe, secure environment free of as many anxieties as possible.

Medicare covers nursing care at the SNF level only. This coverage is basically intended for one situation: you need more care to recuperate, but less-intensive care than that provided in a hospital. For the first 8 days of SNF care, a co-payment ($25.50 per day in 1989) is required. Medicare covers the next 142 days in full. After 151 days, Medicare pays nothing. You are once again eligible for another 150 days of SNF care in the next calendar year.

So the bad news is that Medicare covers very few nursing home costs. In fact, less than 2 percent of nursing home revenues comes from Medicare.

However, there is some good news. Medicaid, another program, will pay for nursing home care if you are eligible.

Medicaid is intended for the very poor who have nowhere else to turn, but not all of the very poor are covered. It is a state-run program that receives federal funds. States make most of the rules, and the trend in recent years has been to make Medicaid requirements more stringent. Up until 1989, the law virtually guaranteed that the spouse who stayed at home would have to impoverish himself or herself to pay for the care of the spouse in the nursing home.

Despite repeal of the Medicare Catastrophic Act the following provisions were retained. These provisions greatly reduce the burden but can still lead to a substantial loss of assets. As of January 1, 1989:

• In any month in which a married person is in a nursing home, no income of the at-home spouse is to be considered available to the spouse in the nursing home.

• Income is considered the property of the person to whom it is paid. Income paid to both spouses is attributed 50 percent to each.

• The home, household goods, and personal effects of both spouses are not counted in considering Medicaid eligibility.

• All assets other than these will be counted and divided in two. If the at-home spouse has less than $12,000, the spouse in the nursing home may transfer assets to him or her to make up to $12,000 available to the at-home spouse. (States may, at their option, raise this figure to any amount less than $60,000. The $12,000 amount will be indexed to inflation.)

• The assets that remain in the name of the spouse in the nursing home are considered available to pay for his or her nursing home care. All assets in excess of $60,000 are attributed to the spouse in the nursing home and are considered available to pay for nursing care.

• States must allow nursing home residents to retain certain sums for medical expenses not covered by Medicare or Medicaid before contributing to the expense of their nursing home care. The states may place "reasonable limits" on the amounts spent.

• As of September 30, 1989, the states also had to allow the at-home spouse sufficient income from the other spouse to bring total household income of the at-home spouse to at least 122 percent of the federal poverty level for a two-person household. Until July 1, 1991, this will be $789 per month. On July 1, 1991, it will be raised to 133 percent of the poverty level, and to 150 percent on July 1, 1992. States will not be required to allow more than $1,500 per month, except by court order or change in regulations.

These requirements dramatically reduce the economic stress on the spouse who remains at home, but they still may require parting with large amounts of income and assets. Your spouse does not actually have to give anything toward the cost of your care, but your eligibility is determined as though he or she did. The exact requirements, as well as the amount of assets and income you may retain and still be eligible, vary from state to state. Check with your state Medicaid office.

You are automatically eligible for Medicaid if you are eligible for, or receiving, Supplemental Security Income (SSI) payments for the aged, blind, and disabled, but you must apply to a state welfare office. If you have met the requirements for SSI, there is little chance that you would have to give up additional income or assets to qualify for Medicaid.

If your income, less certain deductions and medical bills, is within certain (low) limits, you may be eligible for Medicaid as "medically needy." You must "spend down" to pay medical bills to the point at which you are eligible; after that, Medicaid pays for all of them as long as you are eligible.

Here are answers to some other frequently asked questions:

I don't have the money to pay my medical bills now. Do I have to pay them all off in order to get Medicaid to pay for future ones?

No. This is a common misunderstanding. The requirement for the medically needy spend-down is that you have incurred enough medical bills so that your income, minus allowances and the medical bills, is less than the income limit for eligibility. Medicaid pays all of the bills, both current and future, if you meet this test, have assets under the asset limit, and meet other requirements, such as age and residency, which your particular state may impose.

Now that I am in a nursing home, I am shocked at the conditions. What rights do I have?

It is difficult for nursing home residents to be effective advocates for themselves. If they are on Medicaid, they may have surrendered all their assets to obtain funding for their nursing home stay and may, in effect, be trapped in the home. They do not complain, simply because they do not want to make a bad situation worse. The same applies, to a lesser degree, to just about everyone else in the home. Even if they are economically able to move, there may be long waiting lists at the homes they want to move to.

But that is no excuse for a mediocre nursing home. At a minimum, no nursing home should ever fall below these standards:

• No resident should be allowed to remain in a soiled bed for a moment longer than absolutely necessary.

• It is close to impossible to prevent all pressure sores in totally bed-ridden people, but they should be small in size and promptly treated by repositioning the patient, use of special mattresses, and immediate attention by a doctor when needed.

• Food should be hot or cold as appropriate and of better than just-acceptable quality.

• Dehydration and malnutrition should not develop and should be promptly and vigorously treated if found.

• Medications should be given, and given reasonably close to the prescribed schedule. Drug reactions should be noted in writing and reported to the doctor quickly.

The best way to make sure that a friend or relative is getting the required services is by visiting frequently and randomly. It is a good idea to arrange visits so that promised events can be checked on. If a particular program is scheduled, such as a movie, visit when it is scheduled and make sure it happens. Some cancellations are unavoidable due to weather and so on, but the general program the home promises should be carried out.

In Appendix B, we publish the Patient Bill of Rights for Nursing Homes suggested by the Health Care Financing Administration. If you find serious violations of the rights suggested in the Bill, report them to the state authorities. They are also listed in Appendix A.

Generally, it is best to deal with problems by pointing them out, politely but firmly, to the appropriate person — the nurse, the administrator, the billing office. The approach of being firm but not antagonistic works best. Keep repeating, in a polite manner, the problem you see and the solution you want.

An important point to remember is this: don't let the nursing home personnel blame you for the problem. Often they try to turn the situation around by saying that families don't visit enough or support their loved ones adequately. You do not have to solve, or even sympathize with, their difficulties.

Finally, it is not useful to threaten to move a resident. Besides the antagonism this may create, it may mean nothing in a community where there is a waiting list for space. But do not hesitate to pull your loved one out if there is an immediate danger to the patient's health and welfare.

Also, do not hesitate to contact a lawyer if you think legal action may be warranted.

Supplemental Medicare Insurance (Medigap)

Supplemental insurance policies, known as Medigap insurance, are designed to offset the deductible and co-payments required by Medicare: the gaps. They may also offer additional benefits, depending on the policy. In 1988, new requirements were imposed for all Medicare supplemental insurance polices and the Secretary of the Department of Health and Human Services was directed to develop minimum coverage standards to be met by all supplemental policies. As a result, there are certain things you should know concerning your rights as they relate to supplemental insurance.

• Every time there is a change in Medicare coverage, there must be a corresponding change in the coverage offered by supplemental policies. For example, if the hospital deductible is increased, then carriers must adjust their supplemental insurance policies to reflect the change. As a policyholder, you must be advised of these changes in writing, and you must also be told how they will affect your premium.

• Not all health insurance policies are Medicare supplements. No policy may be legally advertised as a Medicare supplemental policy unless it meets the minimum standards and has been approved by your state's insurance commissioner.

• The Secretary of Health and Human Services and the National Association of Insurance Commissioners developed the following minimum standards for all supplemental policies. These standards apply to Medicare Part A and Part B. Remember, supplemental insurance is designed to fill in the "gaps" left open under the Medicare program. So we will list the gaps first, then what the policies must contain.

MEDICARE COVERAGE *GAPS* (What Medicare does not pay)

Part A

• Hospital yearly deductible of $560 (1989 dollar figures used)

• Skilled nursing facility co-payment of $25.50/day for days 1 through 8

• Blood services deductible equal to the cost of the first three pints of blood or packet of red cells. (If any portion of this deductible was met under Part B, it counts toward this blood deductible.)

Part B

• Physician/outpatient services:
$75.00 annual deductible
20 percent of Medicare-approved charges

SUPPLEMENTAL INSURANCE MINIMUM COVERAGE (What must be covered)

Part A

• All or none of the hospital inpatient deductible

• Daily co-payment for skilled nursing facility care days 1 through 8

• Coverage of the cost of the first three pints of blood or packed red cells, whether received under Parts A or B

Part B

• Must cover the 20 percent co-payment that Medicare does not pay, but only up to $5,000 in total benefits. (Note: depending on the terms of your policy you may be required to pay up to $200 out of pocket, including the $75 Part B deductible.)

Here are some additional points concerning minimum benefits:

Part A
Hospital Inpatient Deductible
    If your policy covers the annual deductible, it must pay for the full amount. (Remember this changes each year.)
Blood Service Deductible

This is equal to the cost of the first three pints of whole blood or packed red cells. The deductible is waived if you replace the blood by arranging for donors. If you receive blood on an outpatient basis, (under PART B) this cost counts toward the total blood services deductible.

Part B

Physician/Outpatient Services.

Your policy must pay the 20 percent co-payment on the Medicare-approved charges after an out-of-pocket expense of $200. This means that your insurance policy may or may not cover the Part B deductible of $75 and the first $125 of co-payment.

Health Maintenance Organizations (HMOs) for Medicare Beneficiaries

Since 1985, Health Maintenance Organizations (HMOs) have been interested in enrolling significant numbers of senior citizens. That year, the Health Care Financing Administration (HCFA) opened the door for Medicare beneficiaries to enroll in HMOs. As a result, more and more senior citizens have the opportunity to enroll in a Medicare HMO program and have a choice of HMOs. Also, retiring employees in some companies who belong to an HMO can retire into the Medicare HMO program.

Of course, whether you want to join an HMO is up to you. Quality of care should be the number-one consideration. But if you have decided that a Medicare HMO is for you, here are some points concerning your rights that you should be aware of:

• HMO Medicare coverage is a *supplement* to, not a *substitute* for your Medicare coverage. When you join the HMO, you do not give up your Medicare Part A Hospital Insurance or Part B Medical Insurance coverage. You continue to pay your Part B Medical Insurance premium as you always did, and continue to be covered under Part B. The HMO program is supplemental or "wrap-around" insurance, which covers the costs of hospital and/or medical services not covered by Medicare. You should consider an HMO plan in competition with other Medicare Supplemental Insurance plans, but you do not give up Medicare to join an HMO. Neither do you give up any part of your monthly Social Security check to an HMO.

• You may be required to pay the HMO a monthly premium for coverage of hospital and medical expenses over and above basic Medicare coverage. This payment will probably cost $20 to $50 per month, with the exact amount determined by the HMO. Some company retirement plans contribute all or a portion of the HMO monthly payments.

The Medicare HMO plan will cover all basic Medicare services and additional services, usually including:

1. Deductible for hospital and skilled nursing services

2. Deductible and co-payment for physician services in hospital and office settings

3. Diagnostic and rehabilitation services, prescription drugs and pharmaceuticals (sometimes an extra fee)

Make sure you understand the exact benefits and services provided by the HMO as well as the cost of the monthly premium.

An HMO cannot deny you membership because of your medical condition with only two exceptions: those with end-stage renal disease (chronic kidney failure) and those receiving hospice benefits. Note that HMOs cannot require you to have a medical examination as a condition of considering your application.

If you join an HMO and don't like it, you may withdraw at any time for any reason and return to your previous Medicare status. If you join the HMO and have problems, first try to work them out through the HMO grievance process. If you decide that you want to quit the HMO, you simply fill out a withdrawal form, which will take 30 to 60 days to process. Conversely, an HMO can drop you only if you move out of its service area or if it documents a complete lack of cooperation with its administrative rules (e.g., you don't pay your monthly premium, you permit misuse of your membership card, etc.).

Special Rights Issues for Senior Citizens

Obviously, Medicare and Medicaid are not the only medical rights issues that affect the elderly. Most states offer special health and medical programs for senior citizens. These programs range from prescription-drug programs to free (or reduced-cost) inoculations. There are also special programs for medically needy individuals that many senior citizens qualify for.

The important point is to find out what your state offers (sometimes county and local governments offer programs as well) and what your rights are concerning those programs.

The best way to find out what is available is to call the area agency on aging in your community. It is listed in the phone book, often under the "government" section. You might also try a local senior citizens' center. Often the staff of these programs are well versed in available programs. Also, call the local office of your *state* representative or *state* senator. Since these programs are state operated or sponsored, calling your federal representative will probably not produce very much information.

Do not be hesitant to use these programs if you are eligible. They are not charity. They are government-sponsored programs — insurance for those who need or can benefit from them. They are a lot like Social Security; not everyone needs it, but everyone who worked or was a dependent of a worker can collect.

Senior citizens have the same medical rights as people under age 65. While this may seem obvious, many senior citizens believe that turning age 65, or becoming a Medicare beneficiary, automatically limits their rights. In fact, because of the increased interaction seniors have with the health care system, it is even more important for senior citizens to be vigilant in protecting and exercising their medical rights.

Sadly, many providers of health care, retailers of medical equipment, and insurance salespersons take advantage of older medical consumers. They often prey on their diminished faculties (when such a condition exists) or attempt to intimidate the elder consumer with confusing jargon. Of course, these are the minority of providers, but with 37 million senior citizens in the medical marketplace, those whose rights are abused add up quickly.

Several years ago, a Congressional committee took a look at the question of why senior citizens sue doctors for malpractice less often than younger consumers. In assisting the staff of the committee to find victims of bad medicine to testify, the People's Medical Society spoke with many elderly Americans who had been harmed by medical service. When asked why they did not pursue legal action against the offending party, most said they feared the repercussions that might follow. Leading the list was fear that no other doctor would again treat them. Others believed that if they lost their cases they would lose Medicare benefits. Still others said that they were fearful the doctor might harm them later — out of spite. As absurd as one might think those answers are, for those individuals it was reality, or at least perceived reality.

But failure to exercise your medical rights will only permit such violations to continue and to flourish. It is especially important as a senior citizen to stand up for your medical rights and not be intimidated by the system. It may not be easy to fight back, but fight you must if your rights are threatened or violated. And don't be afraid to seek help. There are many places one can turn for assistance, beginning with a family member or friend and ending with a lawyer. In between, there are organizations like the People's Medical Society and other groups who can help guide and assist you.

Being older does not have to mean losing your dignity and rights. Knowing the rules and having the fortitude to stand up for what is rightfully yours will make your encounters with the medical system more healing ones.

CHAPTER TEN

"Oops . . . Sorry!"

In 1985, a House Select Committee on Aging study determined that "at least 23 percent of the 1 million [cataract lens] implants performed may not be necessary." Heading the list of reasons for these unnecessary procedures were fraud, abuse, and waste that took the form of high markups, manufacturer kickbacks, and other enticements.

A 1986 National Institute for Health Statistics report said that of 750,000 hysterectomies performed in the United States each year, 22 percent are unnecessary. ". . . in only 10 percent of the cases were the indications for a hysterectomy so clear-cut that all doctors would agree to perform the operation," according to the Institute.

If you were one of those 230,000 people who had an unnecessary implant or 150,000 women who had unnecessary hysterectomies, would an "Oops . . . Sorry!" be an acceptable apology from the practitioner who performed the deed?

As we discussed in an earlier chapter, being prepared for what is medically in front of you is important. Knowing as much as you can about the doctor, hospital, treatment plan, and your condition itself is the vital first line of defense in protecting your medical rights.

But no matter how well prepared you are, problems may arise. Medicine is still essentially a secret state where even the most aggressive and assertive consumers can easily become victims of misdeed and misinformation.

Cesarean sections provide a powerful contemporary example of how medical consumers are often deceived into one course of treatment when another, less invasive, less expensive, one may be appropriate.

In 1989, nearly 25 percent of all children delivered in America were by cesarean section. The C-section rate has skyrocketed over the past 20 years. By comparison, England's C-section rate reached 11 percent in 1988. The British medical press called it a crisis, and much was written and discussed on how this horrible rate could be decreased.

While some experts argue that the U.S. rate is almost twice the number it should be, others defend it. The defenders blame defensive medicine. They contend that consumers are overly litigious. Doctors, they say, are afraid of being sued by mothers and fathers who expect the "perfect" baby.

All through the medical press, the litigious consumer is cited as the major cause for the increase in C-section rates. At medical meetings, obstetricians rail about the high-risk patient — but in this instance high risk is the likelihood that the patient will sue rather then have complications in delivering.

That's what the "experts" report to one another. It is not quite the same story told to the mother-to-be.

The most resourceful investigative reporter would have a difficult time locating even one woman who delivered by cesarean section and was told that the delivery was necessary because of the practitioner's fear of a lawsuit. In fact, the reason always cited to the mother is risk either to the baby or to the woman herself.

Why this discrepancy? How can the doctors say one thing to their colleagues and something completely different to their patients? Are they lying? If so, to whom?

Dr. Colin Francome, a senior sociology lecturer, pointed to this dichotomy in an article about "needless births by cesarean" in the London newspaper *The Sunday Times:*

"If you ask doctors why the cesarean rate is up they say it is because we are scared of being sued, or because of time pressures or staff shortages. But when you ask women, they are never told this. They say it is because the baby had problems or because they needed it. It is obvious they are not being told the truth."

At least one study has noted that about half of Americans' cesarean sections are unnecessary. Did the doctors intentionally lie to those hundreds of thousands of women?

Obviously some did. Clearly, they knew that delivering the child by C-section was more beneficial to themselves than to the baby or the mother. But the others, while in fact lying, may actually believe they are operating in the best interest of the mother. In other words, they believe their own lies.

The late medical critic Robert S. Mendelsohn, M.D., whose book *Confessions of a Medical Heretic* rocked the often smug, self-satisfied world of medicine when first published in 1979, often spoke on this subject.

Mendelsohn, while not defending the culprit practitioners, noted that doctors who gave their patients misinformation, or guided them into procedures more risky than necessary, in fact believed their own words. They had fallen into a way of thinking that, as long as nobody got hurt, what harm was the more invasive procedure.

In fact, when challenged about whether a possible unnecessary procedure has been performed, most practitioners retreat to the old, "In my best judgment it was the best course of action for the patient."

In other words, "Sorry," but of course no "Oops."

So what does the consumer do? Clearly, many treatments, tests, and procedures are being done unnecessarily. The consent by the consumer to have such a "service" performed is done on the basis of misinformation or lack of information.

The dilemma, the burden, that confronts most people is whether they can prove the doctor committed malpractice by performing the procedure knowing it was unnecessary. And this is quite difficult: especially if the consumer can show no physical harm. As noted earlier, the doctor can retort with a defense that is based on both "no harm done" and "in my best judgment." That is mighty powerful stuff in a courtroom.

Of course, proving that the doctor lied with intent is like trying to climb Everest; possible for a few but beyond the strength of the average.

But that is if malpractice is what one is seeking to prove. There are other routes one can pursue.

As we note elsewhere in the book, many consumers who believe they were wronged by a hospital or practitioner are not seeking monetary damages. What these individuals want is to protect others from having the same thing happen to them.

Their avenues of recourse are different from those of the individual who is seeking to prove malpractice and win a monetary award. First, they can file a complaint with the state medical licensing board or other appropriate agency. (See Chapter 12, How to File a Complaint, to learn how this is done.)

Second, they can utilize the consumer protection bureaus that exist in most states. These agencies of government investigate claims of misrepresentation, fraud, and other potentially illegal or shady actions that may have been perpetrated against a consumer.

While these avenues should be pursued, it is important to note that success rates are not overwhelming in the consumer column. To prove that a doctor intentionally misrepresented the need for a particular treatment or procedure is difficult. But what the attempt accomplishes is the launching of an investigation. Such an investigation is on the record; in most cases a filed complaint is noted and reported publicly if requested; and it serves notice to the practitioner that a customer has gone beyond his office receptionist to report an outrage.

Still another approach is to bring the matter to the attention of the press. An example of this is the case of a physician in Ohio who performed unnecessary and mutilating procedures on thousands of women, some unknown to the women themselves, who was able to avoid any accountability for his actions for many years. No other doctor would testify that his actions were outside the scope of normal practice. The women were afraid of and intimidated by the doctor's reputation. Finally, someone listened, and the story came out in a nationally broadcast television newsmagazine. As a result, more victims came forth, and soon the licensing board and others in the state were looking into taking disciplinary action against him. The doctor, however, surrendered his license before any action was taken and agreed not to practice in the United States again.

A victory for American jurisprudence? No! A pat on the back for a medical disciplinary system operating at full steam? Of course not! But a victory nonetheless. And a sign to other quacks that they can be held accountable.

Filing complaints, seeking disciplinary actions, even suing a practitioner or hospital, are important steps if you believe or know you have been wronged. And being wronged does not necessarily mean the offending party physically harmed you.

Pursuing justice is the most important way to keep the medical profession honest. Medicine polices itself, for the most part, and, some would argue, not too well. State medical licensing boards are made up almost exclusively of doctors. In 1986, for example, less than .5 percent of the over 600,000 doctors in America were disciplined, in any form, by such boards. It is hard to believe any profession would have such a low rate of error that this figure would truthfully represent its failures.

Therefore, pursuing action when something has occurred that is out of the ordinary is important to maintain some checks and balances in the system. And these are not just the words of a consumer advocate and a trial lawyer.

Robert Mendelsohn often pointed out the importance of pursuing lawsuits and other forms of action against less than competent or reputable practitioners. Such acts, or even the knowledge that they might be pursued, keep most of the profession honest, he often noted.

But what do you do if you have been physically or mentally hurt by something a doctor did to you? What if something happens at the hospital that should not have occurred, or you were injured?

Let's start with the doctor. Obviously, physicians can make errors. Some are minor and cause no harm or damage. Others, however, are major and can lead to death or permanent injury.

Some errors are quite obvious. The doctor performed a procedure that did not work, and the patient was injured. Others are not quite as obvious. A doctor prescribes a medication which causes the patient to have a violent reaction, and permanent brain damage results. On first blush one cannot blame the doctor. But a second look finds that the doctor had been advised that the patient was allergic to the major ingredient in that particular medication. Therefore, what may appear as "just one of those things" turns out to be very serious negligence on the part of the doctor.

Medicine has a term for harm done by doctors. It is *iatrogenesis,* and it is a bigger problem than most people think. Iatrogenesis is a Greek word meaning "doctor-caused" or "doctor-produced."

In one major study conducted at a teaching hospital, researchers from Boston University Medical Center found that of 815 consecutive admissions, 36 percent were for iatrogenic conditions. Nine percent of the 815 patients were seriously ill because of the problem; in 2 percent iatrogenesis contributed to the patient's death.

Iatrogenesis comes in many forms. It occurs when a doctor performs a procedure that has a greater risk than benefit and the gamble doesn't work. It happens when the doctor hasn't prepared for the unexpected complication, although the distinct possibility of its occurring was well known. Of course, there is also the iatrogenic mishap caused by a doctor's mistake in judgment or in handiwork.

Many of these iatrogenic incidents are isolated occurrences in which a single doctor creates a medical condition in a patient who previously did not have it. But others are more widespread, more epidemic in nature.

Stanford Medical School Professor Eugene D. Robin, M.D., in his book *Matters of Life and Death* (1984), also describes what he calls "iatroepidemics." Iatroepidemics are epidemics or plagues caused by doctors. He describes them as "systematic errors incorporated into medical practice." For example, doctors agree that a procedure or series of steps is the way to treat a problem and incorporate them into their practice. They become generally accepted. The problem is that these procedures and steps, though officially sanctioned, kill or harm patients. As Inlander and Weiner noted in *Take This Book to the Hospital with You* (1985), "They are very often crackpot schemes dressed up in pseudoscientific robes or insufficiently tested operations and drugs that are used anyway because word gets around that they might be valuable. A jump-on-the-bandwagon mentality."

Robin's list of iatroepidemics includes mastectomies, the prescribing of DES (diethylstilbestrol) to prevent spontaneous abortions (which led to genital cancers in some of the children of mothers who took it), tonsillectomies, brain surgery for schizophrenia, the prescribing of thalidomide for acne, and others.

One of the problems iatrogenesis presents is that often the patient is unaware that he or she is a victim of it. Very few physicians are willing to acknowledge that they have made a mistake. Often, in order to remove any thoughts of blaming the doctor from the patient's mind, they will reverse the logic and blame the patient. "I told you to call me if there was a problem!" (I did, Doctor, but your nurse would not put me through. She said keep taking the pills.) Other times they will pooh-pooh the matter, wave it off as nothing important. "That's a normal complication, Mr. Jones. Lots of patients get infections in their wounds." (But, Doctor, I read that most wound infections are the result of negligence in sterilization practices.)

The dilemma is what to do if you know you have been harmed.

First and foremost, seek medical attention to correct the problem, if possible. While you may want to go back to the doctor who caused the problem, it may be wise to find someone else. If the doctor is reluctant to acknowledge that he made an error, he may not take the problem, complication, or setback seriously.

Next, get as much information as possible to document the source of your problem. Are there others who can attest to the fact that the doctor did you harm? Is there a written record at the hospital or the doctor's office showing what happened?

Documentation is critical if you are going to prove that something a doctor did to you has harmed you. Keep track of the course of your problem. Do not wait to take action, if action is necessary to ensure your health.

Here is an example of a man who took steps right away to correct a physician-caused error. The individual was severely burned on his back. He received treatment at a local hospital and was released with instructions on caring for himself. His condition worsened at home, and he called the doctor, who said, "Don't worry, these things are painful." Not satisfied, he had himself taken 50 miles away to another hospital, which had a burn center. He was immediately admitted and informed that the earlier treatment was causing more harm than good. Eventually, he recovered, but only thanks to his realization that what the first practitioner had done was causing more harm than the burn itself. Did he sue the doctor? No. Did he file a grievance with the medical licensing board? Yes. The result was an investigation of the hospital and the doctor, with a number of improvements made at the originating hospital for dealing with similar patients.

All errors or mistakes do not happen as a result of negligence or incompetent actions. But a good number do. The next important step is to determine if negligence or incompetence did come into play. This can be tricky. Remember, it is rare for a physician to acknowledge an error.

Your first step is to get a copy of your medical record. We discussed how to do this in chapter 3.

Next, have someone with medical knowledge look at it. Your interpretation may not be the same as a medical expert's. Also, there are some occurrences that are viewed as within the realm of acceptable standards of practice. We discussed this earlier, and it is important to understand. While in fact you may have been injured or harmed, the damage may be viewed by a court as within acceptable standards, given the knowledge, state-of-the-art, and experience of medicine in dealing with the problem. That is not to say they are right and you are wrong. Instead, it is one of those times when "Oops . . . Sorry!" is an acceptable excuse — legally. However, we do recommend that you file a grievance with the proper state board, since these "standards" are more a picture of the state of the art than science. Standards change, and more reports of problems may, in fact, force a look at these occurrences.

Even untoward events that happen under the guise of acceptable standards of practice may be grounds for a lawsuit or claim if it can be shown that the practitioner performed the procedure knowing there was a risk present that should have been considered before treatment. An example is hospital staph infections.

As we noted in an earlier chapter, most victims of hospital staph infections have found little relief in courts. The exception has been when the court was shown that the physician or hospital knew that the patient was at high risk because of other circumstances. In one case, a hospital knew that more than a dozen patients had acquired a staph infection within the previous week and they had not identified the source nor reported the infection to the state or county health departments. Several additional patients later came down with it after surgery. In this case, both the doctor and the hospital were found guilty of negligence.

Hospitals present other, less obvious, risks. Malpractice insurance companies report that a large percentage of settlements and judgments against hospitals have to do with patients falling down. These falls are the result of slippery floors, patients attempting to walk unattended, or any number of other similar reasons.

Another hospital problem area has been the patient injured while trying to climb out of bed. Many hospital beds come equipped with cage-like railings. These can be raised and lowered, but only from the outside. In the middle of the night, a patient who wants to use the bathroom and is getting no response from the nurses' station often attempts to scale these barriers. The result may require longer hospital stays, according to what insurers report.

The point is that the medical-surgical wings of the hospital are not the only danger zone.

If you suspect that you or a family member have been harmed, it is advisable to seek an attorney. There are several reasons to pursue this route.

First, an attorney can help you determine what the important facts are. He can advise you on the documents and evidence you will need. He will help you focus your case in the right direction.

Second, an attorney, particularly one who specializes in medical malpractice litigation, will be forthcoming in discussing the merits of your case. Unfortunately, many people, when they suspect medical malpractice, turn to the attorney they used to settle on their home or who drew up their will. Often, these lawyers are competent but have no skills or experience in the complex world of medical malpractice. Often they accept the case as a favor, hoping for a settlement, only to find later they are in over their heads.

Third, an experienced malpractice attorney will reject your case if he does not believe it is winnable. While this may seem harsh, the fact is, consumers lose 70 percent of the malpractice cases they file. This means that a great deal of pain, anguish, and money is spent to get nothing. Therefore, if several competent malpractice attorneys turn you down, there is a very good chance your case was not good enough for a court.

In the next chapter, we guide you in detail through the process of how to seek, select, and retain an attorney.

CHAPTER ELEVEN

Selecting the Right Lawyer

How do you find a good medical malpractice lawyer? Once you've found him, what can you expect?

It's vitally important to understand the process. A competent lawyer can be invaluable in your fight to preserve your rights as a health care consumer. He can make the difference between winning and losing a case, between a large and a small settlement, between allowing an incompetent physician to get off scot-free or be punished.

Let's say you have been the victim of what you suspect is medical malpractice. What's the first thing you should do?

Resources

In virtually every major city, there are hundreds of personal injury lawyers. Very few of them specialize solely in medical malpractice. They'll probably also handle everything from workmen's compensation to product liability cases.

Begin your search for a lawyer the same way you would for a doctor. Find someone you know who can refer you to a personal injury lawyer. Ideally, the person will have worked with that lawyer in a medical malpractice situation and will recommend him.

If you have no luck with that route, there are a number of reference books in law libraries that might help you. Bar associations usually have referral lists, though they often don't screen those lists carefully. The Martindale-Hubbell legal directory and *Markham's Negligence Counsel* are two other references.

In these directories, you'll find all sorts of credentials: education, speeches, publications, memberships. Though it's difficult to evaluate some of the credentials, pay attention to whether the attorney belongs to prestigious trial societies such as the American College of Trial Lawyers, the International Academy of Trial Lawyers, and the International Society of Barristers. It is especially noteworthy if a lawyer is a fellow of one of these groups; a fellow has over 15 years of experience and has been thoroughly screened by colleagues and judges.

You should also look to see if a lawyer is a member of his state trial lawyers' association and the Association of Trial Lawyers of America. Also see if he is a present or past officer of these organizations.

Finally, note the articles and speeches listed in the directories. It's possible that an attorney has written or spoken on a subject relevant to your case. If, for instance, an attorney has published an article on medical negligence, he is probably qualified to help you.

Initial Meeting

Schedule appointments with the lawyer or lawyers who seem best suited to your needs. When you meet with them, you'll want to ask some key questions, including:

• What sorts of medical malpractice cases have they handled? How much experience do they have, and what were the outcomes of some of the cases?

• Who will actually try the case? Many successful personal injury attorneys have staffs, and they frequently divide responsibility for a case among staffers. That's fine, providing the staff is competent and the attorney you hired is involved in the case, especially in the courtroom.

• You should also determine whether you feel comfortable with the lawyer. This is more important than it might seem. Some lawyers communicate frequently and well with their clients; others do not. Some are autocratic; others are down-to-earth. Your relationship with the attorney might last years. The more you trust and like the attorney, the better that relationship will be.

• Is your lawyer competent to handle your type of case? In most instances, he'll be able to if he's an experienced medical malpractice attorney. If you want to sue a hospital because of a particular surgical error, you don't need an attorney who's handled the exact type of case. The only exception might be if yours is a drug case: for example, a pharmaceutical company marketed a drug with harmful effects they didn't warn the public about. Usually, there are one or two attorneys who have done the exhaustive research necessary to litigate these cases, and it might be wise to contact them.

Fees

The standard contingency-fee contract calls for an attorney to receive one-third of all monies awarded to a client. However, that percentage can vary from attorney to attorney. In medical malpractice cases, the percentage is often as high as 40 percent or 45 percent because of the extensive amount of time and outside costs such cases require. You might also live in a state that provides for graduated percentages based on award amounts. In Illinois, for instance, lawyers are allowed 33 percent of the first $150,000, 25 percent over $150,000, and 20 percent over $1 million. (If you see this in your contract with a lawyer, don't automatically assume you have a chance of gaining a million bucks; the amounts are inserted because of the law rather than because of the lawyer's expectations.)

According to the attorney's code of professional responsibility and the laws of every state, clients are responsible for costs. Those costs can be high, easily topping $10,000 in many cases. They entail a variety of expenses, including expert testimony, filing fees, reprints of records, and reporting of depositions.

What are you to do if you don't have the thousands of dollars required? Here are some options.

Suggest to a lawyer that he advance you the money to pay for costs and subtract that "advance" from the final settlement or judgment. This is a fairly common practice, and many lawyers will suggest it to clients. What happens if you lose the case and there is no settlement? Though lawyers aren't legally permitted to absorb the costs, many will offer verbal assurances such as, "I've never sued a client for costs," or something to that effect. In most instances, it's not an empty promise. From a purely practical standpoint, attorneys recognize that they're not going to collect from a penniless client.

Another option is to put a clause in your contract with the lawyer that limits costs. If, for instance, you have some available cash, you might want to insert a clause that stipulates that any costs over a certain amount ($7,500, for instance) will be deducted from the lawyer's fee. Again, this is an accepted practice that many lawyers will agree to.

A third option involves marginal cases — ones the attorney is reluctant to take on. If you believe your case has merit, you might persuade him to review the case by offering an advance ($2,500 is a typical amount). That will enable him to spend sufficient time to determine whether you have a chance of winning and will also limit your costs.

What to Bring with You

Don't arrive in your attorney's office empty-handed. The more information your attorney has and the faster he gets it, the better your chances for a favorable resolution of the case.

Here's what you should bring:

• All records available to you: medical history, hospital and office visits.

• A written chronology of events that led up to your problem. Dates, times, places, and people involved should be clearly listed.

• Copies of relevant prescriptions.

• Bills received from doctors, hospitals, and other health care facilities.

Putting a Case Together

Cases are won or lost based on a lawyer's preparation. You should expect and demand that your lawyer leave no stone unturned. His ability to prepare a case thoroughly will have a tremendous impact on the outcome.

Let's look at depositions. These pretrial examinations of experts and potential witnesses are extraordinarily important. If your lawyer is able to obtain the right information in a deposition, he'll have a powerful weapon to use in court.

For instance, a man was pushed into a door after an argument with a store owner. The police came, and the man told them he was hurt, that he couldn't move his arms or legs. The police threw him into a patrol wagon. In the hospital, doctors told the man that as a result of his injuries, he would be a quadriplegic.

The man decided to sue the city, claiming his condition was the result of mishandling by the police. The defense's neurosurgeon maintained in his deposition that the man's injuries were an irreversible result of the fall into the door, that the man had suffered a burst fracture. During the deposition, the lawyer questioned the doctor about the nature of a burst fracture, eliciting the response that a burst fracture is "a rare, highly unstable fracture."

During the trial, the lawyer questioned the neurosurgeon again, pulling out a medical textbook the doctor had referred to in the deposition as the "bible."

"Doctor," the lawyer said, "you maintained a burst fracture is rare and uncommon, correct?"

"Yes," the doctor replied.

"But, Doctor," the lawyer continued, "isn't it true that this is a common fracture known by other names?"

"Absolutely not true," the doctor insisted.

"Well, Doctor, I refer you to page 52 of your bible, which states that a burst fracture is also known as a vertical compression fracture. It says that it's not at all uncommon; that when a burst fracture occurs, the lateral ligaments of the neck are seldom interrupted or damaged, so that if a person is treated properly, he won't have as much damage."

Because of the deposition in which he referred to the text as his "bible," the lawyer sounded foolish to the neurosurgeon when he took issue with the statement in the text.

The man received a verdict from the jury against the city.

Many cases hinge on a lawyer's aggressiveness. Your lawyer should act quickly to get the information he needs. He shouldn't be intimidated by closemouthed health care professionals, and he should take what they say with more than a few grains of salt.

Here's a fascinating case that illustrates the point.

A mother took her 6-month-old child to the hospital because she was spitting up blood. The bleeding was stopped but a new problem developed: the child's right hand was turning blue.

The attending physician noticed the circulation problem and noted on the chart that he wasn't sure what was going on; he questioned on the chart whether he should call in a vascular surgeon. A full six hours later, he did so.

Shortly thereafter, the doctor called the mother and told her a blood clot had developed and they'd have to operate; there was a chance the child might lose her arm.

Subsequently, the mother received an anonymous phone call, the caller saying, "I was in the operating room and the butchers cut a vein, and that's why your child will lose an arm; they're covering it up."

The mother tape-recorded the phone call and brought it with her to the lawyer. The mother then received another anonymous phone call, the voice saying that a bottle that had been assumed to be a glucose solution had been mislabeled, and a corroding drug was mistakenly injected into the baby's arm, resulting in the circulation problem.

Subsequently, the child's arm was amputated.

Once the amputation was performed, the lawyer acted quickly. He had the mother sign a letter messengered to the hospital's department of legal affairs. The letter requested that the amputated arm be sent to an independent pathologist for examination.

At first, the hospital refused. The lawyer then sent another letter, threatening the hospital with a lawsuit for punitive damages if they didn't turn over the arm.

The letter worked. The report of the pathologist who examined the arm for the lawyer, combined with the delay in contacting the vascular specialist, provided substantial evidence of negligence. The lawyer won a substantial settlement for the client.

Do You Need Perry Mason?

Many people believe that a lawyer's courtroom oratory can sway a jury.

This happens rarely, especially in medical malpractice cases. Years ago, spellbinding courtroom oratory had more of an impact on decisions. A great deal of information was privileged, and our system was, out of necessity, a battle of wits between opposing attorneys.

Today, each side knows generally what the other is going to do before the trial begins. It's like a play that's been well rehearsed. The jury is an audience, and they will decide based on how well each "actor" has prepared for his role. Jurors, too, are far more sophisticated than they used to be. Study after study demonstrates that juries usually reach decisions based on the evidence they hear and not on a lawyer's histrionics.

Therefore, don't choose a lawyer because he has a mesmerizing manner or a commanding baritone. Don't make your choice because he has received favorable publicity about his courtroom antics. It's all sizzle. Far better to have a dull, mousy lawyer who prepares his cases well than a flamboyant showman who misses crucial details.

Settlements

In many medical malpractice suits, defendants wish to settle out of court. At some point during the legal process, you might be confronted with a settlement decision.

It's a tough, tricky one.

If the situation arises, here are some things you should consider.

First, remember it's your decision, not your lawyer's, the defendant's, or the judge's (though the judge can decide about a settlement if a minor is involved). A settlement can't be imposed upon you.

Second, before making that decision, be sure you have all the facts. Just as you wouldn't agree to an operation without all the facts, neither should you agree to a settlement without sufficient information. The informed consent principle is applicable here, as well.

To ensure that you are fully informed, ask the following questions as soon as a lawyer proposes a settlement:

• What, if any, limitations does the state law impose on the amount of money that is recoverable? (In recent years, in response to medical lobbies, many state legislatures have passed damage limits in medical malpractice cases.)

• Is there a likelihood that more money might be offered?

• Is it likely that additional money will be offered before, or during, the trial?

• How long will the settlement offer be on the table? In many instances, the offer will change or be withdrawn depending on what develops as the case evolves.

• If you reject the settlement, what are your chances for losing the case and receiving nothing?

Be wary of hospital administrators overeager to settle. You might find that they'll contact you before you have contacted a lawyer. They'll usher you into their plush conference room, apologize profusely for your loss, and pull out a check with a number of zeros that has your name on it. They'll tell you this is a neat, clean way of settling the case and you won't have to pay attorney fees. Before letting you have the check, they'll insist you sign a form releasing the hospital of all liability for negligence and stating that you won't sue them.

Don't fall victim to this ploy. When hospitals make these offers, they almost always offer less than they should. They're counting on your naïveté.

If you do sign the release and accept the money, however, you might still be able to file a suit. In a number of instances, the courts have set aside these releases when they've determined that the hospital paid the victim an unfairly small amount

What a Jury Might Award

During your initial interview with a lawyer, you might be tempted to ask him what your case is worth, what a jury might give you.

Your lawyer shouldn't tell you. If he quotes a specific amount — if he says you're looking at seven figures — don't believe him. Until he spends the necessary time poring over documents and interviewing experts and witnesses, he cannot give you even an educated guess. The amount you're likely to receive is directly related to the strength of your legal case, the extent of your injuries, and your ultimate damages, and that's something the lawyer can't possibly know at the outset.

On the other hand, you are entitled to know what your lawyer thinks about your case. Is his initial impression positive or negative? Does he believe damages are extensive? What are those damages as defined by the law, and what does the law allow you to recover?

Let's say the client comes to a lawyer with a claim for the wrongful death of a spouse. He should tell him that wrongful death involves a pecuniary loss, that the next of kin may recover for loss of services, and that an economist may be called in to estimate what the value of those services are. He should explain that in most states, juries are instructed not to award anything for grief or emotional suffering in wrongful death cases. They are, however, generally allowed to give awards for loss of society and companionship.

At the very least, ask your lawyer for his impressions of your case. He might be able to tell you something like, "If we can prove that the hospital ignored your warning that you were allergic to the medication, then we've got a strong case"; Or, "If the nurse is willing to testify that the doctor was drunk in the operating room, we can expect a sizable award from the jury."

Time Frame

Don't expect to resolve your case quickly. The fastest resolutions usually take at least a year. Some cases drag on for five years. Only if both parties agree to a settlement in the early stages of a case — a rare occurrence — do medical malpractice cases end in less than a year.

Why does it take so long? A number of reasons. For one thing, the extent of a plaintiff's injuries often aren't known immediately; it can take months until someone's condition stabilizes and the damages (both physical and financial) can be assessed. Another problem is that most medical malpractice cases — especially ones involving serious injuries — are complicated. It takes time for both sides to compile evidence, interview experts, etc. Finally, conflicting schedules must be reconciled before a trial date is set — schedules of defendants, plaintiffs, witnesses, lawyers, and judges.

Some cases reach the courts faster than others. Generally, because of volume, cases in large cities go more slowly than those in smaller communities; federal courts often work faster than metropolitan state courts; smaller claims move through the system faster than larger claims.

Incompetent Lawyers

It's not only physicians who are incompetent. What happens if you suspect your lawyer is negligent?

You have every right to discharge your lawyer. If you're considering this action, think hard and long before doing so. Changing lawyers in midcase can be costly and counterproductive.

Many clients feel their lawyers are incompetent because months pass with seemingly little activity; or because their lawyers don't return phone calls quickly; or because they find themselves dealing with an associate of the original lawyer they hired.

Try to resolve miscommunication with your lawyer before dismissing him. Many times, he's unaware that there's a communication problem, and if you inform him of the problem, more often than not he'll correct it.

If, however, you're certain that your attorney is incompetent, fire him and look for a new attorney. Your former lawyer might insist on being paid for work to date. If you have proof that he was truly incompetent, he should receive little, if anything. The law provides that attorneys in contingency fee cases should be paid for efforts that have reasonably contributed to the successful conclusion of a case. Your new lawyer will help you resolve any fee problems.

CHAPTER TWELVE

How to File a Complaint Against a Practitioner

No ONE LIKES TO SUE a doctor, a hospital, or any other medical service provider. In fact, a Rand Corporation study found that only about 10 percent of the cases that might merit a suit are ever filed. This underscores both the trust and the intimidation the medical world breeds.

And, as we noted earlier, trial lawyers often hear their clients say they are not interested in collecting money from a malpractitioner, but rather in seeing that some form of punishment or action is taken that will prevent the same thing from happening to some other unsuspecting victim.

At the People's Medical Society, we hear similar statements. People write to ask how they can file a complaint against a practitioner or facility for harm they believe has been done to them.

Consumers also write to ask where they can report an act, event, or condition that they have witnessed concerning a doctor, hospital, or other medical provider. These may not be things that have happened directly to the individual wishing to lodge the complaint, but rather items noted during a hospital stay or a physician's office visit.

For example, what do you do if you suspect your physician was inebriated during an office visit? Where do you complain if you noticed hospital staff mishandling a fellow patient? Who investigates what you perceive to be a deficiency in service or care?

Many of these complaints may be violations of your rights or those of other consumers, but they do not necessarily warrant hiring an attorney or filing a lawsuit. They are, however, violations that should be investigated. Then, if guilt is determined, the appropriate action should be taken.

Good News and Bad News

Filing a complaint about a medical practitioner or facility is your right in every state. Each state has boards and agencies, all part of the state government, whose responsibilities include the investigation and sanctioning of medical personnel and facilities providing care. In Appendix A you will find a listing of the names, addresses, and phone numbers of the boards and agencies in your state to whom you should address your complaint. You will note that no state has a single agency that handles all practitioners and all facilities. That is why we list each of the organizations in each state by the type of practitioner or facilities they oversee.

That's the good news. At least these organizations exist.

The bad news is that most consumers who file complaints with these organizations are extremely dissatisfied with the action that results from their complaint. And the facts about the failure to act by most medical licensing boards bear out consumer claims.

Despite the lofty titles of such agencies — such as the Board of Medical Quality Assurance or the Board of Medical Education and Licensure — many, if not most, of these entities see their function as rehabilitative, rather than disciplinary. Most sanctioning and licensing bodies are made up of members of the profession being regulated. While they are officially state agencies, they are in fact extensions of the profession itself. Thus, conflict-of-interest problems tend to arise. How objective can a group of physicians be about other physicians? How willing are they to be generous in their protection of the consumer versus protecting one of their own?

Or, as one prominent health care official put it when asked to explain why medical boards do so little sanctioning: "Who would expect a college fraternity to ban beer from one of its own parties?"

The record is replete with failures of medical licensing boards and hospital oversight entities to take action against practitioners or facilities who have clearly ignored the law, violated someone's rights, or consistently performed below accepted standards. As some have put it, medicine operates under an acknowledged "conspiracy of silence" that protects its own out of fear that public exposure of the bad apples will make everyone in the profession suspect. Sadly, such thinking actually does the opposite. Because medical licensing boards fail to meet their statutory obligation to protect the public from bad practitioners, the public becomes suspicious of all doctors. And with most studies showing that between 5 and 10 percent of the doctors commit over 50 percent of the malpractice, it is apparent that the world of medicine is doing the majority of its members a great disservice.

But change does seem to be on the horizon. Since the advent of medical consumerism in the early 1980s, much has been written and exposed about the failure of state licensing and quality assurance agencies to take action. And while the system is not perfect, it is getting a little bit better.

It is also improving because of the pressure consumers are putting on state governments and organized medicine to be more publicly accountable. The media has picked up on the issue as well and has brought forth vivid, and often tragic, examples of state agencies originally created to protect the medical consumer failing to do so.

As a result, regulatory agencies are beginning to improve their act. While it is just a start, the outlook is promising.

Thus, despite past history, as a consumer you have an obligation to file a complaint when you believe your rights or those of others have been or are being violated by any medical practitioner or facility. It won't be fun; you may not win, but unless you take action, the incompetence or mistreatment that you received will happen to others unchecked.

Filing the Complaint

If you find yourself in a situation in which you feel you have been wronged, it is within your rights to file a complaint against the offending medical practitioner, hospital, health care facility, or health care insurance company.

Keep in mind that if you decide to file a formal complaint, you should be prepared to follow through with the process. When you contact the proper agency to lodge your complaint, make sure that you ask for any special forms that must be completed when your complaint is filed. Failure to file the necessary forms could delay action on your complaint.

Keep in mind that ultimately your complaint will most likely need to be in writing. Agency personnel might listen to your complaint or situation over the phone, then ask you to write it down. Don't let this dissuade you from making the complaint. Putting it in writing may take a while and may involve a good deal of work on your part, but at least it sets up a paper trail that can be traced should the agency to which you are complaining fail to respond or act.

We suggest you do the following:

1. Select the proper agency from Appendix A. (Generally speaking, your complaint will most likely involve a licensed professional. Therefore, the first agencies to review are those involved with licensing. If you cannot locate what you think is the proper agency in Appendix A, then call the information operator listed under Agency Locator at the beginning of each state's listing in the Appendix.)

2. Contact the proper agency and explain that you want to file a complaint. Be sure to ask for any special forms that must be filed with your complaint. You may contact the agency either by phone or by mail.

3. Make sure that you include the following information in your complaint:

• Name of the offending party

• Date when the incident occurred

• Where the incident occurred (as specifically as possible)

• Nature of the incident (listing every detail and including other witnesses, if any)

4. Make sure you have all the pertinent records relating to the incident, such as medical records, laboratory reports, hospital records, billing statements, and so forth. If you do not have direct access to the applicable documents but know they exist, indicate where such records can be found.

5. If the incident was extremely serious, you may want to consider consulting or retaining an attorney.

While the above information is general in nature and may not apply to all situations, it will serve as a basic guide to filing a complaint about a practitioner, facility, or health care insurer. Understand that this is not legal advice but rather a guide to the process. Procedures vary from state to state, so be sure to follow the procedure required by your state. The agencies you contact will outline that procedure.

If you are unable to reach the agency you desire, it may be because of a change in address or telephone numbers. (The agency names, addresses, and telephone numbers listed in Appendix A were updated at the time this book went to press.) Call the information operator in the city where the agency is listed for an up-to-date listing if you find the number no longer in service.

Some Words of Caution

When filing a complaint, use the agencies we list in Appendix A for your state. These are the entities that have a legal mandate to protect the consumer or regulate the professionals or facilities.

Many consumers have complained to the American Medical Association, a state medical society, or a local medical society. While these organizations will be happy to receive your complaint, they are merely trade associations for the medical profession. They may have standards of conducts and committees that review doctors, but the reality is that a complaint to a medical society is like complaining about nuclear power to a utility company that operates a nuclear plant.

Another point to keep in mind: if you file your complaint with the proper agency and do not receive a response or are not satisfied with their response and feel something more should be done, contact your state senator or state representative (not your federal legislators). "State" is the key word here. Remember, physicians, other medical professionals, and hospitals are regulated and licensed by the state, not the federal government. Complaining to your federal representative will only be wasting your time and possibly delaying any action that should be taken.

Conclusion

Knowing and exercising your medical rights is your key to a successful encounter with the world of medicine.

Being an informed medical consumer is your best defense against bad and incompetent medicine.

As we noted in the first chapter, knowledge is power. Knowing about your condition, practitioner, and community medical facilities is one level of power. Knowing about the risks of tests and treatments, alternative methods of dealing with your medical problem, and where to turn for more information or another medical opinion provides even greater control. Being armed with information gives you the data you need to make your own medical decisions and, most likely, the right ones.

The journey to medical knowledge is not an easy one for most consumers. Aside from not being medically trained, most laypeople are not willingly provided with adequate information to make reasonable and informed decisions about the medical course of action most appropriate to their conditions. Physicians are generally not forthcoming with all the information one needs to make an independent choice. In fact, most practitioners disclose just enough for the consumer to choose the treatment option presented by the disclosing physician.

Throughout this book, we have emphasized steps and actions you should take to prevent becoming a medical mishap. We have focused on problem areas that most consumers encounter. Obviously, a great deal more might have been covered, but no book can cover every situation. Nor are there definitive answers to every problem. While general rules may apply, every person is different and every case has its own circumstances medically and legally.

More important, though, is the concept of empowerment. This book is designed to empower you, the medical consumer, to be the driving force in your own health care. The concept of empowerment means that you know not only what needs to be done but what can be done and where you can turn for answers and assistance.

Empowerment means that you understand concepts and ideas and are well-versed enough to encompass them in your travels through the medical system.

But empowerment does not mean you need to be a walking encyclopedia. No one can be expected to know everything about his illnesses or injuries, the treatments available, or the debates that may be swirling around medical meetings concerning new ways to treat longstanding conditions. Simply put, empowerment is knowing where to get the answer when you need an answer.

And one way to make sure that you are an empowered medical consumer is to know what questions to ask and of whom to ask them. That is what *Your Medical Rights* is designed to do.

As you clearly noticed while reading *Your Medical Rights,* there are more questions posed than answers. That is because your situation is unique; your relationship with your practitioner or hospital is singular; the circumstances surrounding your care are not necessarily the same as someone else's. By the same token, we have written the book on the assumption that you are an intelligent human being, capable of making your own decisions, given the proper information.

But we also recognize that no matter how informed you may be, something can go wrong in the course of your medical care. We have tried to assist you in better understanding in the event that a mistake or error crosses the line between unavoidable or within a reasonable level of expectation, and gross negligence or incompetence. We have also tried to direct you in the most straightforward way possible to the resources available to seek redress or compensation for damages done to you.

An important final point must be made. It would be nice if we could have simply listed the laws and presented your medical rights in alphabetical order. Unfortunately, no such easy method is possible. Your medical rights are intertwined with many types of laws, most of which were not written with medical problems in mind.

Being an assertive, informed, and empowered medical consumer involves work. It means you have to ask a lot of questions of people and institutions that easily intimidate. It means you have to take your medical practitioner off any pedestal you may have elevated him to. It means you have to be tenacious, persistent, and, on occasion, disagreeable in order to get the information and response you deserve. It also means you have to be willing to accept the proposition that medicine is a business, the biggest business in America, and as such must be held accountable for all it does to people.

You should not be afraid to exercise your medical rights. From questioning a doctor to suing him — these are your rights as a medical consumer. The laws granting you these rights were designed to protect you and make those who provide the services accountable. You should not be intimidated by a physician's diplomas, office building, or cavalier manner. Nor should you be overly impressed by a hospital with hundreds of beds, names of community philanthropists plastered about the walls, or beautiful tree-lined grounds.

As a medical consumer, it is your right to have competent, high-quality medical care delivered by persons accountable to you in settings that meet the highest standards of health, safety, and public disclosure. To expect anything less is potentially to receive inadequate care.

Appendix A
State Agencies

NOTE: *If an Agency cannot be reached at the address or telephone number given, the Agency Locator/Information Operator should be contacted.*

ALABAMA

Type of Agency/Comments	*Organization and Address*	*Phone*
AGENCY LOCATOR *For Agencies & telephone numbers not listed*	Information Operator State Capitol Montgomery, AL 36130	205-261-2500
AGING *Provides programs & services to senior citizens*	Commission on Aging 136 Catoma St. Montgomery, AL 36130	205-261-5743
ALCOHOLISM *Provides assistance to alcohol abusers*	Mental Illness & Substance Abuse Programs Dept. of Mental Health 200 Interstate Park Dr. P.O. Box 3710 Montgomery, AL 36193	205-271-9253
ATTORNEY GENERAL *Chief law enforcement officer*	Attorney General's Office 11 South Union St. Montgomery, AL 36130	205-261-7305
CHILD WELFARE *Provides services to children and youths*	Div. of Family & Children's Services Dept. of Human Resources Administrative Bldg., Rm. 503 64 North Union St. Montgomery, AL 36130	205-261-3409

Type of Agency/Comments	*Organization and Address*	*Phone*
COMMUNITY AFFAIRS *Provides programs to communities*	Community Services Div. Dept. of Economic & Community Affairs 3465 Norman Bridge Rd. Montgomery, AL 36105	205-248-8957
CONSUMER ADVOCATE *Investigates consumer complaints*	Div. of Consumer Protection Attorney General's Office State House 11 South Union St., Rm. 335 Montgomery, AL 36130	205-261-7334
DEPARTMENT OF HEALTH *Supervises health activities in the state*	Dept. of Public Health State Office Bldg., Rm. 381 434 Monroe St. Montgomery, AL 36130	205-261-5052
DEVELOPMENTAL DISABILITIES *Provides services to the developmentally disabled*	Dept. of Mental Health & Retardation 200 Interstate Park Dr. P.O. Box 3710 Montgomery, AL 36193	205-271-9295
DRUG ABUSE *Provides assistance to drug abusers*	Substance Abuse Commission Programs Dept. of Mental Health 200 Interstate Park Dr. P.O. Box 3710 Montgomery, AL 36193	205-271-9253
FOOD AND DRUGS *Registers food and drug items*	Dept. of Agriculture & Industries Richard Beard Bldg. 1445 Federal Dr. P.O. Box 3336 Montgomery, AL 36193	205-261-2631
GOVERNOR *Citizens access to the governor*	Office of the Governor State House 11 South Union St. Montgomery, AL 36130	205-261-7150
INSURANCE *Regulates the insurance industry*	Dept. of Insurance Retirement Systems Bldg. 135 South Union St. Montgomery, AL 36130	205-269-3550
LICENSING: DENTISTS *Report complaints about dentists to this office*	Board of Dental Examiners Exec. Secretary 2308 B Starmount Cir. Huntsville, AL 35801	205-533-4638

Type of Agency/Comments	Organization and Address	Phone
LICENSING: HOSPITALS *Report complaints about hospitals to this office*	Dept. of Public Health/Bur. of Licensure & Certification 654 State Office Bldg. Montgomery, AL 36130	205-261-5113
LICENSING: NURSES *Report complaints about nurses to this office*	Alabama Board of Nursing Attn: Legal Division 500 East Blvd., Suite 213 Montgomery, AL 36130	205-261-4060
LICENSING: NURSING HOMES *Report complaints about nursing homes to this office*	Nursing Home Licensure Office Div. of Licensure & Certification Dept. of Health State Office Bldg., Rm. 654 Montgomery, AL 36103	205-261-5113
LICENSING: PHARMACISTS *Report complaints about pharmacists to this office*	Board of Pharmacy City Federal Bldg. Birmingham, AL 35302	205-252-8976
LICENSING: PHYSICIANS *Report complaints about doctors to this office*	Medical Licensure Commission P.O. Box 887 Montgomery, AL 36101	205-261-4116
MEDICAID OFFICE *Administers Medicaid program*	Alabama Medicaid Agency 2500 Fairland Dr. Montgomery, AL 36130	205-277-2710
MEDICARE PART B CARRIER *Processes Medicare claims*	Medicare/Blue Cross-Shield of Alabama P.O. Box C-140 Birmingham, AL 35238	205-998-2244 800-292-8855
MENTAL HEALTH *Provides patient services*	Dept. of Mental Health & Mental Retardation Interstate Park Dr., Rm. 200 P.O. Box 3710 Montgomery, AL 36193	205-271-9208
OCCUPATIONAL SAFETY & HEALTH *Inspects worksites*	Div. of Safety & Inspection Dept. of Industrial Relations 1816 8th Ave. North P.O. Box 10444 Birmingham, AL 35202	205-251-1181

Type of Agency/Comments	Organization and Address	Phone
OMBUDSMAN (NURSING HOMES) *Investigates complaints from nursing home residents*	Commission on Aging 136 Catoma St. Montgomery, AL 36130	205-261-5743
SOCIAL SERVICES *Provides support services and counseling*	Dept. of Human Rights Folsom Administrative Bldg. 64 North Union St. Montgomery, AL 36130	205-261-3190
VETERANS AFFAIRS *Provides assistance to veterans*	Dept. of Veterans Affairs State Office Bldg., Rm. 186 501 Dexter Ave. P.O. Box 1509 Montgomery, AL 36192	205-261-5077
VITAL STATISTICS *Maintains birth & death records*	Bureau of Vital Statistics Dept. of Public Health State Office Bldg., Rm. 381 434 Monroe St. Montgomery, AL 36130	205-261-5052
VOCATIONAL REHABILITATION *Provides information on rehabilitation programs*	Div. of Rehab. Dept. of Education 2129 East South Blvd. Montgomery, AL 36111	205-281-8780
WELFARE *Administers income programs*	Public Assistance Div. Dept. of Human Resources One Court Square 64 North Union St. Montgomery, AL 36130	205-261-2875
WORKER'S COMPENSATION *Provides income for injured workers*	Worker's Compensation Div. Dept. of Industrial Relations Industrial Relations Bldg. 649 Monroe St. Montgomery, AL 36130	205-261-2868

ALASKA

Type of Agency/Comments	Organization and Address	Phone
AGENCY LOCATOR *For Agencies & telephone numbers not listed*	Information Operator State Capitol 120 Fourth St. Juneau, AK 99811	907-465-2111

Type of Agency/Comments	Organization and Address	Phone
AGING *Provides programs &* *services to senior citizens*	Older Alaskans Commission Dept. of Administration 2600 Denali St. Suite 403 Anchorage, AK 99503	907-279-2232

ALCOHOLISM
 	
Provides assistance to
alcohol abusers
	Office of Alcoholism & Drug
	   Abuse
	Dept. of Health & Social
	   Services
	114 Second St.
	Juneau, AK 99811
		907-586-6201

ATTORNEY GENERAL *Chief law enforcement* *officer*	Dept. of Law State Capitol, Rm. 412 120 4th St. P.O. Box K Juneau, AK 99811	907-465-3600

CHILD WELFARE
 	
Provides services to children
and youths
	Div. of Family & Youth
	   Services
	Dept. of Health & Social
	   Services
	Alaska Office Bldg., Rm. 404
	350 Main St.
	Juneau, AK 99811
		907-465-3170

COMMUNITY AFFAIRS *Provides programs to* *communities*	Dept. of Community & Regional Affairs Community Bldg., Rm. 217 150 Third St. Juneau, AK 99811	907-465-4700
CONSUMER ADVOCATE *Investigates consumer* *complaints*	Consumer Protection Section Attorney General's Office 1031 West Fourth Ave. Suite 110 Anchorage, AK 99501	907-276-3550
DEPARTMENT OF HEALTH *Supervises health activities* *in the state*	Dept. of Health & Social Services Alaska Office Bldg., Rm. 503 350 Main St. Juneau, AK 99811	907-465-3030

DEVELOPMENTAL
  DISABILITIES
 	
Provides services to the
developmentally disabled
	Div. of Mental Health/
	   Developmental Disabilities
	Dept. of Health & Social
	   Services
	350 Main St.
	Juneau, AK 99811
		907-465-3370

Type of Agency/Comments	Organization and Address	Phone
DRUG ABUSE *Provides assistance to drug abusers*	Office of Alcoholism & Drug Abuse Dept. of Health & Social Services 114 Second St. Juneau, AK 99811	907-586-6201
GOVERNOR *Citizen's access to the governor*	Office of the Governor State Capitol 120 Fourth St. P.O. Box A Juneau, AK 99811	907-465-3500
INSURANCE *Regulates the insurance industry*	Div. of Insurance Dept. of Commerce 333 Willoughby Ave. P.O. Box D, Mail Stop 0800 Juneau, AK 99811	907-465-2515
LICENSING: DENTISTS *Report complaints about dentists to this office*	Board of Dental Examiners Dept. of Commerce Div. of Occupational Licensing P.O. Box D Juneau, AK 99811	907-465-2544
LICENSING: HOSPITALS *Report complaints about hospitals to this office*	Alaska Health Facilities Licensing & Certification 4041 B St. Suite 101 Anchorage, AK 99503	907-561-2171
LICENSING: NURSES *Report complaints about nurses to this office*	Alaska Div. of Occupational Licensing 3601 C St. Suite 722 Anchorage, AK 99503	907-561-2878
LICENSING: NURSING HOMES *Report complaints about nursing homes to this office*	Dept. of Health & Social Services Health Facilities Licensing 4041 B St. Suite 101 Anchorage, AK 99503	907-561-2171
LICENSING: PHARMACISTS *Report complaints about pharmacists to this office*	Alaska Board of Pharmacy P.O. Box 3728 Anchorage, AK 99501	907-465-2541

Type of Agency/Comments	Organization and Address	Phone
LICENSING: PHYSICIANS *Report complaints about doctors to this office*	Dept. of Commerce & Economic Development State Medical Board P.O. Box D Juneau, AK 99811	907-465-2541
LICENSING: PROFESSIONALS *Contact for information on other health professionals*	Div. of Occupational Licensing Dept. of Commerce State Office Bldg. 333 Willoughby Ave. Juneau, AK 99811	907-465-2534
MEDICAID OFFICE *Administers Medicaid program*	Dept. of Health & Social Services Div. of Medical Assistance P.O. Box H-07 Juneau, AK 99811	907-465-3355
MEDICARE PART B CARRIER *Processes Medicare claims for Alaska residents*	Aetna Life & Casualty Co. 200 SW Market St. Portland, OR 97207	800-547-6333
MENTAL HEALTH *Provides patient services*	Div. of Mental Health & Developmental Disabilities Alaska Office Bldg., Rm. 214 350 Main St. Juneau, AK 99811	907-465-3370
OCCUPATIONAL SAFETY & HEALTH *Inspects worksites*	Occupational Safety & Health Section Dept. of Labor 1111 West Eighth St. P.O. Box 1149 Juneau, AK 99802	907-465-4855
OMBUDSMAN (GENERAL) *Citizens access to government officials*	Office of the Ombudsman 240 Main St., Rm. 702 P.O. Box WO, MS 3000 Juneau, AK 99811	907-465-4970 800-478-4970
OMBUDSMAN (NURSING HOMES) *Investigates complaints from nursing home residents*	Older Alaskans Commission Dept. of Administration 2600 Denali St. Suite 403 Anchorage, AK 99503	907-279-2232

Type of Agency/Comments	*Organization and Address*	*Phone*
SOCIAL SERVICES *Provides support services and counseling*	Div. of Family & Youth Services Dept. of Health & Social Services Alaska Office Bldg., Rm. 404 350 Main St. Juneau, AK 99811	907-465-3170
VETERANS AFFAIRS *Provides assistance to veterans*	Veterans Affairs Div. Military & Veterans Affairs Frontier Bldg., Rm. 650 3601 C St. Anchorage, AK 99503	907-249-1241
VITAL STATISTICS *Maintains birth & death records*	Bur. of Vital Records Dept. of Health & Social Services Alaska Office Bldg., Rm. 114 350 Main St. Juneau, AK 99811	907-465-3391
VOCATIONAL REHABILITATION *Provides information on rehabilitation programs*	Div. of Vocational Rehab. Dept. of Education Goldbelt Bldg., First Floor 801 West Tenth St. Juneau, AK 99811	907-465-2814
WELFARE *Administers income programs*	Div. of Public Assistance Dept. of Health & Social Services Alaska Office Bldg., Rm. 309 350 Main St. Juneau, AK 99811	907-465-3347
WORKER'S COMPENSATION *Provides income for injured workers*	Div. of Worker's Compensation Dept. of Labor 1111 West 8th St. P.O. Box 1149 Juneau, AK 99811	907-465-2790

ARKANSAS

Type of Agency/Comments	*Organization and Address*	*Phone*
AGENCY LOCATOR *For Agencies & telephone numbers not listed*	Information Operator State Capitol 5th & Woodlane Little Rock, AR 72201	501-371-3000

Type of Agency/Comments	Organization and Address	Phone
AGING *Provides programs & services for senior citizens*	Div. of Aging & Adult Services Dept. of Human Services Donaghey Bldg., Rm. 1417 7th & Main Sts. Little Rock, AR 72203	501-682-2441
ALCOHOLISM *Provides assistance to alcohol abusers*	Office on Alcohol & Drug Abuse Prevention Dept. of Human Services 7th & Main Sts. Little Rock, AR 72203	501-682-6650
ATTORNEY GENERAL *Chief law enforcement officer*	Office of Attorney General 200 Tower Bldg. 4th & Center Sts. Little Rock, AR 72201	501-682-2007
CHILD WELFARE *Provides services to children and youths*	Div. of Children & Family Services Dept. of Human Services 7th & Main Sts. Little Rock, AR 72203	501-682-8772
COMMUNITY AFFAIRS *Provides programs to communities*	Div. of Economic & Medical Services Dept. of Human Services Donaghey Bldg., Rm. 1306 7th & Main Sts. Little Rock, AR 72203	501-682-8375
CONSUMER ADVOCATE *Investigates consumer complaints*	Consumer Protection Div. Office of Attorney General 4th & Center Sts. Little Rock, AR 72201	501-682-2341
DEPARTMENT OF HEALTH *Supervises health activities in the state*	Dept. of Health State Health Bldg. 4815 West Markham St. Little Rock, AR 72205	501-661-2112

DEVELOPMENTAL
  DISABILITIES
 	
*Provides services to the
developmentally disabled*
	Developmental Disabilities
	  Services Div.
	Dept. of Human Services
	Donaghey Plaza North, 5th
	  Floor
	7th & Main Sts.
	Little Rock, AR 72203
		501-682-8662

Type of Agency/Comments	Organization and Address	Phone
DRUG ABUSE *Provides assistance to drug abusers*	Office on Alcohol & Drug Abuse Prevention Dept. of Human Services 7th & Main Sts. Little Rock, AR 72203	501-682-6650
FOOD AND DRUGS *Registers food items*	Food & Dairy Products Section Div. of Sanitation Services Dept. of Health 4815 West Markham St. Little Rock, AR 72205	501-661-2171
FOOD AND DRUGS *Registers drug items*	Div. of Pharmacy Services Dept. of Health 4815 West Markham St. Little Rock, AR 72205	501-661-2325
GOVERNOR *Citizens access to the governor*	Office of the Governor State Capitol Rm. 250 Little Rock, AR 72201	501-682-2345
INSURANCE *Regulates the insurance industry*	Insurance Dept. University Tower Bldg., Rm. 400 12th & University Ave. Little Rock, AR 72204	501-371-1325
LICENSING: DENTISTS *Report complaints about dentists to this office*	Board of Dental Examiners Tower Bldg., Suite 1200 Little Rock, AR 72202	501-682-2085
LICENSING: HOSPITALS *Report complaints about hospitals to this office*	Dept. of Health Div. of Health Facilities Service 4815 West Markham St. Little Rock, AR 72205	501-661-2201
LICENSING: NURSES *Report complaints about nurses to this office*	Board of Nursing Towers Bldg. 1123 South University Suite 800 Little Rock, AR 72204	501-371-2751
LICENSING: NURSING HOMES *Report complaints about nursing homes to this office*	Dept. of Health Certification & Licensing Section Office of Long Term Care P.O. Box 8059 Little Rock, AR 72203	501-682-8430

Type of Agency/Comments	Organization and Address	Phone
LICENSING: PHARMACISTS *Report complaints about pharmacists to this office*	Board of Pharmacy 320 West Capitol, Suite 802 Little Rock, AR 72201	501-371-3050
LICENSING: PHYSICIANS *Report complaints about doctors to this office*	Board of Medical Examiners P.O. Box 102 Harrisburg, AR 72432	501-578-2448
MEDICAID OFFICE *Administers Medicaid program*	Dept. of Human Services Information & Referral P.O. Box 1437 Little Rock, AR 72203	501-682-1001
MEDICARE PART B CARRIER *Processes Medicare claims*	Arkansas Blue Cross/Shield P.O. Box 1418 Little Rock, AR 72203	501-378-2320 800-482-5525
MENTAL HEALTH *Provides patient services*	Div. of Mental Health Services Dept. of Human Services 4313 West Markham St. Little Rock, AR 72205	501-682-9164
OCCUPATIONAL SAFETY & HEALTH *Inspects worksites*	Safety Div. Dept. of Labor 1022 High St. Little Rock, AR 72202	501-682-4522
OMBUDSMAN (GENERAL) *Citizens access to government officials*	State Claims Commission State Capitol, Rm. 021 5th & Woodlane Little Rock, AR 72201	501-682-1619
OMBUDSMAN (NURSING HOMES) *Investigates complaints from nursing home residents*	Div. of Aging & Adult Services Dept. of Human Services Donaghey Bldg. 7th & Main Sts. Little Rock, AR 72203	501-682-2441
SOCIAL SERVICES *Provides support services and counseling*	Div. of Economic & Medical Services Dept. of Human Services Donaghey Bldg., Rm. 316 7th & Main Sts. Little Rock, AR 72201	501-682-8375

Type of Agency/Comments	Organization and Address	Phone
VETERANS AFFAIRS *Provides assistance to veterans*	Dept. of Veterans Affairs VA Regional Office Bldg. Rm. 118 P.O. Box 1280 North Little Rock, AR 72115	501-370-3820
VITAL STATISTICS *Maintains birth & death records*	Office of Vital Records Dept. of Health State Health Bldg. 4815 West Markham St. Little Rock, AR 72205	501-661-2134
VOCATIONAL REHABILITATION *Provides information on rehabilitation programs*	Rehab. Services Dept. Dept. of Human Services 1401 Brookwood Dr. P.O. Box 3781 Little Rock, AR 72203	501-682-6709
WELFARE *Administers income programs*	Div. of Economic & Medical Services Dept. of Human Services Donaghey Bldg., Rm. 316 P.O. Box 1437 Little Rock, AR 72201	501-682-8375
WORKER'S COMPENSATION *Provides income for injured workers*	Worker's Compensation Commission Justice Bldg. Capitol Grounds Little Rock, AR 72201	501-682-3930 800-622-4472

ARIZONA

Type of Agency/Comments	Organization and Address	Phone
AGENCY LOCATOR *For Agencies & telephone numbers not listed*	Information Operator State Capitol 1700 West Washington St. Phoenix, AZ 85007	602-542-4900
AGING *Provides programs for senior citizens*	Div. of Aging, Family & Children Dept. of Economic Security 1400 West Washington St. P.O. Box 6123 Phoenix, AZ 85007	602-542-4446

Type of Agency/Comments	Organization and Address	Phone
ALCOHOLISM *Provides assistance to alcohol abusers*	Office of Community Behavioral Services Dept. of Health Services 411 North 24th St. Phoenix, AZ 85304	602-220-6478
ATTORNEY GENERAL *Chief law enforcement officer*	Attorney General's Office Dept. of Law 1275 West Washington St. Phoenix, AZ 85007	602-542-4266
CHILD WELFARE *Provides services to children and youths*	Div. of Aging, Family & Children Services Dept. of Economic Security 1400 West Washington St. Phoenix, AZ 85007	602-255-3569
COMMUNITY AFFAIRS *Provides programs to communities*	Community Assistance Div. Dept. of Commerce State Capitol, Rm. 505 1700 West Washington St. Phoenix, AZ 85007	602-542-5434
CONSUMER ADVOCATE *Report consumer complaints*	Financial Fraud Div. Attorney General's Office Dept. of Law 1275 West Washington St. Phoenix, AZ 85007	602-542-3702 800-352-8431
DEPARTMENT OF HEALTH *Supervises health activities in the state*	Dept. of Health Services 1740 West Adams St. Phoenix, AZ 85007	602-542-1024
DEVELOPMENTAL DISABILITIES *Provides services to the developmentally disabled*	Div. of Developmental Disabilities Dept. of Economic Security 1841 West Buchanan St. Phoenix, AZ 85007	602-258-0419
DRUG ABUSE *Provides assistance to drug abusers*	Office of Community Behavioral Health Services Dept. of Health Services 411 North 24th St. Phoenix, AZ 85304	602-220-6478
FOOD AND DRUGS *Registers food & drug items*	Dept. of Health Services 1740 West Adams St. Phoenix, AZ 85007	602-542-1024

Type of Agency/Comments	*Organization and Address*	*Phone*
GOVERNOR *Citizens access to the governor*	Office of the Governor State Capitol 1700 West Washington St. Phoenix, AZ 85007	602-255-1343
INSURANCE *Regulates insurance industry*	Office of the Director Insurance Dept. 3030 North 3rd St. Phoenix, AZ 85012	602-255-5400
LICENSING: DENTISTS *Report complaints about dentists to this office*	Arizona State Board of Dental Examiners 5060 North 19th Ave. Rm. 406 Phoenix, AZ 85015	602-255-3696
LICENSING: HOSPITALS *Report complaints about hospitals to this office*	Arizona Dept. of Health Services Bur. of Health Care Institutions Licensing 1740 West Adams St. Phoenix, AZ 85007	602-542-1000
LICENSING: NURSES *Report complaints about nurses to this office*	Arizona Board of Nursing 2001 W. Camelback Suite 350 Phoenix, AZ 85015	602-255-5092
LICENSING: NURSING HOMES *Report complaints about nursing homes to this office*	Dept. of Health Services Office of Health Care Licensure 701 East Jefferson St. Suite 300 Phoenix, AZ 85034	602-255-1177
LICENSING: PHARMACISTS *Report complaints about pharmacists to this office*	Board of Pharmacy 5060 19th Ave. Suite 101 Phoenix, AZ 85007	602-255-5125
LICENSING: PHYSICIANS *Report complaints about doctors to this office*	Arizona Board of Medical Examiners 2001 West Camelback Rd. Suite 300 Phoenix, AZ 85015	602-255-3751
LICENSING: PROFESSIONALS *Licenses other health care professionals*	State Boards Office Dept. of Administration 1645 West Jefferson St. Rm. 410 Phoenix, AZ 85007	602-542-3095

Type of Agency/Comments	*Organization and Address*	*Phone*
MEDICAID OFFICE *Administers Medicaid program*	Arizona Health Care Cost Containment System 801 East Jefferson St. Phoenix, AZ 85034	602-234-3655
MEDICARE PART B CARRIER *Processes Medicare claims*	Medicare/Aetna Life & Casualty Co. P.O. Box 37200 Phoenix, AZ 85069	602-861-1968 800-352-0411
MENTAL HEALTH *Provides patient services*	Office of Community Behavioral Health Services Dept. of Health 411 North 24th St. Phoenix, AZ 85304	602-220-6478
OCCUPATIONAL SAFETY & HEALTH *Inspects worksites*	Div. of Occupational Safety & Health Industrial Commission 800 West Washington St., Rm. 202 P.O. Box 19070 Phoenix, AZ 85007	602-542-5795
OMBUDSMAN (NURSING HOMES) *Investigates complaints from nursing home residents*	Aging & Adult Administration Dept. of Economic Security 1400 West Washington St. Phoenix, AZ 85007	602-542-4446
SOCIAL SERVICES *Provides support services and counseling*	Admin. for Children, Youth & Families Div. of Aging, Family & Children's Services Dept. of Economic Security 1400 West Washington St. Phoenix, AZ 85007	602-542-3981
VETERANS AFFAIRS *Provides assistance to veterans*	Veterans Service Commission 3225 North Central Suite 910 Phoenix, AZ 85012	602-255-4713
VITAL STATISTICS *Maintains birth & death records*	Office of Vital Records Dept. of Admin. 1740 West Adams St. Phoenix, AZ 85007	602-542-1084

Type of Agency/Comments	Organization and Address	Phone
VOCATIONAL REHABILITATION *Provides information on retraining programs*	Rehab. Services Bur. 1300 West Washington St. Rm. 93A Phoenix, AZ 85007	602-542-3332
WELFARE *Administers income programs*	Div. of Aging, Family & Children's Services Dept. of Economic Security 1400 West Washington St. Phoenix, AZ 85007	602-255-3596
WORKER'S COMPENSATION *Provides income for injured workers*	State Compensation Fund 3031 North Second St. Phoenix, AZ 85012	602-631-2050

CALIFORNIA

Type of Agency/Comments	Organization and Address	Phone
AGENCY LOCATOR *For Agencies & telephone numbers not listed*	Information Operator State Capitol Sacramento, CA 95814	916-322-9900
AGING *Provides programs & services for senior citizens*	Dept. of Aging 1020 19th St. Sacramento, CA 95814	916-322-5290
ALCOHOLISM *Provides assistance to alcohol abusers*	Dept. of Alcohol & Drug Programs 111 Capitol Mall Sacramento, CA 95814	916-445-0834
ATTORNEY GENERAL *Chief law enforcement officer*	Attorney General's Office Dept. of Justice 1515 K St. Suite 511 Sacramento, CA 95814	916-445-9555
CHILD WELFARE *Provides services to children and youths*	Adult & Family Services Div. Dept. of Social Services State Office Bldg. 9 744 P St. Sacramento, CA 95814	916-445-7653

Type of Agency/Comments	*Organization and Address*	*Phone*
COMMUNITY AFFAIRS *Provides programs to communities*	Div. of Community Affairs Dept. of Housing & Community Development 921 10th St., Rm. 401 Sacramento, CA 95814	916-322-1560
CONSUMER ADVOCATE *Investigates consumer complaints*	Dept. of Consumer Affairs 1020 N St. Rm. 516 Sacramento, CA 95814	916-445-4465
DEPARTMENT OF HEALTH *Supervises health activities in the state*	Dept. of Health Services 714 P St. Rm. 1253 Sacramento, CA 95814	916-445-1248
DEVELOPMENTAL DISABILITIES *Provides services to the developmentally disabled*	Dept. of Developmental Services Health & Welfare Agency 1600 9th St. Sacramento, CA 95814	916-323-3131
DRUG ABUSE *Provides assistance to drug abusers*	Dept. of Alcohol & Drug Programs 111 Capitol Mall Sacramento, CA 95814	916-445-0834
FOOD AND DRUGS *Registers food & drug items*	Food & Drug Branch Environmental Health Div. State Office Bldg. 8, Rm. 400 714 P St. Sacramento, CA 95814	916-445-2263
GOVERNOR *Citizen's access to the governor*	Office of the Governor State Capitol First Floor Sacramento, CA 95814	916-445-4571
INSURANCE DEPARTMENT *Regulates insurance industry*	Office of the Commissioner Dept. of Insurance 600 South Commonwealth Ave. 14th Floor Los Angeles, CA 90005	213-736-2551
LICENSING: DENTISTS *Report complaints about dentists to this office*	California State Board of Dental Examiners 1430 Howe St. Suite 85 B Sacramento, CA 95825	916-920-7451

Type of Agency/Comments	*Organization and Address*	*Phone*
LICENSING: HOSPITALS *Report complaints about hospitals to this office*	California Dept. of Health Services Div. of Licensing & Certification 714 P St. Sacramento, CA 95814	916-445-2070
LICENSING: NURSES *Report complaints about nurses to this office*	California Board of Registered Nursing 1030 13th St. Rm. 200 Sacramento, CA 95814	916-322-3350
LICENSING: NURSING HOMES *Report complaints about nursing homes to this office*	Nursing Home Licensure Office Licensure & Certification Div. Facilities Licensing Section 714 P St., Rm. 823 Sacramento, CA 95814	916-445-3281
LICENSING: PHARMACISTS *Report complaints about pharmacists to this office*	State Board of Pharmacy 1021 O St. Sacramento, CA 95814	916-445-5014
LICENSING: PHYSICIANS *Report complaints about doctors to this office*	California Board of Medical Quality Assurance 1430 Howe Ave. Sacramento, CA 95825	916-920-6393
LICENSING: PROFESSIONALS *Licenses other health care professionals*	Office of the Director Dept. of Consumer Affairs 1020 N St. Rm. 516 Sacramento, CA 95814	916-445-4465
MEDICAID OFFICE *Administers Medicaid program*	Dept. of Health Services Referral Office for Medi-Cal 714-744 P St. P.O.Box 942732 Sacramento, CA 94234	916-445-4171
MEDICARE PART B CARRIER *Check your area for specific coverage and toll-free number*	Blue Shield of California Medicare Claims Dept. Chico, CA 95976	916-743-1583 714-824-0900

Type of Agency/Comments	Organization and Address	Phone
MEDICARE PART B CARRIER *Check your area for exact coverage*	Medicare/Transamerica Occidental Life Insurance Co. P.O. Box 50061 Upland, CA 91785	213-748-2311 800-252-9020
MENTAL HEALTH *Provides patient services*	Dept. of Mental Health Gregory Bateson Bldg. Rm. 151 1600 Ninth St. Sacramento, CA 95814	916-323-8173
OCCUPATIONAL SAFETY & HEALTH *Inspects worksites*	Occupational Safety & Health Standards Board Dept. of Industrial Relations 1006 Fourth St. Sacramento, CA 95814	916-322-3640
OMBUDSMAN (NURSING HOMES) *Investigates complaints from nursing home residents*	California Dept. of Aging Office of LTC Ombudsman 1600 K St. Sacramento, CA 95814	916-322-3887 800-231-4024
SOCIAL SERVICES *Provides support services and counseling*	Dept. of Social Services State Office Bldg. 9 744 P St. Sacramento, CA 95814	916-445-2077
VETERANS AFFAIRS *Provides assistance to veterans*	Dept. of Veterans Affairs Veterans Affairs Bldg. 1227 O St. P.O. Box 94295-0001 Sacramento, CA 94295	916-445-3111

VITAL STATISTICS
 	
Maintains birth & death records
	Health Data & Statistics
	   Branch
	Rural & Community Health
	   Div.
	Dept. of Health Services
	410 N St.
	Sacramento, CA 95814
		916-445-1719

VOCATIONAL REHABILITATION *Provides information on rehabilitation services*	Dept. of Rehab. 830 K St. Mall Sacramento, CA 95814	916-445-3971

Type of Agency/Comments	*Organization and Address*	*Phone*
WELFARE *Administers income programs*	Dept. of Social Services State Office Bldg. 9 744 P St. Sacramento, CA 95814	916-445-2077
WORKER'S COMPENSATION *Provides income for injured workers*	Div. of Industrial Accidents Dept. of Industrial Relations 525 Golden Gate Ave., Rm. 103 P.O. Box 603 San Francisco, CA 94101	415-557-3542

COLORADO

Type of Agency/Comments	*Organization and Address*	*Phone*
AGENCY LOCATOR *For Agencies & telephone numbers not listed*	Information Operator State Capitol 200 East Colfax Ave. Denver, CO 80203	303-866-5000
AGING *Provides programs & services to senior citizens*	Aging & Adult Services Div. Dept. of Social Services State Social Services Bldg. 1575 Sherman St. Denver, CO 80203	303-866-5905
ALCOHOLISM *Provides assistance to alcohol abusers*	Alcohol & Drug Abuse Div. Dept. of Health 4210 East 11th Ave. Denver, CO 80220	303-331-8201
ATTORNEY GENERAL *Chief law enforcement officer*	Attorney General's Office Dept. of Law 1525 Sherman St., 3rd Floor Denver, CO 80203	303-866-3611
CHILD WELFARE *Provides services to children and youths*	Div. of Family-Children Services Dept. of Social Services 1575 Sherman St. Denver, CO 80218	303-866-5957
COMMUNITY AFFAIRS *Provides programs to communities*	Dept. of Local Affairs State Centennial Bldg., Rm. 518 1313 Sherman St. Denver, CO 80203	303-866-2205

Type of Agency/Comments	Organization and Address	Phone
CONSUMER ADVOCATE *Investigates consumer complaints*	Consumer Protection Unit Office of Attorney General State Services Bldg., Rm. 215 1525 Sherman St. Denver, CO 80203	303-866-5168
DEPARTMENT OF HEALTH *Supervises health activities in the state*	Dept. of Health 4210 East 11th Ave. Denver, CO 80220	303-331-4602
DEVELOPMENTAL DISABILITIES *Provides services to the developmentally disabled*	Div. for Developmental Disabilities Dept. of Institutions 3824 West Princeton Cir. Denver, CO 80236	303-762-4550
DRUG ABUSE *Provides assistance to drug abusers*	Alcohol & Drug Abuse Div. Dept. of Health 4210 East 11th Ave. Denver, CO 80220	303-331-8201
FOOD AND DRUGS *Registers food & drug items*	Consumer Protection Div. Office of Health Protection Dept. of Health 4210 East 11th Ave. Denver, CO 80220	303-320-8333
GOVERNOR *Citizens access to the governor*	Office of the Governor State Capitol Rm. 136 Denver, CO 80203	303-866-2471
INSURANCE *Regulates the insurance industry*	Div. of Insurance Dept. of Regulatory Agencies First Western Plaza Bldg., Rm. 500 303 West Colfax Ave. Denver, CO 80204	303-866-3201
LICENSING: DENTISTS *Report complaints about dentists to this office*	Board of Dental Examiners 1525 Sherman St. Rm. 132 Denver, CO 80203	303-866-5807
LICENSING: HOSPITALS *Report complaints about hospitals to this office*	Dept. of Health Div. of Health Facilities Regulation 4210 East 11th Ave. Denver, CO 80220	303-331-4930

Type of Agency/Comments	*Organization and Address*	*Phone*
LICENSING: NURSES *Report complaints about nurses to this office*	Board of Nursing 1560 Broadway Suite 670 Denver, CO 80203	303-894-2430
LICENSING: NURSING HOMES *Report complaints about nursing homes to this office*	Colorado Dept. of Health Health Facilities Div. Evaluation & Licensure Section 4210 East 11th Ave., Rm. 254 Denver, CO 80220	303-331-4930
LICENSING: PHARMACISTS *Report complaints about pharmacists to this office*	State Board of Pharmacy 1525 Sherman St. Denver, CO 80203	303-866-2526
LICENSING: PHYSICIANS *Report complaints about doctors to this office*	Board of Medical Examiners 1525 Sherman St. Suite 132 Denver, CO 80203	303-866-2468
LICENSING: PROFESSIONALS *Licenses other health care professionals*	Dept. of Regulatory Agencies State Services Bldg., Rm. 110 1525 Sherman St. Denver, CO 80203	303-866-3304
MEDICAID OFFICE *Administers Medicaid program*	Dept. of Social Services Div. of Medical Services 717 17th St. Denver, CO 80218	303-294-5700
MEDICARE PART B CARRIER *Processes Medicare claims*	Blue Shield of Colorado 700 Broadway Denver, CO 80273	303-831-2661 800-332-6681
MENTAL HEALTH *Provides patient services*	Div. of Mental Health Dept. of Institutions Ft. Logan Mental Health Center 3520 West Oxford Ave. Denver, CO 80236	303-762-4073
OMBUDSMAN (NURSING HOMES) *Investigates complaints*	State Ombudsman Program 455 Sherman St. Denver, CO 80218	303-722-0300 800-582-7410

Type of Agency/Comments	*Organization and Address*	*Phone*
SOCIAL SERVICES *Provides support services and counseling*	Dept. of Social Services 1575 Sherman St. Social Services Bldg. Denver, CO 80203	303-866-5800
VETERANS AFFAIRS *Provides assistance to veterans*	Director of Veterans Affairs Dept. of Social Services Social Services Bldg., Rm. 122 1575 Sherman St. Denver, CO 80203	303-866-2494
VITAL STATISTICS *Maintains birth & death records*	Health Policy, Planning & Statistics Div. Dept. of Health 4210 East 11th Ave. Denver, CO 80220	303-320-8475
VOCATIONAL REHABILITATION *Provides information on rehabilitation programs*	Div. of Rehab. Dept. of Social Services 1575 Sherman St. Social Services Bldg. Denver, CO 80218	303-866-5186
WELFARE *Administers income programs*	Program Admin. Dept. of Social Services 1575 Sherman St. Social Services Bldg. Denver, CO 80203	303-866-5981
WORKER'S COMPENSATION *Provides income for injured workers*	Div. of Labor Dept. of Labor & Employment State Centennial Bldg. 1313 Sherman St. Denver, CO 80203	303-866-2782

CONNECTICUT

Type of Agency/Comments	*Organization and Address*	*Phone*
AGENCY LOCATOR *For Agencies & telephone numbers not listed*	Information Operator State Capitol 210 Capitol Ave. Hartford, CT 06106	203-566-2211
AGING *Provides programs & services for senior citizens*	Dept. on Aging 175 Main St. Hartford, CT 06106	203-566-3238

Type of Agency/Comments	*Organization and Address*	*Phone*
ALCOHOLISM *Provides assistance to alcohol abusers*	Alcohol & Drug Abuse Commission 999 Asylum Ave. Hartford, CT 06105	203-566-4145
ATTORNEY GENERAL *Chief law enforcement officer*	Attorney General's Office 30 Trinity St. Hartford, CT 06106	203-566-3747
CHILD WELFARE *Provides services to children and youths*	Dept. of Children and Youth Services 170 Sigourney St. Hartford, CT 06105	203-566-3536
COMMUNITY AFFAIRS *Provides programs to communities*	Municipal Development Div. Dept. of Economic Development 210 Washington St. Hartford, CT 06106	203-566-3308
CONSUMER ADVOCATE *Investigates consumer complaints*	Dept. of Consumer Protection State Office Bldg. Rm. 105 165 Capitol Ave. Hartford, CT 06106	203-566-4999
DEPARTMENT OF HEALTH *Supervises health activities in the state*	Dept. of Health Services 150 Washington St. Hartford, CT 06106	203-566-2038
DEVELOPMENTAL DISABILITIES *Provides services to the developmentally disabled*	Dept. of Mental Health 90 Pitkin St. East Hartford, CT 06108	203-528-7141
DRUG ABUSE *Provides assistance to drug abusers*	Alcohol & Drug Abuse Commission NCR Bldg. 999 Asylum Ave. Hartford, CT 06105	203-566-4145

Type of Agency/Comments	*Organization and Address*	*Phone*
FOOD AND DRUGS *Registers food & drug items*	Food Div. Dept. of Consumer Protection State Office Bldg. 165 Capitol Ave. Hartford, CT 06106	203-566-3388
GOVERNOR *Citizen's access to the* *governor*	Office of the Governor State Capitol 210 Capitol Ave. Hartford, CT 06106	203-566-4840
INSURANCE *Regulates insurance industry*	Insurance Dept. State Office Bldg., Rm. 425 153 Market St. Hartford, CT 06106	203-299-3800
LICENSING: DENTISTS *Report complaints about* *dentists to this office*	CT Dept. of Health Services Medical Quality Assurance Dental 150 Washington St. Hartford, CT 06106	203-566-1027
LICENSING: HOSPITALS *Report complaints about* *hospitals to this office*	CT Dept. of Health Services Hospital & Medical Care Div. 150 Washington St. Hartford, CT 06106	203-566-1073
LICENSING: NURSES *Report complaints about* *nurses to this office*	CT Dept. of Health Consumer Complaint Div. 150 Washington St. Hartford, CT 06106	203-566-1011
LICENSING: NURSING HOMES *Report complaints about* *nursing homes to this* *office*	Nursing Home Licensure Office State Dept. of Health Hospitals & Medical Care Div. 150 Washington St. Hartford, CT 06106	203-566-5758
LICENSING: PHARMACISTS *Report complaints about* *pharmacists to this office*	State Commission of Pharmacy State Office Bldg. 165 Capitol Ave. Hartford, CT 06106	203-566-3917
LICENSING: PHYSICIANS *Report complaints about* *doctors to this office*	CT Board of Medical Examiners 150 Washington St. Hartford, CT 06106	203-566-1035

Type of Agency/Comments	*Organization and Address*	*Phone*
LICENSING: PROFESSIONALS *Licenses other health care professionals*	Bur. of Licensing & Regulation Dept. of Consumer Protection State Office Bldg., Rm. 101 165 Capitol Ave. Hartford, CT 06106	203-566-7177
MEDICAID OFFICE *Administers Medicaid program*	CT Dept. of Human Resources Bur. of Field Operations 1049 Asylum Ave. Hartford, CT 06105	203-566-4580
MEDICARE PART B CARRIER *Process Medicare claims*	Medicare/The Travelers Insurance Co. P.O. Box 5005 Wallingford, CT 06493	203-728-6783 203-237-8592 800-982-6819
MENTAL HEALTH *Provides patient services*	Dept. of Mental Health 90 Washington St. Hartford, CT 06106	203-566-3650
OCCUPATIONAL SAFETY & HEALTH *Inspects worksites*	Div. of Occupational Safety & Health Dept. of Labor 200 Folly Brook Blvd. Wethersfield, CT 06109	203-566-4550
OMBUDSMAN (NURSING HOMES) *Investigates complaints from nursing home residents*	Dept. of Aging 175 Main St. Hartford, CT 06106	203-566-7770
SOCIAL SERVICES *Provides support services and counseling*	Dept. of Human Resources 1049 Asylum Ave. Hartford, CT 06105	203-566-3318
VETERANS AFFAIRS *Provides assistance to veterans*	Veterans Home & Hospital 287 West St. Rocky Hill, CT 06067	203-529-2571
VITAL STATISTICS *Maintains birth & death records*	Div. of Health Policy, Planning & Statistics 150 Washington St. Hartford, CT 06106	203-566-1188

Type of Agency/Comments	*Organization and Address*	*Phone*
VOCATIONAL REHABILITATION *Provides information on rehabilitation programs*	Governor's Committee on Employment of the Handicapped 200 Folly Brook Blvd. Wethersfield, CT 06109	203-566-8061
WELFARE OFFICE *Administers income programs*	Dept. of Income Maintenance 110 Bartholomew Ave. Hartford, CT 06106	203-566-2008
WORKER'S COMPENSATION *Provides income for injured workers*	Worker's Compensation Commission 1890 Dixwell Ave. Hamden, CT 06514	203-789-7783

DISTRICT OF COLUMBIA

Type of Agency/Comments	*Organization and Address*	*Phone*
AGENCY LOCATOR *For Agencies & telephone numbers not listed*	Information Operator District Bldg. 1350 Pennsylvania Ave., NW Washington, DC 20004	202-727-1000
AGING *Provides programs & services to senior citizens*	Office on Aging Executive Office of the Mayor 1424 K St., NW Second Floor Washington, DC 20005	202-724-5622
ALCOHOLISM *Provides assistance to alcohol abusers*	Alcohol & Drug Abuse Admin. Dept. of Human Services 1301 1st St., NE Rm. 319 Washington, DC 20002	202-727-1762
ATTORNEY GENERAL *Chief law enforcement officer*	Attorney General's Office 329 District Bldg. 1350 Pennsylvania Ave., NW Washington, DC 20004	202-727-6248
CHILD WELFARE *Provides services to children and youths*	Family Services Admin. Dept. of Human Services Randall School Bldg. 1st and I Sts., SW Washington, DC 20024	202-727-5947

Type of Agency/Comments	Organization and Address	Phone
COMMUNITY AFFAIRS *Provides programs to communities*	Dept. of Housing and Community Development 1133 North Capitol St., NE Suite 217 Washington, DC 20002	202-535-1500
CONSUMER ADVOCATE *Investigates consumer complaints*	Office of Consumer Affairs Consumer & Regulatory Affairs North Potomac Bldg. 614 H St., NW Washington, DC 20001	202-727-7170
DEPARTMENT OF HEALTH *Supervises health activities in the District*	Commission of Public Health Dept. of Human Services 1660 L St., NW 12th Floor Washington, DC 20009	202-673-7700
DEVELOPMENTAL DISABILITIES *Provides services to the developmentally disabled*	Mental Retardation & Developmental Disabilities Dept. of Human Services 429 O St., NW Washington, DC 20001	202-673-7657
DRUG ABUSE *Provides assistance to drug abusers*	Alcohol & Drug Abuse Admin. Dept. of Human Services 1301 1st St., NE Rm. 319 Washington, DC 20002	202-727-1762
FOOD AND DRUGS *Registers food and drug items*	Business Inspection Div. Dept. of Consumer & Regulatory Affairs North Potomac Bldg., Rm. 616 614 H St., NW Washington, DC 20001	202-724-7260
INSURANCE *Regulates the insurance industry*	Insurance Admin. Dept. of Consumer & Regulatory Affairs P.O. Box 37200 Washington, DC 20013	202-727-8001
LICENSING: DENTISTS *Report complaints about dentists to this office*	Dept. of Consumer & Regulatory Affairs 614 H St., NW Rm. 104 Washington, DC 20001	202-727-7823

Type of Agency/Comments	*Organization and Address*	*Phone*
LICENSING: HOSPITALS *Report complaints about hospitals to this office*	Consumer & Regulatory Affairs Facilities Regulations Admin. 614 H St., NW Washington, DC 20001	202-727-7190
LICENSING: NURSES *Report complaints about nurses to this office*	Dept. of Consumer & Regulatory Affairs Attn: Complaint Div. 614 H St., NW, Rm. 104 Washington, DC 20001	202-727-7107
LICENSING: NURSING HOMES *Report complaints about nursing homes to this office*	Office of Licensing & Certification Nursing Home Div. Dept. of Consumer & Regulatory Affairs 614 H St., NW, Suite 1014 Washington, DC 20001	202-727-7190
LICENSING: PHARMACISTS *Report complaints about pharmacists to this office*	DC Board of Pharmacy 614 H St., NW Washington, DC 20001	202-727-7455
LICENSING: PHYSICIANS *Report complaints about doctors to this office*	Occupational & Professional Licensing Div. 614 H St., NW Rm. 904 Washington, DC 20001	202-727-7480
MAYOR *Citizens access to the mayor*	Office of the Mayor District Bldg. 14th & E Sts., NW Washington, DC 20004	202-727-6319
MEDICAID OFFICE *Administers Medicaid program*	Dept. of Human Services Commission of Public Health Central Referral Bur. Two DC Village La. Washington, DC 20032	202-767-8356
MEDICARE PART B CARRIER *Processes Medicare claims for District residents*	Blue Shield of Pennsylvania P.O. Box 65 Camp Hill, PA 17011	800-233-1124

Type of Agency/Comments	Organization and Address	Phone
MENTAL HEALTH *Provides patient services*	Mental Health Services Admin. Dept. of Human Services A Bldg., Rm. 105 2700 Martin Luther King Ave., SE Washington, DC 20032	202-373-7166
OCCUPATIONAL SAFETY & HEALTH *Inspects worksites*	Occupational Safety & Health Div. Dept. of Employment Services 950 Upshur St., NW Washington, DC 20011	202-576-6339
OMBUDSMAN (GENERAL) *Citizens access to government officials*	Office of Corporation Counsel Executive Office of the Mayor District Bldg., Rm. 329 1350 Pennsylvania Ave., NW Washington, DC 20004	202-727-6248
OMBUDSMAN (NURSING HOMES) *Investigates complaints from nursing home residents*	Office on Aging 1424 K St., NW Washington, DC 20005	202-724-5622
SOCIAL SERVICES *Provides support services and counseling*	Dept. of Human Services 801 North Capitol St., NE Rm. 700 Washington, DC 20002	202-727-0310
VETERANS AFFAIRS *Provides assistance to veterans*	Office of Veterans Affairs Dept. of Human Services Union Center Plaza, Rm. 1211 F 941 North Capitol St., NE Washington, DC 20421	202-727-0328
VITAL STATISTICS *Maintains birth & death records*	Vital Records Branch Dept. of Human Services Chester A. Arthur Bldg. 425 I St., NW Washington, DC 20001	202-727-5319
VOCATIONAL REHABILITATION *Provides information on rehabilitation programs*	Rehab. Services Admin. Dept. of Human Services East Potomac Bldg., Rm. 1100 605 G St., NW Washington, DC 20001	202-737-3227

Type of Agency/Comments	*Organization and Address*	*Phone*
WELFARE *Administers income programs*	Commission on Social Services Dept. of Human Services 609 H St., NE 5th Floor Washington, DC 20024	202-727-5930
WORKER'S COMPENSATION *Provides income for injured workers*	Office of Worker's Compensation 1100 L St., NW Room 9101 Washington, DC 20211	202-724-0702

DELAWARE

Type of Agency/Comments	*Organization and Address*	*Phone*
AGENCY LOCATOR *For Agencies & telephone numbers not listed*	Information Operator Legislative Hall Dover, DE 19901	302-736-4000
AGING *Provides programs & services to senior citizens*	Div. of Aging Dept. of Health & Social Services CT Bldg., State Hospital 1901 North DuPont Hwy. New Castle, DE 19720	302-421-6791
ALCOHOLISM *Provides assistance to alcohol abusers*	Bur. of Alcohol & Drug Abuse Dept. of Health & Social Services CT Bldg., State Hospital 1901 North DuPont Hwy. New Castle, DE 19720	302-421-6107
ATTORNEY GENERAL *Chief law enforcement officer*	Dept. of Justice Elbert N. Carvel Office Bldg. 820 North French St. Wilmington, DE 19801	302-571-3838
CHILD WELFARE *Provides services to children and youths*	Div. of Child Protective Services Dept. of Services for Children Youth & Families 330 East 30th St. Wilmington, DE 19802	302-571-6410

Type of Agency/Comments	*Organization and Address*	*Phone*
COMMUNITY AFFAIRS *Provides programs to communities*	Dept. of Community Affairs Priscilla Bldg. 156 South State St. Dover, DE 19903	302-736-4456
CONSUMER ADVOCATE *Investigates consumer complaints*	Div. of Consumer Affairs Dept. of Community Affairs Elbert N. Carvel Bldg., 4th Floor 820 North French St. Wilmington, DE 19801	302-571-3250
DEPARTMENT OF HEALTH *Supervises health activities in the state*	Div. of Public Health Dept. of Health & Social Services Jessie S. Cooper Bldg. P.O. Box 637 Dover, DE 19901	302-736-4701
DEVELOPMENTAL DISABILITIES *Provides services to the developmentally disabled*	Div. of Mental Retardation Dept. of Health & Social Services Robbins Bldg. 820 Silver Lake Rd. Dover, DE 19901	302-736-4386
DRUG ABUSE *Provides assistance to drug abusers*	Bur. of Alcoholism & Drug Abuse Dept. of Health & Social Services CT Bldg., State Hospital 1901 North DuPont Hwy. New Castle, DE 19720	302-421-6107
FOOD AND DRUGS *Registers food & drug items*	Office of Food Protection Div. of Public Health Robbins Bldg. 802 Silver Lake Blvd. Dover, DE 19903	302-736-4731
GOVERNOR *Citizen's access to the governor*	Office of the Governor Legislative Hall Legislative Ave. Dover, DE 19901	302-736-4101
INSURANCE *Regulates the insurance industry*	Delaware Insurance Dept. Rodney Bldg., Suite 100 841 Silver Lake Blvd. Dover, DE 19903	302-736-4251 800-282-8611

Type of Agency/Comments	*Organization and Address*	*Phone*
LICENSING: DENTISTS *Report complaints about dentists to this office*	Board of Dental Examiners P.O. Box 1401 O'Neill Bldg. Dover, DE 19903	302-736-3029
LICENSING: HOSPITALS *Report complaints about hospitals to this office*	Dept. of Health Office of Health Facilities Licensing & Certification 3000 Newport Gap Pike Wilmington, DE 19808	302-571-3499
LICENSING: NURSES *Report complaints about nurses to this office*	Board of Nursing Margaret O'Neill Bldg. P.O. Box 1401 Dover, DE 19903	302-736-4522
LICENSING: NURSING HOMES *Report complaints about nursing homes to this office*	Office of Health Facility Licensing & Certification Nursing Home Div. Div. of Public Health 3000 Newport Gap Pike Wilmington, DE 19808	302-571-3499
LICENSING: PHARMACISTS *Report complaints about pharmacists to this office*	State Board of Pharmacy Jessie S. Cooper Bldg. Dover, DE 19901	302-736-4708
LICENSING: PHYSICIANS *Report complaints about doctors to this office*	Board of Medical Practice Margaret O'Neill Bldg. Second Floor Dover, DE 19903	302-736-4522
LICENSING: PROFESSIONALS *Licenses other health care professionals*	Div. of Business & Occupational Regulation Margaret O'Neill Bldg. Court & Federal Sts. Dover, DE 19903	302-736-4522
MEDICAID OFFICE *Administers Medicaid program*	Dept. of Health & Social Services Div. of Economic Services Biggs Bldg. State Hospital, P.O. Box 906 New Castle, DE 19720	302-421-6139
MEDICARE PART B CARRIER *Processes Medicare claims for Delaware*	Pennsylvania Blue Shield P.O. Box 890200 Camp Hill, PA 17089-0200	800-851-3535

Type of Agency/Comments	*Organization and Address*	*Phone*
MENTAL HEALTH *Provides services to patients*	Div. of Alcoholism, Drug Abuse & Mental Health CT Bldg., State Hospital 1901 North DuPont Hwy. New Castle, DE 19720	302-421-6107
OCCUPATIONAL SAFETY & HEALTH *Inspects worksites*	Occupational Safety & Health Industrial Affairs Div. Elbert N. Carvel Bldg. 820 North French St. Wilmington, DE 19801	302-571-3908

OMBUDSMAN (NURSING
    HOMES)
 	
Investigates complaints
    (Northern Office)
	Div. of Aging
	Delaware State Hospital
	1901 North DuPont Hwy.
	New Castle, DE 19720
		302-421-6791

OMBUDSMAN (NURSING
    HOMES)
 	
Investigates complaints
    (Southern Office)
	Div. of Aging
	Milford State Services Center
	11-13 Church St.
	Milford, DE 19963
		302-422-1386

SOCIAL SERVICES
 	
Provides support services
    and counseling
	Div. of Economic Services
	Dept. of Health & Social
	    Services
	CT Bldg., State Hospital
	1901 North DuPont Hwy.
	New Castle, DE 19720
		302-421-6734

VETERANS AFFAIRS *Provides assistance to* *veterans*	Veterans Affairs Agency Old State House P.O. Box 1401 Dover, DE 19903	302-736-2792
VITAL STATISTICS *Maintains birth & death* *records*	Office of Vital Statistics Div. of Public Health Robbins Bldg. 802 Silver Lake Blvd. Dover, DE 19903	302-736-4721

VOCATIONAL
    REHABILITATION
 	
Provides information on
    rehabilitation programs
	Div. of Vocational Rehab.
	Dept. of Labor
	Elwyn Delaware Bldg.
	321 East 11th St.
	Wilmington, DE 19801
		302-571-3915

Type of Agency/Comments	*Organization and Address*	*Phone*
WELFARE *Administers income programs*	Div. of Economic Services Dept. of Health & Social Services CT Bldg., State Hospital 1901 North DuPont Hwy. New Castle, DE 19720	302-421-6734
WORKER'S COMPENSATION *Provides income for injured workers*	Industrial Accident Board Dept. of Labor Elbert N. Carvel Bldg. 820 North French St. Wilmington, DE 19801	302-571-3594

FLORIDA

Type of Agency/Comments	*Organization and Address*	*Phone*
AGENCY LOCATOR *For Agencies & telephone numbers not listed*	Information Operator State Capitol Tallahassee, FL 32301	904-488-1234

AGING
 	
Provides programs & services for senior citizens
	Aging & Adult Services
	  Programs
	Dept. of Health & Rehab.
	  Services
	Bldg. II, Rm. 323
	1317 Winewood Blvd.
	Tallahassee, FL 32301
		904-488-8922

ALCOHOLISM
 	
Provides assistance to alcohol abusers
	Alcohol & Drug Abuse
	  Program
	Dept. of Health & Rehab.
	  Services
	Bldg. VI, Rm. 156
	1317 Winewood Blvd.
	Tallahassee, FL 32399-0700
		904-488-0900

ATTORNEY GENERAL *Chief law enforcement officer*	Attorney General's Office Dept. of Legal Affairs The Capitol Plaza Level I Tallahassee, FL 32399-1050	904-487-1963

Type of Agency/Comments	*Organization and Address*	*Phone*
CHILD WELFARE *Provides services to children and youths*	Children, Youth & Family Services Dept. of Health & Rehab. Services Bldg. VIII 1317 Winewood Blvd. Tallahassee, FL 32399	904-488-8763
COMMUNITY AFFAIRS *Provides programs to communities*	Dept. of Community Affairs The Rhyne Bldg. 2740 Centerview Dr. Tallahassee, FL 32399	904-488-8466
CONSUMER ADVOCATE *Investigates complaints*	Div. of Consumer Services Dept. of Agriculture & Consumer Services Mayo Bldg., Rm. 508 407 South Calhoun St. Tallahassee, FL 32301	904-488-2226 800-327-3382
DEPARTMENT OF HEALTH *Supervises health activities in the state*	Health Program Office Dept. of Health & Rehab. Services Bldg. I, Rm. 115 1323 Winewood Blvd. Tallahassee, FL 32399-0700	904-488-4115
DEVELOPMENTAL DISABILITIES *Provides services to the developmentally disabled*	Governor's Commission on Developmental Disabilities Bldg. V, Rm. 215 1311 Winewood Blvd. Tallahassee, FL 32399-0700	904-488-4257
DRUG ABUSE *Provides assistance to drug abusers*	Alcohol & Drug Abuse Program Dept. of Health & Rehab. Services Bldg. VI, Rm. 156 1317 Winewood Blvd. Tallahassee, FL 32399	904-488-0900
FOOD AND DRUGS *Register food and drug items*	Food Grades & Standards Bur. Div. of Inspection Dept. of Agriculture & Consumer Services 3125 Conner Bldg., M-A Tallahassee, FL 32399-1650	904-488-3951

Type of Agency/Comments	*Organization and Address*	*Phone*
GOVERNOR *Citizen's access to the* *governor*	Office of the Governor State Capitol Tallahassee, FL 32399	904-488-5394
INSURANCE *Regulates insurance industry*	Office of the Commissioner Dept. of Insurance The Capitol Plaza Level II Tallahassee, FL 32399-0300	904-488-3440
LICENSING: DENTISTS *Report complaints about* *dentists to this office*	Dept. of Professional Regulation 1940 North Monroe St. Suite 225 Tallahassee, FL 32399-0750	904-488-6015

LICENSING: HOSPITALS
 	
Report complaints about
hospitals to this office
	Dept. of Health & Rehab.
	  Services
	Office of Licensure &
	  Certification
	2727 Mahan Dr.
	Tallahassee, FL 32308
		904-487-3513

LICENSING: NURSES *Report complaints about* *nurses to this office*	Dept. of Professional Regulation 1940 North Monroe St. Tallahassee, FL 32399-0750	904-487-2252
LICENSING: NURSING HOMES *Report complaints about* *nursing homes to this* *office*	Nursing Home Licensure Office Licensure & Certification Div. of Health 2727 Mahan Dr. Tallahassee, FL 32308	904-487-3513
LICENSING: PHARMACISTS *Report complaints about* *pharmacists to this office*	Board of Pharmacy 1940 North Monroe St. Tallahassee, FL 32399-0775	904-488-7546
LICENSING: PHYSICIANS *Report complaints about* *doctors to this office*	Board of Medical Examiners 1940 North Monroe St. Tallahassee, FL 32399-0750	904-488-0595

Type of Agency/Comments	*Organization and Address*	*Phone*
LICENSING: PROFESSIONALS *Licenses other health care professionals*	Dept. of Professional Regulation Old Courthouse Square Bldg. 1940 North Monroe St. Tallahassee, FL 32399-0750	904-487-2252
MEDICAID OFFICE *Administers Medicaid program*	Dept. of Health & Rehab. Services Medicaid Program Office Bldg. VI, Rm. 233 1317 Winewood Blvd. Tallahassee, FL 32399-0750	904-488-3560
MEDICARE PART B CARRIER *Processes Medicare claims*	Medicare Blue Shield of FL P.O. Box 2525 Jacksonville, FL 32231	904-355-3680 800-333-7586

MENTAL HEALTH
 	
Provides patient services
	Alcohol, Drug Abuse &
	  Mental Health Program
	  Office
	Bldg. VI, Rm. 183
	1317 Winewood Blvd.
	Tallahassee, FL 32301
		904-488-8304

OCCUPATIONAL SAFETY &
  HEALTH
 	
Inspects worksites
	Bur. of Industrial Safety &
	  Health
	Dept. of Labor & Employment
	  Security
	349 Forrest Bldg.
	2728 Centerview Dr.
	Tallahassee, FL 32399
		904-488-7421

OMBUDSMAN (GENERAL) *Citizens access to government officials*	Citizen's Assistance Program Exec. Office of the Governor The Capitol, Rm. 207S Tallahassee, FL 32399	904-488-7146

OMBUDSMAN (NURSING
  HOMES)
 	
*Investigates complaints from
nursing home residents*
	Long Term Care Ombudsman
	  Council
	Bldg. I, Rm. 308
	1323 Winewood Blvd.
	Tallahassee, FL 32399-0700
		904-488-6190

SOCIAL SERVICES *Provides support services and counseling*	Div. of Economic Services Dept. of Health & Rehab. Services Bldg. V, Rm. 205 1311 Winewood Blvd. Tallahassee, FL 32399-0700	904-488-3271

Type of Agency/Comments	*Organization and Address*	*Phone*
VETERANS AFFAIRS *Provides assistance to veterans*	Div. of Veterans Affairs Dept. of Admin. 144 First Ave. South P.O. Box 1437 St. Petersburg, FL 33731	813-898-4443
VITAL STATISTICS *Maintains birth & death records*	Office of Vital Statistics Dept. of Health & Rehab. Services Porter Bldg. 1217 Pearl St. Jacksonville, FL 32231	904-359-6971

VOCATIONAL
    REHABILITATION
 	
Provides information on rehabilitation programs
	Div. of Vocational Rehab.
	Dept. of Labor & Employment
	    Security
	1709-A Mahan Dr.
	Tallahassee, FL 32399
		904-488-6210

WELFARE *Administers income programs*	Bur. of Public Assistance Div. of Economic Security Bldg. VI, Rm. 432 1317 Winewood Blvd. Tallahassee, FL 32399	904-487-1597

WORKER'S COMPENSATION
 	
Provides income for injured workers
	Div. of Worker's
	    Compensation
	Dept. of Labor & Employment
	    Security
	301 Forrest Bldg.
	2728 Centerview Dr.
	Tallahassee, FL 32399
		904-488-2514

GEORGIA

Type of Agency/Comments	*Organization and Address*	*Phone*
AGENCY LOCATOR *For Agencies & telephone numbers not listed*	Information Operator State Capitol Atlanta, GA 30334	404-656-2000
AGING *Provides programs & services to senior citizens*	Office of Aging Dept. of Human Resources 878 Peachtree St., NE Suite 632 Atlanta, GA 30309	404-894-5333

Type of Agency/Comments	*Organization and Address*	*Phone*
ALCOHOLISM *Provides assistance to alcohol abusers*	Div. of Mental Health, Retardation & Substance Abuse Dept. of Human Resources 878 Peachtree St., NE, Suite 319 Atlanta, GA 30309	404-894-4785
ATTORNEY GENERAL *Chief law enforcement officer*	Attorney General's Office Law Dept. Judicial Bldg., Rm. 132 40 Capitol Sq., SW Atlanta, GA 30334	404-656-4586
CHILD WELFARE *Provides services to children and youths*	Assistance Payments Bur. Div. of Family & Children Services Dept. of Human Resources 878 Peachtree St., NE, Suite 406 Atlanta, GA 30309	404-894-5505
COMMUNITY AFFAIRS *Provides programs to communities*	Dept. of Community Affairs Equitable Bldg., Rm. 1200 100 Peachtree St., NW Atlanta, GA 30303	404-656-3836
CONSUMER ADVOCATE *Investigates consumer complaints*	Governor's Office of Consumer Affairs Floyd Memorial Bldg. East Tower, Plaza Level 2 Martin Luther King, Jr., Dr., SE Atlanta, GA 30334	404-656-1790
DEPARTMENT OF HEALTH *Supervises health activities in the state*	Div. of Public Health Dept. of Human Resources 878 Peachtree St., NE Suite 201 Atlanta, GA 30309	404-894-7505
DEVELOPMENTAL DISABILITIES *Provides services to the developmentally disabled*	Dept. of Human Resources 878 Peachtree St., NW Suite 306 Atlanta, GA 30309	404-894-6313

Type of Agency/Comments	Organization and Address	Phone
DRUG ABUSE *Provides assistance to drug abusers*	Div. of Mental Health, Retardation & Substance Abuse Dept. of Human Resources 878 Peachtree St., NE, Suite 319 Atlanta, GA 30309	404-894-4785
FOOD AND DRUGS *Registers drug items in state*	Drugs & Narcotics Agency Board of Pharmacy Mitchell-Pryor Bldg., Rm. 503 166 Pryor St., SW Atlanta, GA 30303	404-656-5100
FOOD AND DRUGS *Registers food items in state*	Consumer Protection Field Forces Agriculture Bldg., Rm. 306 19 Martin Luther King, Jr., Dr., SE Atlanta, GA 30334	404-656-3627
GOVERNOR *Citizens access to the governor*	Office of the Governor State Capitol Rm. 203 Atlanta, GA 30334	404-656-1776
INSURANCE *Regulates the insurance industry*	Office of the Commissioner Floyd Memorial Bldg. 716 West Tower 2 Martin Luther King, Jr., Dr., SE Atlanta, GA 30334	404-656-2056
LICENSING: DENTISTS *Report complaints about dentists to this office*	Board of Dentistry 166 Pryor St., SW Atlanta, GA 30303	404-656-3925
LICENSING: HOSPITALS *Report complaints about hospitals to this office*	Dept. of Human Resources Standards & Licensure Section Attn: Complaints Unit 878 Peachtree St., NE Atlanta, GA 30309	404-894-5137
LICENSING: NURSES *Report complaints about nurses to this office*	Board of Nursing 166 Pryor St., SW Atlanta, GA 30303	404-656-3943

Type of Agency/Comments	*Organization and Address*	*Phone*
LICENSING: NURSING HOMES *Report complaints about nursing homes to this office*	Standards & Licensure Unit Office of Regulatory Services 878 Peachtree St., NE Suite 803 Atlanta, GA 30309	404-894-5137
LICENSING: PHARMACISTS *Report complaints about pharmacists to this office*	Board of Pharmacy 166 Pryor St., SW Atlanta, GA 30303	404-656-3912
LICENSING: PHYSICIANS *Report complaints about doctors to this office*	Composite State Board of Medical Examiners 166 Pryor St., SW Atlanta, GA 30303	404-656-3913
LICENSING: PROFESSIONALS *Licenses other health care professionals*	Examining Boards Div. Office of the Secretary of State 166 Pryor St., SW Atlanta, GA 30303	404-656-3900
MEDICAID OFFICE *Administers Medicaid program*	Dept. of Medical Assistance West Tower 2 Martin Luther King, Jr., Dr., SE Atlanta, GA 30334	404-656-4479
MEDICARE PART B CARRIER *Processes Medicare claims*	Medicare/Aetna Life & Casualty P.O. Box 3018 Savannah, GA 31402-3018	912-927-0934 800-727-0827

MENTAL HEALTH
 	
Provides patient services
	Mental Health Services Section
	Div. of Mental Health,
	  Retardation & Substance
	  Abuse
	878 Peachtree St., NE,
	  Suite 304
	Atlanta, GA 30309
		404-894-6307

OCCUPATIONAL SAFETY & HEALTH *Inspects worksites*	Environmental Health Section Div. of Public Health Dept. of Human Resources 878 Peachtree St., NE, Suite 100 Atlanta, GA 30309	404-894-6644
OMBUDSMAN (GENERAL) *Citizens access to government officials*	Governor's Office of Consumer Affairs 2 Martin Luther King, Jr., Dr., SE Atlanta, GA 30334	404-656-1760

Type of Agency/Comments	Organization and Address	Phone
OMBUDSMAN (NURSING HOMES) *Investigates complaints from nursing home residents*	Office of Aging Dept. of Human Resources 878 Peachtree St., NE Rm. 642 Atlanta, GA 30309	404-894-5336
SOCIAL SERVICES *Provides support services and counseling*	Div. of Family & Children Services Dept. of Human Resources 878 Peachtree St., NE Rm. 624 Atlanta, GA 30309	404-894-2009
VETERANS AFFAIRS *Provides assistance to veterans*	Dept. of Veterans Services Floyd Memorial Bldg. East Tower, Suite 970 205 Butler St., SE Atlanta, GA 30334	404-656-2300
VITAL STATISTICS *Maintains birth & death records*	Vital Records Service Div. of Public Health Health Bldg., Rm. 217-H 47 Trinity Ave., SW Atlanta, GA 30334	404-656-4750
VOCATIONAL REHABILITATION *Provides information on rehabilitation programs*	Div. of Rehab. Services Dept. of Human Services 878 Peachtree St., NE Atlanta, GA 30309	404-894-6670
WELFARE *Administers income programs*	Div. of Family & Children Services Dept. of Human Resources 878 Peachtree St., NE Rm. 421 Atlanta, GA 30309	404-894-6386
WORKER'S COMPENSATION *Provides income for injured workers*	Board of Worker's Compensation One CNN Center South Tower Suite 1000 Atlanta, GA 30303	404-656-2034

HAWAII

Type of Agency/Comments	*Organization and Address*	*Phone*
AGENCY LOCATOR *For Agencies & telephone* *numbers not listed*	Information Operator State Capitol 415 South Beretania St. Honolulu, HI 96813	808-548-2211
AGING *Provides programs &* *services to senior citizens*	Executive Office on Aging Office of the Governor 335 Merchant St. Rm. 241 Honolulu, HI 96813	808-548-2593
ALCOHOLISM *Provides assistance to* *alcohol abusers*	Alcohol & Drug Abuse Branch Dept. of Health 1270 Queen Emma St. Suite 706 Honolulu, HI 96801	808-548-4280
ATTORNEY GENERAL *Chief law enforcement* *officer*	Dept. of Attorney General State Capitol 415 South Beretania St. Rm. 405 Honolulu, HI 96813	808-548-4740
CHILD WELFARE *Provides services to children* *and youths*	Office of Children & Youth Office of the Governor Kapuaiwa Bldg. 426 Queen St. Honolulu, HI 96802	808-548-7582
COMMUNITY AFFAIRS *Provides programs to* *communities*	Community Development 　Authority Planning & Economic 　Development 677 Ala Moana Blvd. Suite 1001 Honolulu, HI 96813	808-548-7180
CONSUMER ADVOCATE *Investigates consumer* *complaints*	Office of Consumer Protection Dept. of Commerce & 　Consumer Affairs 828 Fort St. Mall Suite 600B Honolulu, HI 96813	808-548-2560
DEPARTMENT OF HEALTH *Supervises health activities* *in the state*	Dept. of Health Kinau Hall 1250 Punchbowl St. Honolulu, HI 96801	808-548-6505

Type of Agency/Comments	Organization and Address	Phone
DEVELOPMENTAL DISABILITIES *Provides assistance to the developmentally disabled*	Developmental Disabilities Div. Dept. of Health 741-A Sunset Ave., Rm. 208 Honolulu, HI 96816	808-732-0935
DRUG ABUSE *Provides assistance to drug abusers*	Drug Control Program Office of Narcotics Enforcement Dept. of Health 1100 Ward Ave., Suite 875 Honolulu, HI 96814	808-548-7186
FOOD AND DRUGS *Registers food & drug items*	Food Products Section Sanitation Branch Dept. of Health 591 Ala Moana Blvd. Honolulu, HI 96813	808-548-3280
GOVERNOR *Citizen's access to the governor*	Office of the Governor State Capitol Bldg. Fourth Floor 415 Beretania St. Honolulu, HI 96813	808-548-2651
INSURANCE *Regulates the insurance industry*	Insurance Div. Dept. of Commerce 250 S. King St. Honolulu, HI 96811	808-548-6522
LICENSING: DENTISTS *Report complaints about dentists to this office*	Professional & Vocational Licensing P.O. Box 3469 Honolulu, HI 96801	808-548-4100
LICENSING: HOSPITALS *Report complaints about hospitals to this office*	Dept. of Health Hospital & Medical Facilities Branch P.O. Box 3378 Honolulu, HI 96801	808-548-5935
LICENSING: NURSES *Report complaints about nurses to this office*	Board of Nursing P.O. Box 3469 Honolulu, HI 96809	808-548-3086

Type of Agency/Comments	Organization and Address	Phone
LICENSING: NURSING HOMES *Report complaints about nursing homes to this office*	Nursing Home Licensure Office Hospital & Medical Facilities Branch Dept. of Health P.O. Box 3378 Honolulu, HI 96801	808-548-5935
LICENSING: PHARMACISTS *Report complaints about pharmacists to this office*	Board of Pharmacy P.O. Box 3469 Honolulu, HI 96801	808-548-8590
LICENSING: PHYSICIANS *Report complaints about doctors to this office*	Board of Medical Examiners P.O. Box 3469 Honolulu, HI 96801	808-548-4100
LICENSING: PROFESSIONALS *Licenses other health care professionals*	Professional & Vocational Licensing Div. Dept. of Commerce & Consumer Affairs Kamamalu Bldg. 1010 Richards St. Honolulu, HI 96801	808-548-6520
MEDICAID OFFICE *Administers Medicaid program*	Health Care Admin. Div. Dept. of Social Services & Housing P.O. Box 339 Honolulu, HI 96809	808-548-6584
MEDICARE PART B CARRIER *Process Medicare claims*	Aetna Life & Casualty P.O. Box 3947 Honolulu, HI 96812	808-524-1240 800-272-5242
MENTAL HEALTH *Provides patient services*	Mental Health Div. Dept. of Health 1250 Punchbowl St. Honolulu, HI 96801	808-548-6335
OCCUPATIONAL SAFETY & HEALTH *Inspects worksites*	Occupational Safety & Health Div. Dept. of Labor & Industry Keelikolani Bldg. 830 Punchbowl St., Rm. 423 Honolulu, HI 96813	808-548-7510

Type of Agency/Comments	*Organization and Address*	*Phone*
OMBUDSMAN (GENERAL) *Citizens access to government officials*	Office of the Ombudsman 465 South King St. Fourth Floor Honolulu, HI 96813	808-548-7811
OMBUDSMAN (NURSING HOMES) *Investigates complaints from nursing home residents*	Executive Office on Aging Office of the Governor 335 Merchant St. Rm. 241 Honolulu, HI 96813	808-548-2593
SOCIAL SERVICES *Provides support services and counseling*	Dept. of Social Services Queen Liliuokalani Bldg. Rm. 209 1390 Miller St. Honolulu, HI 96809	808-548-6260
VETERANS SERVICES *Provides assistance to veterans*	Adult Services Program Development Office Dept. of Human Services Queen Liliuokalani Bldg. 1390 Miller St. Honolulu, HI 96809	808-548-5976
VITAL STATISTICS *Maintains birth & death records*	Research & Statistics Office Dept. of Health 1250 Punchbowl St. Honolulu, HI 96801	808-548-6454
VOCATIONAL REHABILITATION *Provides information on rehabilitation programs*	Commission on the Handicapped Dept. of Health Old Federal Court House 335 Merchant St. Honolulu, HI 96813	808-548-7606
WELFARE *Administers income programs*	Public Welfare Division Dept. of Social Services 1390 Miller St. Honolulu, HI 96809	808-548-5908
WORKER'S COMPENSATION *Provides income for injured workers*	Disability Compensation Div. Dept. of Labor Keelikolani Bldg. 830 Punchbowl St. Honolulu, HI 96812	808-548-5414

IDAHO

Type of Agency/Comments	Organization and Address	Phone
AGENCY LOCATOR *For Agencies & telephone numbers not listed*	Information Operator State Capitol 700 West Jefferson St. Boise, ID 83720	208-334-2411
AGING *Provides programs & services to senior citizens*	Office on Aging State Office Bldg., Rm. 114 700 West State St. Boise, ID 83720	208-334-3833
ALCOHOLISM *Provides assistance to alcohol abusers*	Bur. of Social Services Dept. of Health & Welfare Towers Bldg., Seventh Floor 450 West State St. Boise, ID 83720	208-334-5934
ATTORNEY GENERAL *Chief law enforcement officer*	Attorney General's Office 210 State Capitol Bldg. 700 West Jefferson St. Boise, ID 83720	208-334-2400
CHILD WELFARE *Provides services to children and youths*	Bur. of Social Services Dept. of Health & Welfare Towers Bldg. 450 West State St. Boise, ID 83720	208-334-5688
COMMUNITY AFFAIRS *Provides programs to communities*	Dept. of Commerce Hall of Mirrors 700 West State St. Boise, ID 83720	208-334-2470
CONSUMER ADVOCATE *Investigates consumer complaints*	Attorney General's Office State Capitol Bldg. Rm. 210 700 West Jefferson St. Boise, ID 83720	208-334-2400
DEPARTMENT OF HEALTH *Supervises health activities in the state*	Div. of Health Dept. of Health & Welfare Towers Bldg., Fourth Floor 450 West State St. Boise, ID 83720	208-334-5930

Type of Agency/Comments	Organization and Address	Phone
DEVELOPMENTAL DISABILITIES *Provides services to the developmentally disabled*	Council on Developmental Disabilities Towers Bldg. 450 West State St. Boise, ID 83720	208-334-5509
DRUG ABUSE *Provides assistance to drug abusers*	Bur. of Social Services Dept. of Health & Welfare Towers Bldg., Seventh Floor 450 West State St. Boise, ID 83720	208-334-5934
FOOD AND DRUGS *Registers food and drug items*	Bur. of Preventive Medicine Div. of Health Towers Bldg., Fourth Floor 450 West State St. Boise, ID 83720	208-334-5930
GOVERNOR *Citizens access to the governor*	Office of the Governor State Capitol Bldg. Second Floor Boise, ID 83720	208-334-2249
INSURANCE *Regulates the insurance industry*	Dept. of Insurance State Office Bldg. 500 South 10th St. Boise, ID 83720	208-334-2250
LICENSING: DENTISTS *Report complaints about dentists to this office*	State Board of Dentistry State House Mail Boise, ID 83720	208-334-2369
LICENSING: HOSPITALS *Report complaints about hospitals to this office*	Dept. of Health & Welfare Facilities Standards Program 450 West State St. Boise, ID 83720	208-334-6626
LICENSING: NURSES *Register complaints about nurses to this office*	Idaho Board of Nursing 500 South 10th St. Suite 102 Boise, ID 83720	208-334-3110
LICENSING: NURSING HOMES *Report complaints about nursing homes to this office*	Nursing Home Licensure Office Facilities Standards & Development Dept. of Health & Welfare 450 West State St. Boise, ID 83720	208-334-6626

Type of Agency/Comments	Organization and Address	Phone
LICENSING: PHARMACISTS *Report complaints about pharmacists to this office*	Board of Pharmacy 500 South 10th St. Boise, ID 83720	208-334-2356
LICENSING: PHYSICIANS *Report complaints about doctors to this office*	State Board of Medicine 500 South 10th St. Suite 103 Boise, ID 83720	208-334-2822
LICENSING: PROFESSIONALS *Licenses other health care professionals*	Bur. of Occupational Licenses Dept. of Self-Governing Agencies 2417 Bank Dr. Rm. 312 Boise, ID 83705	208-334-3233
MEDICAID OFFICE *Administers Medicaid program*	Dept. of Health & Welfare Bur. of Medical Assistance 450 West State St. Sixth Floor Boise, ID 83720	208-334-5794
MEDICARE PART B CARRIER *Processes Medicare claims*	Equicor P.O. Box 8048 Boise, ID 83707	208-342-7763 800-632-6574
MENTAL HEALTH *Provides services to patients*	Bur. of Mental Health Dept. of Health & Welfare 450 West State St. Boise, ID 83720	208-334-5531
OCCUPATIONAL SAFETY & HEALTH *Inspects worksites*	Dept. of Labor & Industrial Services 277 North Sixth St. Boise, ID 83720	208-334-3950
OMBUDSMAN (NURSING HOMES) *Investigates complaints from nursing home residents*	Office on Aging State Office Bldg. Rm. 108 Boise, ID 83720	208-334-3833
SOCIAL SERVICES *Provides support services and counseling*	Bur. of Social Services Dept. of Health & Welfare Towers Bldg., Seventh Floor 450 West State St. Boise, ID 83720	208-334-5934

Type of Agency/Comments	Organization and Address	Phone
VETERANS AFFAIRS *Provides assistance to veterans*	Div. of Veterans Services Dept. of Health & Welfare 320 Collins Rd. Boise, ID 83707	208-334-5000
VITAL STATISTICS *Maintains birth & death records*	Bur. of Vital Statistics Div. of Health Towers Bldg. 450 West State St. Boise, ID 83720	208-334-5976
VOCATIONAL REHABILITATION *Provides information on rehabilitation programs*	Div. of Vocational Rehab. State Board of Education Leon B. Jordan Bldg., Rm. 150 650 West State St. Boise, ID 83720	208-334-3390
WELFARE *Administers income programs*	Div. of Welfare Dept. of Health & Welfare Towers Bldg. 450 West State St. Boise, ID 83720	208-334-6630
WORKER'S COMPENSATION *Provides income for injured workers*	Industrial Commission Industrial Admin. Bldg. 317 Main St. Boise, ID 83720	208-334-6000

ILLINOIS

Type of Agency/Comments	Organization and Address	Phone
AGENCY LOCATOR *For Agencies & telephone numbers not listed*	Information Operator State Capitol Springfield, IL 62706	217-782-2000
AGING *Provides programs for senior citizens*	Dept. on Aging Old Herndon Bldg. 421 East Capitol Ave. Springfield, IL 62701	217-785-3356
ALCOHOLISM *Provides assistance to alcohol abusers*	Dept. of Alcoholism & Substance Abuse State of Illinois Center, Rm. 5-600 100 West Randolph St. Chicago, IL 60601	312-814-3840

Type of Agency/Comments	Organization and Address	Phone
ATTORNEY GENERAL *Chief law enforcement officer*	Office of Attorney General 500 South Second St. Springfield, IL 62706	217-782-1090
CHILD WELFARE *Provides services to children and youths*	Dept. of Children & Family Services 406 East Monroe St. Springfield, IL 62701	217-785-2509
COMMUNITY AFFAIRS *Provides programs to communities*	Program Admin. Dept. of Commerce & Community Affairs 620 East Adams St. Springfield, IL 62701	217-782-6136
CONSUMER ADVOCATE *Investigates consumer complaints*	Consumer Protection Div. Office of Attorney General 500 South Second St. Springfield, IL 62706	217-782-9011
DEPARTMENT OF HEALTH *Supervises health activities in the state*	Dept. of Public Health 535 West Jefferson St. Springfield, IL 62761	217-782-4977
DEVELOPMENTAL DISABILITIES *Provides services to the developmentally disabled*	Dept. of Mental Health & Developmental Disabilities William G. Stratton Bldg. 401 Spring St. Springfield, IL 62706	217-782-0638
DRUG ABUSE *Provides assistance to drug abusers*	Dept. of Alcoholism & Substance Abuse State of Illinois Center, Rm. 5-600 100 West Randolph St. Chicago, IL 60610	312-814-3840
FOOD AND DRUGS *Registers food and drug items*	Div. of Food, Drugs & Dairies Dept. of Public Health 525 West Jefferson St. Springfield, IL 62761	217-785-2439
GOVERNOR *Citizens access to the governor*	Office of the Governor State Capitol Rm. 207 Springfield, IL 62706	217-782-7355

Type of Agency/Comments	Organization and Address	Phone
INSURANCE *Regulates the insurance industry*	Dept. of Insurance Bicentennial Bldg. 320 West Washington St. Springfield, IL 62767	217-782-4515
LICENSING: DENTISTS *Report complaints about dentists to this office*	Dept. of Registration & Education Attn: Dental Unit State of Illinois Center Rm. 9-300 100 West Randolph St. Chicago, IL 60601	312-814-4481
LICENSING: HOSPITALS *Report complaints about hospitals to this office*	Dept. of Public Health Div. of Health Facilities 525 West Jefferson St. Fourth Floor Springfield, IL 62761	217-782-7412
LICENSING: NURSES *Report complaints about nurses to this office*	Illinois Nursing Committee Dept. of Registration & Education 320 West Washington St. Springfield, IL 62786	217-782-7116
LICENSING: NURSING HOMES *Report complaints about nursing homes to this office*	Nursing Home Licensure Office Dept. of Public Health Facilities & Quality of Care 525 West Jefferson St. Springfield, IL 62761	217-782-5180
LICENSING: PHARMACISTS *Report complaints about pharmacists to this office*	Board of Pharmacy Dept. of Registration & Education 320 West Washington St. Springfield, IL 62786	217-782-0458
LICENSING: PHYSICIANS *Report complaints about doctors to this office*	Dept. of Registration & Education 320 West Washington St. Springfield, IL 62786	217-785-0800
LICENSING: PROFESSIONALS *Licenses other health care professionals*	Dept. of Registration & Education 320 West Washington St. Springfield, IL 62786	217-785-0800

Type of Agency/Comments	*Organization and Address*	*Phone*
MEDICAID OFFICE *Administers Medicaid program*	Dept. of Public Aid Div. of Medical Programs 201 South Grand Ave. East Springfield, IL 62743	217-782-2570
MEDICARE PART B CARRIER *Processes Medicare claims*	Medicare Claims Blue Cross & Shield of Illinois P.O. Box 4422 Marion, IL 62959	312-938-8000 800-642-6930
MENTAL HEALTH *Provides patient services*	Dept. of Mental Health & Developmental Disabilities William G. Stratton Bldg. 401 South Spring St. Springfield, IL 62706	217-782-7179
OMBUDSMAN (GENERAL) *Citizens access to government officials*	Office of Citizens Assistance & Consumer Affairs Office of the Governor 201 West Monroe St. Springfield, IL 62706	217-782-0244
OMBUDSMAN (NURSING HOMES) *Investigates complaints from nursing home residents*	Dept. on Aging 421 East Capitol Ave. Springfield, IL 62701	217-785-3140
SOCIAL SERVICES *Provides support services and counseling*	Dept. of Children & Family Services 406 East Monroe St. Springfield, IL 62701	217-785-2509
VETERANS AFFAIRS *Provides assistance to veterans*	Dept. of Veterans Affairs 208 West Cook St. P.O. Box 19432 Springfield, IL 62794	217-782-6641
VITAL STATISTICS *Maintains birth & death records*	Div. of Vital Records Office of Admin. Services Dept. of Public Health 605 West Jefferson St. Springfield, IL 62702	217-782-6553
VOCATIONAL REHABILITATION *Provides information on rehabilitation programs*	Dept. of Rehab. Services 623 East Adams St. P.O. Box 1587 Springfield, IL 62705	217-782-2093 800-233-DIAL

Type of Agency/Comments	*Organization and Address*	*Phone*
WELFARE *Administers income programs*	Dept. of Public Aid Harris II Bldg. 100 South Grand Ave. East Springfield, IL 62762	217-782-6716
WORKER'S COMPENSATION *Provides income for injured workers*	Illinois Industrial Commission State of Illinois Center Rm. 8-272 100 West Randolph St. Chicago, IL 60601	312-814-6500 800-972-4604

INDIANA

Type of Agency/Comments	*Organization and Address*	*Phone*
AGENCY LOCATOR *For Agencies & telephone numbers not listed*	Information Operator State House 200 West Washington St. Indianapolis, IN 46204	317-232-3140
AGING *Provides programs for senior citizens*	Dept. of Human Services 251 North Illinois St. P.O. Box 7083 Indianapolis, IN 46207	317-232-7000
ALCOHOLISM *Provides assistance to alcohol abusers*	Div. of Addiction Services Dept. of Mental Health 117 East Washington St. Indianapolis, IN 46204	317-232-7816
ATTORNEY GENERAL *Chief law enforcement officer*	Office of the Attorney General State House Rm. 219 200 West Washington St. Indianapolis, IN 46204	317-232-6201
CHILD WELFARE *Provides services to children and youths*	Child Welfare/Social Services Div. Dept. of Public Welfare 141 South Meridian St. 6th Floor Indianapolis, IN 46225	317-232-4420
COMMUNITY AFFAIRS *Provides programs to communities*	Dept. of Human Services 251 North Illinois St. P.O. Box 7083 Indianapolis, IN 46207	317-232-7000

Type of Agency/Comments	Organization and Address	Phone
CONSUMER ADVOCATE *Investigates consumer complaints*	Consumer Protection Div. Attorney General's Office State House Rm. 219 200 West Washington St. Indianapolis, IN 46204	317-232-6330
DEPARTMENT OF HEALTH *Supervises health activities in the state*	State Board of Health Health Bldg. 1330 West Michigan St. P.O. Box 1964 Indianapolis, IN 46206	317-633-8400
DEVELOPMENTAL DISABILITIES *Provides services to the developmentally disabled*	Div. of Developmental Disabilities Dept. of Mental Health 117 East Washington St. Indianapolis, IN 46204	317-232-7836
DRUG ABUSE *Provides assistance to drug abusers*	Div. of Addiction Services Dept. of Mental Health 117 East Washington St. Indianapolis, IN 46204	317-232-7816
FOOD AND DRUGS *Registers food and drug items*	Bur. of Laboratories State Board of Health Health Bldg. 1330 West Michigan St. Indianapolis, IN 46206	317-633-0720
GOVERNOR *Citizens access to governor*	Office of the Governor State House Rm. 206 Indianapolis, IN 46204	317-232-4584
INSURANCE *Regulates insurance industry*	Office of the Commissioner Dept. of Insurance 311 West Washington St. Indianapolis, IN 46204	317-232-2386
LICENSING: DENTISTS *Report complaints about dentists to this office*	Indiana Consumer Protection Health Professionals Bur. One American Square, Suite 1020 Indianapolis, IN 46282	317-232-2960
LICENSING: HOSPITALS *Report complaints about hospitals to this office*	Indiana Board of Health Div. of Acute Care Services 1330 West Washington St. Rm. 236 Indianapolis, IN 46206	317-633-8472

Type of Agency/Comments	*Organization and Address*	*Phone*
LICENSING: NURSES *Report complaints about nurses to this office*	Consumer Protection Div. 219 State House Indianapolis, IN 46204	317-232-6330
LICENSING: NURSING HOMES *Report complaints about nursing homes to this office*	Nursing Home Licensure Office Div. of Health Facilities Indiana State Board of Health 1330 West Michigan St. Indianapolis, IN 46206	317-633-8442
LICENSING: PHARMACISTS *Report complaints about pharmacists to this office*	Indiana Board of Pharmacy One American Square Suite 1020 Indianapolis, IN 46282	317-232-2960
LICENSING: PHYSICIANS *Report complaints about doctors to this office*	Indiana Consumer Protection Div. 219 State House Indianapolis, IN 46204	317-232-6330
LICENSING: PROFESSIONALS *Licenses other health care professionals*	Professional Licensing Agency State Office Bldg., Rm. 1021 100 North Senate Ave. Indianapolis, IN 46204	317-232-2980
MEDICAID OFFICE *Administers Medicaid program*	Indiana Dept. of Public Welfare Medical Assistance Unit 100 North Senate Ave. Rm. 702 Indianapolis, IN 46204	317-232-4333
MEDICARE PART B CARRIER *Processes Medicare claims*	Medicare Part B Assoc. Insurance Companies P.O. Box 7073 Indianapolis, IN 46207	317-842-4151 800-622-4792
MENTAL HEALTH *Provides patient services*	Office of the Commissioner Dept. of Mental Health 117 East Washington St. Indianapolis, IN 46204	317-232-7844

OCCUPATIONAL SAFETY &
  HEALTH
 	
Inspects worksites
	Div. of Industrial Hygiene &
	  Radiological Health
	State Board of Health
	1330 West Michigan St.
	Indianapolis, IN 46206
		317-633-0147

Type of Agency/Comments	Organization and Address	Phone
OMBUDSMAN (GENERAL) *Citizens access to government officials*	Office of the Ombudsman Dept. of Commerce One North Capitol St. Suite 700 Indianapolis, IN 46204	317-232-8798
OMBUDSMAN (NURSING HOMES) *Investigates complaints from nursing home residents*	Dept. of Human Services 251 North Illinois St. P.O. Box 7083 Indianapolis, IN 46207	317-232-1223
SOCIAL SERVICES *Provides support services and counseling*	Dept. of Human Services 251 North Illinois St. P.O. Box 7083 Indianapolis, IN 46207	317-232-7000
VETERANS AFFAIRS *Provides assistance to veterans*	Dept. of Veterans Affairs State Office Bldg., Rm. 707 100 North Senate Ave. Indianapolis, IN 46204	317-232-3910
VITAL STATISTICS *Maintains birth & death records*	Public Health Statistics State Board of Health Health Bldg. 1330 West Michigan St., Rm. 236 Indianapolis, IN 46206	317-633-8512
VOCATIONAL REHABILITATION *Provides information on rehabilitation programs*	Dept. of Human Services 251 North Illinois St. P.O. Box 7083 Indianapolis, IN 46207	317-232-7000
WELFARE *Administers income programs*	Dept. of Public Welfare State Office Bldg., Rm. 701 100 North Senate Ave. Indianapolis, IN 46204	317-232-4705
WORKER'S COMPENSATION *Provides income for injured workers*	Industrial Board State Office Bldg., Rm. 601 100 North Senate Ave. Indianapolis, IN 46204	317-232-3808

IOWA

Type of Agency/Comments	Organization and Address	Phone
AGENCY LOCATOR *For Agencies & telephone numbers not listed*	Information Operator State Capitol Bldg. 10th & Grand Ave. Des Moines, IA 50319	515-281-5011
AGING *Provides programs & services to senior citizens*	Dept. of Elder Affairs Jewett Bldg., Rm. 236 914 Grand Ave. Des Moines, IA 50319	515-281-5187
ALCOHOLISM *Provides assistance to alcohol abusers*	Substance Abuse Div. Dept. of Public Health Lucas State Office Bldg., 4th Floor 321 East 12th St. Des Moines, IA 50319	515-281-3641
ATTORNEY GENERAL *Chief law enforcement officer*	Attorney General's Office Hoover State Office Bldg. 1300 East Walnut St. Des Moines, IA 50319	515-281-5164
CHILD WELFARE *Provides services to children and youths*	Bur. of Children's Services Div. of Social Services Hoover State Office Bldg. 1300 East Walnut St. Des Moines, IA 50319	515-281-5521
COMMUNITY AFFAIRS *Provides programs to communities*	Div. for Community Progress Dept. of Economic Development 200 East Grand Avenue Des Moines, IA 50309	515-281-3536
CONSUMER ADVOCATE *Investigates consumer complaints*	Consumer Protection Div. Attorney General's Office Hoover State Office Bldg. 1300 East Walnut St. Des Moines, IA 50319	515-281-5926
DEPARTMENT OF HEALTH *Supervises health activities in the state*	Dept. of Public Health Lucas State Office Bldg. 321 East 12th St. Des Moines, IA 50319	515-281-5605

Type of Agency/Comments	*Organization and Address*	*Phone*
DEVELOPMENTAL DISABILITIES *Provides services to the developmentally disabled*	Div. of Mental Health & Developmental Disabilities Hoover State Office Bldg., 5th Floor 1300 East Walnut St. Des Moines, IA 50319	515-281-6003
DRUG ABUSE *Provides assistance to drug abusers*	Substance Abuse Div. Dept. of Public Health Lucas State Office Bldg. 321 East 12th St. Des Moines, IA 50319	515-281-3641
FOOD AND DRUGS *Registers food & drug items*	Bur. of Food & Licensing Div. of Investigation Dept. of Inspection & Appeals Lucas State Office Bldg., 3rd Floor Des Moines, IA 50319	515-281-4192
GOVERNOR *Citizens access to the governor*	Office of the Governor State Capitol Des Moines, IA 50319	515-281-3150
INSURANCE *Regulates the insurance industry*	Div. of Insurance Dept. of Commerce Lucas State Office Bldg. 321 East 12th St. Des Moines, IA 50319	515-281-5705
LICENSING: DENTISTS *Report complaints about dentists to this office*	Board of Dental Examiners Exec. Hills West 1209 East Court Des Moines, IA 50319	515-281-5157
LICENSING: HOSPITALS *Report complaints about hospitals to this office*	Dept. of Health Div. of Health Facilities Dept. of Inspections & Appeals Lucas State Office Bldg., 3rd Floor 321 East 12th St. Des Moines, IA 50319	515-281-4120
LICENSING: NURSES *Report complaints about nurses to this office*	Board of Nursing State Capitol Complex 1223 East Court Ave. Des Moines, IA 50319	515-281-3255

Type of Agency/Comments	Organization and Address	Phone
LICENSING: NURSING HOMES *Report complaints about nursing homes to this office*	Nursing Home Licensure Office Dept. of Health Div. of Health Facilities 321 East 12th St. Des Moines, IA 50319	515-281-4115
LICENSING: PHARMACISTS *Report complaints about pharmacists to this office*	Board of Pharmacy 1209 East Court Exec. Hills West Des Moines, IA 50319	515-281-5944
LICENSING: PHYSICIANS *Report complaints about doctors to this office*	Board of Medical Examiners Exec. Hills West 1209 East Court Des Moines, IA 50319	515-281-5171
LICENSING: PROFESSIONALS *Licenses other health care professionals*	Dept. of Public Health Lucas State Office Bldg. 321 East 12th St. Des Moines, IA 50319	515-281-5787
MEDICAID OFFICE *Administers Medicaid program*	Bur. of Medical Services Dept. of Human Services Hoover State Office Bldg. Des Moines, IA 50319	515-281-8794
MEDICARE PART B CARRIER *Processes Medicare claims*	Blue Shield of Iowa 636 Grand Ave. Des Moines, IA 50309	515-245-4785 800-532-1285
MENTAL HEALTH *Provides patient services*	Div. of Mental Health Dept. of Human Services Hoover State Office Bldg., 5th Floor 1300 East Walnut St. Des Moines, IA 50319	515-281-6003

OCCUPATIONAL SAFETY &
   HEALTH
 	
Inspects worksites
	Employment Appeal Board/
	   OSHA
	Dept. of Inspections &
	   Appeals
	Lucas State Office Bldg.
	321 East 12th St.
	Des Moines, IA 50319
		515-281-4159

Type of Agency/Comments	*Organization and Address*	*Phone*
OMBUDSMAN (GENERAL) *Handles citizens complaints*	Citizens' Aide/Ombudsman Citizens' Aide Office 515 East 12th St. Des Moines, IA 50319	515-281-3592 800-358-5510
OMBUDSMAN (NURSING HOMES) *Investigates complaints from nursing home residents*	Dept. of Elder Affairs 236 Jewett Bldg. 914 Grand Ave. Des Moines, IA 50319	515-281-5187
SOCIAL SERVICES *Provides support services and counseling*	Dept. of Human Services Div. of Social Services Hoover State Office Bldg. 1300 East Walnut St. Des Moines, IA 50319	515-281-5758
VETERANS AFFAIRS *Provides assistance to veterans*	Veterans Affairs Div. Dept. of Public Defense 7700 NW Beaver Dr. Johnston, IA 50131	515-278-9333
VITAL STATISTICS *Maintains birth & death records*	Vital Records Section Dept. of Public Health Lucas State Office Bldg. 321 East 12th St. Des Moines, IA 50319	515-281-5604
VOCATIONAL REHABILITATION *Provides information on rehabilitation programs*	Commission, Persons w/ Disabilities Dept. of Human Rights Lucas State Office Bldg., 1st Floor 321 East 12th St. Des Moines, IA 50319	515-281-5238
WELFARE *Administers income programs*	Bur. of Economic Assistance Dept. of Human Services Hoover State Office Bldg. 1300 East Walnut St. Des Moines, IA 50319	515-281-8629
WORKER'S COMPENSATION *Provides income for injured workers*	Div. of Industrial Services Dept. of Employment Services 1000 East Grand Ave. Des Moines, IA 50319	515-281-5934

KANSAS

Type of Agency/Comments	Organization and Address	Phone
AGENCY LOCATOR *For Agencies & telephone numbers not listed*	Information Operator State House Topeka, KS 66612	913-296-0111
AGING *Provides programs & services for senior citizens*	Dept. on Aging Docking State Office Bldg. 915 SW Harrison Topeka, KS 66612	913-296-4986
ALCOHOLISM *Provides assistance to alcohol abusers*	Alcohol-Drug Abuse Services Div. of Social & Rehab. Biddle Bldg., 2nd Floor 300 SW Oakley Topeka, KS 66606	913-296-3925
ATTORNEY GENERAL *Chief law enforcement officer*	Attorney General's Office Kansas Judicial Center 2nd Floor 301 West 10th St. Topeka, KS 66612	913-296-2215
CHILD WELFARE *Provides services to children and youths*	Children in Need of Care Dept. of Social & Rehab. Smith-Wilson Bldg. 300 SW Oakley Topeka, KS 66606	913-296-3282
COMMUNITY AFFAIRS *Provides programs to communities*	Community Development Div. Dept. of Economic Development 400 West 8th St. Suite 500 Topeka, KS 66603	913-296-3485
CONSUMER ADVOCATE *Investigates consumer complaints*	Consumer Protection & Anti- Trust Div. Office of Attorney General 301 West 10th St. Topeka, KS 66612	913-296-3751
DEPARTMENT OF HEALTH *Supervises health activities in the state*	Div. of Health Dept. of Health & Environment Bldg. 740, Forbes Field Topeka, KS 66620	913-296-1500

Type of Agency/Comments	*Organization and Address*	*Phone*
DEVELOPMENTAL DISABILITIES *Provides services to the developmentally disabled*	Kansas Planning Council on Developmental Disabilities Dept. of Social & Rehab. Docking State Office Bldg. 915 Harrison St. Topeka, KS 66612	913-296-2608
DRUG ABUSE *Provides assistance to drug abusers*	Alcohol-Drug Abuse Services Dept. of Social & Rehab. Biddle Bldg., 2nd Floor 300 SW Oakley Topeka, KS 66606	913-296-3925
FOOD AND DRUGS *Registers food and drug items*	Bur. of Food, Drug & Lodging Dept. of Health & Environment 109 SW 9th St., Suite 604 Topeka, KS 66612	913-296-5600
GOVERNOR *Citizens access to the governor*	Office of the Governor State House 2nd Floor Topeka, KS 66612	913-296-4034
INSURANCE *Regulates the insurance industry*	Insurance Dept. State Office Bldg. 420 West 9th St. Topeka, KS 66612	913-296-3071
LICENSING: DENTISTS *Report complaints about dentists to this office*	Board of Dental Examiners 4301 Huntoon Suite 4 Lower Level Topeka, KS 66604	913-273-0780
LICENSING: HOSPITALS *Report complaints about hospitals to this office*	Dept. of Health & Environment Bur. of Adult & Child Facilities Landon State Office Bldg. 900 SW Jackson Topeka, KS 66612	913-296-1265
LICENSING: NURSES *Report complaints about nurses to this office*	Board of Nursing 900 SW Jackson Suite 551-S Topeka, KS 66612	913-296-4929

Type of Agency/Comments	Organization and Address	Phone
LICENSING: NURSING HOMES *Report complaints about nursing homes to this office*	Dept. of Health & Environment Bur. of Adult & Child Care Landon State Office Bldg. 900 SW Jackson, Suite 1001 Topeka, KS 66612	913-296-1240
LICENSING: PHARMACISTS *Report complaints about pharmacists to this office*	State Board of Pharmacy 900 Jackson, Rm. 513 Topeka, KS 66612	913-296-4056
LICENSING: PHYSICIANS *Report complaints about doctors to this office*	Board of Healing Arts 900 SW Jackson Suite 553 Topeka, KS 66612	913-296-7413
MEDICAID OFFICE *Administers Medicaid program*	Dept. of Social & Rehab. Services Div. of Income Maintenance Docking State Office Bldg. Rm. 624 South Topeka, KS 66612	913-296-3981
MEDICARE PART B CARRIER *Processes Medicare claims for rest of state*	Blue Shield of Kansas City P.O. Box 239 Topeka, KS 66601	800-432-3531 913-232-3773
MEDICARE PART B CARRIER *Processes Medicare claims for Johnson & Wyandotte counties*	Blue Shield of Kansas City P.O. Box 169 Kansas City, MO 64141	800-892-5900 816-561-0900
MENTAL HEALTH *Provides patient services*	Mental Health & Retardation Services & Developmental Disabilities State Office Bldg., 5th Floor 915 Harrison St. Topeka, KS 66612	913-296-3471
OCCUPATIONAL SAFETY & HEALTH *Inspects worksites*	Industrial Safety & Health Dept. of Human Resources 512 West 6th St. Topeka, KS 66603	913-296-4386

Type of Agency/Comments	Organization and Address	Phone
OMBUDSMAN (GENERAL) *Handles citizens complaints*	Constituent Services Office of the Governor State House, 2nd Floor East Wing Topeka, KS 66612	913-296-4030
OMBUDSMAN (NURSING HOMES) *Investigates complaints from nursing home residents*	Dept. on Aging Docking State Office Bldg. 915 SW Harrison St. Topeka, KS 66612	913-296-4986
SOCIAL SERVICES *Provides support services and counseling*	Dept. of Social & Rehab. Services State Office Bldg. Sixth Floor 915 Harrison St. Topeka, KS 66612	913-296-3271
VETERANS AFFAIRS *Provides assistance to veterans*	Commission on Veterans Affairs Jayhawk Towers, Suite 701 700 SW Jackson St. Topeka, KS 66603	913-296-3976
VITAL STATISTICS *Maintains birth & death records*	Office of Vital Statistics Div. of Information Systems Landon State Office Bldg. 900 SW Jackson St. Topeka, KS 66612	913-296-1415
VOCATIONAL REHABILITATION *Provides information on rehabilitation programs*	KACEH Dept. of Human Resources 1400 SW Topeka Ave. Topeka, KS 66612	913-296-1722

WELFARE
 	
Administers income program
	Income Maintenance &
	   Medical Services
	Dept. of Social & Rehab.
	   Services
	Docking State Office Bldg.
	915 Harrison St.
	Topeka, KS 66612
		913-296-6750

Type of Agency/Comments	*Organization and Address*	*Phone*
WORKER'S COMPENSATION *Provides income for injured workers*	Div. of Worker's Compensation Dept. of Human Resources Landon State Office Bldg. 900 SW Jackson St. Topeka, KS 66612	913-296-3441

KENTUCKY

Type of Agency/Comments	*Organization and Address*	*Phone*
AGENCY LOCATOR *For Agencies & telephone numbers not listed*	Information Operator State Capitol Bldg. Frankfort, KY 40601	502-564-2500
AGING *Provides programs & services for senior citizens*	Div. for Aging Services Dept. for Social Services Human Resources Bldg., 6th Floor 275 East Main St. Frankfort, KY 40621	502-564-6930
ALCOHOLISM *Provides assistance to alcohol abusers*	Div. of Substance Abuse Dept. of Health Services Health Services Bldg. 275 East Main St. Frankfort, KY 40621	502-564-2880
ATTORNEY GENERAL *Chief law enforcement officer*	Office of Attorney General State Capitol Bldg. Room 116 Frankfort, KY 40601	502-564-7600
CHILD WELFARE *Provides services to children and youths*	Div. of Family Services Dept. of Social Services Human Resources Bldg., 6th Floor 275 East Main St. Frankfort, KY 40621	502-564-6852
COMMUNITY AFFAIRS *Provides programs to communities*	Div. of Community Programs Dept. of Local Government Office of the Governor Capitol Plaza, 2nd Floor Frankfort, KY 40601	502-564-2382

Type of Agency/Comments	*Organization and Address*	*Phone*
CONSUMER ADVOCATE *Investigates consumer complaints*	Div. of Consumer Protection Office of Attorney General Exec. Bldg. 209 St. Clair St. Frankfort, KY 40601	502-564-2200
DEPARTMENT OF HEALTH *Supervises health activities in the state*	Office of the Commissioner Cabinet for Human Resources Health Services Bldg. 275 East Main St. Frankfort, KY 40621	502-564-3970
DEVELOPMENTAL DISABILITIES *Provides services to the developmentally disabled*	Div. of Mental Retardation Cabinet for Human Resources Health Services Bldg. 275 East Main St. Frankfort, KY 40621	502-564-7700
DRUG ABUSE *Provides assistance to drug abusers*	Div. of Substance Abuse Dept. of Mental Health Health Services Bldg. 275 East Main St. Frankfort, KY 40621	502-564-2880
FOOD AND DRUGS *Registers food & drug items*	Div. of Food & Sanitation Dept. of Health Services Health Services Bldg. 275 East Main St. Frankfort, KY 40621	502-564-3722
GOVERNOR *Citizens access to the governor*	Office of the Governor State Capitol Room 100 Frankfort, KY 40601	502-564-2611
INSURANCE *Regulates the insurance industry*	Dept. of Insurance Fitzgerald Bldg. 229 West Main St. Frankfort, KY 40602	502-564-3630
LICENSING: DENTISTS *Report complaints about dentists to this office*	Board of Dental Examiners 2106 Bardstown Rd. Louisville, KY 40205	502-451-6832

Type of Agency/Comments	Organization and Address	Phone
LICENSING: HOSPITALS *Report complaints about hospitals to this office*	Cabinet for Human Resources Div. of Licensing & Regulation 275 East Main St. Fourth Floor Frankfort, KY 40621	502-564-2800
LICENSING: NURSES *Report complaints about nurses to this office*	Kentucky Board of Nursing 4010 Dupont Circle Suite 430 Louisville, KY 40207	502-897-5143
LICENSING: NURSING HOMES *Report complaints about nursing homes to this office*	Office of the Inspector General Div. of Licensing & Regulation Human Resources Bldg., 4 East 275 East Main St. Frankfort, KY 40621	502-564-2800
LICENSING: PHARMACISTS *Report complaints about pharmacists to this office*	Board of Pharmacy 1228 US 127 South Frankfort, KY 40601	502-564-3833
LICENSING: PHYSICIANS *Report complaints about doctors to this office*	Board of Medical Licensure 400 Sherburn Lane, Suite 2222 Louisville, KY 40207	502-896-1516
LICENSING: PROFESSIONALS *Licenses other health care professionals*	Div. of Occupational & Professional Licensing Berry Hill Annex P.O. Box 456 Frankfort, KY 40602	502-564-3296
MEDICAID OFFICE *Administers Medicaid program*	Cabinet for Human Resources Dept. for Medicaid Services 275 East Main St. Frankfort, KY 40621	502-564-4321
MEDICARE PART B CARRIER *Processes Medicare claims*	Blue Cross/Shield Kentucky 100 East Vine St. Lexington, KY 40507	606-223-1441 800-432-9255
MENTAL HEALTH *Provides patient services*	Div. of Mental Health Dept. for Mental Health Services Health Services Bldg. 275 East Main St. Frankfort, KY 40621	502-564-4448

Type of Agency/Comments	Organization and Address	Phone
OCCUPATIONAL SAFETY & HEALTH *Inspects worksites*	Occupational Safety & Health Review Commission 4 Millcreek Park Rte. 3, Millville Rd. Frankfort, KY 40601	502-564-6892
OMBUDSMAN (NURSING HOMES) *Investigates complaints from nursing home residents*	Dept. of Social Services Div. of Aging Services C Human Resources Bldg., 6 West 275 East Main St. Frankfort, KY 40621	502-564-6930
SOCIAL SERVICES *Provides support services and counseling*	Dept. for Social Services Cabinet for Human Resources Human Resources Bldg., 6th Floor 275 East Main St. Frankfort, KY 40621	502-564-4650
VETERANS AFFAIRS *Provides assistance to veterans*	Center for Veterans Affairs Dept. for Military Affairs 600 Federal Place Room 136-J Louisville, KY 40202	502-588-4447
VITAL STATISTICS *Maintains birth & death records*	Office of Vital Statistics Dept. for Health Services Human Resources Bldg., 1st Floor 275 East Main St. Frankfort, KY 40621	502-564-4212
VOCATIONAL REHABILITATION *Provides information on rehabilitation programs*	Office of Vocational Rehab. Dept. of Education Capital Plaza Tower 9th Floor Frankfort, KY 40601	502-564-4440
WELFARE *Administers income programs*	Dept. for Social Insurance Human Resources Bldg. 275 East Main St. Frankfort, KY 40621	502-564-3703
WORKER'S COMPENSATION *Provides income for injured workers*	Worker's Compensation Board Dept. of Worker's Claims 1270 Perimeter Park West US Hwy. 60 Frankfort, KY 40601	502-564-5550

LOUISIANA

Type of Agency/Comments	Organization and Address	Phone
AGENCY LOCATOR *For Agencies & telephone numbers not listed*	Information Operator State Capitol 900 Riverside North Baton Rouge, LA 70804	504-342-6600
AGING *Provides programs & services to senior citizens*	Office of Elderly Affairs Office of the Governor 4528 Bennington Ave. Baton Rouge, LA 70898	504-925-1700
ALCOHOLISM *Provides assistance to alcohol abusers*	Alcohol & Drug Abuse Office Dept. of Health & Human Resources 2744-B Wooddale Blvd. P.O. Box 53129 Baton Rouge, LA 70892	504-922-0730
ATTORNEY GENERAL *Chief law enforcement officer*	Attorney General's Office State Capitol 900 Riverside North Baton Rouge, LA 70804	504-342-7013

CHILD WELFARE
 	
Provides services to children and youths
	Div. of Children, Youth and
	  Family Services
	Dept. of Health & Human
	  Services
	1967 North St.
	Baton Rouge, LA 70821
		504-342-2297

COMMUNITY AFFAIRS *Provides programs to communities*	Dept. of Urban/Community Affairs Capitol Annex, Rm. 501 Riverside Mall P.O. Box 94455 Baton Rouge, LA 70804	504-342-9787
CONSUMER ADVOCATE *Investigates consumer complaints*	Consumer Protection Section Dept. of Justice P.O. Box 94005, Capitol Station Baton Rouge, LA 70804	504-342-7013
DEPARTMENT OF HEALTH *Supervises health activities in the state*	Office of Public Health Services Dept. of Hospitals 325 Loyola Ave. P.O. Box 60630 Baton Rouge, LA 70160	504-568-5052

Type of Agency/Comments	*Organization and Address*	*Phone*
DEVELOPMENTAL DISABILITIES *Provides services to the developmentally disabled*	Office of Mental Regardation and Developmental Disabilities Schwing Bldg., Rm. 305 721 Government St. Baton Rouge, LA 70802	504-342-6811
DRUG ABUSE *Provides assistance to drug abusers*	Alcohol & Drug Abuse Office Dept. of Health & Human Resources 2744-B Wooddale Blvd. P.O. Box 53129 Baton Rouge, LA 70892	504-922-0730
FOOD AND DRUGS *Registers food & drug items*	Food and Drug Unit State Office Bldg., Rm. 414 325 Loyola Ave. New Orleans, LA 70112	504-568-5402
GOVERNOR *Citizens access to the governor*	Office of the Governor State Capitol 900 Riverside North P.O. Box 94004 Baton Rouge, LA 70804	504-342-7015
INSURANCE *Regulates the insurance industry*	Dept. of Insurance Insurance Bldg. 950 North 5th St. P.O. Box 94214 Baton Rouge, LA 70804	504-342-5900
LICENSING: DENTISTS *Report complaints about dentists to this office*	Board of Dental Examiners 1515 Poydras St. Suite 2240 New Orleans, LA 70112	504-568-8574
LICENSING: HOSPITALS *Report complaints about hospitals to this office*	Dept. of Health & Human Resources Div. of Licensing and Certification P.O. Box 3767 Baton Rouge, LA 70821	504-342-6448
LICENSING: NURSES *Report complaints about nurses to this office*	Board of Nursing 907 Pere Marquette Bldg. 150 Baronne St. New Orleans, LA 70112	504-568-5464

Type of Agency/Comments	Organization and Address	Phone
LICENSING: NURSING HOMES *Report complaints about nursing homes to this office*	Nursing Home Licensure Office DHH, Bureau of Health Services Health Standards Financing Section Baton Rouge, LA 70821	504-342-5774
LICENSING: PHARMACISTS *Report complaints about pharmacists to this office*	State Board of Pharmacy 5615 Corporate Blvd. Baton Rouge, LA 70808	504-925-6496
LICENSING: PHYSICIANS *Report complaints about doctors to this office*	Board of Medical Examiners 830 Union St. Suite 100 Baton Rouge, LA 70112	504-524-6763
LICENSING: PROFESSIONALS *Licenses other health care professionals*	Div. of Licensing & Certification Dept. of Health & Human Resources 1201 Capitol Access Rd. Baton Rouge, LA 70822	504-342-6448
MEDICAID OFFICE *Administers Medicaid program*	Dept. of Health & Human Resources Office of Family Security P.O. Box 91030 Baton Rouge, LA 70821-9030	504-342-3891
MEDICARE PART B CARRIER *Processes Medicare claims*	Blue Cross/Blue Shield of Louisiana Medicare Admin. P.O. Box 95024 Baton Rouge, LA 70895	504-272-1242 800-462-9666
MENTAL HEALTH *Provides patient services*	Office of Mental Health Dept. of Health & Human Resources 755 Riverside Baton Rouge, LA 70821	504-342-6717
OCCUPATIONAL SAFETY & HEALTH *Inspects worksites*	Occupational Safety & Health Survey Dept. of Labor Employment Security Bldg. 1001 North 23rd St. Baton Rouge, LA 94094	504-342-3126

Type of Agency/Comments	*Organization and Address*	*Phone*
OMBUDSMAN (NURSING HOMES) *Investigates complaints from nursing home residents*	Governor's Office of the Elderly P.O. Box 80374 Baton Rouge, LA 70898	504-925-1700
SOCIAL SERVICES *Provides support services and counseling*	Div. of Children, Youth & Family Dept. of Health & Human Resources 1967 North St. P.O. Box 3318 Baton Rouge, LA 70821	504-342-2297
VETERANS AFFAIRS *Provides assistance to veterans*	Dept. of Veterans Affairs Hoover Bldg., Rm. 211-A 8312 Florida Blvd. Baton Rouge, LA 70804	504-342-5863
VITAL STATISTICS *Maintains birth & death records*	Vital Records Section Dept. of Health & Human Resources State Office Bldg., Rm. 103 325 Loyola Ave. New Orleans, LA 70160	504-568-8353
VOCATIONAL REHABILITATION *Provides information on rehabilitation programs*	Div. of Rehab. Services Dept. of Health & Human Resources 1755 Florida Blvd. Baton Rouge, LA 70804	504-342-9409
WELFARE *Administers income programs*	Office of Family Security Dept. of Health & Human Resources 755 Riverside North P.O. Box 94065 Baton Rouge, LA 70804	504-342-3947
WORKER'S COMPENSATION *Provides income for injured workers*	Office Worker's Compensation Admin. Dept. of Labor 1001 North 23rd St. Baton Rouge, LA 70806	504-342-7555 800-824-4592

MAINE

Type of Agency/Comments	*Organization and Address*	*Phone*
AGENCY LOCATOR *For Agencies & telephone numbers not listed*	Information Operator State House Augusta, ME 04333	207-289-1110
AGING *Provides programs & services to senior citizens*	Bur. of Maine's Elderly Dept. of Human Services One Amherst St. State House Station 11 Augusta, ME 04333	207-289-2561
ALCOHOLISM *Provides assistance to alcohol abusers*	Office of Alcoholism Prevention Dept. of Human Services 235 State St. State House Station 11 Augusta, ME 04333	207-289-2781
ATTORNEY GENERAL *Chief law enforcement officer*	Dept. of the Attorney General State Office Bldg., 6th Floor State House Station 6 Augusta, ME 04333	207-289-3661
CHILD WELFARE *Provides services to children and youths*	Div. of Child & Family Services Human Services Bldg. 221 State St. State House Station 11 Augusta, ME 04333	207-289-5060
COMMUNITY AFFAIRS *Provides programs to communities*	Div. of Community Services Hallowell Annex State House Station 73 Augusta, ME 04333	207-289-3771

CONSUMER ADVOCATE
 	
Investigates consumer complaints
	Bur. of Consumer Credit
	  Protection
	Dept. of Professional and
	  Financial Regulation
	Hallowell Annex
	State House Station 35
	Augusta, ME 04333
		207-582-8718

Type of Agency/Comments	*Organization and Address*	*Phone*
DEPARTMENT OF HEALTH *Supervises health activities in the state*	Bur. of Health Dept. of Human Services 157 Capitol St. State House Station 11 Augusta, ME 04333	207-289-3201
DEVELOPMENTAL DISABILITIES *Provides services to the developmentally disabled*	Planning & Advisory Council on Developmental Disabilities Nash Bldg. 102 Sewall St. Augusta, ME 04333	207-289-4213
DRUG ABUSE *Provides assistance to drug abusers*	Office of Drug Abuse Prevention Dept. of Human Services 235 State St. State House Station 11 Augusta, ME 04333	207-289-2781
FOOD AND DRUGS *Registers food & drug items*	Div. of Regulation Dept. of Agriculture Deering Bldg., AMHI Complex State House Station 28 Augusta, ME 04333	207-289-3841
GOVERNOR *Citizens access to the governor*	Office of the Governor State House Station 1 Augusta, ME 04333	207-289-2531
INSURANCE *Regulates the insurance industry*	Bur. of Insurance Dept. of Professional and Financial Regulation State House Station 34 Augusta, ME 04333	207-582-8707
LICENSING: DENTISTS *Report complaints about dentists to this office*	Board of Dental Examiners State House Station 143 Augusta, ME 04333	207-289-3333
LICENSING: HOSPITALS *Report complaints about hospitals to this office*	Dept. of Human Resources Div. of Licensing & Certification 249 Western Ave. State House Station 11 Augusta, ME 04333	207-289-2606

Type of Agency/Comments	*Organization and Address*	*Phone*
LICENSING: NURSES *Report complaints about nurses to this office*	Board of Nursing 295 Water St. Augusta, ME 04330	207-289-5324
LICENSING: NURSING HOMES *Report complaints about nursing homes to this office*	Nursing Home Licensure Office Div. of Licensure & Certification 249 Water St. State House Station 11 Augusta, ME 04333	207-289-2606
LICENSING: PHARMACISTS *Report complaints about pharmacists to this office*	Commission on Pharmacy State House Station 35 Augusta, ME 04333	207-582-8723
LICENSING: PHYSICIANS *Report complaints about doctors to this office*	Board of Registration in Medicine State House Station 137 Augusta, ME 04333	207-289-3601
LICENSING: PROFESSIONALS *Licenses other health care professionals*	Div. of Licensing & Enforcement Dept. of Professional & Financial Regulation State House Station 35 Augusta, ME 04333	207-582-8723
MEDICAID OFFICE *Administers Medicaid program*	Bur. of Medical Services Dept. of Human Services State House Station 11 Augusta, ME 04333	207-289-2736
MEDICARE PART B CARRIER *Administers Medicare claims*	Blue Shield of Massachusetts P.O. Box 1010 Biddeford, ME 04005	800-492-0919 207-282-5991
MENTAL HEALTH *Provides services to patients*	Bur. of Mental Health Dept. of Mental Health-Retardation State Office Bldg., Rm. 411 State House Station 40 Augusta, ME 04333	207-289-4230

Type of Agency/Comments	*Organization and Address*	*Phone*
OCCUPATIONAL SAFETY & HEALTH *Inspects worksites*	Bur. of Labor Standards Div. of Safety Dept. of Labor State House Station 82 Augusta, ME 04333	207-289-2591
OMBUDSMAN (GENERAL) *Provides assistance to citizens*	Div. of Community Services Exec. Dept. Hallowell Annex State House Station 73 Augusta, ME 04333	207-289-3771
OMBUDSMAN (NURSING HOMES) *Investigates complaints*	LTC Ombudsman Program Maine Committee on Aging State House Station 127 Augusta, ME 04333	207-289-3658
SOCIAL SERVICES *Provides support services and counseling*	Bur. of Social Services Dept. of Human Services Human Services Bldg. 221 State St. Augusta, ME 04333	207-289-5060
VETERANS AFFAIRS *Provides assistance to veterans*	Bur. of Veterans Services Dept. of Defense & Veterans Services State Office Bldg. State House Station 117 Augusta, ME 04333	207-289-4060
VITAL STATISTICS *Maintains birth & death records*	Office of Data, Research & Vital Records Dept. of Human Services 151 Capitol St. State House Station 11 Augusta, ME 04333	207-289-3001
VOCATIONAL REHABILITATION *Provides information on rehabilitation programs*	Bur. of Rehab. 32 Winthrop St. Augusta, ME 04330	207-289-2266

Type of Agency/Comments	Organization and Address	Phone
WELFARE *Administers income programs*	Bur. of Income Maintenance Dept. of Human Services State House Station 11 Augusta, ME 04333	207-289-2415
WORKER'S COMPENSATION *Provides income for injured workers*	Worker's Compensation Commission Deering Bldg. AMHI Complex State House Station 27 Augusta, ME 04333	207-289-3751

MARYLAND

Type of Agency/Comments	Organization and Address	Phone
AGENCY LOCATOR *For Agencies & telephone numbers not listed*	Information Operator State House Annapolis, MD 21401	301-974-2000
AGING *Provides programs & services to senior citizens*	Office on Aging State Office Bldg. 301 West Preston St. Baltimore, MD 21201	301-225-1100
ALCOHOLISM *Provides assistance to alcohol abusers*	Alcohol Control Commission Dept. of Health & Mental Hygiene H. R. O'Connor Office Bldg. 201 West Preston St. Baltimore, MD 21201	301-225-6441
ATTORNEY GENERAL *Chief law enforcement officer*	Law Department Attorney General's Office Munsey Bldg. Seven North Calvert St. Baltimore, MD 21202	301-576-6300
CHILD WELFARE *Provides services to children and youths*	Office for Children & Youth Exec. Dept. 1502 State Office Bldg. 301 West Preston St. Baltimore, MD 21201	301-225-1460

Type of Agency/Comments	*Organization and Address*	*Phone*
COMMUNITY AFFAIRS *Provides programs to communities*	Community Development Admin. Dept. of Economic and Community Development 45 Calvert St. Annapolis, MD 21401	301-974-3161
CONSUMER ADVOCATE *Investigates consumer complaints*	Consumer Protection Div. Attorney General's Office Munsey Bldg. 7 North Calvert St. Baltimore, MD 21202	301-528-8662
DEPARTMENT OF HEALTH *Supervises health activities in the state*	Dept. of Health and Mental Hygiene 201 West Preston St. Baltimore, MD 21201	301-225-6500
DEVELOPMENTAL DISABILITIES *Provides services to the developmentally disabled*	Developmental Disabilities Admin. H. R. O'Connor Office Bldg. 201 West Preston St. Baltimore, MD 21201	301-225-5600
DRUG ABUSE *Provides assistance to drug abusers*	Drug Abuse Admin. Dept. of Health & Mental Hygiene H. R. O'Connor Office Bldg. 201 West Preston St. Baltimore, MD 21201	301-225-6441
FOOD AND DRUGS *Registers food & drug items*	Community Health Management Office of Environmental Programs 201 West Preston St. Baltimore, MD 21201	301-333-3154
GOVERNOR *Citizens access to the governor*	Office of the Governor State House Annapolis, MD 21404	301-974-2316

Type of Agency/Comments	*Organization and Address*	*Phone*
INSURANCE *Regulates the insurance industry*	Div. of Insurance Dept. of Licensing & Regulation Stanbalt Bldg. 501 St. Paul St. Baltimore, MD 21202	301-333-6300
LICENSING: DENTISTS *Report complaints about dentists to this office*	Board of Dental Examiners 4201 Patterson Ave. Baltimore, MD 21215	301-764-4730
LICENSING: HOSPITALS *Report complaints about hospitals to this office*	Dept. of Health 4201 Patterson Ave. Baltimore, MD 21215	301-764-2750
LICENSING: NURSES *Report complaints about nurses to this office*	Board of Nursing 4201 Patterson Ave. Baltimore, MD 21215	301-764-4747
LICENSING: NURSING HOMES *Report complaints about nursing homes to this office*	Dept. of Health Office of Licensing & Certification Metro Executive Center 4201 Patterson Ave. Baltimore, MD 21215	301-764-2770
LICENSING: PHARMACISTS *Report complaints about pharmacists to this office*	State Board of Pharmacy 4201 Patterson Ave. Baltimore, MD 21201	301-764-4755
LICENSING: PHYSICIANS *Report complaints about doctors to this office*	Maryland Physician Quality Assurance P.O. Box 2571 Baltimore, MD 21215	301-764-4777
LICENSING: PROFESSIONALS *Licenses other health care professionals*	Dept. of Licensing & Regulation Stanbalt Bldg. 501 St. Paul St. Baltimore, MD 21202	301-333-6322
MEDICAID OFFICE *Administers Medicaid program*	Medical Assistance Unit Office of Income Maintenance Dept. of Human Resources 201 West Preston St., Rm. 525 Baltimore, MD 21201	301-225-6535

Type of Agency/Comments	Organization and Address	Phone
MEDICARE PART B CARRIER *Processes Medicare claims*	[Rest of Maryland] Maryland Blue Shield Inc. 700 East Joppa Rd. Towson, MD 21204	301-561-4160 800-492-4795
MEDICARE PART B CARRIER *Serves Montgomery and Prince Georges counties only*	Pennsylvania Blue Shield P.O. Box 890100 Camp Hill, PA 17089-0100	800-233-1124
MENTAL HEALTH *Provides patient services*	Mental Hygiene Admin. Dept. of Health & Mental Hygiene H. R. O'Connor Office Bldg. 201 West Preston St. Baltimore, MD 21201	301-225-6611
OCCUPATIONAL SAFETY & HEALTH *Inspects worksites*	Div. of Labor & Industry Dept. of Licensing & Regulation 501 St. Paul St. Baltimore, MD 21202	301-333-4182
OMBUDSMAN (GENERAL) *Provides assistance to citizens*	Office of the State Prosecutor Investment Bldg., Rm. 103 One Investment Place Towson, MD 21204	301-321-4067
OMBUDSMAN (NURSING HOMES) *Investigates complaints from nursing home residents*	Office of Aging 301 West Preston St. Rm. 1004 Baltimore, MD 21201	301-225-1083
SOCIAL SERVICES *Provides support services and counseling*	Social Services Admin. Dept. of Human Resources Saratoga State Center, Rm. 578 Baltimore, MD 21201	301-333-0103
VETERANS AFFAIRS *Provides assistance to veterans*	Maryland Veterans Commission Federal Bldg. 31 Hopkins Plaza Baltimore, MD 21201	301-962-4700

Type of Agency/Comments	Organization and Address	Phone
VITAL STATISTICS *Maintains birth & death records*	Div. of Vital Records Dept. of Health & Mental Hygiene H. R. O'Connor Office Bldg. 201 West Preston St. Baltimore, MD 21203	301-225-5974
VOCATIONAL REHABILITATION *Provides information on rehabilitation programs*	Governor's Committee on Employment of the Handicapped One Market Center 300 West Lexington St. Baltimore, MD 21201	301-333-2264
WELFARE *Administers income programs*	Social Services Admin. Dept. of Human Resources 300 West Preston St. Baltimore, MD 21201	301-576-5201
WORKERS' COMPENSATION *Provides income for injured workers*	Worker's Compensation Commission Six North Liberty St. Baltimore, MD 21201	301-659-4775

MASSACHUSETTS

Type of Agency/Comments	Organization and Address	Phone
AGENCY LOCATOR *For Agencies & telephone numbers not listed*	Information Operator State House Beacon St. Boston, MA 02133	617-727-2121
AGING *Provides programs & services to senior citizens*	Dept. of Elder Affairs 38 Chauncy St. 2nd Floor Boston, MA 02111	617-727-7750
ALCOHOLISM *Provides assistance to alcohol abusers*	Div. of Alcoholism Dept. of Public Health 150 Tremont St. Boston, MA 02111	617-727-8614
ATTORNEY GENERAL *Chief law enforcement officer*	Dept. of the Attorney General J. W. McCormack Office Bldg. One Ashburton Place Boston, MA 02108	617-727-2200

Type of Agency/Comments	*Organization and Address*	*Phone*
CHILD WELFARE *Provides services to children and youths*	Office for Children 10 West St. Boston, MA 02111	617-727-8900
COMMUNITY AFFAIRS *Provides programs to communities*	Exec. Office of Communities & Development Leverett Saltonstall Bldg. Rm. 1404 100 Cambridge St. Boston, MA 02202	617-727-7765
CONSUMER ADVOCATE *Investigates consumer complaints*	Exec. Office of Consumer Affairs McCormack State Office Bldg. Rm. 1411 One Ashburton Place Boston, MA 02108	617-727-7755
DEPARTMENT OF HEALTH *Supervises health activities in the state*	Dept. of Public Health 150 Tremont St. Boston, MA 02111	617-727-0201
DEVELOPMENTAL DISABILITIES *Provides services*	Exec. Office of Human Services Dept. of Mental Retardation 160 North Washington St. Boston, MA 02114	617-727-5608 617-227-7548
DRUG ABUSE *Provides assistance to drug abusers*	Div. of Alcoholism and Drug Rehab. Dept. of Public Health 150 Tremont St. Boston, MA 02111	617-727-8614
FOOD AND DRUGS *Registers food & drug items*	Div. of Food & Drugs Dept. of Public Health Institute Labs 305 South St. Jamaica Plain, MA 02130	617-727-2670
GOVERNOR *Citizens access to the governor*	Office of the Governor State House Rm. 360 Boston, MA 02133	617-727-2759

Type of Agency/Comments	*Organization and Address*	*Phone*
INSURANCE *Regulates the insurance industry*	Div. of Insurance 280 Friend St. Boston, MA 02114	617-727-7189
LICENSING: DENTISTS *Report complaints about dentists to this office*	Board of Registration in Dentistry 100 Cambridge St. Rm. 1509 Boston, MA 02202	617-727-7406
LICENSING: HOSPITALS *Report complaints about hospitals to this office*	Dept. of Public Health Div. of Health Care Quality 80 Boylston St. 11th Floor Boston, MA 02116	617-727-1296 800-462-5540
LICENSING: NURSES *Report complaints about nurses to this office*	Board of Registration in Nursing 100 Cambridge St. Rm. 1509 Boston, MA 02202	617-727-9961
LICENSING: NURSING HOMES *Report complaints about nursing homes to this office*	Nursing Home Licensure Office LTC Facilities Program Dept. of Public Health 80 Boylston St., 11th Floor Boston, MA 02116	617-727-5864
LICENSING: PHARMACISTS *Report complaints about pharmacists to this office*	Board of Registration in Pharmacy 100 Cambridge St. Boston, MA 02202	617-727-3076
LICENSING: PHYSICIANS *Report complaints about doctors to this office*	Board of Registration in Medicine 10 West St. Boston, MA 02111	617-727-3086
LICENSING: PROFESSIONALS *Licenses other health care professionals*	Board of Allied Health Profession Div. of Registration 100 Cambridge St. Boston, MA 02202	617-727-3071

Type of Agency/Comments	Organization and Address	Phone
MEDICAID OFFICE *Administers Medicaid program*	Dept. of Public Welfare 180 Tremont St., 13th Floor Boston, MA 02111	617-574-0205
MEDICARE PART B CARRIER *Processes Medicare claims*	Blue Shield of Massachusetts 1022 Hingham St. Rockland, MA 02371	800-882-1228 617-956-3994
MENTAL HEALTH *Provides patient services*	Dept. of Mental Health Hoffman Bldg. 160 North Washington St. Boston, MA 02114	617-727-5600
OCCUPATIONAL SAFETY & HEALTH *Inspects worksites*	Div. of Industrial Safety Dept. of Labor & Industries Leverett Saltonstall Bldg. 100 Cambridge St. Boston, MA 02202	617-727-3567
OMBUDSMAN (GENERAL) *Provides assistance to consumers*	Exec. Office of Consumer Affairs and Business Regulation McCormack Bldg., Rm. 1141 One Ashburton Place Boston, MA 02108	617-727-7755
OMBUDSMAN (NURSING HOMES) *Investigates complaints from nursing home residents*	Exec. Offices — Elder Affairs 38 Chauncy St. Boston, MA 02111	617-727-7750
SOCIAL SERVICES *Provides support services and counseling*	Dept. of Social Services 150 Causeway St. Rm. 1109 Boston, MA 02114	617-727-0900
VETERANS AFFAIRS *Provides assistance to veterans*	Office of Veterans Services Leverett Saltonstall Bldg. Rm. 1002 100 Cambridge St. Boston, MA 02202	617-727-3570

Type of Agency/Comments	*Organization and Address*	*Phone*
VITAL STATISTICS *Maintains birth & death records*	Registry of Vital Records & Statistics Dept. of Public Health 150 Tremont St. Boston, MA 02111	617-727-0036
VOCATIONAL REHABILITATION *Provides information on rehabilitation programs*	Rehab. Commission Fort Point Place 27–43 Wormwood St. Boston, MA 02210	617-727-2172
WELFARE *Administers income programs*	Dept. of Public Welfare 180 Tremont St. 13th Floor Boston, MA 02111	617-574-0213
WORKER'S COMPENSATION *Provides income for injured workers*	Industrial Accident Board 600 Washington St. 7th Floor Boston, MA 02111	617-727-4900

MICHIGAN

Type of Agency/Comments	*Organization and Address*	*Phone*
AGENCY LOCATOR *For Agencies & telephone numbers not listed*	Information Operator State Capitol Bldg. Lansing, MI 48909	517-373-1837
AGING *Provides programs to senior citizens*	Office of Services to the Aging 300 East Michigan Ave. P.O. Box 30026 Lansing, MI 48909	517-373-8230
ALCOHOLISM *Provides assistance to alcohol abusers*	Substance Abuse Services Dept. of Public Health 3423 North Logan St. P.O. Box 30035 Lansing, MI 48909	517-373-8809
ATTORNEY GENERAL *Chief law enforcement officer*	Attorney General's Office Law Bldg., 7th Floor 525 West Ottawa St. Lansing, MI 48909	517-373-1110

Type of Agency/Comments	*Organization and Address*	*Phone*
CHILD WELFARE *Provides services to children and youths*	Children and Youth Services Dept. of Social Services Commerce Center Bldg. 300 South Capitol Ave. Lansing, MI 48909	517-373-0093
COMMUNITY AFFAIRS *Provides programs to communities*	Community and Business Assistance Div. Dept. of Commerce 525 West Ottawa St. Lansing, MI 48909	517-373-0601
CONSUMER ADVOCATE *Investigates consumer complaints*	Michigan Consumers Council Hollister Bldg., Rm. 414 106 West Allegan St. Lansing, MI 48933	517-373-0701
DEPARTMENT OF HEALTH *Supervises health activities in the state*	Dept. of Public Health Baker-Olin West Bldg. 3423 North Logan St. P.O. Box 30195 Lansing, MI 48909	517-335-8000
DEVELOPMENTAL DISABILITIES *Provides services to the developmentally disabled*	Dept. of Mental Health Lewis Cass Bldg. 5th Floor Lansing, MI 48913	517-373-3500
DRUG ABUSE *Provides assistance to drug abusers*	Substance Abuse Services Dept. of Public Health 3423 North Logan St. P.O. Box 30035 Lansing, MI 48909	517-373-8809
FOOD AND DRUGS *Registers food & drug items*	Food Div. Dept. of Agriculture 611 West Ottawa St. P.O. Box 30017 Lansing, MI 48909	517-373-1060
GOVERNOR *Citizens access to the governor*	Office of the Governor State Capitol Lansing, MI 48909	517-373-7956

Type of Agency/Comments	*Organization and Address*	*Phone*
INSURANCE *Regulates the insurance industry*	Insurance Bureau Dept. of Licensing & Regulation 611 West Ottawa St. P.O. Box 30220 Lansing, MI 48909	517-373-9273
LICENSING: DENTISTS *Report complaints about dentists to this office*	Dept. of Licensing & Regulation Health Investigation Div. P.O. Box 30018 Lansing, MI 48909	517-373-9196
LICENSING: HOSPITALS *Report complaints about hospitals to this office*	Dept. of Public Health Patients & Complaints 3500 North Logan St. Lansing, MI 48909	517-335-8511
LICENSING: NURSES *Report complaints about nurses to this office*	Board of Nursing 611 West Ottawa St. P.O. Box 30193 Lansing, MI 48909	517-373-1600
LICENSING: NURSING HOMES *Report complaints about nursing homes to this office*	Nursing Home Licensure Office Bur. of Health Care Admin. Dept. of Public Health 3423 North Logan St. Lansing, MI 48909	517-335-8505
LICENSING: PHARMACISTS *Report complaints about pharmacists to this office*	Michigan Board of Pharmacy Dept. of Licensing & Regulation 611 West Ottawa St. P.O. Box 30018 Lansing, MI 48909	517-373-0620
LICENSING: PHYSICIANS *Report complaints about doctors to this office*	State Board of Medicine 611 West Ottawa St. P.O. Box 30018 Lansing, MI 48909	517-373-1870
LICENSING: PROFESSIONALS *Licenses other health care professionals*	Dept. of Licensing & Regulation Ottawa Bldg. North 611 West Ottawa St. Lansing, MI 48909	517-373-1870

Type of Agency/Comments	Organization and Address	Phone
MEDICAID OFFICE *Administers Medicaid program*	Dept. of Social Services Citizen's & Legislative Inquiry Lansing, MI 48910	517-334-7262 800-638-6414
MEDICARE PART B CARRIER *Processes Medicare claims*	Michigan Blue Cross/Shield P.O. Box 2201 Detroit, MI 48231	313-225-8200
MENTAL HEALTH *Provides services to patients*	Dept. of Mental Health Lewis Cass Bldg. 6th Floor 320 Walnut St. Lansing, MI 48926	517-373-3500
OCCUPATIONAL SAFETY & HEALTH *Inspects worksites*	Bur. of Environment and Occupational Health Dept. of Public Health 3500 North Logan St. Lansing, MI 48909	517-335-9218
OMBUDSMAN (GENERAL) *Provides assistance to citizens*	Office of the Ombudsman Dept. of Civil Service 320 South Walnut St. Lansing, MI 48909	517-373-6497
OMBUDSMAN (NURSING HOMES) *Investigates complaints from nursing home residents*	Citizens for Better Care 1553 Woodward, Suite 525 David Whitney Bldg. Detroit, MI 48226	313-962-5968
SOCIAL SERVICES *Provides support services and counseling*	Dept. of Social Services Commerce Center 300 South Capitol Ave. P.O. Box 30037 Lansing, MI 48909	517-373-2000
VETERANS AFFAIRS *Provides assistance to veterans*	Veterans Trust Fund Dept. of Management & Budget Ottawa Bldg. North 611 West Ottawa St. Lansing, MI 48909	517-373-3133
VITAL STATISTICS *Maintains birth & death records*	Center for Health Statistics Dept. of Public Health 3423 North Logan St. P.O. Box 30035 Lansing, MI 48909	517-225-8676

Type of Agency/Comments	*Organization and Address*	*Phone*
VOCATIONAL REHABILITATION *Provides information on rehabilitation programs*	Commission on Handicapped Concerns Dept. of Labor 201 North Washington Square Lansing, MI 48909	517-373-8397
WELFARE *Administers income programs*	Dept. of Social Services Commerce Center 300 South Capitol St. P.O. Box 30037 Lansing, MI 48909	517-373-2000
WORKER'S COMPENSATION *Provides income for injured workers*	Bur. of Workers Disability Dept. of Labor 201 North Washington Square P.O. Box 30016 Lansing, MI 48909	517-373-3490

MINNESOTA

Type of Agency/Comments	*Organization and Address*	*Phone*
AGENCY LOCATOR *For Agencies & telephone numbers not listed*	Information Operator State Capitol Aurora Ave. & Park St. St. Paul, MN 55155	612-296-6013
AGING *Provides programs & services to senior citizens*	Minnesota Board of Aging Dept. of Human Services Human Services Bldg. 444 Lafayette Rd. St. Paul, MN 55155	612-296-2544
ALCOHOLISM *Provides assistance to alcohol abusers*	Chemical Dependency Program Dept. of Public Welfare Space Center Bldg. 444 Lafayette Rd. St. Paul, MN 55155	612-296-3991
ATTORNEY GENERAL *Chief law enforcement officer*	Attorney General's Office State Capitol Rm. 102 Aurora Ave. & Park St. St. Paul, MN 55155	612-296-6196

Type of Agency/Comments	*Organization and Address*	*Phone*
CHILD WELFARE *Provides services to children and youths*	Office of Children & Youth Services Dept. of Social Services Commerce Center Bldg., 9th Floor 300 South Capitol Ave. St. Paul, MN 55155	612-296-5960
COMMUNITY AFFAIRS *Provides programs to communities*	Small Cities Development Program Community Development Div. American Center Bldg., 9th Floor 150 East Kellogg Blvd. St. Paul, MN 55101	612-297-3172
CONSUMER ADVOCATE *Investigates consumer complaints*	Consumer Div. Office of Attorney General Ford Bldg., Rm. 124 117 University Ave. St. Paul, MN 55155	612-296-3353
DEPARTMENT OF HEALTH *Supervises health activities in the state*	Dept. of Health 717 Delaware St., NE P.O. Box 9441 Minneapolis, MN 55440	612-623-5460
DEVELOPMENTAL DISABILITIES *Provides services to the developmentally disabled*	Div. for Persons with Developmental Disabilities Dept. of Human Services 444 Lafayette Rd. St. Paul, MN 55155	612-296-1898
DRUG ABUSE *Provides assistance to drug abusers*	Chemical Dependency Program Dept. of Public Welfare Space Center Bldg. 444 Lafayette Rd. St. Paul, MN 55155	612-296-3991
FOOD AND DRUGS *Registers food & drug items*	Food Inspection Div. Dept. of Agriculture 90 West Plato Blvd. St. Paul, MN 55107	612-296-2627
GOVERNOR *Citizens access to the governor*	Office of the Governor State Capitol St. Paul, MN 55155	612-296-3391

Type of Agency/Comments	*Organization and Address*	*Phone*
INSURANCE *Regulates the insurance industry*	Insurance Div. Dept. of Commerce Metro Square Bldg., Rm. 500 7th & Roberts Sts. St. Paul, MN 55101	612-296-4026
LICENSING: DENTISTS *Report complaints about dentists to this office*	Board of Dentistry 2700 University Ave. West Suite 109 Minneapolis, MN 55414	612-642-0579
LICENSING: HOSPITALS *Report complaints about hospitals to this office*	Minnesota Dept. of Health Office of Health Facility Complaints Central Medical Bldg. 393 Dunlap St. St. Paul, MN 55164	612-643-2520
LICENSING: NURSES *Report complaints about nurses to this office*	Board of Nursing 2700 University Ave. West Rm. 108 St. Paul, MN 55114	612-642-0552
LICENSING: NURSING HOMES *Report complaints about nursing homes to this office*	Nursing Home Licensure Office Dept. of Health Survey & Compliance Section 393 Dunlap St. St. Paul, MN 55164	612-643-2101
LICENSING: PHARMACISTS *Report complaints about pharmacists to this office*	Minnesota Board of Pharmacy 2700 University Ave. West Rm. 107 St. Paul, MN 55114	612-642-0541
LICENSING: PHYSICIANS *Report complaints about doctors to this office*	Board of Medical Examiners 2700 University Ave. West Rm. 106 St. Paul, MN 55114	612-642-0538
LICENSING: PROFESSIONALS *Licenses other health care professionals*	Dept. of Commerce Metro Square Bldg., Rm. 500 7th & Roberts Sts. St. Paul, MN 55101	612-296-4026
MEDICAID OFFICE *Administers Medicaid program*	Dept. of Human Services Health Care & Residential Program 444 Lafayette Rd. St. Paul, MN 55155	612-296-2766

Type of Agency/Comments	*Organization and Address*	*Phone*
MEDICARE PART B CARRIER *Processes Medicare claims* *Check for coverage area*	Blue Shield of Minnesota P.O. Box 64357 St. Paul, MN 55164	612-456-5070 800-392-0343
MEDICARE PART B CARRIER *Processes Medicare claims* *Check for coverage area*	Travelers Insurance Co. 8120 Penn Ave. South South Bloomington, MN 55431	612-884-7171 800-352-2762
MENTAL HEALTH *Provides patient services*	Mental Health Bur. Dept. of Human Services 444 Lafayette Rd. St. Paul, MN 55155	612-296-4497
OCCUPATIONAL SAFETY & HEALTH *Inspects worksites*	Occupational Safety & Health Div. Dept. of Labor and Industry 444 Lafayette Rd. St. Paul, MN 55101	612-296-2116
OMBUDSMAN (GENERAL) *Provides assistance to* *citizens*	Office of the Lieutenant Governor State Capitol, Rm. 121 Aurora Ave. & Park St. St. Paul, MN 55155	612-296-2374
OMBUDSMAN (NURSING HOMES) *Investigates complaints from* *nursing home residents*	Minnesota Board on Aging Human Services Bldg. 444 Lafayette Rd. St. Paul, MN 55155	612-296-2770
SOCIAL SERVICES *Provides support services* *and counseling*	Bur. of Social Services Dept. of Human Services 444 Lafayette Rd. St. Paul, MN 55155	612-296-2701
VETERANS AFFAIRS *Provides assistance to* *veterans*	Dept. of Veterans Affairs State Veterans Service Bldg. Second Floor 20 West 12th St. St. Paul, MN 55155	612-296-2562
VITAL STATISTICS *Maintains birth & death* *records*	Registrar of Vital Statistics Dept. of Health 717 Delaware St. SE Minneapolis, MN 55440	612-623-5121

Type of Agency/Comments	Organization and Address	Phone
VOCATIONAL REHABILITATION *Provides information on rehabilitation programs*	Council on Disability Metro Square Bldg. 7th Place & Jackson St. St. Paul, MN 55101	612-296-6785
WELFARE *Administers income programs*	Dept. of Human Services 444 Lafayette Rd. St. Paul, MN 55155	612-296-2701
WORKER'S COMPENSATION *Provides income for injured workers*	Worker's Compensation Div. Dept. of Labor & Industry 444 Lafayette Rd. St. Paul, MN 55101	612-296-6490

MISSISSIPPI

Type of Agency/Comments	Organization and Address	Phone
AGENCY LOCATOR *For Agencies & telephone numbers not listed*	Information Operator New Capitol Bldg. 400 High St. Jackson, MS 39202	601-354-7011
AGING *Provides programs & services to senior citizens*	Council on Aging Office of Federal State Programs Office of the Governor 301 West Pearl St. Jackson, MS 39203	601-949-2013
ALCOHOLISM *Provides assistance to alcohol abusers*	Div. of Alcohol & Drug Abuse Dept. of Mental Health 239 North Lamar St. Jackson, MS 39201	601-359-1288
ATTORNEY GENERAL *Chief law enforcement officer*	Attorney General's Office Carroll Gartin Justice Bldg. 450 High St. Jackson, MS 39205	601-359-3680
COMMUNITY AFFAIRS *Provides programs to communities*	Research & Development Center 3825 Ridgewood Rd. Jackson, MS 39211	601-982-6456

Type of Agency/Comments	*Organization and Address*	*Phone*
CONSUMER ADVOCATE *Investigates consumer complaints*	Regulatory Services Div. Dept. of Agriculture & Commerce Stillers State Office Bldg. 550 High St. Jackson, MS 39215	601-359-3636
DEPARTMENT OF HEALTH *Supervises health activities in the state*	State Board of Health 2423 North State St. P.O. Box 1700 Jackson, MS 39215	601-960-7400
DEVELOPMENTAL DISABILITIES *Provides services to the developmentally disabled*	Developmental Disabilities Dept. of Mental Health 1101 Robert E. Lee Bldg. 239 North Lamar St. Jackson, MS 39201	601-359-1288
DRUG ABUSE *Provides assistance to drug abusers*	Div. of Alcohol & Drug Abuse Dept. of Mental Health 239 North Lamar St. Jackson, MS 39201	601-359-1288
GOVERNOR *Citizens access to the governor*	Office of the Governor State Capitol Jackson, MS 39205	601-359-3111
INSURANCE *Regulates the insurance industry*	Insurance Dept. 1804 Sillers Bldg. 550 High St. Jackson, MS 39205	601-359-3569
LICENSING: DENTISTS *Report complaints about dentists to this office*	Board of Dental Examiners P.O. Box 1960 Clinton, MS 39060	601-924-9622
LICENSING: HOSPITALS *Report complaints about hospitals to this office*	Health Care Commission Div. of Licensure & Certification P.O. Box 1700 Rm. 101 Jackson, MS 39215	601-960-7769
LICENSING: NURSES *Report complaints about nurses to this office*	Board of Nursing 239 North Lamar St. Jackson, MS 39201	601-359-6170

Type of Agency/Comments	Organization and Address	Phone
LICENSING: NURSING HOMES *Report complaints about nursing homes to this office*	Nursing Home Licensure Office Facilities Licensure & Certification Board of Health P.O. Box 1700 Jackson, MS 39215	601-960-7769
LICENSING: PHARMACISTS *Report complaints about pharmacists to this office*	Board of Pharmacy 2310 Highway 80 West Jackson, MS 39204	601-354-6750
LICENSING: PHYSICIANS *Report complaints about doctors to this office*	Board of Medical Licensure 2688 D Insurance Center Dr. Jackson, MS 39216	601-354-6645
LICENSING: PROFESSIONALS *Licenses other health care professionals*	Board of Medical Licensure 2688 D Insurance Center Dr. Jackson, MS 39216	601-354-6645
MEDICAID OFFICE *Administers Medicaid program*	Dept. of Public Welfare Div. of Medicaid 239 North Lamar St. Suite 801 Jackson, MS 39201	601-359-6050
MEDICARE PART B CARRIER *Processes Medicare claims*	Travelers Insurance Co. P.O. Box 22545 Jackson, MS 39205	601-956-0372 800-682-5417
MENTAL HEALTH *Provides patient services*	Dept. of Mental Health Robert E. Lee Bldg., Rm. 1101 239 North Lamar St. Jackson, MS 39201	601-359-1288
OCCUPATIONAL SAFETY & HEALTH *Inspects worksites*	Occupational Safety & Health Branch State Board of Health 305 West Lorenz Blvd. Jackson, MS 39206	601-987-3981
OMBUDSMAN (NURSING HOMES) *Investigates complaints from nursing home residents*	Aging and Adult Services 421 West Pascagoula St. Jackson, MS 39203	601-949-2029

Type of Agency/Comments	*Organization and Address*	*Phone*
SOCIAL SERVICES *Provides support services and counseling*	Social Services Dept. of Public Welfare 515 East Amite St. Jackson, MS 39205	601-354-0341
VETERANS AFFAIRS *Provides assistance to veterans*	Veterans Affairs Commission State Veterans Bldg. 4607 Lindberg Rd. Jackson, MS 39209	601-354-7205
VITAL STATISTICS *Maintains birth & death records*	Office of Public Health Statistics Dept. of Health Underwood Bldg., Rm. 110 Jackson, MS 39215	601-690-7960
WELFARE *Administers income program*	Dept. of Public Welfare 515 East Amite St. Jackson, MS 39205	601-354-0341
WORKER'S COMPENSATION *Provides income for injured workers*	Worker's Compensation Commission 1428 Lakeland Dr. P.O. Box 5300 Jackson, MS 39216	601-987-4200

MISSOURI

Type of Agency/Comments	*Organization and Address*	*Phone*
AGENCY LOCATOR *For Agencies & telephone numbers not listed*	Information Operator State Capitol Bldg. Jefferson City, MO 65101	314-751-2000
AGING *Provides programs & services to senior citizens*	Div. of Aging Dept. of Social Services 2701 West Main St. Jefferson City, MO 65102	314-751-3082
ALCOHOLISM *Provides assistance to alcohol abusers*	Div. of Alcohol & Drug Abuse Dept. of Mental Health 1915 Southridge Dr. Jefferson City, MO 65102	314-751-4942

Type of Agency/Comments	*Organization and Address*	*Phone*
ATTORNEY GENERAL *Chief law enforcement officer*	Attorney General's Office Supreme Court Bldg. Jefferson City, MO 65102	314-751-3321
CHILD WELFARE *Provides services to children and youths*	Div. of Family Services Dept. of Social Services Broadway State Office Bldg. 221 West High St. Jefferson City, MO 65103	314-751-4247

COMMUNITY AFFAIRS
 	
Provides programs to communities
	Economic Development
	  Programs
	Dept. of Economic
	  Development
	Truman State Office Bldg.
	301 West High St.
	Jefferson City, MO 65102
		314-751-2133

CONSUMER ADVOCATE *Investigates consumer complaints*	Consumer Protection Div. Supreme Court Bldg. P.O. Box 899 Jefferson City, MO 65102	314-751-3321
DEPARTMENT OF HEALTH *Supervises health activities in the state*	Dept. of Health P.O. Box 570 Jefferson City, MO 65102	314-751-6001
DEVELOPMENTAL DISABILITIES *Provides services to the developmentally disabled*	Div. of Mental Health & Developmental Disabilities Dept. of Mental Health 1915 Southridge Dr. Jefferson City, MO 65102	314-751-4505
DRUG ABUSE *Provides assistance to drug abusers*	Div. of Alcohol & Drug Abuse Dept. of Mental Health 1915 Southridge Dr. Jefferson City, MO 65102	314-751-4942
FOOD AND DRUGS *Registers food & drug items*	Bur. of Community Sanitation Dept. of Health 1730 East Elm Jefferson City, MO 65102	314-751-6090
GOVERNOR *Citizens access to the governor*	Office of the Governor State Capitol Rm. 216 Jefferson City, MO 65102	314-751-3222

Type of Agency/Comments	*Organization and Address*	*Phone*
INSURANCE *Regulates the insurance industry*	Div. of Insurance Dept. of Economic Development Truman State Office Bldg. 301 West High St. Jefferson City, MO 65102	314-751-4126
LICENSING: DENTISTS *Report complaints about dentists to this office*	Missouri Dental Board P.O. Box 1367 Jefferson City, MO 65102	314-751-2334
LICENSING: HOSPITALS *Report complaints about hospitals to this office*	Dept. of Health Bur. of Hospital Licensing P.O. Box 570 Jefferson City, MO 65102	314-751-6302
LICENSING: NURSES *Report complaints about nurses to this office*	Board of Nursing P.O. Box 656 Jefferson City, MO 65102	314-751-2334
LICENSING: NURSING HOMES *Report complaints about nursing homes to this office*	Dept. of Social Services Div. of Aging 1440 Arron Court P.O. Box 1337 Jefferson City, MO 65102	314-751-2712
LICENSING: PHARMACISTS *Report complaints about pharmacists to this office*	Board of Pharmacy P.O. Box 625 Jefferson City, MO 65101	314-751-2334
LICENSING: PHYSICIANS *Report complaints about doctors to this office*	State Board of Regulation for the Healing Arts P.O. Box 4 Jefferson City, MO 65102	314-751-2334
LICENSING: PROFESSIONALS *Licenses other health care professionals*	Div. of Professional Registration Dept. of Economic Development 3523 North Ten Mile Dr. Jefferson City, MO 65109	314-751-2334
MEDICAID OFFICE *Administers Medicaid program*	Dept. of Social Services Div. of Family Services P.O. Box 6500 Jefferson City, MO 65103	314-751-6529 800-392-1261

Type of Agency/Comments	Organization and Address	Phone
MEDICARE PART B CARRIER *Processes Medicare claims*	Blue Shield of Kansas City P.O. Box 169 Kansas City, MO 64141	816-561-0900 800-892-5900
MEDICARE PART B CARRIER *Processes Medicare claims*	General American Life Insurance Co. P.O. Box 505 St. Louis, MO 63166	314-843-8880 800-392-3070
MENTAL HEALTH *Provides patient services*	Dept. of Mental Health 1915 Southridge Dr. P.O. Box 678 Jefferson City, MO 65102	314-751-3070
OCCUPATIONAL SAFETY & HEALTH *Inspects worksites*	Safety and Health Consultation Services Dept. of Labor & Industry 621 East McCarthy St. Jefferson City, MO 65102	314-751-3403
OMBUDSMAN (GENERAL) *Provides assistance to citizens*	Lieutenant Governor's Office State Capitol, Rm. 326 Jefferson City, MO 65102	314-751-3000
OMBUDSMAN (NURSING HOMES) *Investigates complaints from nursing home residents*	Dept. of Social Services Div. of Aging 2701 West Main St. Jefferson City, MO 65102	314-751-3082
SOCIAL SERVICES *Provides support services and counseling*	Dept. of Social Services Broadway State Office Bldg. 221 West High St. Jefferson City, MO 65102	314-751-4815
VETERANS AFFAIRS *Provides assistance to veterans*	Div. of Veterans Affairs Office of Adjutant General 911 B Leslie Pl. Jefferson City, MO 65102	314-751-3779
VITAL STATISTICS *Maintains birth & death records*	Bur. of Vital Records Dept. of Health 1730 East Elm St. Jefferson City, MO 65102	314-751-6400
VOCATIONAL REHABILITATION *Provides information on rehabilitation programs*	Governor's Committee on Employment of the Handicapped 1904 Missouri Blvd. Jefferson City, MO 65102	314-751-2600 800-392-8249

Type of Agency/Comments	Organization and Address	Phone
WELFARE *Administers income program*	Dept. of Social Services Div. of Family Services Broadway State Office Bldg. 221 West High St. Jefferson City, MO 65103	314-751-4247

WORKER'S COMPENSATION
 	
Provides income for injured workers
	Div. of Worker's
	   Compensation
	Dept. of Labor and Industrial
	   Relations
	722 Jefferson St.
	Jefferson City, MO 65102
		314-751-4231

MONTANA

Type of Agency/Comments	Organization and Address	Phone
AGENCY LOCATOR *For Agencies & telephone numbers not listed*	Information Operator Capitol Bldg. Helena, MT 59620	406-444-2511
AGING *Provides programs & services to senior citizens*	Aging Services Coordinator Office of the Governor Capitol Bldg. Helena, MT 59620	406-444-3111
ALCOHOLISM *Provides assistance to alcohol abusers*	Treatment Services Div. Alcohol & Drug Abuse Div. Dept. of Institutions 1539 11th Ave. Helena, MT 59620	406-444-3904
ATTORNEY GENERAL *Chief law enforcement officer*	Dept. of Justice Justice Bldg. Rm. 317 215 North Sanders St. Helena, MT 59620	406-444-2026
CHILD WELFARE *Provides services to children*	Dept. of Family Services 48 North Last Chance Gulch P.O. Box 8005 Helena, MT 59601	406-444-5900

Type of Agency/Comments	Organization and Address	Phone
COMMUNITY AFFAIRS *Provides programs to communities*	Local Government Assistance Div. Dept. of Commerce Cogswell Bldg., Rm. C-211 Lockey St. Helena, MT 59620	406-444-3757
CONSUMER ADVOCATE *Investigates consumer complaints*	Consumer Affairs Unit Dept. of Commerce 1424 9th Ave. Helena, MT 59620	406-444-4312
DEPARTMENT OF HEALTH *Supervises health activities in the state*	Dept. of Health and Environment Cogswell Bldg. Lockey St. Helena, MT 59620	406-444-2544
DEVELOPMENTAL DISABILITIES *Provides services to the developmentally disabled*	Developmental Disabilities Div. Dept. of Social & Rehab. Services SRS Bldg. 111 Sanders St. Helena, MT 59604	406-444-2995
DRUG ABUSE *Provides assistance to drug abusers*	Treatment Services Div. Alcohol & Drug Abuse Div. Dept. of Institutions 1539 11th Ave. Helena, MT 59620	406-444-3904
FOOD AND DRUGS *Registers food & drug items*	Food & Consumer Safety Bur. Dept. of Health & Environment Cogswell Bldg., Rm. A-201 Lockey St. Helena, MT 59620	406-444-2408
GOVERNOR *Citizens access to the governor*	Office of the Governor Capitol Bldg. Helena, MT 59620	406-444-3111
INSURANCE *Regulates the insurance industry*	Commissioner of Insurance State Auditor's Office 205 Roberts St. Helena, MT 59620	406-444-2040

Type of Agency/Comments	Organization and Address	Phone
LICENSING: DENTISTS *Report complaints about dentists to this office*	Dept. of Commerce 1424 9th Ave. Helena, MT 59620	406-444-3745
LICENSING: HOSPITALS *Report complaints about hospitals to this office*	Dept. of Health & Environment Medical Facilities Div. Cogswell Bldg. Helena, MT 59620	406-444-2037
LICENSING: NURSES *Report complaints about nurses to this office*	Board of Nursing 1424 9th Ave. Helena, MT 59620	406-444-4279
LICENSING: NURSING HOMES *Report complaints about nursing homes to this office*	Dept. of Health & Environment Bur. of Licensing & Certification Cogswell Bldg. Helena, MT 59620	406-444-2037
LICENSING: PHARMACISTS *Report complaints about pharmacists to this office*	Board of Pharmacy 510 1st Ave. North Great Falls, MT 59401	406-761-5131
LICENSING: PHYSICIANS *Report complaints about doctors to this office*	Board of Medical Licensure 1424 9th Ave. Helena, MT 59620	406-444-4284
LICENSING: PROFESSIONALS *Licenses other health care professionals*	Professional & Occupational Licensing Bur. Dept. of Commerce 1424 9th Ave. Helena, MT 59620	406-444-3737
MEDICAID OFFICE *Administers Medicaid program*	Dept. of Social and Rehab. Services Economic Assistance Div. 111 Sanders St. Helena, MT 59604	406-444-4540
MEDICARE PART B CARRIER *Processes Medicare claims*	Blue Shield of Montana P.O. Box 4310 Helena, MT 59604	406-444-8350 800-332-6146

Type of Agency/Comments	Organization and Address	Phone
MENTAL HEALTH *Provides patient services*	Mental Health Services Div. Dept. of Institutions 1539 11th Ave. Helena, MT 59620	406-444-3969
OCCUPATIONAL SAFETY & HEALTH *Inspects worksites*	Occupational Health Bur. Dept. of Health & Environment Cogswell Bldg., Rm. A-113 Lockey St. Helena, MT 59620	406-444-3671
OMBUDSMAN (GENERAL) *Provides assistance to citizens*	Office of Citizen's Advocate Office of the Governor Capitol Bldg., Rm. 213 Helena, MT 59620	406-444-3468
OMBUDSMAN (NURSING HOMES) *Investigates complaints from nursing home residents*	Seniors Office Legal & Ombudsman Services Capitol Station Helena, MT 59620	406-444-4676
SOCIAL SERVICES *Provides support services and counseling*	Dept. of Family Services 48 North Last Chance Gulch P.O. Box 8005 Helena, MT 59601	406-444-5900
VETERANS AFFAIRS *Provides assistance to veterans*	Veterans Affairs Div. Dept. of Military Affairs State Armory 1100 North Last Chance Gulch Helena, MT 59604	406-444-6926
VITAL STATISTICS *Maintains birth & death records*	Records & Statistics Bur. Financial Management Div. Cogswell Bldg. Lockey St. Helena, MT 59620	406-444-2614
VOCATIONAL REHABILITATION *Provides information on rehabilitation programs*	Rehab. Services Div. P.O. Box 4210 Helena, MT 59601	406-444-2590

Type of Agency/Comments	Organization and Address	Phone
WELFARE *Administers income programs*	Economic Assistance Div. Dept. of Social and Rehab. Services 111 Sanders St. Helena, MT 59604	406-444-4540
WORKER'S COMPENSATION *Provides income for injured workers*	Div. of Worker's Compensation Dept. of Labor & Industry 5 South Last Chance Gulch Helena, MT 59601	406-444-6518

NEBRASKA

Type of Agency/Comments	Organization and Address	Phone
AGENCY LOCATOR *For Agencies & telephone numbers not listed*	Information Operator State Capitol 1445 K St. Lincoln, NE 68509	402-471-2311
AGING *Provides programs & services to senior citizens*	Dept. on Aging State Office Bldg. 301 Centennial Mall South Lincoln, NE 68509	402-471-2306
ALCOHOLISM *Provides assistance to alcohol abusers*	Div. of Alcoholism & Drug Abuse Dept. of Public Institutions West Van Dorn & Folsom Sts. Lincoln, NE 68509	402-471-2851
ATTORNEY GENERAL *Chief law enforcement officer*	Attorney General's Office Dept. of Justice State Capitol, Rm. 2115 1445 K St. Lincoln, NE 68509	402-471-2682
CHILD WELFARE *Provides services to children and youths*	Div. of Human Services Dept. of Social Services 2320 North 57th St. Lincoln, NE 68504	402-471-3305
COMMUNITY AFFAIRS *Provides programs to communities*	Div. of Community Affairs Dept. of Economic Development 301 Centennial Mall South Lincoln, NE 68509	402-471-3762

Type of Agency/Comments	*Organization and Address*	*Phone*
CONSUMER ADVOCATE *Investigates consumer complaints*	Consumer Fraud Div. Office of Attorney General 1445 K St. Lincoln, NE 68509	402-471-4723
DEPARTMENT OF HEALTH *Supervises health activities in the state*	Dept. of Health State Office Bldg. 301 Centennial Mall South Lincoln, NE 68509	402-471-2133
DEVELOPMENTAL DISABILITIES *Provides services to the developmentally disabled*	Office of Mental Retardation Dept. of Public Institutions West Van Dorn & Folsom Sts. Lincoln, NE 68509	402-471-2851
DRUG ABUSE *Provides assistance to drug abusers*	Div. of Alcoholism & Drug Abuse Dept. of Public Institutions West Van Dorn & Folsom Sts. Lincoln, NE 68509	402-471-2851
FOOD AND DRUGS *Registers food & drug items*	Bur. of Dairies & Foods Dept. of Agriculture 301 Centennial Mall South Lincoln, NE 68509	402-471-2536
GOVERNOR *Citizens access to the governor*	Office of the Governor State Capitol Lincoln, NE 68509	402-471-2244
INSURANCE *Regulates the insurance industry*	Dept. of Insurance State Office Bldg. 941 O St. Lincoln, NE 68508	402-471-2201
LICENSING: DENTISTS *Report complaints about dentists to this office*	Board of Dental Examiners Bur. of Examining Boards P.O. Box 95007 Lincoln, NE 68506	402-471-2115
LICENSING: HOSPITALS *Report complaints about hospitals to this office*	Dept. of Health Div. of Licensure and Standards 301 Centennial Mall South Lincoln, NE 68509	402-471-2946

Type of Agency/Comments	Organization and Address	Phone
LICENSING: NURSES *Report complaints about nurses to this office*	Bur. of Examining Boards Nursing Board Dept. of Health 301 Centennial Mall South Lincoln, NE 68509	402-471-4921
LICENSING: NURSING HOMES *Report complaints about nursing homes to this office*	Bur. of Health Facilities Standards 301 Centennial Mall South P.O. Box 95007 Lincoln, NE 68509	402-471-2946
LICENSING: PHARMACISTS *Report complaints about pharmacists to this office*	Bur. of Examining Boards P.O. Box 95007 Lincoln, NE 68509	402-471-2115
LICENSING: PHYSICIANS *Report complaints about doctors to this office*	Board of Medical Examiners State Office Bldg. 301 Centennial Mall South Lincoln, NE 68509	402-471-2115
MEDICAID OFFICE *Administers Medicaid program*	Dept. of Social Services Medical Assistance Unit 301 Centennial Mall South Lincoln, NE 68509	402-471-9330
MEDICARE PART B CARRIER *Processes Medicare claims for Nebraska*	Blue Cross/Blue Shield of Nebraska P.O. Box 3106 Omaha, NE 68103	800-633-1113
MENTAL HEALTH *Provides services to patients*	Office of Community Mental Health Dept. of Public Institutions West Van Dorn & Folsom Sts. Lincoln, NE 68509	402-471-2851
OCCUPATIONAL SAFETY & HEALTH *Inspects worksites*	Div. of Safety Dept. of Labor 301 Centennial Mall South Lincoln, NE 68509	402-471-2239
OMBUDSMAN (GENERAL) *Provides assistance to citizens*	Office of the Ombudsman Legislative Council State Capitol, 8th Floor 1445 K St. Lincoln, NE 68509	402-471-2035

Type of Agency/Comments	*Organization and Address*	*Phone*
OMBUDSMAN (NURSING HOMES) *Investigates complaints from nursing home residents*	Dept. on Aging State Office Bldg. 301 Centennial Mall South P.O. Box 95044 Lincoln, NE 68509	402-471-2307
SOCIAL SERVICES *Provides support services and counseling*	Div. of Human Services Dept. of Social Services 301 Centennial Mall South P.O. Box 95026 Lincoln, NE 68509	402-471-3121
VETERANS AFFAIRS *Provides assistance to veterans*	Dept. of Veterans Affairs State Office Bldg. 301 Centennial Mall South P.O. Box 95083 Lincoln, NE 68509	402-471-2458
VITAL STATISTICS *Maintains birth & death records*	Bur. of Vital Statistics Dept. of Health 301 Centennial Mall South Lincoln, NE 68509	402-471-2871
VOCATIONAL REHABILITATION *Provides information on rehabilitation programs*	Governor's Committee on Employment of the Handicapped Dept. of Labor 550 South 16th St. Lincoln, NE 68509	402-475-8451
WELFARE *Administers income programs*	Dept. of Social Services State Office Bldg. 301 Centennial Mall South P.O. Box 95026 Lincoln, NE 68509	402-471-3121
WORKER'S COMPENSATION *Provides income for injured workers*	Worker's Compensation Court State Capitol 1445 K St. Lincoln, NE 68509	402-471-2568

NEVADA

Type of Agency/Comments	*Organization and Address*	*Phone*
AGENCY LOCATOR *For Agencies & telephone numbers not listed*	Information Operator State Capitol Bldg. Carson City, NV 89710	702-885-5000

Type of Agency/Comments	Organization and Address	Phone
AGING *Provides programs & services to senior citizens*	Div. for Aging Services Dept. of Human Resources Cannon Center, Suite 114 340 North 11th St. Las Vegas, NV 89109	702-486-3545
ALCOHOLISM *Provides assistance to alcohol abusers*	Bur. of Alcohol & Drug Abuse Dept. of Human Resources 505 East King St. Capitol Complex Carson City, NV 89710	702-885-4790
ATTORNEY GENERAL *Chief law enforcement officer*	Attorney General's Office Capitol Complex Carson City, NV 89710	702-885-4170
CHILD WELFARE *Provides services to children and youths*	Social Services Div. Dept. of Human Services 2527 North Carson St. Carson City, NV 89710	702-885-4766
COMMUNITY AFFAIRS *Provides programs to communities*	Office of Community Services 1100 East William St. Suite 109 Carson City, NV 89710	702-885-4990
CONSUMER ADVOCATE *Investigates consumer complaints*	Consumer Affairs Div. Dept. of Commerce 2601 East Sahara Ave. Las Vegas, NV 89158	702-486-4150
DEPARTMENT OF HEALTH *Supervises health activities in the state*	Health Div. Dept. of Human Resources 505 East King St. Carson City, NV 89710	702-885-4740
DEVELOPMENTAL DISABILITIES *Provides services to the developmentally disabled*	Div. of Mental Health/ Retardation Dept. of Human Services Kinkead Bldg., Rm. 403 505 East King St. Carson City, NV 89710	702-885-5943
DRUG ABUSE *Provides assistance to drug abusers*	Bur. of Alcohol & Drug Abuse Dept. of Human Services 505 East King St. Carson City, NV 89710	702-885-4790

Type of Agency/Comments	*Organization and Address*	*Phone*
FOOD AND DRUGS *Registers food & drug items*	Consumer Health Protection Div. of Health 505 East King St. Carson City, NV 89710	702-885-4750
GOVERNOR *Citizens access to the governor*	Office of the Governor State Capitol Carson City, NV 89710	702-885-5670
INSURANCE *Regulates the insurance industry*	Insurance Div. Dept. of Commerce 201 South Fall St. Carson City, NV 89710	702-885-4270
LICENSING: DENTISTS *Report complaints about dentists to this office*	Board of Dental Examiners P.O. Box 80360 Las Vegas, NV 89180	702-258-4230
LICENSING: HOSPITALS *Report complaints about hospitals to this office*	Div. of Health Bur. of Regulatory Health Services 505 East King St., Rm. 202 Carson City, NV 89710	702-885-4475
LICENSING: NURSES *Report complaints about nurses to this office*	Board of Nursing 1281 Terminal Way Rm. 116 Reno, NV 89502	702-786-2778
LICENSING: NURSING HOMES *Report complaints about nursing homes to this office*	Bur. of Regulatory Health Services 505 East King St., Rm. 202 Carson City, NV 89710	702-885-4475
LICENSING: PHARMACISTS *Report complaints about pharmacists to this office*	Board of Pharmacy 1201 Terminal Way Reno, NV 89502	702-322-0691
LICENSING: PHYSICIANS *Report complaints about doctors to this office*	Board of Medical Examiners P.O. Box 7238 Reno, NV 89510	702-329-2559

Type of Agency/Comments	*Organization and Address*	*Phone*
MEDICAID OFFICE *Administers Medicaid program*	Dept. of Human Resources Welfare Div. Medicaid Section 2527 North Carson St. Carson City, NV 89710	702-885-4378
MEDICARE PART B CARRIER *Processes Medicare claims for Nevada residents*	Aetna Life & Casualty Co. P.O. Box 37320 Phoenix, AZ 85069	800-528-0311
MENTAL HEALTH *Provides patient services*	Div. of Mental Hygiene Dept. of Human Resources Kinkead Bldg., Rm. 403 505 East King St. Carson City, NV 89710	702-885-5943
OCCUPATIONAL SAFETY & HEALTH *Inspects worksites*	Div. of Occupational Safety & Health Dept. of Industrial Relations 1370 South Curry St. Carson City, NV 89714	702-885-5240
OMBUDSMAN (GENERAL) *Provides assistance to citizens*	Consumer Advocate Office of Attorney General 1931 Sutro St. Suite 203A Reno, NV 89512	702-789-0220
OMBUDSMAN (NURSING HOMES) *Investigates complaints from nursing home residents*	Div. for Aging Services 505 East King St. Rm. 101 Carson City, NV 89710	702-885-4210
SOCIAL SERVICES *Provides support services and counseling*	Welfare Div. Dept. of Human Resources 2527 North Carson St. Carson City, NV 89710	702-885-4766
VETERANS AFFAIRS *Provides assistance to veterans*	Veterans Affairs Commission 1201 Terminal Way Reno, NV 89520	702-789-0155
VITAL STATISTICS *Maintains birth & death records*	Vital Statistics Section Div. of Health 505 East King St. Kinkead Bldg., Rm. 102 Carson City, NV 89710	702-885-4480

Type of Agency/Comments	*Organization and Address*	*Phone*
VOCATIONAL REHABILITATION *Provides information on rehabilitation programs*	Rehab. Div. Dept. of Human Resources Kinkead Bldg., 5th Floor 505 East King St. Carson City, NV 89710	702-885-4440
WELFARE *Administers income programs*	Welfare Div. Dept. of Human Resources 2527 North Carson St. Carson City, NV 89710	702-885-4128
WORKER'S COMPENSATION *Provides income for injured workers*	State Industrial Insurance SIIS Bldg. 515 East Musser St. Carson City, NV 89710	702-885-5284

NEW HAMPSHIRE

Type of Agency/Comments	*Organization and Address*	*Phone*
AGENCY LOCATOR *For Agencies & telephone numbers not listed*	Information Operator State House 107 North Main St. Concord, NH 03301	603-271-1110
AGING *Provides programs & services to senior citizens*	Div. of Elderly & Adult Services Dept. of Health & Human Services Health & Human Services Bldg. 6 Hazen Dr. Concord, NH 03301	603-271-4680
ALCOHOLISM *Provides assistance to alcohol abusers*	Office of Alcohol & Drug Abuse Prevention Dept. of Health & Human Services 6 Hazen Dr. Concord, NH 03301	800-852-3345 603-271-4627
ATTORNEY GENERAL *Chief law enforcement officer*	Attorney General's Office 208 State House Annex 25 Capitol St. Concord, NH 03301	603-271-3655

Type of Agency/Comments	Organization and Address	Phone
CHILD WELFARE *Provides services to children and youths*	Bur. of Program Development and Client Services Dept. of Health & Human Services 6 Hazen Dr. Concord, NH 03301	603-271-4456
COMMUNITY AFFAIRS *Provides programs to communities*	Office of State Planning Office of the Governor 2½ Beacon St. Concord, NH 03301	603-271-2155
CONSUMER ADVOCATE *Investigates consumer complaints*	Consumer Protection Div. Attorney General's Office 25 Capitol St. Concord, NH 03301	603-271-3641
DEPARTMENT OF HEALTH *Supervises health activities in the state*	Div. of Public Health Services Dept. of Health & Human Services 6 Hazen Dr. Concord, NH 03301	603-271-4501
DEVELOPMENTAL DISABILITIES *Provides services to the developmentally disabled*	Div. of Mental Health & Developmental Services Dept. of Health & Human Services 105 Pleasant St. Concord, NH 03301	603-271-5007
DRUG ABUSE *Provides assistance to drug abusers*	Office of Alcohol & Drug Abuse Prevention Dept. of Health & Human Services 6 Hazen Dr. Concord, NH 03301	800-852-3345 603-271-4627
FOOD AND DRUGS *Registers food & drug items*	Office of Disease Prevention Health & Welfare Bldg. Div. of Public Health Services 6 Hazen Dr. Concord, NH 03301	603-271-4671
GOVERNOR *Citizens access to the governor*	Office of the Governor State House Concord, NH 03301	603-271-2121

Type of Agency/Comments	*Organization and Address*	*Phone*
INSURANCE *Regulates the insurance industry*	Insurance Dept. 169 Manchester St. Concord, NH 03301	603-271-2261
LICENSING: DENTISTS *Report complaints about dentists to this office*	Board of Dental Examiners Health & Welfare Bldg. 6 Hazen Dr. Concord, NH 03301	603-271-4561
LICENSING: HOSPITALS *Report complaints about hospitals to this office*	Dept. of Public Health Bur. of Health Facilities Health & Welfare Bldg. 6 Hazen Dr. Concord, NH 03301	603-271-4592
LICENSING: NURSES *Report complaints about nurses to this office*	State Nurses Registration Div. of Public Health Health & Welfare Bldg. 6 Hazen Dr. Concord, NH 03301	603-271-2323

LICENSING: NURSING HOMES
 	
*Report complaints about
   nursing homes to this
   office*
	Dept. of Health & Human
	   Services
	Bur. of Health Facilities
	Health & Welfare Bldg.
	6 Hazen Dr.
	Concord, NH 03301
		603-271-4592

LICENSING: PHARMACISTS *Report complaints about pharmacists to this office*	Board of Pharmacy Health & Welfare Bldg. 6 Hazen Dr. Concord, NH 03301	603-271-2350

LICENSING: PHYSICIANS
 	
*Report complaints about
   doctors to this office*
	Board of Registration in
	   Medicine
	Health & Welfare Bldg.
	6 Hazen Dr.
	Concord, NH 03301
		603-271-1203

MEDICAID OFFICE
 	
*Administers Medicaid
   program*
	Dept. of Health & Human
	   Services
	Office of Economic Assistance
	Health & Welfare Bldg.
	6 Hazen Dr.
	Concord, NH 03301
		800-852-3345
		603-271-4353

Type of Agency/Comments	*Organization and Address*	*Phone*
MEDICARE PART B CARRIER *Processes Medicare claims for New Hampshire residents*	Blue Shield of Massachusetts P.O. Box 1010 Biddeford, ME 04005	800-447-1142
MENTAL HEALTH *Provides services to patients*	Div. of Mental Health & Development Services Dept. of Health & Human Services 105 Pleasant St. Concord, NH 03301	800-852-3345 603-271-5041
OCCUPATIONAL SAFETY & HEALTH *Inspects worksites*	Inspection Div. Dept. of Labor 19 Pillsbury St. Concord, NH 03301	603-271-2024
OMBUDSMAN (GENERAL) *Provides assistance to citizens*	State Ombudsman Office of the Governor State House 107 North Main St. Concord, NH 03301	603-271-3130
OMBUDSMAN (NURSING HOMES) *Investigates complaints from nursing home residents*	Long Term Care Ombudsman Dept. of Elderly & Adult Services Health & Welfare Bldg. 6 Hazen Dr. Concord, NH 03301	603-271-4375
SOCIAL SERVICES *Provides support services and counseling*	Div. of Human Services Dept. of Health & Human Services Health & Welfare Bldg. 6 Hazen Dr. Concord, NH 03301	800-852-3345 603-271-4321
VETERANS AFFAIRS *Provides assistance to veterans*	State Veterans Council 359 Lincoln St. Manchester, NH 03103	603-624-9230
VITAL STATISTICS *Maintains birth & death records*	Bur. of Vital Records Health & Welfare Bldg. 6 Hazen Dr. Concord, NH 03301	603-271-4650

Type of Agency/Comments	Organization and Address	Phone
VOCATIONAL REHABILITATION *Provides information on rehabilitation programs*	Governor's Commission for the Handicapped Park Plaza 85 Manchester St. Concord, NH 03301	603-271-2773 800-852-3405
WELFARE *Administers income programs*	Div. of Human Services Dept. of Health & Human Services Health & Welfare Bldg. 6 Hazen Dr. Concord, NH 03301	800-852-3345 603-271-4321
WORKER'S COMPENSATION *Provides income programs for injured workers*	Dept. of Labor 19 Pillsbury St. Concord, NH 03301	603-271-3176

NEW JERSEY

Type of Agency/Comments	Organization and Address	Phone
AGENCY LOCATOR *For Agencies & telephone numbers not listed*	Information Operator State House Trenton, NJ 08625	609-292-2121
AGING *Provides programs & services to senior citizens*	Div. on Aging Dept. of Community Affairs South Broad & Front Sts. CN 807 Trenton, NJ 08625	609-292-4833
ALCOHOLISM *Provides assistance to alcohol abusers*	Alcohol & Drug Abuse Unit Dept. of Health 129 Hanover St., CN 362 Trenton, NJ 08608	609-292-8949
ATTORNEY GENERAL *Chief law enforcement officer*	Attorney General's Office Dept. of Law and Public Safety R. J. Hughes Justice Complex 25 Market St. Trenton, NJ 08625	609-292-4925

Type of Agency/Comments	*Organization and Address*	*Phone*
CHILD WELFARE *Provides services to children and youths*	Div. of Youth and Family Services Dept. of Human Services 1 South Montgomery St. CN 717 Trenton, NJ 08625	609-292-6920
COMMUNITY AFFAIRS *Provides programs to communities*	Dept. of Community Affairs South Broad & Front Sts. Trenton, NJ 08625	609-292-6429
CONSUMER ADVOCATE *Investigates consumer complaints*	Div. of Consumer Affairs Dept. of Law & Public Safety 1100 Raymond Blvd. Rm. 504 Newark, NJ 07102	201-648-4010
DEPARTMENT OF HEALTH *Supervises health activities in the state*	Dept. of Health Health & Agriculture Bldg. John Fitch Plaza CN 360 Trenton, NJ 08625	609-292-7837
DEVELOPMENTAL DISABILITIES *Provides services to the developmentally disabled*	Div. of Developmental Disabilities Capitol Place One 222 South Warren St. Trenton, NJ 08625	609-292-3742
DRUG ABUSE *Provides assistance to drug abusers*	Alcohol & Drug Abuse Unit Dept. of Health 129 East Hanover St. CN 362 Trenton, NJ 08608	609-292-5760
FOOD AND DRUGS *Registers food & drug items*	Environmental Health Services Dept. of Health Uptown Bldg. 120 South Stockton St. Trenton, NJ 08625	609-984-0794
GOVERNOR *Citizens access to the governor*	Office of the Governor State House Trenton, NJ 08625	609-292-8956

Type of Agency/Comments	Organization and Address	Phone
INSURANCE *Regulates the insurance industry*	Div. of Administration Dept. of Insurance Arnold Constable Bldg., Rm. 307 20 West State St. Trenton, NJ 08625	609-292-5360
LICENSING: DENTISTS *Report complaints about dentists to this office*	Board of Examiners 1100 Raymond Blvd. Rm. 321 Newark, NJ 07102	201-648-7087
LICENSING: HOSPITALS *Report complaints about hospitals to this office*	N.J. Dept. of Health Health Facilities Evaluation Licensing & Standards CN 367 Trenton, NJ 08625	800-792-9770 609-588-7726
LICENSING: NURSES *Report complaints about nurses to this office*	State Board of Nursing 1100 Raymond Blvd. Newark, NJ 07102	201-648-2570
LICENSING: NURSING HOMES *Report complaints about nursing homes to this office*	Nursing Home Licensure Office Dept. of Health Licensing, Certification & Standards Trenton, NJ 08625	609-588-7726
LICENSING: PHARMACISTS *Report complaints about pharmacists to this office*	Board of Pharmacy 1100 Raymond Blvd. Newark, NJ 07102	201-648-2433
LICENSING: PHYSICIANS *Report complaints about doctors to this office*	Board of Medical Examiners 28 West State St. Rm. 914 Trenton, NJ 08608	609-292-4843
LICENSING: PROFESSIONALS *Licenses other health care professionals*	N.J. State Dept. of Health c/o Consumer Office CN 360 Trenton, NJ 08625	609-292-7837
MEDICAID OFFICE *Administers Medicaid program*	Dept. of Human Services Div. of Medical Assistance & Health Services Seven Quakerbridge Plaza Trenton, NJ 08625	609-588-2602

Type of Agency/Comments	*Organization and Address*	*Phone*
MEDICARE PART B CARRIER *Processes Medicare claims*	Medicare/PA Blue Shield Box 400010 Camp Hill, PA 17140-0010	800-462-9306
MENTAL HEALTH *Provides services to patients*	Div. of Mental Health & Hospitals Dept. of Human Services 13 Roszel Rd. Princeton, NJ 08540	609-987-0888
OCCUPATIONAL SAFETY & HEALTH *Inspects worksites*	Workplace Standards Div. Dept. of Labor Labor & Industry Bldg. CN 011 Trenton, NJ 08625	609-292-2313
OMBUDSMAN (GENERAL) *Assists citizens*	Div. of Citizen Complaints and Dispute Settlement Dept. of Public Advocate 25 Market St. Trenton, NJ 08625	609-292-1770 800-792-8600
OMBUDSMAN (NURSING HOMES) *Investigates complaints*	Ombudsman for the Elderly 28 West State St. Rm. 305 Trenton, NJ 08624	609-292-8016
SOCIAL SERVICES *Provides support services and counseling*	Dept. of Human Services Capitol Place One 222 South Warren St. CN 700 Trenton, NJ 08625	609-292-3717
VETERANS AFFAIRS *Provides assistance to veterans*	Div. of Veterans Programs and Special Services Dept. of Human Services Broad Street Bank Bldg., Rm. 505 143 East State St. Trenton, NJ 08608	609-292-9303
VITAL STATISTICS *Maintains birth & death records*	Bur. of Vital Statistics Dept. of Health John Fitch Plaza, CN 360 Trenton, NJ 08625	609-292-4087
VOCATIONAL REHABILITATION *Provides information on rehabilitation programs*	Div. of Vocational Rehab. 1005 Labor & Industry Bldg. CN 398 Trenton, NJ 08625	609-292-5987

Type of Agency/Comments	Organization and Address	Phone
WELFARE *Administers income programs*	Div. of Public Welfare Dept. of Human Services Six Quakerbridge Plaza CN 716 Trenton, NJ 08625	609-588-2401
WORKER'S COMPENSATION *Provides income for injured workers*	Div. of Worker's Compensation Dept. of Labor Labor & Industry Bldg. CN 381 Trenton, NJ 08625	609-292-2414

NEW MEXICO

Type of Agency/Comments	Organization and Address	Phone
AGENCY LOCATOR *For Agencies & telephone numbers not listed*	Information Operator State Capitol Santa Fe, NM 87503	505-827-4011
AGING *Provides programs & services to senior citizens*	State Agency on Aging La Villa Rivers Bldg., 4th Floor 224 East Palace Ave. Santa Fe, NM 87501	505-827-7640
ALCOHOLISM *Provides assistance to alcohol abusers*	Substance Abuse Bur. Behavioral Health Services Harold Runnels Bldg., Rm. 3350 1190 St. Francis Dr. Santa Fe, NM 87503	505-827-2589
ATTORNEY GENERAL *Chief law enforcement officer*	Attorney General's Office 260 Bataan Memorial Bldg. Santa Fe, NM 87504	505-827-6000
CHILD WELFARE *Provides services to children and youths*	Social Services Div. Human Services Dept. 2009 South Pacheco P.O. Box 2348 Santa Fe, NM 87504	505-827-8439

Type of Agency/Comments	*Organization and Address*	*Phone*
CONSUMER ADVOCATE *Investigates consumer complaints*	Consumer Protection & Economic Crimes Div. Office of Attorney General Bataan Memorial Bldg. Santa Fe, NM 87504	505-827-6060
DEPARTMENT OF HEALTH *Supervises health activities in the state*	Public Health Div. Health & Environment Dept. Harold Runnels Bldg. 1190 St. Francis Dr. Santa Fe, NM 87503	505-827-0020
DEVELOPMENTAL DISABILITIES *Provides services to the developmentally disabled*	Developmental Disabilities Bur. Health & Environment Dept. Harold Runnels Bldg. 1190 St. Francis Dr. Santa Fe, NM 87503	505-827-2573
DRUG ABUSE *Provides assistance to drug abusers*	Substance Abuse Bur. Behavioral Health Services Harold Runnels Bldg., Rm. 3350 1190 St. Francis Dr. Santa Fe, NM 87503	505-827-2589
FOOD AND DRUGS *Registers food & drug items*	Food Quality Section Health & Environment Dept. Harold Runnels Bldg. 1190 St. Francis Dr. Santa Fe, NM 87503	505-827-2785
GOVERNOR *Citizens access to the governor*	Office of the Governor Exec. Legislative Bldg. State Capitol Santa Fe, NM 87503	505-827-3000
INSURANCE *Regulates the insurance industry*	Dept. of Insurance Corporation Commission Old Santa Fe Trail Santa Fe, NM 87504	505-827-4500
LICENSING: DENTISTS *Report complaints about dentists to this office*	Board of Dental Examiners P.O. Box 25101 Santa Fe, NM 87504	505-827-6207

Type of Agency/Comments	Organization and Address	Phone
LICENSING: HOSPITALS *Report complaints about hospitals to this office*	Dept. of Health & Environment Health Services Div. Federal Program Certification 1190 St. Francis Dr. Santa Fe, NM 87503	505-827-2416
LICENSING: NURSES *Report complaints about nurses to this office*	Board of Nursing 4125 Carlisle, NE Albuquerque, NM 87107	505-841-6314
LICENSING: NURSING HOMES *Report complaints about nursing homes to this office*	Nursing Home Licensure Health & Environment Licensing & Certification Bur. Harold Runnels Bldg. 1190 St. Francis Dr. Santa Fe, NM 87503	505-827-2434
LICENSING: PHARMACISTS *Report complaints about pharmacists to this office*	Board of Pharmacy 4125 Carlisle, NE Albuquerque, NM 87107	505-841-6311
LICENSING: PHYSICIANS *Report complaints about doctors to this office*	Board of Medical Examiners P.O. Box 20001 Santa Fe, NM 87504	505-827-9933
LICENSING: PROFESSIONALS *Licenses other health care professionals*	Regulation & Licensing Dept. 725 St. Michael's Dr. Santa Fe, NM 87503	505-827-7160
MEDICAID OFFICE *Administers Medicaid program*	Dept. of Human Services Medical Assistance Div. P.O. Box 2348 Santa Fe, NM 87504	505-827-4315
MEDICARE PART B CARRIER *Processes Medicare claims for New Mexico*	Aetna Life and Casualty P.O. Box 25500 Oklahoma City, OK 73125	800-423-2925 505-843-7771
MENTAL HEALTH *Provides patient services*	Mental Health Bur. Behavioral Health Services Harold Runnels Bldg. 1190 St. Francis Dr. Santa Fe, NM 87503	505-827-2647

Type of Agency/Comments	Organization and Address	Phone
OCCUPATIONAL SAFETY & HEALTH *Inspects worksites*	Occupational Safety and Health Bur. Health & Environment Dept. Harold Runnels Bldg. 1190 St. Francis Dr. Santa Fe, NM 87503	505-827-2888
OMBUDSMAN (GENERAL) *Provides assistance to citizens*	Constituents Services Agency Office of the Governor State Capitol Santa Fe, NM 87503	505-827-3000
OMBUDSMAN (NURSING HOMES) *Investigates complaints from nursing home residents*	State Agency on Aging 224 East Palace Ave. Santa Fe, NM 87501	505-827-7640
SOCIAL SERVICES *Provides support services and counseling*	Social Services Div. Human Services Dept. 725 St. Michael's Drive Santa Fe, NM 87503	505-827-8464
VETERANS AFFAIRS *Provides assistance to veterans*	Veterans Service Commission Bataan Memorial Bldg. Rm. 142 Santa Fe, NM 87503	505-827-6300
VITAL STATISTICS *Maintains birth & death records*	Vital Statistics Bur. Health & Environment Dept. Harold Runnels Bldg. 1190 St. Francis Dr. Santa Fe, NM 87503	505-827-2342
VOCATIONAL REHABILITATION *Provides information on rehabilitation programs*	Div. of Vocational Rehab. 604 West San Mateo Santa Fe, NM 87503	505-982-4555
WELFARE *Administers income programs*	Human Services Dept. 1105 St. Francis Dr. Santa Fe, NM 87502	505-827-8720
WORKER'S COMPENSATION *Provides income for injured workers*	Worker's Compensation Div. 401 Broadway, NE P.O. Box 27190 Albuquerque, NM 87125	505-841-8790

NEW YORK

Type of Agency/Comments	*Organization and Address*	*Phone*
AGENCY LOCATOR *For Agencies & telephone numbers not listed*	Information Operator State Capitol Albany, NY 12224	518-474-2121
AGING *Provides programs & services to senior citizens*	Office for the Aging Exec. Dept. Agency Bldg. 2 Empire State Plaza Albany, NY 12223	800-342-9871 518-474-4425
ALCOHOLISM *Provides assistance to alcohol abusers*	Div. of Alcohol Abuse Alcoholism & Substance Abuse 194 Washington Ave. Albany, NY 12210	518-474-5417
ATTORNEY GENERAL *Chief law enforcement officer*	Attorney General's Office Dept. of Law 221 State Capitol Albany, NY 12224	518-474-7330
CHILD WELFARE *Provides services to children and youths*	Div. of Children & Family Services Dept. of Social Services Ten Eyck Bldg. 40 North Pearl St. Albany, NY 12243	518-474-9607
COMMUNITY AFFAIRS *Provides programs to communities*	Office for Local Government Services Dept. of State 162 Washington Ave. Albany, NY 12231	518-474-3355
CONSUMER ADVOCATE *Investigates consumer complaints*	Consumer Protection Board Exec. Dept. 1020 Twin Towers 99 Washington Ave. Albany, NY 12210	518-474-3514
DEPARTMENT OF HEALTH *Supervises health activities in the state*	Dept. of Health Corning Tower, Rm. 1408 Empire State Plaza Albany, NY 12237	518-474-2011

Type of Agency/Comments	Organization and Address	Phone
DEVELOPMENTAL DISABILITIES *Provides services to the developmentally disabled*	Div. of Operations Dept. of Social Services Ten Eyck Bldg. 40 North Pearl St. Albany, NY 12243	518-473-1997
DRUG ABUSE *Provides assistance to drug abusers*	Div. of Substance Abuse Services Office of Alcoholism & Substance Abuse Exec. Park South, 2nd Floor Stuyvesant Plaza Albany, NY 12203	518-457-2061
FOOD AND DRUGS *Registers food & drug items*	Div. of Food Inspection Services Dept. of Agriculture & Markets Capitol Plaza One Winners Cir. Albany, NY 12235	518-457-5368
GOVERNOR *Citizens access to the governor*	Office of the Governor State Capitol Albany, NY 12224	518-474-8418
INSURANCE *Regulates the insurance industry*	Insurance Dept. 160 West Broadway New York, NY 10013	212-602-0429
LICENSING: DENTISTS *Report complaints about dentists to this office*	New York State Education Dept. Office of Professional Discipline 622 Third Ave. New York, NY 10017	800-442-8106 212-557-2100
LICENSING: HOSPITALS *Report complaints about hospitals to this office*	New York Dept. of Health Bur. of Hospital Services Empire State Plaza Albany, NY 12237	518-474-5013
LICENSING: NURSES *Report complaints about nurses to this office*	State Education Dept. Office of Professional Discipline 622 Third Ave. New York, NY 10017	212-557-2100

Type of Agency/Comments	Organization and Address	Phone
LICENSING: NURSING HOMES *Report complaints about nursing homes to this office*	Bur. of Long Term Care Services Corning, Second Tower Empire State Plaza Albany, NY 12237	518-473-1564
LICENSING: PHARMACISTS *Report complaints about pharmacists to this office*	State Board of Pharmacy Cultural Education Center Albany, NY 12230	518-474-3848

LICENSING: PHYSICIANS
 	
Report complaints about doctors to this office
	New York State Dept. of
	  Health
	Office of Professional Medical
	  Conduct
	Empire State Plaza
	Albany, NY 12237
		518-474-8357

LICENSING: PROFESSIONALS *Licenses other health care professionals*	Div. of Professional Licensing Service State Education Dept. Cultural Education Center Rm. 3021, Empire State Plaza Albany, NY 12230	518-474-3830
MEDICAID OFFICE *Administers Medicaid program*	Div. of Medical Assistance Dept. of Social Services 40 North Pearl St. Albany, NY 12243	800-342-3715 518-474-9132
MEDICARE PART B CARRIER *Processes Medicare claims for Borough of Queens*	Groups Health Incorporated P.O. Box 1608 Ansonia Station New York, NY 10023	212-721-1770
MEDICARE PART B CARRIER *Processes Medicare claims (Check for coverage area)*	Blue Shield of Western NY P.O. Box 5600 Binghamton, NY 13902	800-252-6550 607-772-6906
MEDICARE PART B CARRIER *Processes claims for Bronx, Kings, New York, Richmond*	Empire Blue Cross/Blue Shield P.O. Box 100 Yorktown Heights, NY 10598	212-490-4444
MEDICARE PART B CARRIER *Processes Medicare claims (Check for coverage area)*	Empire Blue Cross/Blue Shield P.O. Box 100 Yorktown Heights, NY 10598	800-442-8430 212-490-4444

Type of Agency/Comments	Organization and Address	Phone
MENTAL HEALTH *Provides patient services*	Office of Mental Health 44 Holland Ave. Albany, NY 12229	518-474-4403
OCCUPATIONAL SAFETY & HEALTH *Inspects worksites*	Div. of Safety and Health Dept. of Labor State Office Bldg. Rm. 512 Albany, NY 12240	518-457-3518
OMBUDSMAN (GENERAL) *Provides assistance to* *citizens*	Office of the Ombudsman Secretary of State 162 Washington Ave. Albany, NY 12231	518-474-4750
OMBUDSMAN (NURSING HOMES) *Investigates complaints from* *nursing home residents*	Office for the Aging Agency Bldg. 2, Second Floor Empire State Plaza Albany, NY 12223	518-474-7329
SOCIAL SERVICES *Provides support services* *and counseling*	Dept. of Social Services Ten Eyck Bldg., 16th Floor 40 North Pearl St. Albany, NY 12243	518-474-9475
VETERANS AFFAIRS *Provides assistance to* *veterans*	Div. of Veterans Affairs Exec. Dept. 194 Washington Ave. Fifth Floor Albany, NY 12210	518-474-3752 800-635-6534
VITAL STATISTICS *Maintains birth & death* *records*	Vital Statistics Dept. of Health Corning Tower, Rm. 321 Empire State Plaza Albany, NY 12237	518-474-2026
VOCATIONAL REHABILITATION *Provides information on* *rehabilitation programs*	Office of Vocational Rehab. One Commerce Plaza Albany, NY 12230	518-473-4595

Type of Agency/Comments	Organization and Address	Phone
WELFARE *Administers income programs*	Dept. of Social Services Ten Eyck Bldg., 16th Floor 40 North Pearl St. Albany, NY 12243	518-474-9475
WORKER'S COMPENSATION *Provides income for injured workers*	Worker's Compensation Board 180 Livingston St. Brooklyn, NY 11248	718-802-6700

NORTH CAROLINA

Type of Agency/Comments	Organization and Address	Phone
AGENCY LOCATOR *For Agencies & telephone numbers not listed*	Information Operator State Capitol Raleigh, NC 27611	919-733-1110
AGING *Provides programs & services to senior citizens*	Div. of Aging Dept. of Human Resources 1985 Umstead Dr. Raleigh, NC 27603	919-733-3983
ALCOHOLISM *Provides assistance to alcohol abusers*	Alcohol & Drug Abuse Section Dept. of Human Resources Albemarle Bldg., Rm. 1124 325 North Salisbury St. Raleigh, NC 27611	919-733-4670
ATTORNEY GENERAL *Chief law enforcement officer*	Attorney General's Office Dept. of Justice 2 West Morgan St. Raleigh, NC 27602	919-733-3377
CHILD WELFARE *Provides services to children and youths*	Youth Advocacy and Involvement Office Dept. of Admin. 121 West Jones St. Raleigh, NC 27603	919-733-9296
COMMUNITY AFFAIRS *Provides programs to communities*	Div. of Community Assistance Dept. of Natural Resources and Community Development 512 North Salisbury St. Raleigh, NC 27687	919-733-2850

Type of Agency/Comments	*Organization and Address*	*Phone*
CONSUMER ADVOCATE *Investigates consumer complaints*	Special Deputy Attorney General Consumer Protection Section Dept. of Justice 104 Fayettville St. Raleigh, NC 27602	919-733-7741
DEPARTMENT OF HEALTH *Supervises health activities in the state*	Office of the State Health Director Archdale Bldg. 512 North Salisbury St. Raleigh, NC 27611	919-733-3446
DEVELOPMENTAL DISABILITIES *Provides services to the developmentally disabled*	Council on Developmental Disabilities Dept. of Human Resources 1508 Western Blvd. Raleigh, NC 27606	919-733-6566
DRUG ABUSE *Provides assistance to drug abusers*	Alcohol & Drug Abuse Section Dept. of Human Resources Albemarle Bldg., Rm. 1124 325 North Salisbury St. Raleigh, NC 27611	919-733-4670
FOOD AND DRUGS *Registers food & drug items*	Food & Drug Protection Div. Dept. of Agriculture 4000 Reedy Creek Rd. Raleigh, NC 27611	919-733-7366
GOVERNOR *Citizens access to the governor*	Office of the Governor State Capitol Raleigh, NC 27611	919-733-5612
INSURANCE *Regulates the insurance industry*	Dept. of Insurance Dobbs Bldg., Rm. 4071 430 North Salisbury St. Raleigh, NC 27611	919-733-7487
LICENSING: DENTISTS *Report complaints about dentists to this office*	Board of Dental Examiners P.O. Box 32270 Raleigh, NC 27622	919-781-4901
LICENSING: HOSPITALS *Report complaints about hospitals to this office*	Dept. of Human Resources Health Care Facility Branch 701 Barbour Dr. Raleigh, NC 27603	919-733-2786

Type of Agency/Comments	*Organization and Address*	*Phone*
LICENSING: NURSES *Report complaints about nurses to this office*	Board of Nursing P.O. Box 2129 Raleigh, NC 27602	919-782-3211
LICENSING: NURSING HOMES *Report complaints about nursing homes to this office*	Nursing Home Licensure Office Licensure & Certification Section Health Care Facilities Branch 701 Barbour Dr. Raleigh, NC 27603	919-733-2786
LICENSING: PHARMACISTS *Report complaints about pharmacists to this office*	Board of Pharmacy P.O. Box 459 Carrboro, NC 27510	919-942-4454
LICENSING: PHYSICIANS *Report complaints about doctors to this office*	Board of Medical Examiners P.O. Box 26808 Raleigh, NC 27611	919-876-3885
MEDICAID OFFICE *Administers Medicaid program*	Dept. of Human Resources Div. of Medical Assistance 1985 Umstead Dr. Raleigh, NC 27603	919-733-2060
MEDICARE PART B CARRIER *Processes Medicare claims*	Equicor, Inc. P.O. Box 671 Nashville, TN 37202	800-672-3071
MENTAL HEALTH *Provides patient services*	Div. of Mental Health Dept. of Human Resources 325 North Salisbury St. Raleigh, NC 27611	919-733-7011
OCCUPATIONAL SAFETY & HEALTH *Inspects worksites*	Div. of Occupational Safety & Health Dept. of Labor Shore Bldg. 214 West Jones St. Raleigh, NC 27603	919-733-2385
OMBUDSMAN (GENERAL) *Provides assistance to citizens*	Office of the Ombudsman Office of the Governor Admin. Bldg. 116 West Jones St. Raleigh, NC 27611	919-733-2391

Type of Agency/Comments	*Organization and Address*	*Phone*
OMBUDSMAN (NURSING HOMES) *Investigates complaints from nursing home residents*	Div. of Aging Dept. of Human Resources 1985 Umstead Dr. Raleigh, NC 27603	919-733-3983
SOCIAL SERVICES *Provides support services and counseling*	Div. of Social Services Dept. of Human Resources 325 North Salisbury St. Raleigh, NC 27611	919-733-3055
VETERANS AFFAIRS *Provides assistance to veterans*	Div. of Veterans Affairs Dept. of Admin. Heart of Raleigh Bldg. 227 East Edenton St. Raleigh, NC 27601	919-733-3851
VITAL STATISTICS *Maintains birth & death records*	Vital Records Branch Div. of Health Services 225 North McDowell St. Raleigh, NC 27602	919-733-3000
VOCATIONAL REHABILITATION *Provides information on rehabilitation programs*	Advocacy Council for Persons with Disabilities Dept. of Admin. 1318 Dale St. Raleigh, NC 27605	919-733-9250
WELFARE *Administers income programs*	Div. of Social Services Dept. of Human Resources Albemarle Bldg., Rm. 813 325 North Salisbury St. Raleigh, NC 27611	919-733-3055
WORKER'S COMPENSATION *Provides income for injured workers*	NC Industrial Commission Dept. of Commerce 430 North Salisbury St. Raleigh, NC 27611	919-733-4820

NORTH DAKOTA

Type of Agency/Comments	*Organization and Address*	*Phone*
AGENCY LOCATOR *For Agencies & telephone numbers not listed*	Information Operator State Capitol Bismarck, ND 58505	701-224-2000

Type of Agency/Comments	Organization and Address	Phone
AGING *Provides programs and service to senior citizens*	Aging Services Bur. Dept. of Human Services Bismarck, ND 58505	701-224-2577
ALCOHOLISM *Provides assistance to alcohol abusers*	Div. of Alcoholism & Drug Abuse Dept. of Human Services 1839 East Capitol Ave. Bismarck, ND 58505	701-224-2769
ATTORNEY GENERAL *Chief law enforcement officer*	Attorney General's Office State Capitol Bismarck, ND 58505	701-224-2210
CHILD WELFARE *Provides services to children and youths*	Children & Family Services Social Services Div. Dept. of Human Services Bismarck, ND 58505	701-224-4811
COMMUNITY AFFAIRS *Provides programs to local communities*	Office of Intergovernmental Assistance Office of Management & Budget State Capitol, 14th Floor Bismarck, ND 58505	701-224-2094
CONSUMER ADVOCACY *Investigates consumer complaints*	Consumer Fraud Div. Attorney General's Office State Capitol Bismarck, ND 58505	701-224-3404
DEPARTMENT OF HEALTH *Supervises health activities in the state*	Dept. of Health State Capitol 600 East Blvd. Bismarck, ND 58505	701-224-2372
DEVELOPMENTAL DISABILITIES *Provides services to the developmentally disabled*	Developmental Disabilities Div. Dept. of Human Services State Capitol Bismarck, ND 58505	701-224-2768
DRUG ABUSE *Provides assistance to drug abusers*	Div. of Alcoholism & Drug Abuse Dept. of Human Services 1839 East Capitol Ave. Bismarck, ND 58505	701-224-2769

Type of Agency/Comments	*Organization and Address*	*Phone*
FOOD AND DRUGS *Registers food & drug items*	Laboratories Dept. 2635 East Main St. Bismarck, ND 58501	701-221-6140
GOVERNOR *Citizens access to the* *governor*	Office of the Governor State Capitol Bismarck, ND 58505	701-224-2209
INSURANCE *Regulates the insurance* *industry*	Insurance Dept. State Capitol, 5th Floor Bismarck, ND 58505	701-224-2440
LICENSING: DENTISTS *Report complaints about* *dentists to this office*	Board of Dental Examiners P.O. Box 179 Valley City, ND 58072	701-845-3708
LICENSING: HOSPITALS *Report complaints about* *hospitals to this office*	Dept. of Health Div. of Health Facilities State Capitol Bismarck, ND 58505	701-224-2352
LICENSING: NURSES *Report complaints about* *nurses to this office*	Board of Nursing 919 South 7th St. Suite 504 Bismarck, ND 58504	701-224-2974

LICENSING: NURSING HOMES
 	
Report complaints about
  nursing homes to this
  office
	Div. of Health Facilities
	Dept. of Health
	Judicial Wing, 2nd Floor
	Bismarck, ND 58505
		701-224-2352

LICENSING: PHARMACISTS *Report complaints about* *pharmacists to this office*	Board of Pharmacy P.O. Box 1354 Bismarck, ND 58501	701-258-1535
LICENSING: PHYSICIANS *Report complaints about* *doctors to this office*	Board of Medical Examiners City Center Plaza 418 East Broadway Ave. Suite C-18 Bismarck, ND 58501	701-223-9485
LICENSING: PROFESSIONALS *Licenses other health care* *professionals*	Licensing Dept. Office of the Attorney General 600 East Blvd. Bismarck, ND 58505	701-224-2219

Type of Agency/Comments	Organization and Address	Phone
MEDICAID OFFICE *Administers Medicaid program*	Dept. of Human Services Medical Services 600 East Blvd. Bismarck, ND 58505	701-224-2321
MEDICARE PART B CARRIER *Processes Medicare claims*	Blue Shield of North Dakota 4510 13th Ave., SW Fargo, ND 58121	800-247-2267 701-282-1100
MENTAL HEALTH *Provides patient services*	Div. of Mental Health Dept. of Human Services Bismarck, ND 58505	701-224-2766
OCCUPATIONAL SAFETY & HEALTH *Inspects worksites*	Occupational Safety & Health Programs Dept. of Health 1200 Missouri Ave. Bismarck, ND 58502	701-224-2348
OMBUDSMAN (NURSING HOMES) *Investigates complaints from nursing home residents*	Long Term Care Ombudsman Aging Services Div. 600 East Blvd. State Capitol Bismarck, ND 58505	701-224-2577
SOCIAL SERVICES *Provides support services and counseling*	Dept. of Human Services State Capitol Bismarck, ND 58505	701-224-2310
VETERANS AFFAIRS *Provides assistance to veterans*	Dept. of Veterans Affairs 15 Broadway, 6th Floor Fargo, ND 58102	701-237-8383
VITAL STATISTICS *Maintains birth & death records*	Div. of Vital Records Dept. of Health Bismarck, ND 58505	701-224-2360
VOCATIONAL REHABILITATION *Provides information on rehabilitation programs*	Div. of Vocational Rehabilitation Dept. of Human Services State Capitol Bismarck, ND 58505	701-224-2907

Type of Agency/Comments	Organization and Address	Phone
WELFARE	Public Assistance	701-224-2332
	Dept. of Human Services	
Administers income	State Capitol	
programs	Bismarck, ND 58505	
WORKER'S COMPENSATION	Worker's Compensation Bur.	701-224-2700
	Russel Bldg.	
Provides income for injured	4007 North State St.	
workers	Bismarck, ND 58501	

OHIO

Type of Agency/Comments	Organization and Address	Phone
AGENCY LOCATOR	Information Operator	614-466-2000
	State House	
For Agencies & telephone	Broad and High Sts.	
numbers not listed	Columbus, OH 43215	
AGING	Commission on Aging	614-466-5500
	50 West Broad St.	
Provides programs &	9th Floor	
services to senior citizens	Columbus, OH 43215	
ALCOHOLISM	Div. of Alcoholism	614-466-3445
	Dept. of Health	
Provides assistance to	170 North High St., 3rd Floor	
alcohol abusers	Columbus, OH 43266	
ATTORNEY GENERAL	Attorney General's Office	614-466-3376
	State Office Tower	
Chief law enforcement	30 East Broad St.	
officer	Columbus, OH 43215	
CHILD WELFARE	Div. of Family, Children &	614-466-1213
	Adult Services	
Provides services to children	Dept. of Human Services	
and youths	State Office Tower, 30th Floor	
	30 East Broad St.	
	Columbus, OH 43215	
COMMUNITY AFFAIRS	Div. of Community	614-466-5863
	Development	
Provides programs to	Vern Riffe Office Tower	
communities	77 South High St.	
	Columbus, OH 43215	

Type of Agency/Comments	Organization and Address	Phone
CONSUMER ADVOCATE *Investigates consumer complaints*	Consumer Frauds & Crimes Section Attorney General's Office State Office Tower 30 East Broad St. Columbus, OH 43215	614-466-8831
DEPARTMENT OF HEALTH *Supervises health activities in the state*	Dept. of Health 246 North High St. Columbus, OH 43266	614-466-3543
DEVELOPMENTAL DISABILITIES *Provides services to the developmentally disabled*	Dept. of Mental Retardation/ Developmental Disabilities State Office Tower, Rm. 1280 30 East Broad St. Columbus, OH 43215	614-466-5214
DRUG ABUSE *Provides assistance to drug abusers*	Bur. of Drug Abuse Dept. of Health 170 North High St., 3rd Floor Columbus, OH 43266	614-466-3445
FOOD AND DRUGS *Registers food and drug items*	Div. of Foods, Dairies & Drugs Dept. of Agriculture 8995 East Main St. Reynoldsburg, OH 43068	614-866-6361
GOVERNOR *Citizens access to the governor*	Office of the Governor State House Columbus, OH 43215	614-466-1722
INSURANCE *Regulates the insurance industry*	Dept. of Insurance 2100 Stella Ct. Columbus, OH 43266	614-644-2658
LICENSING: DENTISTS *Report complaints about dentists to this office*	Ohio State Dental Board 77 South High St., 18th Floor Columbus, OH 43266-0306	614-466-2580
LICENSING: HOSPITALS *Report complaints about hospitals to this office*	Dept. of Health Survey Operations 246 North High St. P.O. Box 118 Columbus, OH 43266-0118	614-644-7935

Type of Agency/Comments	Organization and Address	Phone
LICENSING: NURSES *Report complaints about nurses to this office*	Ohio Board of Nursing 77 South High St., 17th Floor Columbus, OH 43266-0316	614-466-3947
LICENSING: NURSING HOMES *Report complaints about nursing homes to this office*	Nursing Home Licensure Office Licensing & Certification Div. Dept. of Health 246 North High St., 8th Floor P.O. Box 118 Columbus, OH 43266-0118	614-466-2070
LICENSING: PHARMACISTS *Report complaints about pharmacists to this office*	Ohio State Board of Pharmacy 77 South High St., 17th Floor Columbus, OH 43266-0320	614-466-4143
LICENSING: PHYSICIANS *Report complaints about doctors to this office*	Ohio State Medical Board 77 South High St. Columbus, OH 43215	614-466-3938
LICENSING: PROFESSIONALS *Licenses other health care professionals*	Div. of Licensing Dept. of Commerce 77 South High St., 23rd Floor Columbus, OH 43266-0546	614-466-4130
MEDICAID OFFICE *Administers Medicaid program*	Dept. of Human Services Benefits Admin. 30 East Broad St., 31st Floor Columbus, OH 43215	614-466-3196
MEDICARE CARRIER PART B *Processes Medicare claims*	Nationwide Mutual Insurance P.O. Box 57 Columbus, OH 43216	800-282-0530 614-249-7157
MENTAL HEALTH *Provides patient services*	Dept. of Mental Health 1180 State Office Tower 30 East Broad St. Columbus, OH 43215	614-466-2337
OCCUPATIONAL SAFETY & HEALTH *Inspects worksites*	Div. of Safety & Hygiene Industrial Commission of Ohio 246 North High St. Columbus, OH 43266	614-466-1276
OMBUDSMAN (GENERAL) *Provides assistance to citizens*	State Ombudsman Office of the Governor State House Columbus, OH 43215	614-466-4363

Type of Agency/Comments	Organization and Address	Phone
OMBUDSMAN (NURSING HOMES) *Investigates complaints from nursing home residents*	Ohio Dept. on Aging State Ombudsman 50 West Broad St., 9th Floor Columbus, OH 43215	614-466-1220
SOCIAL SERVICES *Provides support services and counseling*	Div. of Social Services Dept. of Human Services State Office Tower 30 East Broad St. Columbus, OH 43215	614-466-6282
VETERANS AFFAIRS *Provides assistance to veterans*	Div. of Veterans Affairs Adjutant General's Dept. State House Annex, Rm. 11 Columbus, OH 43215	614-466-5453
VITAL STATISTICS *Maintains birth & death records*	Div. of Vital Statistics Dept. of Health 65 South Front St. Columbus, OH 43266	614-466-2531
VOCATIONAL REHABILITATION *Provides information on rehabilitation programs*	Rehab. Services Commission 400 East Campus View Dr. Columbus, OH 43229	614-438-1210
WELFARE *Administers income programs*	Div. of Public Assistance Dept. of Human Services State Office Tower, 27th Floor 30 East Broad St. Columbus, OH 43215	614-466-4815
WORKER'S COMPENSATION *Provides income program for injured workers*	Bur. of Worker's Compensation 246 North High St. Columbus, OH 43266	614-466-2950

OKLAHOMA

Type of Agency/Comments	Organization and Address	Phone
AGENCY LOCATOR *For Agencies & telephone numbers not listed*	Information Operator State Capitol Lincoln Blvd. Oklahoma City, OK 73105	405-521-2011

Type of Agency/Comments	Organization and Address	Phone
AGING *Provides programs &* *services for senior citizens*	Aging Services Div. Dept. of Human Services 312 NE 28th St. Oklahoma City, OK 73125	405-521-2327
ALCOHOLISM *Provides assistance to* *alcohol abusers*	Alcohol & Drug Abuse Bur. Dept. of Mental Health 12 NE 13th St. Oklahoma City, OK 73152	405-271-7474
ATTORNEY GENERAL *Chief law enforcement* *officer*	Attorney General's Office 112 State Capitol Lincoln Blvd. Oklahoma City, OK 73105	405-521-3921
CHILD WELFARE *Provides services to children* *and youths*	Div. of Child Welfare Dept. of Human Services 2400 North Lincoln Blvd. Oklahoma City, OK 73125	405-521-3777
COMMUNITY AFFAIRS *Provides programs to* *communities*	Industrial and Community Development Div. Dept. of Commerce 6601 Broadway Ext. Oklahoma City, OK 73116	405-841-9326 800-443-6552
CONSUMER ADVOCATE *Investigates consumer* *complaints*	Dept. of Consumer Credit Jim Thorpe Office Bldg. 2101 North Lincoln Blvd. Oklahoma City, OK 73105	405-521-3653
DEPARTMENT OF HEALTH *Supervises health activities* *in the state*	Dept. of Health 1000 NE 10th St. P.O. Box 53551 Oklahoma City, OK 73152	405-271-4200

DEVELOPMENTAL
  DISABILITIES
 	
Provides services to the
developmentally disabled
	Services for the
	  Developmentally Disabled
	Dept. of Human Services
	2401 N. Lincoln Blvd.
	Oklahoma City, OK 73125
		405-521-3617

DRUG ABUSE	Alcohol & Drug Abuse Bur. Dept. of Mental Health 12 NE 13th St. Oklahoma City, OK 73152	405-271-7474

Type of Agency/Comments	Organization and Address	Phone
FOOD AND DRUGS *Registers food & drug items*	Food Protection Service Dept. of Health 1000 NE 10th St. Rm. 355 Oklahoma City, OK 73152	405-271-5243
GOVERNOR *Citizens access to the governor*	Office of the Governor State Capitol Oklahoma City, OK 73105	405-521-3208
INSURANCE *Regulates the insurance industry*	Insurance Dept. State Insurance Bldg. 1901 North Walnut Blvd. Oklahoma City, OK 73152	405-521-2828
LICENSING: DENTISTS *Report complaints about dentists to this office*	Board of Dental Examiners 2726 North Oklahoma Oklahoma City, OK 73105	405-521-2350
LICENSING: HOSPITALS *Report complaints about hospitals to this office*	Dept. of Health Institutional Services 1000 NE 10th St. Oklahoma City, OK 73152	405-271-6868
LICENSING: NURSES *Report complaints about nurses to this office*	Board of Nurse Registration & Education 2915 North Claussen Blvd. Suite 524 Oklahoma City, OK 73106	405-525-2076
LICENSING: NURSING HOMES *Report complaints about nursing homes to this office*	Nursing Home Licensure Office Special Health Services Dept. of Health 1000 NE 10th St. Oklahoma City, OK 73152	405-271-6868
LICENSING: PHARMACISTS	Oklahoma Board of Pharmacy 4545 Lincoln Blvd. Suite 112 Oklahoma City, OK 73105	405-521-3815
LICENSING: PHYSICIANS *Report complaints about doctors to this office*	Board of Medical Examiners 5104 North Francis Suite C Oklahoma City, OK 73118	405-848-6841

Type of Agency/Comments	Organization and Address	Phone
MEDICAID OFFICE *Administers Medicaid program*	Dept. of Human Services Medical Services Div. P.O. Box 25352 Oklahoma City, OK 73125	405-557-2540
MEDICARE PART B CARRIER *Processes Medicare claims*	Aetna Life & Casualty Co. 701 NW 63rd St. Suite 100 Oklahoma City, OK 73116	800-522-9079 405-848-7711
MENTAL HEALTH *Provides patient services*	Dept. of Mental Health 1200 NE 13th St. Oklahoma City, OK 73152	405-271-7474
OCCUPATIONAL SAFETY & HEALTH *Inspects worksites*	Safety Standards Div. Dept. of Labor 1315 Broadway Place Oklahoma City, OK 73103	405-235-5568
OMBUDSMAN (GENERAL) *Provides assistance to citizens*	Office of the Ombudsman Office of the Governor State Capitol, Rm. 212 Lincoln Blvd. Oklahoma City, OK 73105	405-521-2342
OMBUDSMAN (NURSING HOMES) *Investigates complaints from nursing home residents*	Dept. of Human Services Long Term Care Ombudsman 312 NE 28th St. Oklahoma City, OK 73125	405-521-2281
SOCIAL SERVICES *Provides support services and counseling*	Social Services Income Support Div. Dept. of Human Services 2400 North Lincoln Blvd. Oklahoma City, OK 73125	405-521-3531
VETERANS AFFAIRS *Provides assistance to veterans*	Dept. of Veterans Affairs Veterans Memorial Bldg. 2311 North Central Ave. Oklahoma City, OK 73152	405-521-3684
VITAL STATISTICS *Maintains birth & death records*	Bur. of Vital Statistics Vital Records Div. Dept. of Health 1000 NE 10th St. Oklahoma City, OK 73152	405-271-4040

Type of Agency/Comments	*Organization and Address*	*Phone*
VOCATIONAL REHABILITATION *Provides information on rehabilitation programs*	Governor's Office of Handicapped Concerns 4300 N. Lincoln Blvd. Suite 200 Oklahoma City, OK 73105	405-521-3756
WELFARE *Administers income programs*	Assistance Payments Income Support Div. Dept. of Human Services 2400 Lincoln Blvd. Oklahoma City, OK 73125	405-521-3076
WORKER'S COMPENSATION *Provides income for injured workers*	Worker's Compensation Court Denver N. Davision Bldg. 1915 North Stiles Oklahoma City, OK 73105	405-557-7600

OREGON

Type of Agency/Comments	*Organization and Address*	*Phone*
AGENCY LOCATOR *For Agencies & telephone numbers not listed*	Information Operator State Capitol Salem, OR 97310	503-378-3131
AGING *Provides programs & services for senior citizens*	Senior Services Div. Dept. of Human Resources 313 Public Service Bldg. Capitol Mall Salem, OR 97310	800-232-3020 503-378-4728
ALCOHOLISM *Provides assistance to alcohol abusers*	Alcohol & Drug Abuse Programs Dept. of Human Resources Public Service Bldg., Rm. 301 Capitol Mall Salem, OR 97310	503-378-2163
ATTORNEY GENERAL *Chief law enforcement officer*	Attorney General's Office Dept. of Justice Justice Bldg. Court and 12th Sts. Salem, OR 97310	503-378-6002
CHILD WELFARE *Provides services to children and youths*	Children's Services Div. Dept. of Human Resources 198 Commercial St. SE Salem, OR 97310	503-378-4374

Type of Agency/Comments	Organization and Address	Phone
COMMUNITY AFFAIRS *Provides programs to communities*	Inter-Government Relations Div. Exec. Dept. Capitol Bldg., Rm. 160 Salem, OR 97310	503-378-5937
CONSUMER ADVOCATE *Investigates consumer complaints*	Consumer Affairs Div. Dept. of Justice 100 Justice Bldg. Portland, OR 97310	503-378-4732
DEPARTMENT OF HEALTH *Supervises health activities in the state*	Health Div. Dept. of Human Services State Office Bldg., Rm. 811 1400 SW 5th Ave. Portland, OR 97201	503-229-5032
DEVELOPMENTAL DISABILITIES *Provides services to the developmentally disabled*	Mental Health Div. Dept. of Human Resources 2575 Bittern St., NE Salem, OR 97310	503-378-2429
DRUG ABUSE *Provides assistance to drug abusers*	Alcohol & Drug Abuse Programs Dept. of Human Resources Public Service Bldg., Rm. 301 Capitol Mall Salem, OR 97310	503-378-2163
FOOD AND DRUGS *Registers food & drug items*	Div. of Food & Dairy Dept. of Agriculture 635 Capitol St., NE Salem, OR 97310	503-378-3790
GOVERNOR *Citizens access to the governor*	Office of the Governor State Capitol Salem, OR 97310	503-378-3121
INSURANCE *Regulates insurance industry*	Insurance & Finance Div. 21 Labor & Industry Bldg. Salem, OR 97310	503-378-4474
LICENSING: DENTISTS *Report complaints about dentists to this office*	Oregon Board of Dentistry 1515 SW 5th Ave. Suite 400 Portland, OR 97201	503-229-5520

Type of Agency/Comments	Organization and Address	Phone
LICENSING: HOSPITALS *Report complaints about hospitals to this office*	Office of Environmental & Health Services Health Facilities Section P.O. Box 231 Portland, OR 97207	503-229-5686
LICENSING: NURSES *Report complaints about nurses to this office*	Board of Nursing 1400 SW 5th Ave. Rm. 904 Portland, OR 97201	503-229-5653
LICENSING: NURSING HOMES *Report complaints about nursing homes to this office*	Senior Services Div. Long Term Care Licensing Licensing & Certification 313 Public Service Bldg. Portland, OR 97310	503-378-3751
LICENSING: PHARMACISTS *Report complaints about pharmacists to this office*	Board of Pharmacy P.O. Box 231 Portland, OR 97207	503-229-5849
LICENSING: PHYSICIANS *Report complaints about doctors to this office*	Board of Medical Examiners 1500 SW 1st Ave. Portland, OR 97201	503-229-5770
MEDICAID OFFICE *Administers Medicaid program*	Dept. of Human Resources Adult and Family Services 313 Public Service Bldg. Salem, OR 97310	503-378-4728
MEDICARE CARRIER PART B *Processes Medicare claims*	Aetna Life & Casualty 200 SW Market St. P.O. Box 1997 Portland, OR 97207	800-452-0125 503-222-6831
MENTAL HEALTH *Provides patient services*	Mental Health Div. Dept. of Human Resources 2575 Bittern St., NE Salem, OR 97310	503-378-2671
OCCUPATIONAL SAFETY & HEALTH *Inspects worksites*	Accident Prevention Div. Worker's Compensation Dept. 204 Labor & Industries Bldg. Capitol Mall Salem, OR 97310	503-378-3272
OMBUDSMAN (GENERAL) *Provides assistance to citizens*	Citizens' Representative Office of the Governor State Capitol, Rm. 160 Salem, OR 97310	503-378-4582

Type of Agency/Comments	*Organization and Address*	*Phone*
OMBUDSMAN (NURSING HOMES) *Investigates complaints from nursing home residents*	Long Term Care Ombudsman 2475 Lancaster Dr., NE Bldg. B, Suite 9 Salem, OR 97310	503-378-6533
SOCIAL SERVICES *Provides support services and counseling*	Dept. of Human Resources 318 Public Service Bldg. Capitol Mall Salem, OR 97310	503-378-3034
VETERANS AFFAIRS *Provides assistance to veterans*	Dept. of Veterans Affairs Oregon Veterans Bldg. 700 Summer St., NE Salem, OR 97310	503-373-2000
VITAL STATISTICS *Maintains birth & death records*	Center for Health Statistics Health Div. State Office Bldg. 1400 SW 5th Ave. Portland, OR 97207	503-229-5895
VOCATIONAL REHABILITATION *Provides information on rehabilitation programs*	Dept. of Human Services Public Service Bldg., Rm. 318 Capitol Mall Salem, OR 97310	503-378-3034
WELFARE *Administers income programs*	Adult & Family Services Div. Dept. of Human Resources 417 Public Service Bldg. Capitol Mall Salem, OR 97310	503-378-6142
WORKER'S COMPENSATION *Provides income for injured workers*	Worker's Compensation Dept. 480 Church St., SE Salem, OR 97310	503-378-3311

PENNSYLVANIA

Type of Agency/Comments	*Organization and Address*	*Phone*
AGENCY LOCATOR *For Agencies and telephone numbers not listed*	Information Operator Main Capitol Bldg. Harrisburg, PA 17120	717-787-2121

Type of Agency/Comments	*Organization and Address*	*Phone*
AGING *Provides programs & services to senior citizens*	Dept. of Aging Barto Bldg. 231 State St. Harrisburg, PA 17101	717-783-1550
ALCOHOLISM *Provides assistance to alcohol abusers*	Drug & Alcohol Programs Dept. of Health 809 Health & Welfare Bldg. Forster & Commonwealth Harrisburg, PA 17108	717-787-9857
ATTORNEY GENERAL *Chief law enforcement officer*	Attorney General's Office Strawberry Square, 16th Floor 4th & Walnut Sts. Harrisburg, PA 17120	717-787-3391
CHILD WELFARE *Provides services to children and youths*	Children, Youth, and Families Dept. of Public Welfare Health & Welfare Bldg. Rm. 131, P.O. Box 2675 Harrisburg, PA 17105	717-787-4756
COMMUNITY AFFAIRS *Provides programs to communities*	Dept. of Community Affairs 317 Forum Bldg. Walnut & Commonwealth Ave. Harrisburg, PA 17120	717-787-7160
CONSUMER ADVOCATE *Investigates consumer complaints*	Bur. of Consumer Affairs Office of the Attorney General Strawberry Square, 14th Floor 4th & Walnut Sts. Harrisburg, PA 17120	717-787-9707
DEPARTMENT OF HEALTH *Supervises health activities in the state*	Dept. of Health 802 Health & Welfare Bldg. Forster & Commonwealth Harrisburg, PA 17108	717-787-6436
DEVELOPMENTAL DISABILITIES *Provides services to the developmentally disabled*	Office of Mental Retardation Dept. of Public Welfare Forster & Commonwealth Sts. Harrisburg, PA 17120	717-787-3700
DRUG ABUSE *Provides assistance to drug abusers*	Drug & Alcohol Programs Dept. of Health 809 Health & Welfare Bldg. Forster & Commonwealth Harrisburg, PA 17108	717-787-9857

Type of Agency/Comments	*Organization and Address*	*Phone*
GOVERNOR *Citizen access to the governor*	Office of the Governor State Capitol Rm. 225 Harrisburg, PA 17120	717-787-1116
INSURANCE *Regulates the insurance industry*	Insurance Dept. 1321 Strawberry Square 4th & Walnut Sts. Harrisburg, PA 17120	717-787-2317
LICENSING: DENTISTS *Report complaints about dentists to this office*	Bur. of Professional & Occupational Affairs Dental Board Complaint Dept. Harrisburg, PA 17105	717-787-8503
LICENSING: HOSPITALS *Report complaints about hospitals to this office*	Dept. of Health Bur. of Quality Assurance Div. of Hospitals Health & Welfare Bldg., Rm. 532 Harrisburg, PA 17108	717-783-8980
LICENSING: NURSES *Report complaints about nurses to this office*	Bur. of Professional & Occupational Affairs P.O. Box 2649 Harrisburg, PA 17105	717-787-8503
LICENSING: NURSING HOMES *Report complaints about nursing homes to this office*	Nursing Home Licensure Office Div. of Long Term Care Health & Welfare Bldg. Rm. 526 Harrisburg, PA 17120	717-787-1816
LICENSING: PHARMACISTS *Report complaints about pharmacists to this office*	State Board of Pharmacy Transportation & Safety Bldg. P.O. Box 2649 Harrisburg, PA 17105	717-783-7157
LICENSING: PHYSICIANS *Report complaints about doctors to this office*	Board of Medical Education & Licensure P.O. Box 2649 Harrisburg, PA 17105	717-787-2381
LICENSING: PROFESSIONALS *Licenses other health care professionals*	Bur. of Professional & Occupational Affairs Dept. of State Transportation & Safety Bldg. Forster & Commonwealth Harrisburg, PA 17105	717-787-8503

Type of Agency/Comments	*Organization and Address*	*Phone*
MEDICAID OFFICE *Administers Medicaid program*	Dept. of Public Welfare Health & Welfare Bldg. Rm. 515 Harrisburg, PA 17120	717-787-1870
MEDICARE CARRIER PART B *Processes Medicare claims*	Pennsylvania Blue Shield P.O. Box 890065 Camp Hill, PA 17089-0065	800-382-1274
MENTAL HEALTH *Provides patient services*	Office of Mental Health Dept. of Public Welfare 308 Health & Welfare Bldg. Forster & Commonwealth Harrisburg, PA 17105	717-787-6443
OCCUPATIONAL SAFETY & HEALTH *Inspects worksites*	Bur. of Occupational & Industrial Safety Dept. of Labor & Industry 7th and Forster Sts. Harrisburg, PA 17120	717-787-3323 800-426-7362
OMBUDSMAN (GENERAL) *Provides assistance to citizens*	Governor's Action Center Office of the Governor Finance Bldg., Rm. 402 Commonwealth & North Sts. Harrisburg, PA 17120	717-783-1198 800-932-0784
OMBUDSMAN (NURSING HOMES *Investigates complaints from nursing home residents*	Dept. of Aging Bur. of Program Field Operations Barto Bldg. 231 State St. Harrisburg, PA 17101	717-783-7247
SOCIAL SERVICES *Provides support services and counseling*	Office of Children, Youth & Family Dept. of Public Welfare Health & Welfare Bldg. Rm. 131 Harrisburg, PA 17105	717-787-4756
VETERANS AFFAIRS *Provides assistance to veterans*	Bur. for Veterans Affairs Dept. of Military Affairs Bldg. S-0-47, Rm. 220 Fort Indiantown Gap Annville, PA 17003	717-865-8901
VITAL STATISTICS *Maintains birth & death records*	Div. of Vital Records Dept. of Health 101 South Mercer St. New Castle, PA 16103	412-656-3111

Type of Agency/Comments	*Organization and Address*	*Phone*
VOCATIONAL REHABILITATION *Provides information on rehabilitation programs*	Bur. of Vocational Rehab. 7th & Forster Sts. Harrisburg, PA 17120	717-787-5244
WELFARE *Administers income programs*	Dept. of Public Welfare Health & Welfare Bldg. Rm. 333 Forster & Commonwealth Harrisburg, PA 17105	717-787-2600
WORKER'S COMPENSATION *Provides income for injured workers*	Bur. of Worker's Compensation Dept. of Labor & Industry 3607 Derry St., 4th Floor Harrisburg, PA 17111	717-783-5421

RHODE ISLAND

Type of Agency/Comments	*Organization and Address*	*Phone*
AGENCY LOCATOR *For Agencies & telephone numbers not listed*	Information Operator State House 82 Smith St. Providence, RI 02903	401-277-2000
AGING *Provides programs & services to senior citizens*	Dept. of Elderly Affairs 160 Pine St. Providence, RI 02903	401-277-6847
ALCOHOLISM *Provides assistance to alcohol abusers*	Div. of Substance Abuse Admin. Bldg. Cranston, RI 02920	401-464-2091
ATTORNEY GENERAL *Chief law enforcement officer*	Attorney General's Office 72 Pine St. Providence, RI 02903	401-274-4400
CHILD WELFARE *Provides services to children and youths*	Dept. for Children and Their Families Bldg. 7 610 Mt. Pleasant Ave. Providence, RI 02908	401-457-7450

Type of Agency/Comments	Organization and Address	Phone
CONSUMER ADVOCATE *Investigates consumer complaints*	Consumer's Council 365 Broadway Providence, RI 02909	401-277-2764
DEPARTMENT OF HEALTH *Supervises health activities in the state*	Dept. of Health 401 Cannon Bldg. Three Capitol Hill Providence, RI 02908	401-277-2231
DEVELOPMENTAL DISABILITIES *Provides services to the developmentally disabled*	Div. of Retardation & Developmental Disabilities Aime J. Forand Bldg. 600 New London Ave. Cranston, RI 02920	401-464-3231
DRUG ABUSE *Provides assistance to drug abusers*	Div. of Substance Abuse Dept. of Mental Health, Retardation, & Hospitals Substance Abuse Admin. Bldg. Cranston, RI 02920	401-464-2091
FOOD AND DRUGS *Registers food items*	Div. of Food Protection Dept. of Health 75 Davis St. Providence, RI 02908	401-277-3118
FOOD AND DRUGS *Registers drug items*	Div. of Drug Control Dept. of Health 75 Davis St. Providence, RI 02908	401-277-2837
GOVERNOR *Citizens access to the governor*	Office of the Governor State House Providence, RI 02903	401-277-2080
INSURANCE *Regulates the insurance industry*	Dept. of Business Regulation 233 Richmond St. Providence, RI 02903	401-277-2246
LICENSING: DENTISTS *Report complaints about dentists to this office*	Div. of Professional Regulation Three Capitol Hill Providence, RI 02908	401-277-2827
LICENSING: HOSPITALS *Report complaints about hospitals to this office*	Dept. of Health Facilities Regulation Three Capitol Hill Providence, RI 02908	401-277-2566

Type of Agency/Comments	Organization and Address	Phone
LICENSING: NURSES *Report complaints about nurses to this office*	Board of Nurse Registration Dept. of Health Cannon Bldg., Rm. 104 Three Capitol Hill Providence, RI 02908	401-277-2827
LICENSING: NURSING HOMES *Report complaints about nursing homes to this office*	Nursing Home Licensure Office Dept. of Health Div. of Facilities Regulation Three Capitol Hill Providence, RI 02908	401-277-2566
LICENSING: PHARMACISTS *Report complaints about pharmacists to this office*	Board of Pharmacy Div. of Drug Control Three Capitol Hill Providence, RI 02908	401-277-2837
LICENSING: PHYSICIANS *Report complaints about doctors to this office*	Div. of Professional Regulation Three Capitol Hill Providence, RI 02908	401-277-2827
LICENSING: PROFESSIONALS *Licenses other health care professionals*	Div. of Professional Regulation Dept. of Health Three Capitol Hill Providence, RI 02908	401-277-2827
MEDICAID OFFICE *Administers Medicaid program*	Dept. of Human Services Div. of Medical Services 600 New London Ave. Cranston, RI 02920	401-464-3575
MEDICARE PART B CARRIER *Processes Medicare claims*	Blue Shield of Rhode Island 444 Westminster Mall Providence, RI 02901	800-662-5170 401-861-2273
MENTAL HEALTH *Provides patient services*	Div. of Mental Health & Community Support Services Aime J. Forand Bldg. 600 New London Ave. Cranston, RI 02920	401-464-2350
OCCUPATIONAL SAFETY & HEALTH *Inspects worksites*	Div. of Occupational Safety Dept. of Labor 220 Elmwood Ave. Providence, RI 02907	401-457-1829

Type of Agency/Comments	Organization and Address	Phone
OMBUDSMAN (NURSING HOMES) *Investigates complaints from nursing home residents*	Dept. of Elderly Affairs 160 Pine St. Providence, RI 02903	401-277-2894
SOCIAL SERVICES *Provides support services and counseling*	Dept. of Human Services Aime J. Forand Bldg. 600 New London Ave. Cranston, RI 02920	401-464-2121
VETERANS AFFAIRS *Provides assistance to veterans*	Div. of Veterans Affairs Dept. of Human Services Metacom Ave. Bristol, RI 02809	401-277-2488
VITAL STATISTICS *Maintains birth & death records*	Vital Statistics Div. Dept. of Health Cannon Bldg. 75 Davis St. Providence, RI 02908	401-277-2811
VOCATIONAL REHABILITATION *Provides information on rehabilitation programs*	Div. of Vocational Rehab. Community Services Div. Gardner Bldg., 2nd Floor 40 Fountain St. Providence, RI 02903	401-421-7005 401-421-7016 (TDD)
WELFARE *Administers income programs*	Assistance Payments Div. of Economic & Social Service Aime J. Forand Bldg. 600 New London Ave. Cranston, RI 02920	401-464-3052
WORKER'S COMPENSATION *Provides income for injured workers*	Dept. of Worker's Compensation Dept. of Labor 610 Manton Ave. Providence, RI 02909	401-272-0700

SOUTH CAROLINA

Type of Agency/Comments	Organization and Address	Phone
AGENCY LOCATOR *For Agencies & telephone numbers not listed*	Information Operator State House Columbia, SC 29201	803-734-1000

Type of Agency/Comments	Organization and Address	Phone
AGING *Provides programs & services to senior citizens*	Commission on Aging 400 Arbor Lake Dr. Suite B-500 Columbia, SC 29223	803-735-0210
ALCOHOLISM *Provides assistance to substance abusers*	Commission on Alcoholism & Drug Abuse 3700 Forest Dr. Suite 300 Columbia, SC 29204	803-734-9520
ATTORNEY GENERAL *Chief law enforcement officer*	Attorney General's Office R. C. Dennis Office Bldg. Rm. 729 1000 Assembly St. Columbia, SC 29211	803-734-3970
CHILD WELFARE *Provides services to children and youths*	Office of Children & Family Services Dept. of Social Services 1535 Confederate Ave. Columbia, SC 29202	803-734-6182
COMMUNITY AFFAIRS *Provides programs to communities*	Div. of Local Government State House Budget & Control Board Columbia, SC 29211	803-734-2382
CONSUMER ADVOCATE *Investigates consumer complaints*	Dept. of Consumer Affairs Carolina Continental Insurance Bldg. 2nd Floor 2801 Devine St. Columbia, SC 29250	803-734-9452 800-922-1594
DEPARTMENT OF HEALTH *Supervises health activities in the state*	Dept. of Health & Environmental Control 2600 Bull St. Columbia, SC 29201	803-734-4880
DEVELOPMENTAL DISABILITIES *Provides services to the developmentally disabled*	Dept. of Mental Retardation 2712 Middleburg Dr. Columbia, SC 29240	803-737-6444
DRUG ABUSE *Provides assistance to substance abusers*	Commission on Alcoholism & Drug Abuse 3700 Forest Dr. Suite 300 Columbia, SC 29204	803-734-9520

Type of Agency/Comments	*Organization and Address*	*Phone*
FOOD AND DRUGS *Registers drug items*	Bur. of Drug Control Office of Health Protection 2600 Bull St. Columbia, SC 29201	803-734-4710
FOOD AND DRUGS *Registers food items*	Div. of Food Protection Office of Health Protection 2600 Bull St. Columbia, SC 29201	803-734-5088
GOVERNOR *Citizens access to the* *governor*	Office of the Governor State House, P.O. Box 11369 Columbia, SC 29211	803-734-9818
INSURANCE *Regulates the insurance* *industry*	Office of the Commissioner Dept. of Insurance 1612 Marion St. P.O. Box 100105 Columbia, SC 29202	803-737-6268
LICENSING: DENTISTS *Report complaints about* *dentists to this office*	Board of Dental Examiners 1315 Blanding St. Columbia, SC 29201	803-734-8904
LICENSING: HOSPITALS *Report complaints about* *hospitals to this office*	Dept. of Health & Environmental Control Div. of Health Licensing 2600 Bull St. Columbia, SC 29201	803-734-4530
LICENSING: NURSES *Report complaints about* *nurses to this office*	Board of Nursing 1777 St. Julian Place Suite 102 Columbia, SC 29204	803-737-6596

LICENSING: NURSING HOMES
 	
Report complaints about
nursing homes to this
office
	Nursing Home Licensure
	  Office
	Div. of Health Facilities &
	  Services
	Dept. of Health Licensing
	2600 Bull St.
	Columbia, SC 29201
		803-734-4680

LICENSING: PHARMACISTS *Report complaints about* *pharmacists to this office*	Board of Pharmacy P.O. Box 11927 Columbia, SC 29211	803-734-1010

Type of Agency/Comments	*Organization and Address*	*Phone*
LICENSING: PHYSICIANS *Report complaints about doctors to this office*	Board of Medical Examiners 1220 Pickins St. Columbia, SC 29201	803-734-8901
MEDICAID OFFICE *Administers Medicaid program*	Dept. of Social Services Div. of Medicaid Eligibility P.O. Box 8206 Columbia, SC 29202-8206	803-253-6100
MEDICARE PART B CARRIER *Processes Medicare claims*	Blue Shield of South Carolina Fontaine Road Business Center 300 Arbor Lake Dr. Suite 1300 Columbia, SC 29223	800-922-2340 803-754-0639
MENTAL HEALTH *Provides patient services*	Dept. of Mental Health 2414 Bull St. Columbia, SC 29202	803-734-7780
OCCUPATIONAL SAFETY & HEALTH *Inspects worksites*	Occupational Safety & Health Labor Dept. 3600 Forest Dr. Columbia, SC 29211	803-734-9643

OMBUDSMAN (GENERAL)
 	
Provides assistance to citizens
	Div. of Ombudsman &
	  Citizens Services
	Edgar A. Brown Bldg., Rm.
	  308
	1205 Pendleton St.
	Columbia, SC 29201
		803-734-0457

OMBUDSMAN (NURSING HOMES) *Investigates complaints from nursing home residents*	Governor's Office Ombudsman Div. Edgar A. Brown Bldg. 1205 Pendleton St. Columbia, SC 29201	803-734-0457
SOCIAL SERVICES *Provides support services and counseling*	Dept. of Social Services North Tower Complex 1535 Confederate Ave., Ext. Columbia, SC 29202	803-734-6173
VETERANS AFFAIRS *Provides assistance to veterans*	Dept. of Veterans Affairs Edgar A. Brown Bldg., Rm. 227 1205 Pendleton St. Columbia, SC 29201	803-734-0200

Type of Agency/Comments	Organization and Address	Phone
VITAL STATISTICS *Maintains birth & death records*	Office of Vital Records & Public Health Statistics J. Marion Sims Bldg., Rm. 105 2600 Bull St. Columbia, SC 29201	803-734-4810
VOCATIONAL REHABILITATION *Provides information on rehabilitation programs*	Vocational Rehabilitation 1410 Boston Ave. P.O. Box 15 West Columbia, SC 29171	803-734-4300
WELFARE *Administers income programs*	Office of Adult, Economic & Medical Services Dept. of Social Services 1535 Confederate Ave. Columbia, SC 29202	803-734-6188
WORKER'S COMPENSATION *Provides income for injured workers*	Worker's Compensation Commission 1612 Marion St. P.O. Box 1715 Columbia, SC 29202	803-737-5697

SOUTH DAKOTA

Type of Agency/Comments	Organization and Address	Phone
AGENCY LOCATOR *For Agencies & telephone numbers not listed*	Information Operator State Capitol 500 East Capitol Ave. Pierre, SD 57501	605-773-3011
AGING *Provides services & programs to senior citizens*	Office of Adult Services & Aging Dept. of Social Services 700 Governors Dr. Pierre, SD 57501	605-773-3656
ALCOHOLISM *Provides assistance to alcohol abusers*	Div. of Alcohol & Drug Abuse Dept. of Health 523 East Capitol Ave. Pierre, SD 57501	605-773-3123
ATTORNEY GENERAL *Chief law enforcement officer*	Attorney General's Office State Capitol Pierre, SD 57501	605-773-3215

Type of Agency/Comments	*Organization and Address*	*Phone*
CHILD WELFARE *Provides services to children and youths*	Child Protection Services Dept. of Social Services Richard F. Kneip Bldg. 700 Governors Dr. Pierre, SD 57501	605-773-3227
COMMUNITY AFFAIRS *Provides programs to local communities*	Intergovernmental Relations Dept. of Exec. Management 500 East Capitol St. Pierre, SD 57501	605-773-3661
CONSUMER ADVOCATE *Investigates consumer complaints*	Div. of Consumer Affairs Attorney General's Office Capitol Bldg. 500 East Capitol Ave. Pierre, SD 57501	605-773-4400
DEPARTMENT OF HEALTH *Supervises health activities in the state*	Dept. of Health 523 East Capitol Ave. Pierre, SD 57501	605-773-3361
DEVELOPMENTAL DISABILITIES *Provides services to the developmentally disabled*	Office of Developmental Disabilities & Mental Health Dept. of Social Services Richard F. Kneip Bldg. 700 Governors Dr. Pierre, SD 57501	605-773-3438
DRUG ABUSE *Provides assistance to drug abusers*	Div. of Alcohol & Drug Abuse Dept. of Health 523 East Capitol Ave. Pierre, SD 57501	605-773-3123
FOOD AND DRUGS *Registers food & drug items*	Dept. of Health 523 East Capitol St. Pierre, SD 57501	605-773-3361
GOVERNOR *Citizens access to the governor*	Office of the Governor State Capitol Pierre, SD 57501	605-773-3212
INSURANCE *Regulates the insurance industry*	Div. of Insurance 910 E. Sioux Ave. Pierre, SD 57501	605-773-3563

Type of Agency/Comments	*Organization and Address*	*Phone*
LICENSING: DENTISTS *Report complaints about dentists to this office*	State Board of Dentistry 1708 Space Court Rapid City, SD 57702	605-342-3026
LICENSING: HOSPITALS *Report complaints about hospitals to this office*	Dept. of Health Licensure and Certification 523 East Capitol Ave. Pierre, SD 57501	605-773-3364
LICENSING: NURSES *Report complaints about nurses to this office*	Board of Nursing 304 South Phillips Ave. Suite 205 Sioux Falls, SD 57102	605-335-4973
LICENSING: NURSING HOMES *Report complaints about nursing homes to this office*	Dept. of Health Div. of Licensure & Certification 523 East Capitol Ave. Pierre, SD 57501	605-773-3364
LICENSING: PHARMACISTS *Report complaints about pharmacists to this office*	State Board of Pharmacy P.O. Box 518 Pierre, SD 57501	605-224-2338
LICENSING: PHYSICIANS *Report complaints about doctors to this office*	State Board of Medical & Osteopathic Examiners 1323 S. Minnesota Ave. Sioux Falls, SD 57105	605-336-1965
LICENSING: PROFESSIONALS *Licenses other health care professionals*	Div. of Professional & Occupational Licensing Dept. of Commerce 910 E. Sioux Ave. Pierre, SD 57501	605-773-3178
MEDICAID OFFICE *Administers Medicaid program*	Dept. of Social Services Office of Medical Services 700 Governors Dr. Pierre, SD 57501	605-773-3495
MEDICARE PART B CARRIER *Processes Medicare claims for South Dakota*	Medicare Part B Blue Shield of North Dakota 4510 13th Ave., SW Fargo, ND 58121	800-437-4762

Type of Agency/Comments	*Organization and Address*	*Phone*
MENTAL HEALTH *Provides patient services*	Office of Developmental Disabilities & Mental Health Dept. of Social Services 700 North Governors Dr. Pierre, SD 57501	605-773-3438
OMBUDSMAN (GENERAL) *Provides assistance to* *citizens*	State Ombudsman Dept. of Social Services Richard F. Kneip Bldg. 700 Governors Dr. Pierre, SD 57501	605-773-3165

OMBUDSMAN (NURSING
  HOMES)
 	
Investigates complaints from
  nursing home residents
	Office of Adult Services &
	  Aging
	State Ombudsman
	700 Governors Dr.
	Pierre, SD 57501
		605-773-3656

SOCIAL SERVICES *Provides support services* *and counseling*	Dept. of Social Services Richard F. Kneip Bldg. 700 Governors Dr. Pierre, SD 57501	605-773-3165

VETERANS AFFAIRS
 	
Provides assistance to
  veterans
	Div. of Veterans Affairs
	Dept. of Military & Veterans
	  Affairs
	523 East Capitol Ave.
	Pierre, SD 57501
		605-773-3269

VITAL STATISTICS *Maintains birth & death* *records*	Center for Health Statistics Dept. of Health Joe Foss Bldg., Rm. 302 523 East Capitol Ave. Pierre, SD 57501	605-773-3355

VOCATIONAL
  REHABILITATION
 	
Provides information on
  rehabilitation programs
	Dept. of Vocational
	  Rehabilitation
	Richard F. Kneip Bldg.
	700 Governors Dr.
	Pierre, SD 57501
		605-773-3125

WELFARE *Administers income* *programs*	Dept. of Social Services Richard F. Kneip Bldg. 700 Governors Dr. Pierre, SD 57501	605-773-3165
WORKER'S COMPENSATION *Provides income for injured* *workers*	Div. of Labor & Management Dept. of Labor Richard F. Kneip Bldg. 700 Governors Dr. Pierre, SD 57501	605-773-3681

TENNESSEE

Type of Agency/Comments	Organization and Address	Phone
AGENCY LOCATOR *For Agencies & telephone numbers not listed*	Information Operator State Capitol Nashville, TN 37219	615-741-3011
AGING *Provides programs & services to senior citizens*	Commission on Aging Doctors Bldg., Rm. 201 706 Church St. Nashville, TN 37219	615-741-2056
ALCOHOLISM *Provides assistance to alcohol abusers*	Div. of Alcohol & Drug Abuse Services Doctors Bldg., 4th Floor 706 Church St. Nashville, TN 37219	615-741-1921
ATTORNEY GENERAL *Chief law enforcement officer*	Attorney General's Office 450 James Robertson Pkwy. Nashville, TN 37219	615-741-3491
CHILD WELFARE *Provides services to children and youths*	Children's Services Commission Office of the Governor 1510 Parkway Towers 404 James Robertson Pkwy. Nashville, TN 37219	615-741-2633
COMMUNITY AFFAIRS *Provides programs to communities*	Div. of Community Development Rachel Jackson Bldg. 6th Floor 320 6th Ave., North Nashville, TN 37219	615-741-2373
CONSUMER ADVOCACY *Investigates consumer complaints*	Div. of Consumer Affairs 500 James Robertson Pkwy. Nashville, TN 37219	800-342-8385 615-741-4737
DEPARTMENT OF HEALTH *Supervises health activities in the state*	Dept. of Health & Environment Cordell Hull Bldg., Rm. 344 Nashville, TN 37219	615-741-3111

Type of Agency/Comments	*Organization and Address*	*Phone*
DEVELOPMENTAL DISABILITIES *Provides services to the developmentally disabled*	Mental Retardation Services Dept. of Mental Health Doctors Bldg., 3rd Floor 706 Church St. Nashville, TN 37219	615-741-3803
DRUG ABUSE *Provides assistance to drug abusers*	Div. of Alcohol & Drug Abuse Services Doctors Bldg., 4th Floor 706 Church St. Nashville, TN 37219	615-741-1921
FOOD AND DRUGS *Registers food & drug items*	Div. of Food and Dairies Dept. of Agriculture Holeman Office Bldg. Hogan Rd. Nashville, TN 37204	615-360-0150
GOVERNOR *Citizens access to the governor*	Office of the Governor State Capitol Nashville, TN 37219	615-741-3763
INSURANCE *Regulates the insurance industry*	Dept. of Commerce & Insurance 500 James Robertson Pkwy. Nashville, TN 37243	615-741-2241
LICENSING: DENTISTS *Report complaints about dentists to this office*	Board of Dental Examiners 282 Plus Park Blvd. Nashville, TN 37219	615-367-6228
LICENSING: HOSPITALS *Report complaints about hospitals to this office*	Dept. of Public Health Div. of Health Care Facilities 287 Plus Park Blvd. Nashville, TN 37217	615-367-6338
LICENSING: NURSES *Report complaints about nurses to this office*	Board of Nursing 283 Plus Park Blvd. Nashville, TN 37219	615-367-6232
LICENSING: NURSING HOMES *Report complaints about nursing homes to this office*	Dept. of Health & Environment Board for Licensing Health Care Facilities 283 Plus Park Blvd. Nashville, TN 37219	615-376-6303

Type of Agency/Comments	*Organization and Address*	*Phone*
LICENSING: PHARMACISTS *Report complaints about pharmacists to this office*	Board of Pharmacy 500 James Robertson Pkwy. Nashville, TN 37243	615-741-2718
LICENSING: PHYSICIANS *Report complaints about doctors to this office*	Board of Medical Examiners 283 Plus Park Blvd. Nashville, TN 37217	615-367-6231
LICENSING: PROFESSIONALS *Licenses other health care professionals*	Regulatory Boards Dept. of Commerce & Insurance 500 James Robertson Pkwy. Nashville, TN 37243	615-741-3449
MEDICAID OFFICE *Administers Medicaid program*	Dept. of Health & Environment Bur. of Medicaid 729 Church St. Nashville, TN 37219	615-741-0213
MEDICARE PART B CARRIER *Processes Medicare claims*	Equicor, Inc. P.O. Box 1465 Nashville, TN 37202	800-342-8900 615-244-5650
MENTAL HEALTH *Provides patient services*	Dept. of Mental Health & Mental Retardation Doctors Bldg., 6th Floor 706 Church St. Nashville, TN 37219	615-741-3107
OCCUPATIONAL SAFETY & HEALTH *Inspects worksites*	Div. of Occupational Health & Safety Dept. of Labor 501 Union Bldg., 6th Floor Nashville, TN 37219	615-741-2793
OMBUDSMAN (GENERAL) *Provides assistance to citizens*	Office of the Ombudsman State Capitol Rm. 10 Nashville, TN 37219	615-741-1208
OMBUDSMAN (NURSING HOMES) *Investigates complaints from nursing home residents*	Commission on Aging 703 Tennessee Bldg. 706 Church St. Nashville, TN 37219	615-741-2056

Type of Agency/Comments	*Organization and Address*	*Phone*
SOCIAL SERVICES *Provides support services and counseling*	Div. of Social Services Policy Development Dept. of Human Services 400 Deaderick St. Nashville, TN 37219	615-741-3443
VETERANS AFFAIRS *Provides assistance to veterans*	Dept. of Veterans Affairs 215 8th Ave., North Nashville, TN 37203	615-741-2345
VITAL STATISTICS *Maintains birth & death records*	Div. of Vital Records Dept. of Health & Environment Cordell Hull Bldg., Rm. C2-242 5th & Gay Aves. Nashville, TN 37219	615-741-1954
VOCATIONAL REHABILITATION *Provides information on rehabilitation programs*	Div. of Rehab. Services Citizens Plaza Bldg. 400 Deaderick St. Nashville, TN 37219	615-741-2019
WELFARE *Administers income programs*	Office of Family Assistance Dept. of Human Services 400 Deaderick St. 15th Floor Nashville, TN 37219	615-741-5463
WORKER'S COMPENSATION *Provides income programs for injured workers*	Worker's Compensation Div. Dept. of Labor 501 Union St. Nashville, TN 37219	615-741-2395

TEXAS

Type of Agency/Comments	*Organization and Address*	*Phone*
AGENCY LOCATOR *For Agencies & telephone numbers not listed*	Information Operator State Capitol Austin, TX 78711	512-463-4630
AGING *Provides programs & services to senior citizens*	Dept. of Aging 1949 IH 35 South, 3rd Floor Austin, TX 78711	800-252-9240 512-444-2727

Type of Agency/Comments	*Organization and Address*	*Phone*
ALCOHOLISM *Provides assistance to* *alcohol abusers*	Commission on Alcohol & Drug Abuse 1705 Guadalupe St. Austin, TX 78701	512-463-5510
ATTORNEY GENERAL *Chief law enforcement* *officer*	Attorney General's Office Supreme Court Bldg. Austin, TX 78711	512-463-2100
CHILD WELFARE *Provides services to children* *and youths*	Service to Families & Children Dept. of Human Services 701 West 51st St. Austin, TX 78769	512-450-3020
COMMUNITY AFFAIRS *Provides programs to* *communities*	Dept. of Community Affairs 8317 Crosspark Dr. Austin, TX 78754	512-834-6010
CONSUMER ADVOCATE *Investigates consumer* *complaints*	Consumer Protection Div. Attorney General's Office American Legion Bldg. 15th St. & Congress Ave. Austin, TX 78711	512-463-2070
DEPARTMENT OF HEALTH *Supervises health activities* *in the state*	Dept. of Health 1100 West 49th St. Austin, TX 78756	512-458-7375
DEVELOPMENTAL DISABILITIES *Provides services to the* *developmentally disabled*	Div. of Mental Retardation Services Dept. of Mental Health 909 W. 45th St. Austin, TX 78711	512-465-4521
DRUG ABUSE *Provides assistance to drug* *abusers*	Commission on Alcohol & Drug Abuse 1705 Guadalupe St. Austin, TX 78701	512-463-5510
FOOD AND DRUGS *Registers food and drug* *items*	Bur. of Consumer Health Protection Div. of Food & Drugs Dept. of Health 1100 West 49th St. Austin, TX 78756	512-458-7248

Type of Agency/Comments	*Organization and Address*	*Phone*
GOVERNOR *Citizens access to the governor*	Office of the Governor State Capitol P.O. Box 12428 Austin, TX 78711	512-463-1826
INSURANCE *Regulates the insurance industry*	State Board of Insurance 1110 San Jacinto Blvd. Austin, TX 78701	512-463-6464
LICENSING: DENTISTS *Report complaints about dentists to this office*	Board of Dental Examiners Capitol Station P.O. Box 13165 Austin, TX 78711	512-834-6021
LICENSING: HOSPITALS *Report complaints about hospitals to this office*	Dept. of Health Health Facility Licensure & Certification 1100 West 49th St. Austin, TX 78756	512-458-7245
LICENSING: NURSES *Report complaints about nurses to this office*	Board of Nurse Examiners 9101 Burnet Rd. Suite 104 Box 140466 Austin, TX 78714	512-835-4880
LICENSING: NURSING HOMES *Report complaints about nursing homes to this office*	Nursing Home Licensure Office Dept. of Health Licensing Div. 1100 West 49th St., Rm. T-201 Austin, TX 78756	512-458-7490
LICENSING: PHARMACISTS *Report complaints about pharmacists to this office*	State Board of Pharmacy 8505 Cross Park Dr. Austin, TX 78754	512-832-0661
LICENSING: PHYSICIANS *Report complaints about doctors to this office*	Board of Medical Examiners P.O. Box 13562 Capitol Station Austin, TX 78711	512-452-1078
MEDICAID OFFICE *Administers Medicaid program*	Medical Assistance Unit Texas Dept. of Human Resources P.O. Box 149030 Austin, TX 78714	512-450-3192

Type of Agency/Comments	*Organization and Address*	*Phone*
MEDICARE CARRIER PART B *Processes Medicare claims*	Blue Cross/Shield of Texas P.O. Box 660031 Dallas, TX 75266	214-235-3433 800-442-2620
MENTAL HEALTH *Provides services to patients*	Div. of Mental Health Services Dept. of Mental Health & Retardation 909 West 45th St. Austin, TX 78711	512-465-4510
OCCUPATIONAL SAFETY & HEALTH *Inspects worksites*	Occupational Safety Div. Dept. of Health 1100 West 49th St. Austin, TX 78756	512-458-7287
OMBUDSMAN (GENERAL) *Provides assistance to* *citizens*	Ombudsman Office of the Governor Governor's Office P.O. Box 12428 Austin, TX 78711	512-463-1780 800-252-9600
OMBUDSMAN (NURSING HOMES) *Investigates complaints from* *nursing home residents*	Dept. of Aging Box 12786, Capitol Station Austin, TX 78711	512-444-2727
SOCIAL SERVICES *Provides support services* *and counseling*	Services to Families & Children Dept. of Human Resources 701 West 51st St. Austin, TX 78769	512-450-3020
VETERANS AFFAIRS *Provides assistance to* *veterans*	Veterans Affairs Commission E.O. Thompson Office Bldg. 920 Colorado St. Austin, TX 78711	512-463-5538
VITAL STATISTICS *Maintains birth & death* *records*	Bur. of Vital Statistics Dept. of Health 1100 West 49th St. Austin, TX 78756	512-458-7692
VOCATIONAL REHABILITATION *Provides information on* *rehabilitation programs*	Texas Rehab. Commission 118 East Riverside Dr. Austin, TX 78704	512-445-8108

Type of Agency/Comments	Organization and Address	Phone
WELFARE

*Administers income
programs* | Dept. of Human Resources
701 West 51st St.
Austin, TX 78769 | 512-450-3040 |
| WORKER'S COMPENSATION

*Provides income for injured
workers* | Industrial Accident Board
Bevington A. Reed Bldg.
200 East Riverside Dr.
Austin, TX 78704 | 512-448-7960 |

UTAH

Type of Agency/Comments	Organization and Address	Phone
AGENCY LOCATOR

*For Agencies & telephone
numbers not listed* | Information Operator
State Capitol
Salt Lake City, UT 84114 | 801-538-3000 |
| AGING

*Provides programs &
services to senior citizens* | Div. of Aging & Adult
Services
Dept. of Social Services
Social Services Bldg.
120 North, 200 West
Salt Lake City, UT 84145-0500 | 801-538-3910 |
| ALCOHOLISM

*Provides assistance to
alcohol abusers* | Div. of Alcoholism & Drugs
Dept. of Social Services
Social Services Bldg.
120 North, 200 West
Salt Lake City, UT 84145-0500 | 801-538-3939 |
| ATTORNEY GENERAL

*Chief law enforcement
officer* | Attorney General's Office
236 State Capitol
Salt Lake City, UT 84114 | 801-538-1324 |
| CHILD WELFARE

*Provides services to children
and youths* | Div. of Family Services
Dept. of Social Services
Social Services Bldg.
120 North, 200 West
P.O. Box 45500
Salt Lake City, UT 84115 | 801-538-4100 |

Type of Agency/Comments	*Organization and Address*	*Phone*
COMMUNITY AFFAIRS *Provides programs to communities*	Div. of Community Development Dept. of Community & Economic Development State Office Bldg., Rm. 6233 Salt Lake City, UT 84114	801-538-3033 800-289-8824
CONSUMER ADVOCATE *Investigates consumer complaints*	Consumer Protection Div. Dept. of Business Regulation Heber M. Wells Bldg., 2nd Floor 160 East 300 South, P.O. Box 45802 Salt Lake City, UT 84145-0801	801-530-6601
DEPARTMENT OF HEALTH *Supervises health activities in the state*	Dept. of Health 288 North 1460 West P.O. Box 16700 Salt Lake City, UT 84116-0700	801-538-6101
DEVELOPMENTAL DISABILITIES *Provides services to the developmentally disabled*	Div. of Services to the Handicapped Dept. of Social Services Social Services Bldg. 120 North, 200 West Salt Lake City, UT 84103	801-538-4200
DRUG ABUSE *Provides assistance to drug abusers*	Div. of Alcoholism & Drugs Dept. of Social Services Social Services Bldg. 120 North, 200 West Salt Lake City, UT 84145-0500	801-538-3939
FOOD AND DRUGS *Registers food & drug items*	Food and Dairy Section Dept. of Agriculture William Spry Bldg. 350 N. Redwood Rd. Salt Lake City, UT 84116	801-538-7124
GOVERNOR *Citizens access to the governor*	Office of the Governor State Capitol Salt Lake City, UT 84114	801-538-1000
INSURANCE *Regulates the insurance industry*	Insurance Dept. Heber M. Wells Bldg. 160 East 300 South P.O. Box 45803 Salt Lake City, UT 84145	801-530-6400

Type of Agency/Comments	*Organization and Address*	*Phone*
LICENSING: DENTISTS *Report complaints about* *dentists to this office*	Dept. of Commerce Heber M. Wells Bldg. 160 East 300 South P.O. Box 45802 Salt Lake City, UT 84145	801-530-6628
LICENSING: HOSPITALS *Report complaints about* *hospitals to this office*	Dept. of Health Facility Standards-Licensure 288 North 1460 West P.O. Box 16660 Salt Lake City, UT 84103	801-538-6152
LICENSING: NURSES *Report complaints about* *nurses to this office*	Dept. of Occupational & Professional Licensing P.O. Box 45802 Salt Lake City, UT 84145	801-530-6628
LICENSING: NURSING HOMES *Report complaints about* *nursing homes to this* *office*	Nursing Home Licensure Office Dept. of Health Bur. of Health Facilities P.O. Box 16660 Salt Lake City, UT 84116-0660	801-538-6152
LICENSING: PHARMACISTS *Report complaints about* *pharmacists to this office*	Board of Pharmacy 160 East, 300 South Salt Lake City, UT 84145	801-530-6633
LICENSING: PHYSICIANS *Report complaints about* *doctors to this office*	Dept. of Commerce Heber M. Wells Bldg. Medical Licensing 160 East 300 South, 4th Floor Salt Lake City, UT 84145	801-530-6628
LICENSING: PROFESSIONALS *Licenses other health care* *professionals*	Div. of Occupational & Professional Licensing Dept. of Business Regulation 160 East 300 South P.O. Box 5802 Salt Lake City, UT 84145-5802	801-530-6628
MEDICAID OFFICE *Administers Medicaid* *program*	Dept. of Health Bur. of Medical Payments Medicaid Information Unit 288 North 1470 West P.O. Box 16580 Salt Lake City, UT 84116-0580	801-538-6155 Salt Lake Area 800-662-9651

Type of Agency/Comments	Organization and Address	Phone
MEDICARE PART B CARRIER *Processes Medicare claims*	Medicare/Blue Shield of Utah 2455 Parley's Way P.O. Box 30269 Salt Lake City, UT 84130-0269	800-426-3477 801-481-6196
MENTAL HEALTH *Provides patient services*	Div. of Mental Health Dept. of Social Services 120 North, 200 West P.O. Box 45500 Salt Lake City, UT 84145-0500	801-538-4270
OCCUPATIONAL HEALTH & SAFETY *Inspects worksites*	Div. of Occupational Safety & Health Industrial Commission 160 East 300 South Salt Lake City, UT 84151	801-530-6901
OMBUDSMAN (NURSING HOMES) *Investigates complaints from nursing home residents*	Div. of Aging & Adult Services Long Term Care Ombudsman 120 North 200 West Rm. 401, 4th Floor Salt Lake City, UT 84103	801-538-3929
SOCIAL SERVICES *Provides support services and counseling*	Dept. of Social Services 310 Social Services Bldg. 120 North, 200 West P.O. Box 45500 Salt Lake City, UT 84145-0500	801-538-4001
VITAL STATISTICS *Maintains birth & death records*	Bur. of Vital Records Dept. of Health Cannon Health Bldg., Rm. 140 288 North 146 West P.O. Box 16700 Salt Lake City, UT 84116-0700	801-538-6186
VOCATIONAL REHABILITATION *Provides information on rehabilitation programs*	Div. of Rehab. Office of Education 250 East 500 South Salt Lake City, UT 84111	801-538-7530
WELFARE *Administers income programs*	Office of Assistance Payments Admin. Dept. of Social Services 120 North 200 West P.O. Box 45500 Salt Lake City, UT 84145-0500	801-538-3970

Type of Agency/Comments	*Organization and Address*	*Phone*
WORKER'S COMPENSATION *Provides income for injured workers*	Worker's Compensation Industrial Commission Heber M. Wells Bldg. 160 East 300 South P.O. Box 45580 Salt Lake City, UT 84145-4580	801-530-6811

VERMONT

Type of Agency/Comments	*Organization and Address*	*Phone*
AGENCY LOCATOR *For Agencies & telephone numbers not listed*	Information Operator State House State St. Montpelier, VT 05620	802-828-1110
AGING *Provides programs & services to senior citizens*	Office on Aging Waterbury Office Complex 103 South Main St. Waterbury, VT 05676	802-241-2400
ALCOHOLISM *Provides assistance to alcohol abusers*	Office of Alcohol & Drug Abuse Programs Waterbury Office Complex 103 South Main St. Waterbury, VT 05676	802-241-2170
ATTORNEY GENERAL *Chief law enforcement officer*	Attorney General's Office Pavillion Office Bldg. 109 State St. Montpelier, VT 05602	802-828-3171
CHILD WELFARE *Provides services to children and youths*	Div. of Social Services Agency for Human Services 103 South Main St. Waterbury, VT 05676	802-241-2131
COMMUNITY AFFAIRS *Provides programs to communities*	Agency for Development & Community Affairs Pavillion Office Bldg. 109 State St. Montpelier, VT 05602	802-828-3211
CONSUMER ADVOCATE *Investigates consumer complaints*	Public Protection Div. Attorney General's Office Pavillion Office Bldg. 109 State St. Montpelier, VT 05602	802-828-3171

Type of Agency/Comments	Organization and Address	Phone
DEPARTMENT OF HEALTH *Supervises health activities in the state*	Dept. of Health Agency for Human Services 60 Main St. Burlington, VT 05402	802-863-7280
DEVELOPMENTAL DISABILITIES *Provides services to the developmentally disabled*	Developmental Disabilities Council Agency for Human Services Waterbury Office Complex 103 S. Main St. Waterbury, VT 05676	802-241-2612
DRUG ABUSE *Provides assistance to drug abusers*	Office of Alcohol & Drug Abuse Programs Waterbury Office Complex 103 South Main St. Waterbury, VT 05676	802-241-2170
FOOD AND DRUGS *Registers food & drug items*	Div. of Environmental Health Dept. of Health Agency for Human Services 60 Main St. Burlington, VT 05402	802-862-7221
GOVERNOR *Citizens access to the governor*	Office of the Governor State House Montpelier, VT 05602	802-828-3333
INSURANCE *Regulates the insurance industry*	Dept. of Banking & Insurance State Office Bldg. 120 State St. Montpelier, VT 05602	802-828-3301
LICENSING: DENTISTS *Report complaints about dentists to this office*	Vermont Secretary of State Complaint Dept. Pavillion Office Bldg. Montpelier, VT 05602	802-828-2390
LICENSING: HOSPITALS *Report complaints about hospitals to this office*	Dept. of Health Medical Care Regulation 60 Main St. Burlington, VT 05401	802-863-7272
LICENSING: NURSES *Report complaints about nurses to this office*	Board of Nursing 26 Terrace St. Montpelier, VT 05602	802-828-2396

Type of Agency/Comments	*Organization and Address*	*Phone*
LICENSING: NURSING HOMES *Report complaints about nursing homes to this office*	Nursing Home Licensure Office Dept. of Rehab. & Aging Medical Regulations 60 Main St., P.O. Box 70 Burlington, VT 05402	802-863-7250
LICENSING: PHARMACISTS *Report complaints about pharmacists to this office*	State Board of Pharmacy Secretary of State's Office Montpelier, VT 05602	802-828-2372
LICENSING: PHYSICIANS *Report complaints about doctors to this office*	Board of Medical Practice Secretary of State's Office Montpelier, VT 05602	802-828-2673
LICENSING: PROFESSIONALS *Licenses other health care professionals*	Secretary of State Restone Bldg. 26 Terrace St. Montpelier, VT 05602	802-828-2363
MEDICAID OFFICE *Administers Medicaid program*	Medicaid Div. Agency for Human Services 103 South Main St. Waterbury, VT 05676	802-241-2880
MEDICARE PART B CARRIER *Processes Medicare claims for Vermont*	Blue Shield of Massachusetts P.O. Box 1010 Biddeford, ME 04005	800-447-1142
MENTAL HEALTH *Provides patient services*	Dept. of Mental Health Agency for Human Services 103 South Main St. Waterbury, VT 05676	802-241-2610
OCCUPATIONAL SAFETY & HEALTH *Inspects worksites*	Occupational Safety & Health Admin. Dept. of Labor & Industry 120 State St. Montpelier, VT 05602	802-828-2765
OMBUDSMAN (NURSING HOMES) *Investigates complaints from nursing home residents*	Dept. of Rehab. & Aging Long Term Care Ombudsman 103 South Main St. Waterbury, VT 05676	802-241-2400

Type of Agency/Comments	Organization and Address	Phone
SOCIAL SERVICES *Provides support services and counseling*	Div. of Social Services Agency for Human Services 103 South Main St. Waterbury, VT 05676	802-241-2131
VETERANS AFFAIRS *Provides assistance to veterans*	Veterans Affairs Div. Military Dept. 118 State St. Montpelier, VT 05602	802-828-3379
VITAL STATISTICS *Maintains birth & death records*	Vital Records Section Div. of Public Health Statistics Dept. of Health 60 Main St. Burlington, VT 05402	802-863-7275
VOCATIONAL REHABILITATION *Provides information on rehabilitation programs*	Vocational Rehab. 103 South Main St. Waterbury, VT 05676	802-241-2211
WELFARE *Administers income programs*	Dept. of Social Welfare Agency for Human Services 103 South Main St. Waterbury, VT 05676	802-241-2852
WORKER'S COMPENSATION *Provides income program for injured workers*	Admin. Div. Dept. of Labor & Industry 120 State St. Montpelier, VT 05602	802-828-2286

VIRGINIA

Type of Agency/Comments	Organization and Address	Phone
AGENCY LOCATOR *For Agencies and telephone numbers not listed*	Information Operator State Capitol Capitol Square Richmond, VA 23219	804-786-0000
AGING *Provides services & programs for senior citizens*	Dept. for the Aging 700 East Franklin St. 10th Floor Richmond, VA 23219-2327	804-225-2271

Type of Agency/Comments	*Organization and Address*	*Phone*
ALCOHOLISM *Provides assistance to alcohol abusers*	Office of Substance Abuse Services James Madison Bldg. 109 Governor St. P.O. Box 1797 Richmond, VA 23214-1797	804-786-3906
ATTORNEY GENERAL *Chief law enforcement officer*	Attorney General's Office Dept. of Law 101 North 8th St. Richmond, VA 23219	804-786-2071
CHILD WELFARE *Provides services to children and youths*	Bur. of Child Welfare Services Dept. of Social Services Nelson Bldg., Suite 244 1503 Santa Rosa Rd. Richmond, VA 23229-8699	804-662-9695
COMMUNITY AFFAIRS *Provides programs to communities*	Dept. of Housing & Community Development Fourth St. Office Bldg. 205 N. 4th St. Richmond, VA 23219-1747	804-786-1575
CONSUMER ADVOCATE *Investigates consumer complaints*	Office of Consumer Affairs Washington Bldg., Capitol Sq. 1100 Bank St. Richmond, VA 23209	800-552-9963 804-786-2042
DEPARTMENT OF HEALTH *Supervises health activities in the state*	Dept. of Health James Madison Bldg. 109 Governor St. Richmond, VA 23219	804-786-3561
DEVELOPMENTAL DISABILITIES *Provides services to the developmentally disabled*	Developmental Disabilities Office Dept. of Mental Health James Madison Bldg. 109 Governor St. Richmond, VA 23214	804-786-5313
DRUG ABUSE *Provides assistance to drug abusers*	Office of Substance Abuse Services James Madison Bldg. 109 Governor St. P.O. Box 1797 Richmond, VA 23214-1797	804-786-3906

Type of Agency/Comments	*Organization and Address*	*Phone*
FOOD AND DRUGS *Registers food and drug items*	Dairy & Foods Div. Dept. of Agriculture & Consumer Services 1100 Bank St. Richmond, VA 23209	804-786-8899
GOVERNOR *Citizens access to the governor*	Office of the Governor State Capitol Richmond, VA 23212	804-786-2211
INSURANCE *Regulates the insurance industry*	Bur. of Insurance State Corporation Commission Jefferson Bldg. 1220 Bank St. Richmond, VA 23209	804-786-3741
LICENSING: DENTISTS *Report complaints about dentists to this office*	Board of Dental Examiners 1601 Rolling Hills Dr. Richmond, VA 23229	804-662-9906
LICENSING: HOSPITALS *Report complaints about hospitals to this office*	Dept. of Health Div. of Licensure & Certification 109 Governor St. Richmond, VA 23219	804-786-2081
LICENSING: NURSES *Report complaints about nurses to this office*	Board of Nursing Health Regulatory Board Enforcement Div. 1601 Rolling Hills Dr. Richmond, VA 23229-5005	804-662-9909

LICENSING: NURSING HOMES
 	
Report complaints about nursing homes to this office
	Nursing Home Licensure
	  Office
	Div. of Licensure &
	  Certification
	1013 Madison Bldg.
	109 Governor St.
	Richmond, VA 23219
		804-786-2081

LICENSING: PHARMACISTS *Report complaints about pharmacists to this office*	Board of Pharmacy 1601 Rolling Hills Dr. Richmond, VA 23229	804-662-9911
LICENSING: PHYSICIANS *Report complaints about doctors to this office*	Board of Medical Examiners 1601 Rolling Hills Dr. Richmond, VA 23229	804-662-9908

Type of Agency/Comments	*Organization and Address*	*Phone*
LICENSING: PROFESSIONALS *Licenses other health care professionals*	Occupational & Professional Licensing Dept. of Commerce 1601 Rolling Hills Dr., Suite 200 Richmond, VA 23229	804-662-9900
MEDICAID OFFICE *Administers Medicaid program*	Dept. of Medical Services Div. of Medical Social Services Eligibility & Appeals Section 600 E. Broad St., Suite 1300 Richmond, VA 23219	804-786-7933
MEDICARE PART B CARRIER *Check for specific coverage areas*	Pennsylvania Blue Shield P.O. Box 890100 Camp Hill, PA 17089-0100	800-233-1124
MEDICARE PART B CARRIER *Processes Medicare claims*	The Travelers Insurance Co. P.O. Box 26463 Richmond, VA 23261	804-254-4130 800-552-3423
MENTAL HEALTH *Provides patient services*	Dept. of Mental Health James Madison Bldg., Rm. 1301 109 Governor St. Richmond, VA 23214	804-786-3921
OCCUPATIONAL SAFETY & HEALTH *Inspects worksites*	Bur. of Occupational Health Dept. of Labor & Industry 205 North Fourth St. P.O. Box 12064 Richmond, VA 23241	804-786-5873
OMBUDSMAN (GENERAL) *Provides assistance to citizens*	State Ombudsman Office of the Governor State Capitol P.O. Box 1475 Richmond, VA 23212-1475	804-786-2211
OMBUDSMAN (NURSING HOMES) *Investigates complaints from nursing home residents*	Dept. for the Aging 700 E. Franklin St. 10th Floor Richmond, VA 23219-2327	804-225-2271

Type of Agency/Comments	*Organization and Address*	*Phone*
SOCIAL SERVICES *Provides support services and counseling*	Div. of Service Programs Dept. of Social Services Nelson Bldg., Suite 212 1503 Santa Rosa Rd. P.O. Box 8007 Richmond, VA 23299-8699	804-662-9308
VETERANS AFFAIRS *Provides assistance to veterans*	Dept. of Veterans Affairs Dept. of Law R H Poff Federal Bldg. 210 Franklin Road, SW P.O. Box 809 Roanoke, VA 24004-0809	703-982-7104
VITAL STATISTICS *Maintains birth and death records*	Div. of Vital Records Dept. of Health James Madison Bldg. 109 Governor St. P.O. Box 1000 Richmond, VA 23208-1000	804-786-6202
VOCATIONAL REHABILITATION *Provides information on rehabilitation programs*	Dept. of Rehab. Services 4901 Fitzhugh Ave. P.O. Box 11045 Richmond, VA 23230	800-552-5019 804-257-0316
WELFARE *Administers income programs*	Dept. of Social Services Blair Bldg. 8007 Discovery Dr. Richmond, VA 23229-8699	804-281-9236
WORKER'S COMPENSATION *Provides income for injured workers*	Industrial Commission 1000 DMV Dr. P.O. Box 1794 Richmond, VA 23214	804-257-8615

WASHINGTON

Type of Agency/Comments	*Organization and Address*	*Phone*
AGENCY LOCATOR *For Agencies & telephone numbers not listed*	Information Operator Legislative Bldg. Olympia, WA 98504	206-753-5000

Type of Agency/Comments	Organization and Address	Phone

AGING
 	
*Provides programs &
services to senior citizens*
	Aging & Adult Services
	   Admin.
	Dept. of Social & Health
	   Services
	Office Bldg. 2
	12th Ave. & Adams St.
	Olympia, WA 98504
		206-586-3768

ALCOHOLISM
 	
*Provides assistance to
abusers*
	Alcohol & Substance Abuse
	Dept. of Social & Health
	   Services
	Office Bldg. 2, Mail Stop OB-
	   44W
	12th Ave. & Franklin St.
	Olympia, WA 98504
		206-753-5866

ATTORNEY GENERAL *Chief law enforcement officer*	Attorney General's Office Highway-Licenses Bldg. Olympia, WA 98504	206-753-2550

CHILD WELFARE
 	
*Provides services to children
and youths*
	Div. of Children & Family
	   Services
	Dept. of Social & Health
	   Services
	Mail Stop OB-41
	Olympia, WA 98504
		206-753-7002

COMMUNITY AFFAIRS *Provides programs to communities*	Dept. of Community Development 9th & Columbia Bldg. Mail Stop GH-51 Olympia, WA 98504	206-753-5625
CONSUMER ADVOCATE *Investigates consumer complaints*	Consumer & Business Practices Div. Dexter Horton Bldg. 710 2nd Ave. Seattle, WA 98104	206-464-7744
DEPARTMENT OF HEALTH *Supervises health activities in the state*	Div. of Health Dept. of Health 1112 South Quince St. Olympia, WA 98504	206-753-5871

Type of Agency/Comments	*Organization and Address*	*Phone*
DEVELOPMENTAL DISABILITIES *Provides services to the developmentally disabled*	Div. of Developmental Disabilities Dept. of Social & Health Services 12th Ave. & Franklin St. Mail Stop OB-42C Olympia, WA 98504	206-753-3900
DRUG ABUSE *Provides assistance to drug abusers*	Alcohol & Substance Abuse Dept. of Social & Health Services Office Bldg. 2, Mail Stop OB-44W 12th Ave. & Franklin St. Olympia, WA 98504	206-753-5866
FOOD AND DRUGS *Registers food & drug items*	Dairy & Food Div. Dept. of Agriculture 11th & Columbia Sts. Gen. Admin. Bldg., Rm. 406 Olympia, WA 98504	206-753-5042
GOVERNOR *Citizens access to the governor*	Office of the Governor State Capitol Legislative Bldg., Rm. AS-13 Olympia, WA 98504	206-753-6780
INSURANCE *Regulates the insurance industry*	Insurance Commissioner Insurance Bldg. Rm. 200 Mail Stop AQ-21 Olympia, WA 98504	206-753-7301
LICENSING: DENTISTS *Report complaints about dentists to this office*	Board of Dental Examiners Dept. of Licensing Program Management Div. P.O. Box 9012 Olympia, WA 98504	206-753-1156
LICENSING: HOSPITALS *Report complaints about hospitals to this office*	Dept. of Social & Health Services Health Facilities Survey Section 1112 South Quince St. ET-31 Olympia, WA 98504	206-753-5851
LICENSING: NURSES *Report complaints about nurses to this office*	Dept. of Licensing Nursing Board Professional Program P.O. Box 9012 Olympia, WA 98504	206-753-3726

Type of Agency/Comments	Organization and Address	Phone
LICENSING: NURSING HOMES *Report complaints about nursing homes to this office*	Nursing Home Licensure Div. Health Services Div. Aging & Adult Services Admin. 623 8th Ave., SE Olympia, WA 98504	206-753-5840
LICENSING: PHARMACISTS *Report complaints about pharmacists to this office*	Board of Pharmacy WEA Bldg. 319 East 7th Ave. Olympia, WA 98504	206-753-6834
LICENSING: PHYSICIANS *Report complaints about doctors to this office*	State Medical Board Div. of Professional Licensing P.O. Box 9012 Olympia, WA 98504	206-753-2205
LICENSING: PROFESSIONALS *Licenses other health care professionals*	Professional Programs Management Div. Dept. of Licensing 1300 Quince St. Olympia, WA 98504	206-753-3234
MEDICAID OFFICE *Administers Medicaid program*	Div. of Medical Assistance Dept. of Social & Health Services 12th Ave. & Franklin St. Mail Stop HB-41 Olympia, WA 98504	206-753-1777
MEDICARE PART B CARRIER *Processes Medicare claims (check for coverage area)*	Washington Physicians' Service 4th & Battery Bldg., 6th Floor 2401 4th Ave. Seattle, WA 98121	206-597-6530 800-422-4087 800-572-5256 800-552-7114
MENTAL HEALTH *Provides patient services*	Mental Health Div. Dept. of Social & Health Services 12th Ave. & Franklin St. ˙ Office Bldg. 2 Mail Stop OB-42F Olympia, WA 98504	206-753-5414
OCCUPATIONAL SAFETY & HEALTH *Inspects worksites*	Industrial Safety & Health Div. Dept. of Labor & Industry Office Bldg. 6 805 Plum St., SE Olympia, WA 98504	206-753-6500

Type of Agency/Comments	*Organization and Address*	*Phone*
OMBUDSMAN (NURSING HOMES) *Investigates complaints from nursing home residents*	Long Term Care Ombudsman 1505 S. 356th St. Federal Way, WA 98003	206-838-6810
OMBUDSMAN (GENERAL) *Provides assistance to citizens*	Staff Assistant for Citizen Relations Office of the Governor Legislative Bldg., 2nd Floor Capitol Campus Olympia, WA 98504	206-753-6780
SOCIAL SERVICES *Provides support services and counseling*	Health & Rehab. Services Dept. of Social & Health Services Office Bldg. 2, 4th Floor Mail Stop OB-44M 12th Ave. & Adams St. Olympia, WA 98504	206-753-3327
VETERANS AFFAIRS *Provides assistance to veterans*	Dept. of Veterans Affairs Republic Bldg., 3rd Floor 505 East Union St. Olympia, WA 98504	206-753-5586
VITAL STATISTICS *Maintains birth & death records*	Vital Records Dept. of Social & Health Services Eastside Plaza, Bldg. A 1112 South Quince St. Olympia, WA 98504	800-551-0562 206-753-5936
VOCATIONAL REHABILITATION *Provides information on rehabilitation programs*	Div. of Vocational Rehab. Services Dept. of Social & Health Services Office Bldg. 2, Mail Stop OB-21C 12th Ave & Franklin St. Olympia, WA 98504	206-753-0293
WELFARE *Administers income programs*	Div. of Income Maintenance Dept. of Social & Health Services Office Bldg. 2, 3rd Floor Mail Stop OB-31C 12th Ave. & Franklin St. Olympia, WA 98504	206-753-3080

Type of Agency/Comments	*Organization and Address*	*Phone*
WORKER'S COMPENSATION *Provides income for injured workers*	Worker's Benefits Dept. of Labor & Industry General Administration Bldg. Mail Stop HC-101 11th Ave. & Columbia St. Olympia, WA 98504	206-753-6376

WEST VIRGINIA

Type of Agency/Comments	*Organization and Address*	*Phone*
AGENCY LOCATOR *For Agencies & telephone numbers not listed*	Information Operator State Capitol Charleston, WV 25305	304-348-3456
AGING *Provides programs & services to senior citizens*	Commission on Aging State Capitol Charleston, WV 25305	800-642-3671 304-348-3317
ALCOHOLISM *Provides assistance to alcohol abusers*	Div. of Alcoholism & Drug Abuse Dept. of Health 1800 Washington St., East Charleston, WV 25305	304-348-2276
ATTORNEY GENERAL *Chief law enforcement officer*	Attorney General's Office State Capitol Room E-26 Charleston, WV 25305	304-348-2021
CHILD WELFARE *Provides services to children and youths*	Families & Children Unit Social Services Div. Dept. of Human Services 1900 Washington St., East Charleston, WV 25305	304-348-7980
COMMUNITY AFFAIRS *Provides programs to communities*	Community Development Div. Governor's Office State Office Bldg. 6, Rm. B-553 1900 Washington St., East Charleston, WV 25305	304-348-4010
CONSUMER ADVOCATE *Investigates consumer complaints*	Consumer Protection Div. Attorney General's Office 812 Quarrier St. Charleston, WV 25301	800-368-8808 304-348-8986

Type of Agency/Comments	*Organization and Address*	*Phone*
DEPARTMENT OF HEALTH *Supervises health activities in the state*	Dept. of Health State Office Bldg. 3 Rm. 206 1800 Washington St., East Charleston, WV 25305	304-348-2971
DEVELOPMENTAL DISABILITIES *Provides services to the developmentally disabled*	Advocates for the Developmentally Disabled 1021 Quarrier St. Suite 407 Charleston, WV 25301	800-642-9205
DRUG ABUSE *Provides assistance to drug abusers*	Div. of Alcoholism & Drug Abuse Dept. of Health 1800 Washington St., East Charleston, WV 25305	304-348-2276
FOOD AND DRUGS *Registers food & drug items*	Public Health Sanitation Office of Environmental Health State Office Bldg. 3, Rm 507 1800 Washington St. East Charleston, WV 25305	304-348-2981
GOVERNOR *Citizens access to the governor*	Office of the Governor State Capitol Charleston, WV 25306	304-348-2015
INSURANCE *Regulates the insurance industry*	Dept. of Insurance 2019 Washington St. East Charleston, WV 25305	304-348-3394
LICENSING: DENTISTS *Report complaints about dentists to this office*	Board of Dental Examiners P.O. Drawer 1459 Beckley, WV 25802	304-252-8266
LICENSING: HOSPITALS *Report complaints about hospitals to this office*	Dept. of Health Health Facilities Licensure & Certification Div. 19 Kanawha Blvd. East Charleston, WV 25305	304-348-0050
LICENSING: NURSES *Report complaints about nurses to this office*	Board of Examiners for Registered Nurses 922 Quarrier St. Suite 309 Charleston, WV 25301	304-348-3728

Type of Agency/Comments	Organization and Address	Phone
LICENSING: NURSING HOMES *Report complaints about nursing homes to this office*	Nursing Home Licensure Office Health Facilities & Certification Section 1900 Kanawha Blvd. Charleston, WV 25305	304-348-0050
LICENSING: PHARMACISTS *Report complaints about pharmacists to this office*	Board of Pharmacy 236 Capitol St. Charleston, WV 25301	304-348-0558
LICENSING: PHYSICIANS *Report complaints about doctors to this office*	Board of Medicine 101 Dee Dr. Charleston, WV 25311	304-348-2921
MEDICAID OFFICE *Administers Medicaid program*	Dept. of Human Services Client Services 1900 Washington St., East Charleston, WV 25305	304-348-8990
MEDICARE PART B CARRIER *Processes Medicare claims for the state of West Virginia*	Nationwide Insurance Co. P.O. Box 57 Columbus, OH 43216	800-848-0106
MENTAL HEALTH *Provides patient services*	Div. of Mental Health Dept. of Health 1800 Washington St. East Charleston, WV 25305	304-348-0627
OCCUPATIONAL SAFETY & HEALTH *Inspects worksites*	Industrial Hygiene Div. Dept. of Health 151 11th Ave. South Charleston, WV 25303	304-348-3526
OMBUDSMAN (NURSING HOMES) *Investigates complaints from nursing home residents*	Commission on Aging State Capitol Charleston, WV 25305	304-348-3317
SOCIAL SERVICES *Provides support services and counseling*	Social Services Div. Dept. of Human Services State Office Bldg. 6 1900 Washington St., East Charleston, WV 25305	304-348-2400

Type of Agency/Comments	*Organization and Address*	*Phone*
VETERANS AFFAIRS *Provides assistance to veterans*	Dept. of Veterans Affairs Atlas Bldg., Rm. 605 1031 Quarrier St. Charleston, WV 25301	304-348-3661
VITAL STATISTICS *Maintains birth & death records*	Div. of Vital Statistics Health Services Section 1800 Washington St., East Charleston, WV 25305	304-348-8800
VOCATIONAL REHABILITATION *Provides information on rehabilitation programs*	Div. of Vocational Rehab. State Capitol Complex Charleston, WV 25305	304-348-2375
WELFARE *Administers income programs*	Dept. of Human Services State Office Bldg. 6 Rm. B-617 1900 Washington St., East Charleston, WV 25305	304-348-2400
WORKER'S COMPENSATION *Provides income program for injured workers*	Worker's Compensation Fund 601 Morris St. Charleston, WV 25301	304-348-2580

WISCONSIN

Type of Agency/Comments	*Organization and Address*	*Phone*
AGENCY LOCATOR *For Agencies & telephone numbers not listed*	Information Operator State Capitol Madison, WI 53702	608-266-2211
AGING *Provides programs & services to senior citizens*	Bur. on Aging 217 South Hamilton St. Suite 300 Madison, WI 53707	608-266-2536

ALCOHOLISM
 	
*Provides assistance to
alcohol abusers*
	Office of Alcohol & Drug
	  Abuse
	Bur. of Community Programs
	Div. of Community Services
	434 Wilson St. State Office
	  Bldg.
	1 West Wilson St., P.O. Box
	  7851
	Madison, WI 53707-7851
		608-266-2717

Type of Agency/Comments	Organization and Address	Phone
ATTORNEY GENERAL *Chief law enforcement officer*	Attorney General's Office Wisconsin Dept. of Justice 114 East State Capitol Madison, WI 53702	608-266-1221
CHILD WELFARE *Provides services to children and youths*	Children, Youth & Families Div. of Community Service Wilson St. State Office Bldg. 1 West Wilson St. Madison, WI 53707	608-266-3036
COMMUNITY AFFAIRS *Provides programs to communities*	Dept. of Development Justice Bldg. 123 West Washington Ave. Madison, WI 53707	608-266-1916
CONSUMER ADVOCATE *Investigates consumer complaints*	Consumer Protection Div. 801 West Badger Road Madison, WI 53708	608-266-7220
DEPARTMENT OF HEALTH *Supervises health activities in the state*	Div. of Health Dept. of Health & Social Services Wilson St. State Office Bldg. 1 West Wilson St. Madison, WI 53701-0309	608-266-7568
DEVELOPMENTAL DISABILITIES *Provides services to the developmentally disabled*	Developmental Disabilities Div. of Community Services Wilson St. State Office Bldg. 1 West Wilson St. Madison, WI 53707	608-266-9329
DRUG ABUSE *Provides assistance to drug abusers*	Office of Alcohol & Drug Abuse Bur. of Community Programs Div. of Community Services P.O. Box 7851 434 Wilson St. Office Bldg. 1 West Wilson St. Madison, WI 53707-7851	608-266-2717
FOOD AND DRUGS *Registers food and drug items*	Food Div. Dept. of Agriculture, Trade & Consumer Protection 801 West Badger Road P.O. Box 8911 Madison, WI 53708	608-266-7240

Type of Agency/Comments	*Organization and Address*	*Phone*
GOVERNOR *Citizens access to governor*	Office of the Governor East State Capitol Rm. 115 Madison, WI 53702	608-266-8110
INSURANCE *Regulates the insurance* *industry*	Commissioner of Insurance Loraine Bldg. 123 West Washington Ave. Madison, WI 53702	608-266-3585
LICENSING: DENTISTS *Report complaints about* *dentists to this office*	Board of Dental Examiners Dept. of Regulation & Licensing P.O. Box 8935 Madison, WI 53708	608-266-1396
LICENSING: HOSPITALS *Report complaints about* *hospitals to this office*	Dept. of Health & Social Services Div. of Health Bur. of Quality Compliance P.O. Box 309 Madison, WI 53701	608-267-7185
LICENSING: NURSES *Report complaints about* *nurses to this office*	Dept. of Licensing Board of Nursing P.O. Box 8935 Madison, WI 53708	608-266-3735
LICENSING: NURSING HOMES *Report complaints about* *nursing homes to this* *office*	Dept. of Health & Social Services Bur. of Quality Compliance 1 West Wilson St. Rm. 150, P.O. Box 309 Madison, WI 53701	608-266-3024
LICENSING: PHARMACISTS *Report complaints about* *pharmacists to this office*	Pharmacy Examining Board 1400 East Washington Ave. Madison, WI 53702	608-266-8794
LICENSING: PHYSICIANS *Report complaints about* *doctors to this office*	Board of Medical Examiners 1400 East Washington Ave. P.O. Box 8935 Madison, WI 53708	608-266-2811
LICENSING: PROFESSIONALS *Licenses other health care* *professionals*	Occupational & Professional Licensing Dept. of Regulation & Licensing 1400 East Washington St. Madison, WI 53708	608-266-8609

Type of Agency/Comments	Organization and Address	Phone
MEDICAID OFFICE *Administers Medicaid program*	Medical Assistance Unit Dept. of Health & Social Services 1 West Wilson St. P.O. Box 309 Madison, WI 53701	608-266-2522
MEDICARE PART B CARRIER *Processes Medicare claims*	Medicare/WPS P.O. Box 1787 Madison, WI 53701	(Madison) 608-221-3330 (Green Bay) 414-931-1071 800-362-7221
MENTAL HEALTH *Provides services to patients*	Office of Mental Health Div. of Community Service 540 Wilson St. Office Bldg. 1 West Wilson St. P.O. Box 7851 Madison, WI 53707-7851	608-266-3249
OCCUPATIONAL SAFETY & HEALTH *Inspects worksites*	Safety & Buildings Div. General Executive Facility 1 201 East Washington Ave. Madison, WI 53707	608-266-1816
OMBUDSMAN (GENERAL) *Provides assistance to citizens*	Ombudsman Office Constituent Relations Office of the Governor State Capitol, Rm. 115 E Madison, WI 53702	608-266-1212
OMBUDSMAN (NURSING HOMES) *Investigates complaints from nursing home residents*	Governor's Ombudsman Program 819 North 6th St. Milwaukee, WI 53203	414-227-4386
SOCIAL SERVICES *Provides support services and counseling*	Div. of Community Services Dept. of Health & Social Services 540 Wilson St. State Off. Bldg. 1 West Wilson St. P.O. Box 7851 Madison, WI 53707-7851	608-266-2701
VETERANS AFFAIRS *Provides assistance to veterans*	Dept. of Veterans Affairs 77 North Dickinson St. Madison, WI 53707	608-266-1311

Type of Agency/Comments	Organization and Address	Phone
VITAL STATISTICS *Maintains birth & death records*	Center for Health Statistics Dept. of Health & Social Services 172 Wilson St. Office Bldg. 1 West Wilson St. P.O. Box 309 Madison, WI 53701	608-266-1334
VOCATIONAL REHABILITATION *Provides information on rehabilitation programs*	Div. of Vocational Rehab. Dept. of Health & Social Services 850 Wilson St. State Office Bldg. 1 West Wilson St. P.O. Box 7852 Madison, WI 53707-7852	608-266-1281
WELFARE *Administers income programs*	Bur. of Economic Assistance Div. of Community Services Dept. of Health & Social Services 358 Wilson St. State Office Bldg. 1 West Wilson St. P.O. Box 7851 Madison, WI 53707-7851	608-266-3035
WORKER'S COMPENSATION *Provides income for injured workers*	Worker's Compensation Div. 161 General Executive Facility 201 East Washington Ave. Madison, WI 53707	608-266-1340

WYOMING

Type of Agency/Comments	Organization and Address	Phone
AGENCY LOCATOR *For Agencies & telephone numbers not listed*	Information Operator State Capitol Cheyenne, WY 82002	307-777-7220
AGING *Provides programs & services to senior citizens*	Commission on Aging Hathaway Bldg. 2300 Capitol Ave. Cheyenne, WY 82002	307-777-7986

Type of Agency/Comments	*Organization and Address*	*Phone*
ALCOHOLISM *Provides assistance to alcohol abusers*	Office of Substance Abuse Dept. of Health & Social Services Hathaway Bldg., Rm. 350 2300 Capitol Ave. Cheyenne, WY 82002-0710	307-777-6945
ATTORNEY GENERAL *Chief law enforcement officer*	Attorney General's Office 123 State Capitol Capitol Ave. at 24th St. Cheyenne, WY 82002	307-777-7841
CHILD WELFARE *Provides services to children and youths*	Div. of Public Assistance Dept. of Health & Social Services Hathaway Bldg., Rm. 318 2300 Capitol Ave. Cheyenne, WY 82002-0710	307-777-6825
COMMUNITY AFFAIRS *Provides programs to communities*	Economic Development & Stabilization Board Herschler Bldg., 3rd Floor East 122 West 25th St. Cheyenne, WY 82002	307-777-7287 800-262-3425
CONSUMER ADVOCATE *Investigates consumer complaints*	Consumer Affairs Div. Attorney General's Office 123 State Capitol Cheyenne, WY 82002	307-777-6286
DEPARTMENT OF HEALTH *Supervises health activities in the state*	Dept. of Health & Social Services 317 Hathaway Bldg. 2300 Capitol Ave. Cheyenne, WY 82002	307-777-7657
DEVELOPMENTAL DISABILITIES *Provides services to the developmentally disabled*	Office of Developmental Disabilities Dept. of Health & Social Services Hathaway Bldg., Rm. 354 2300 Capitol Ave. Cheyenne, WY 82002-0710	307-777-7115
DRUG ABUSE *Provides assistance to drug abusers*	Office of Substance Abuse Dept. of Health & Social Services Hathaway Bldg., Rm. 350 2300 Capitol Ave. Cheyenne, WY 82002-0710	307-777-6945

Type of Agency/Comments	*Organization and Address*	*Phone*
FOOD AND DRUGS *Registers food & drug items*	Food and Drug Section Consumer & Compliance Div. 2219 Carey Ave. Cheyenne, WY 82002	307-777-7321
GOVERNOR *Citizen's access to the governor*	Office of the Governor State Capitol Cheyenne, WY 82002	307-777-7434
INSURANCE *Regulates the insurance industry*	Insurance Dept. Herschler Bldg., 3rd Floor 122 West 25th St. Cheyenne, WY 82002	307-777-7401
LICENSING: DENTISTS *Report complaints about dentists to this office*	Board of Dental Examiners P.O. Box 1024 Powell, WY 82435	307-754-3471
LICENSING: HOSPITALS *Report complaints about hospitals to this office*	Dept. of Health & Social Services Div. of Health & Medical Services Hathaway Bldg., 4th Floor Cheyenne, WY 82002	307-777-7121
LICENSING: NURSES *Report complaints about nurses to this office*	State Board of Nursing Barrett Bldg., 3rd Floor 2301 Central Ave. Cheyenne, WY 82002	307-777-7601
LICENSING: NURSING HOMES *Report complaints about nursing homes to this office*	Dept. of Health & Social Services Div. of Health & Medical Services Medical Facilities Hathaway Bldg., 4th Floor Cheyenne, WY 82002	307-777-7121
LICENSING: PHARMACISTS *Report complaints about pharmacists to this office*	Board of Pharmacy 1720 Poplar St. Casper, WY 82604	307-234-0294
LICENSING: PHYSICIANS *Report complaints about doctors to this office*	Board of Medical Examiners Barrett Bldg., 3rd Floor Cheyenne, WY 82002	307-777-6463

Type of Agency/Comments	Organization and Address	Phone
MEDICAID OFFICE *Administers Medicaid program*	Dept. of Health & Social Services Div. of Public Assistance Hathaway Bldg., 4th Floor 2300 Capitol Ave. Cheyenne, WY 82002	307-777-7531
MEDICARE PART B CARRIER *Processes Medicare claims*	Equicor, Inc. P.O. Box 628 Cheyenne, WY 82003	800-442-2371 307-632-9381
MENTAL HEALTH *Provides patient services*	Mental Health Program Div. of Community Programs Hathaway Bldg., Rm. 358 2300 Capitol Ave. Cheyenne, WY 82002-0710	307-777-7115
OCCUPATIONAL SAFETY & HEALTH *Inspects worksites*	Occupational Safety & Health Commission 604 East 25th St. Cheyenne, WY 82002	307-777-7786
OMBUDSMAN (NURSING HOMES) *Investigates complaints from nursing home residents*	Wyoming Long Term Care Ombudsman P.O. Box 94 Wheatlyn, WY 82201	307-322-5553
SOCIAL SERVICES *Provides support services and counseling*	Dept. of Health & Social Services Div. of Public Assistance & Services Hathaway Bldg., Rm. 318 2300 Capitol Ave. Cheyenne, WY 82002-0710	307-777-6285
VETERANS AFFAIRS *Provides assistance to veterans*	Veterans Home of Wyoming Board of Charities & Reform RFD 1 Buffalo, WY 82834	307-684-5511
VITAL STATISTICS *Maintains birth & death records*	Vital Records Services Hathaway Bldg. 2300 Capitol Ave. Cheyenne, WY 82002	307-777-6464

Type of Agency/Comments	*Organization and Address*	*Phone*
VOCATIONAL REHABILITATION *Provides information on rehabilitation programs*	Div. of Vocational Rehab. Dept. of Health & Social Services Barrett Bldg. 2301 Central Ave. Cheyenne, WY 82002	307-777-7191
WELFARE *Administers income programs*	Div. of Public Assistance Dept. of Health & Social Services Hathaway Bldg., 3rd Floor 2300 Capitol Ave. Cheyenne, WY 82002-0710	307-777-6068
WORKER'S COMPENSATION *Provides income for injured workers*	Worker's Compensation Div. Office of State Treasurer Herschler Bldg., 2nd Floor 122 West 25th St. Cheyenne, WY 82002	307-777-7441

PUERTO RICO

Type of Agency/Comments	*Organization and Address*	*Phone*
AGING *Provides programs & services to senior citizens*	Puerto Rico Gericulture Commission Old Naval Base, Bldg. 2, Wing 6 Majagua St. Santurce, PR 00910	809-722-2429
ALCOHOLISM *Provides assistance to alcohol abusers*	Alcoholism Program Lincoln Bldg. 414 Barbosa Ave. Rio Piedras, PR 00928	809-764-3795
ATTORNEY GENERAL *Chief law enforcement officer*	Secretary of Justice Department of Justice Olimpo and Lindberg Sts. San Juan, PR 00902	809-721-2900
CHILD WELFARE *Provides services to children and youths*	Dept. of Social Services Old Naval Base, Bldg. 10 Miramar Santurce, PR 00910	809-721-4624

Type of Agency/Comments	Organization and Address	Phone
COMMUNITY AFFAIRS *Provides programs to communities*	Municipal Services Admin. Barbosa Plaza Bldg. 306 Barbosa Ave. San Juan, PR 00936	809-753-9151
CONSUMER AFFAIRS *Investigates consumer complaints*	Dept. of Consumer Affairs Minillas Govt. Center, North P.O. Box 41059 Santurce, PR 00940	809-721-3280
DEPARTMENT OF HEALTH *Supervises health activities in the state*	Dept. of Health Call Box 70184 San Juan, PR 00936	809-250-7227
DEVELOPMENTAL DISABILITIES *Provides services to the developmentally disabled*	Vocational Rehab. Program Dept. of Social Services Bldg. 10 Santurce, PR 00907	809-725-1792
DRUG ABUSE *Provides assistance to drug abusers*	Dept. of Addiction Services Lincoln Bldg. 414 Barbosa Ave. Rio Piedras, PR 00928	809-764-3795
FOOD AND DRUGS *Registers food & drug items*	Dept. of Health Torrenos Medical Center, Bldg. A Rio Piedras San Juan, PR 00936	809-751-8394
GOVERNOR *Citizens access to the governor*	Office of the Governor La Fortaleza San Juan, PR 00901	809-721-7000

INSURANCE
 	
Regulates the insurance industry
	Office of the Insurance
	   Commissioner
	 Cobian's Plaza
	 1607 Ponce de Leon Ave.,
	   Stop 23
	 Santurce, PR 00910
		809-722-8686

LICENSING: DENTISTS *Report complaints about dentists to this office*	Puerto Rico Board of Dental Examiners Dept. of Health Call Box 10200 Santurce, PR 00908	809-723-1617

Type of Agency/Comments	*Organization and Address*	*Phone*
LICENSING: HOSPITALS *Report complaints about hospitals to this office*	Puerto Rico Dept. of Health Call Box 70184 San Juan, PR 00936	809-766-1616

LICENSING: NURSES
 	
*Report complaints about
  nurses to this office*
	Office of Regulation &
	  Certification of Health
	Professionals
	Call Box 10200
	Santurce, PR 00908
		809-725-7506

LICENSING: PHARMACISTS
 	
*Report complaints about
  pharmacists to this office*
	Puerto Rico Board of
	  Pharmacy
	P.O. Box 9342
	Santurce, PR 00908
		809-722-2868

LICENSING: PHYSICIANS
 	
*Report complaints about
  doctors to this office*
	Puerto Rico Board of Medical
	  Examiners
	Call Box 10200
	Santurce, PR 00908
		809-725-7903

MEDICAID *Administers Medicaid program*	Medical Assistance Unit Dept. of Health Bldg. A, Call Box 70184 San Juan, PR 00936	809-765-9941
MEDICARE CARRIER PART B *Processes Medicare claims*	Seguros de Service De Salud De Puerto Rico Call Box 71391 San Juan, PR 00936	809-749-4900 800-462-7385
MENTAL HEALTH *Provides patient services*	Dept. of Health Terrenos Medical Center, Bldg. A Rio Piedras San Juan, PR 00936	809-766-1616

OCCUPATIONAL SAFETY &
  HEALTH
 	
Investigates worksites
	Occupational Safety & Health
	  Admin.
	Dept. of Labor & Human
	  Resources
	505 Munoz Rivera Ave.
	Hato Rey, PR 00918
		809-754-2171

OMBUDSMAN (GENERAL)
 	
*Citizens access to
  government officials*
	Office of the Ombudsman
	P.O. Box 41088, Minillas
	  Station
	Santurce, PR 00940
		809-725-1886

Type of Agency/Comments	*Organization and Address*	*Phone*
OMBUDSMAN (NURSING HOMES) *Investigates complaints from nursing home residents*	Office of the Ombudsman San Juan Bank Bldg. 1205 Ponce de Leon Ave. Santurce, PR 00908	809-725-1886
SOCIAL SERVICES *Provides services*	Dept. of Social Services Old Naval Base, Isla Grande Bldg. 10, 2nd Floor Santurce, PR 00910	809-721-4624
VETERANS AFFAIRS *Provides assistance to veterans*	Public Advocate of Puerto Rico Vietnam Veterans Cobian's Plaza, Parada 23 Ponce De Leon 1603 Santurce, PR 00909	809-725-4440
VITAL STATISTICS *Maintains birth & death records*	Demographic Registry Admin. of Facilities & Service P.O. Box 29342 San Juan, PR 00908	809-728-7980
VOCATIONAL REHABILITATION *Provides information on rehabilitation programs*	Office for the Handicapped Office of the Governor 916 Chardon's St. Hato Rey, PR 00918	809-766-2333 800-462-4125
WELFARE *Administers income program*	Dept. of Social Services Old Naval Base, Isla Grande Bldg. 10, 2nd Floor Santurce, PR 00910	809-721-4624
WORKER'S COMPENSATION *Provides income programs for injured workers*	Puerto Rico Industrial Commission GPO Box 4466 San Juan, PR 00936	809-781-0615

VIRGIN ISLANDS

Type of Agency/Comments	*Organization and Address*	*Phone*
AGING *Provides programs & services to senior citizens*	Commission on Aging P.O. Box 550 Charlotte Amalie St. Thomas, VI 00801	809-774-5884

Type of Agency/Comments	Organization and Address	Phone
ALCOHOLISM *Provides assistance to alcohol abusers*	Div. of Mental Health, Alcoholism & Drug Dependency Dept. of Health Knud Hansen Complex St. Thomas, VI 00802	809-774-7265
ATTORNEY GENERAL *Chief law enforcement officer*	Attorney General's Office Dept. of Law 46 Norre Gade St. Thomas, VI 00802	809-774-5666
CHILD WELFARE *Provides services to children and youths*	Dept. of Social Welfare Barbel Plaza South St. Thomas, VI 00802	809-774-4393
COMMUNITY AFFAIRS *Provides programs to communities*	Community Development Programs Planning Board P.O. Box 2626 Charlotte Amalie St. Thomas, VI 00801	809-774-3320
CONSUMER AFFAIRS *Investigates consumer complaints*	Dept. of Licensing & Consumer Affairs St. Thomas, VI 00801	809-774-3130
DEPARTMENT OF HEALTH *Supervises health activities in the state*	Dept. of Health St. Thomas Hospital Charlotte Amalie St. Thomas, VI 00802	809-774-0117
DEVELOPMENTAL DISABILITIES *Provides services to the developmentally disabled*	Special Services Section Dept. of Human Services Barbel Plaza South St. Thomas, VI 00802	809-774-4775
DRUG ABUSE *Provides assistance to drug abusers*	Div. of Mental Health, Alcohol & Drug Dependency Dept. of Health Knud Hansen Complex St. Thomas, VI 00802	809-774-7256
FOOD & DRUGS *Registers food and drug items*	Dept. of Licensing & Consumer Affairs St. Thomas, VI 00801	809-774-3130

Type of Agency/Comments	Organization and Address	Phone
GOVERNOR *Citizen's access to the governor*	Office of the Governor Government House P.O. Box 580 Charlotte Amalie St. Thomas, VI 00801	809-774-0001
INSURANCE *Regulates the insurance industry*	Lieutenant Governor's Office 18 Kongens Gade P.O. Box 450 Charlotte Amalie St. Thomas, VI 00801	809-774-2991
LICENSING: DENTISTS *Report complaints about dentists to this office*	Virgin Islands Dept. of Health St. Thomas Hospital 48 Sugar Estates St. Thomas, VI 00802	809-774-0117
LICENSING: HOSPITALS *Report complaints about hospitals to this office*	Virgin Islands Dept. of Health St. Thomas Hospital 48 Sugar Estates St. Thomas, VI 00801	809-774-0117
LICENSING: NURSES *Report complaints about nurses to this office*	Board of Nurse Examiners P.O. Box 7309 Charlotte Amalie St. Thomas, VI 00801	809-776-7397
LICENSING: PHYSICIANS *Report complaints about doctors to this office*	Dept. of Health P.O. Box 7309 Charlotte Amalie St. Thomas, VI 00801	809-774-0117
MEDICAID *Administers Medicaid program*	Medical Assistance Unit Bur. of Health Insurance P.O. Box 7309 Charlotte Amalie St. Thomas, VI 00801	809-774-4624
MEDICARE CARRIER PART B *Processes Medicare claims*	Medicare/Seguros De Servicio De Salud De Puerto Rico Call Box 71391 San Juan, PR 00936	809-778-2665 809-774-3898
MENTAL HEALTH *Provides patient services*	Div. of Mental Health Dept. of Health 6 & 7 Estate Diamond Ruby St. Croix, VI 00820	809-773-1992

Type of Agency/Comments	*Organization and Address*	*Phone*
OCCUPATIONAL SAFETY & HEALTH *Inspects worksites*	Div. of Occupational Safety Dept. of Labor 207 Bldg. 2, Government Complex Frederiksted St. Croix, VI 00840	809-772-1315
OMBUDSMAN (GENERAL) *Citizens access to* *government officials*	Complaints Line Office of the Governor 21-22 Kongens Gade St. Thomas, VI 00802	809-774-2150
SOCIAL SERVICES *Provides services*	Dept. of Human Services Barbel Plaza South St. Thomas, VI 00802	809-774-0930
VETERANS AFFAIRS *Provides assistance to* *veterans*	Office of Veterans Affairs 22 Hospital St. Christiansted St. Croix, VI 00820	809-773-6663
VITAL STATISTICS *Maintains birth & death* *records*	Health Planning & Statistics Dept. of Health Knud Hansen Complex St. Thomas, VI 00802	809-774-1734
VOCATIONAL REHABILITATION *Provides information on* *rehabilitation programs*	Special Services Section Disabilities & Rehab. Services Dept. of Human Services Barbel Plaza South St. Thomas, VI 00802	809-774-4775
WELFARE *Administers income* *programs*	Income Maintenance Program Dept. of Human Services Barbel Plaza South St. Thomas, VI 00802	809-774-2299
WORKER'S COMPENSATION *Provides income for injured* *workers*	Div. of Worker's Compensation Dept. of Labor Four Winds Plaza Charlotte Amalie St. Thomas, VI 00801	809-775-5747

Appendix B

PATIENT BILL OF RIGHTS FOR
NURSING HOMES

Under federal regulations, nursing homes must have written policies covering the rights of patients. These rights must be posted where residents and visitors can easily see them. A patient bill of rights ensures that each person admitted to a facility will have his/her rights protected. Flagrant violations of these rights should be reported to the proper state authorities listed in Appendix A.

A Patient:
1. is fully informed as evidenced by the resident's written acknowledgment of these rights and of all rules and regulations governing the exercise of these rights.
2. is fully informed of services available in the facility and of related charges for services not covered under Medicare/ Medicaid, or not covered by the facility's basic daily rate.
3. is fully informed of his/her medical condition unless the physician notes in the medical record that it is not in the patient's interest to be told, and is afforded the opportunity to participate in the planning of his/her medical treatment and to refuse to participate in experimental research.
4. is transferred or discharged only for medical reasons, or for his/her welfare or that of other residents, and is given rea-

sonable advance notice to ensure orderly transfer or discharge.

5. is encouraged and assisted, through his/her period of stay to exercise his/her rights as a resident and as a free citizen. To this end he/she may voice grievances and recommend changes in policies and services to facility staff and/or outside representatives of his/her choice without fear of coercion, discrimination, or reprisal.

6. may manage his/her personal financial affairs, or is given at least a quarterly accounting of financial transactions made on his/her behalf if the facility accepts the responsibility to safeguard the funds.

7. is free from mental and physical abuse, and free from chemical and physical restraints except as authorized in writing by a physician for a specified and limited period of time or when necessary to protect patients from injury to themselves or others.

8. is assured confidential treatment of his/her personal and medical records and may approve or refuse their release to any individual outside the facility.

9. is treated with consideration, respect, and full recognition of his/her dignity and individuality, including privacy in treatment and in care of his/her personal needs.

10. is not required to perform services for the facility that are not included for therapeutic purposes in this plan of care.

11. may associate and communicate privately with persons of his/her choice, and send and receive his/her personal mail unopened.

12. may meet with, and participate in activities of social, religious, and community groups at his/her discretion.

13. may retain and use his/her personal clothing and possessions as space permits, unless to do so would infringe upon the rights of other patients, or constitute a hazard of safety.

14. is assured privacy for visits by his/her spouse; if both are inpatients in the facility, they are permitted to share a room.

Source: Suggested by the Health Care Financing Administration, U.S. Department of Health and Human Services, Washington, D.C.

Your Medical Record

Keeping an accurate record of your medical history can be a most valuable asset, yet very few of us keep any more than a billing statement as evidence of our encounter with a doctor. We usually assume that the doctor is paid to keep our medical record and, should we require a copy, we merely make a request and it's given to us. However, this may not always be the case. Very often doctors are reluctant to share your medical record with you, claiming that you might not understand their notes, or that you might be frightened away from a "needed" procedure.

The following section presents all the information you'll need to get started on your medical record. To help you get started we've provided a series of Questions and Answers that explain how to use this section.

Q. Why do I need to maintain my own medical record? Isn't that why I pay the doctor?

A. To a certain extent that is true. But we aren't referring to the medical record your doctor maintains. We're referring to a medical record that you keep and maintain — a medical record that you control and one in which you make the entries.

Q. It sounds difficult. Are you sure it's easy?

A. Yes. Keeping a medical record is no more complicated than maintaining other records. In fact, using this section will make it a snap!

Q. Where do I record the information? Are there special forms?

A. Yes. You will find the easy-to-use forms beginning on page 388. Each form has been designed for a specific purpose, making it easy to keep and maintain your record.

Q. Where do I begin?

A. We suggest that you begin on pages 388 and 389, the "Quick Reference Guide." In the spaces provided you'll be able to list the names, addresses and telephone numbers of all the medical providers you use.

You'll want to list your personal physician and any specialists along with your dentist, chiropractor, optometrist, and so forth.

We've also provided space to list the telephone numbers of police and ambulance services, hospitals, pharmacies, and crisis hot lines. Make sure you keep this record in a convenient place since you never know when a medical emergency might arise.

Q. After I've completed that, what's next?

A. You are now ready to record your own medical history and that of your family. Use the form "Your Medical History" which can be found on pages 390 and 391.

After completing the information at the top of the form you should examine the "Condition Profile Checklist." Place a check mark next to the condition or problem that applies to you.

It's also a good idea to record some of the more pertinent information regarding your family's medical history, so we've provided space for this. Use the "Family Medical History" box near the bottom of page 391. Place a check mark next to the conditions that apply to your father, mother, and siblings.

Q. Where do I record the information that describes my medical problems or symptoms as they do at my doctor's office?

A. "Record of Your Individual Visits," found on page 392, will help you keep track of this important information. This form has three easy-to-use columns where you will record the date, your symptoms or complaints, and the diagnosis and treatment. Make sure you also note any lab tests or diagnostic procedures that may be ordered by your doctor. Pages 390 to 392 are the very heart of your medical record, so you'll want to take your time when making entries.

Q. In addition to these records, what else do you recommend?

A. We strongly recommend that you maintain a record of all prescription and nonprescription medications including vitamins and minerals you are taking. You'll find page 393 helpful when it comes to keeping track of your medications. There is ample space to record the name of the medication, the prescribing physician, the pharmacy where it was filled and any side effects that you may experience.

Q. What other records should I keep?

A. We think it's wise to keep records on your major hospitalizations and laboratory tests, and also your dental and eye examinations. Pages 395 to 398 will be helpful in maintaining these records. Follow the headings on the forms and fill in the blank spaces as necessary.

Q. Do you have any final suggestions?

A. Yes. An individual medical record will be only as good as the information that it contains; therefore, we encourage you to be very careful when making entries. If your record is to be accurate, it must list *all* your visits to different doctors, not just some of them. The same can be said for your medications: Make sure you list all of the prescription and nonprescription medications you are taking.

Outdated and incorrect telephone numbers are of no help when you need them most, so make sure you've got the correct number before you enter it.

Since pages 390 to 392 are the heart of your medical record, and will be used the most, we suggest that you photocopy these pages.

As you use the additional copies, just attach them to the original pages. In this way the most recent sheet will always be on top.

We also suggest that when you record information on pages 390 to 392 that you list any special question or concern that you want to mention to your doctor. This way you'll have it at your fingertips when you see the doctor.

Before you make your first entry, just remember that you are recording this information for your benefit and use. List as much or as little information as you want. You don't need to please anyone but yourself.

Keeping and maintaining a personal medical record isn't difficult. It's the sign of an informed and educated consumer.

Quick Reference Guide

List all of Your Medical Providers and Emergency Telephone Numbers

NAME	SPECIALTY	ADDRESS	TELEPHONE

POLICE / FIRE / AMBULANCE	TELEPHONE	HOSPITAL	TELEPHONE

CRISIS HOT LINES	TELEPHONE	PHARMACIES	TELEPHONE

Your Medical History

This record belongs to:

Date of Birth _____   Place of Birth _____

Insurance Company _____   ID # _____   Telephone (___) _____

Medicare Number _____   Social Security Office Telephone (___) _____

CONDITION PROFILE CHECKLIST*

Indicate by check mark those conditions which you have/had.

Blood
___ Bleeding tendency
___ Bruise easily
___ Hemolytic anemia
___ Other anemia

Bones, Muscles & Joints
___ Arthritis
___ Backache
___ Bone tumors
___ Fractures
___ Muscle pain
___ Osteomyelitis

**Digestive —
Stomach & Intestine**
___ Appetite changes
___ Blood-streaked stools
___ Diverticulitis
___ Gallbladder disease
___ Hemorrhoids

___ Goiter (enlarged thyroid)
___ Persistent fever
___ Protruding eyeballs
___ Sugar in urine
___ Thyroid tumors
___ Unusual thirst
___ Weakness and general tiredness

Heart & Lungs
___ Abnormal electrocardiogram
___ Ankle and leg swelling
___ Asthma
___ Blueness of lips and fingers
___ Bronchitis
___ Chest pain
___ Chest x-ray abnormalities
___ Chronic cough
___ Coughing up blood

___ Sexual impotency
___ Sore on penis
___ Urethral infection

Nerve Disorders
___ Convulsive disorder
___ Difficulty with limb control
___ Extremities fall "asleep"
___ Head trauma
___ Headache
___ Memory problem
___ Muscle weakness
___ Speech problem
___ Stroke
___ Tremor (shaking)
___ Walking disorder

Nose
___ Deviated septum
___ Nosebleeds
___ Polyps

___ Bleeding between periods
___ Menopause
___ Miscarriages
___ Painful intercourse
___ Painful menstruation
___ Post-menopause bleeding
___ Pregnancy
___ Sexual dissatisfaction
___ Tumors — breast, uterus, cervix, ovaries, etc.
___ Vaginal infections

Skin
___ Changes in wart, mole, etc.
___ Chronic skin infections / lesions
___ Common skin infections
___ Psoriasis
___ Skin rash
___ Skin sensitive to light
___ Skin tumors

___ Tarry stools
___ Tumors — stomach, colon, rectum
___ Ulcers
___ Weight gain
___ Weight loss

Ears

___ Deafness
___ Dizziness
___ Drainage from ears
___ Hearing aid
___ Ringing in ears

Eye

___ Blurred vision
___ Cataracts
___ Double vision
___ Eye infection
___ Glaucoma
___ Sudden blindness

Genital and Urinary

___ Bloody urination
___ Excessive urination
___ Kidney stones
___ Losing urine when coughing, straining, laughing, etc.
___ Painful urination
___ Urinary tract infections
___ Urination at night

Glands and Hormones

___ Diabetes

___ Fainting with coughing
___ Heart attack
___ Heart enlargement
___ Heart murmur
___ High blood pressure
___ Irregular heartbeats
___ Leg cramps
___ Low blood pressure
___ Lung tumors
___ Night sweats
___ Pneumonia
___ Shortness of breath at night
___ Shortness of breath lying down
___ Shortness of breath upon exertion
___ TB or TB exposure (tuberculosis)
___ Thrombophlebitis
___ Varicose veins

Infectious Diseases

___ Chicken pox (varicella)
___ German measles (rubella)
___ Gonorrhea
___ Measles (rubeola)
___ Mumps (parotitis)
___ Syphilis

Males

___ Difficulty starting stream
___ Prostate tumor
___ Sexual dissatisfaction

___ Runny nose
___ Sinusitis

Throat

___ Difficulty swallowing
___ Mouth infections
___ Persistent hoarseness
___ Recurrent sore throat
___ Sore tongue
___ Voice change

Obstetrics & Gynecology

___ Abnormal Pap smear
___ Abnormal breast exam
___ Abnormal pelvic exam
___ Age began menstruating

Family Medical History

	FATHER	MOTHER	BROTHERS/SISTERS
Accident			
Alcoholism			
Allergies			
Anemia			
Cancer			
Diabetes			
Headaches			
Hearing Loss			
Heart Attack			
Hypertension			
Kidney			
Obesity			
Psychosis			
Rheumatoid Arthritis			
Stroke			
Tuberculosis			
Age Died			
Cause of Death			

*We gratefully acknowledge Woodbridge Press for permitting us to extract material from Keeping Track: A Personal Health Record System (Santa Barbara: Woodbridge Press, 1980).

Record of Your Individual Visits

DATE	PROBLEMS / COMPLAINTS / SYMPTOMS	DIAGNOSIS AND TREATMENT

Record of Prescription Medications

DATE	MEDICATION	DOCTOR	PHARMACY	SIDE EFFECTS

Record of Over-the-Counter Medications–Include Vitamins and Minerals

DATE	MEDICATION	DATE	MEDICATION	DATE	MEDICATION

Record of Major Hospitalizations

DATE	HOSPITAL	DOCTOR	CONDITION / ILLNESS

Record and Results of Laboratory Tests

DATE	LAB TEST	RESULTS

Record of Dental Examinations

DATE	DENTIST	COMPLAINTS / PROBLEMS / TREATMENTS

Record of Eye Examinations

DATE	RESULTS OF EXAMINATION														

Index